Religious Minorities, Islam and the Law

This book examines the legal conundrum of reconciling international human rights law in a Muslim majority country and identifies a trajectory for negotiating the protection of religious minorities within Islam.

The work explores the history of religious minorities within Islam in Indonesia, which contains the world's largest Muslim population, as well as the present-day ways by which the government may address issues through reconciling international human rights law and Islamic law. Given the context of multiple sets of religious norms in Indonesia, this is a complicated endeavour. In addition to amending and enacting human rights norms, the government is also negotiating with the long history of Islamisation in Indonesia. Particularly relevant is the practice of customary law, which puts the rights of community over individualism. This practice directly affects the rights of religious minorities within Islam. Readers, especially those conducting research, will also be provided with information and references which are relevant to the field of human rights, especially in relation to religious minorities and international law.

The book will be a valuable resource for academics and researchers in the fields of International Human Rights Law, Law and Religion, and Islamic Studies.

Al Khanif is an assistant professor in the Faculty of Law at the University of Jember, Indonesia.

ICLARS Series on Law and Religion

The *ICLARS Series on Law and Religion* is a new series designed to provide a forum for the rapidly expanding field of research in law and religion. The series is published in association with the International Consortium for Law and Religion Studies, an international network of scholars and experts of law and religion founded in 2007 with the aim of providing a place where information, data and opinions can easily be exchanged among members and made available to the broader scientific community. The series aims to become a primary source for students and scholars while presenting authors with a valuable means to reach a wide and growing readership.

Series Editors:

Silvio Ferrari, University of Milan, Italy, Russell Sandberg, Cardiff University, UK, Pieter Coertzen, University of Stellenbosch, South Africa, W. Cole Durham, Jr., Brigham Young University, USA, and Tahir Mahmood, Amity International University, India

Other titles in this series:

The Transition of Religion to Culture in Law and Public Discourse
Lori Beaman

Religious Minorities, Islam and the Law
International Human Rights and Islamic Law in Indonesia
Al Khanif

The Internal Law of Religions
Introduction to a Comparative Discipline
Burkhard Josef Berkmann
Translated by David E. Orton

For more information about this series, please visit:
www.routledge.com/ICLARS-Series-on-Law-and-Religion/book-series/ICLARS

Religious Minorities, Islam and the Law

International Human Rights and Islamic Law in Indonesia

Al Khanif

Routledge
Taylor & Francis Group
LONDON AND NEW YORK

First published 2021
by Routledge
2 Park Square, Milton Park, Abingdon, Oxon OX14 4RN

and by Routledge
605 Third Avenue, New York, NY 10017

First issued in paperback 2022

Routledge is an imprint of the Taylor & Francis Group, an informa business

British Library Cataloguing-in-Publication Data
A catalogue record for this book is available from the British Library

Library of Congress Cataloging-in-Publication Data
Names: Khanif, Al, 1979- author.
Title: Religious minorities, Islam, and the law : international human rights and Islamic law in Indonesia / Al Khanif.
Description: New York : New York, 2020. | Includes bibliographical references and index.
Identifiers: LCCN 2020026079 (print) | LCCN 2020026080 (ebook) | ISBN 9780367500757 (hardback) | ISBN 9781003048695 (ebook)
Subjects: LCSH: Religious minorities–Legal status, laws, etc.–Indonesia. | Religious minorities–Civil rights–Indonesia. | Freedom of religion–Indonesia. | International law and human rights–Indonesia. | Civil rights (Islamic law)–Indonesia. | Customary law–Indonesia. | Religious minorities–Legal status, laws, etc. | International law and human rights.
Classification: LCC KNW2467.M56 K425 2020 (print) | LCC KNW2467.M56 (ebook) | DDC 342.59808/52–dc23
LC record available at https://lccn.loc.gov/2020026079
LC ebook record available at https://lccn.loc.gov/2020026080

ISBN: 978-0-367-50076-4 (pbk)
ISBN: 978-0-367-50075-7 (hbk)
ISBN: 978-1-003-04869-5 (ebk)

DOI: 10.4324/9781003048695

Typeset in Galliard
by Swales & Willis, Exeter, Devon, UK

Contents

Glossary

Abangan	A form of syncretistic religious belief
Abdurrahmah Wahid	Indonesian Muslim thinker and former president of the Republic of Indonesia
Adat	Indonesian customary law
Adatrechtskringen	Adat law region proposed by Cornelis Van Vollenhoven in the era of colonisation
Agama	An organised system of religious belief
Ahad	Narration of a *hadith* by one narrator so that the *hadith* is classified as dubious
Ahlul bait	Members of the Prophet's family
Ahlul kitab	People of the book
Ahmadiyah	A religious minority within Islam founded by Mirza Ghulam Ahmad in India in 1889
AKKBB	*Aliansi Kebangsaan untuk Kebebasan Beragama dan Berkeyakinan* or National Alliance for Freedom of Religion and Belief
Aliran	Religious sect
Aliran Kepercayaan	A form of Indonesian traditional belief
Al-ismah bi al-adamiyah	The universal human rights concept in Islam founded by Imam Abu Hanifa
Al-Qiyadah Al-Islamiyah	A religious sect led by Ahmad Musaddeq, who claims himself as a prophet
Amanah	Instructions made by MUI
Amicus Curiae	Friends of the court
Amir	A concept of commander or leader in the LDII
Aqidah	Creed in Islamic theology
Asas Tunggal	The sole principle in Indonesian statehood
Ashura	The anniversary of the martyrdom of Imam al-Husein at Karbala
Bakorpakem	Badan Koordinasi Pengawasan Aliran dan Kepercayaan or the Joint-Judiciary Committee of Religious Life

Bermasyarakat	An Indonesian concept of the spirit of being with people
Bhinneka Tunggal Ika	A principle of unity in diversity in Indonesian polity
Bid'ah	Innovations or any rituals which were not done by the Prophet
CDHRI	Cairo Declaration of Human Rights in Islam adopted by member states of the OIC in 1990
CERD	Committee on the Elimination of Racial Discrimination
CRCS	Center for Religious and Cross Cultural Studies at Gadjah Mada University
DarulArqam	A Sunni-Messianic Islamic Sect also known as Islam Jamaah or LDII
Dhimmis	Adherents of religions revealed before Islam
Fatwa	Islamic religious ruling, a scholarly opinion on a matter of Islamic law
Fiqh	Islamic jurisprudence
FKKI	Forum Komunikasi Kristen Indonesia or Forum for Christian Communication in Indonesia (FKKI)
FKUB	Forum Kerukunan antar Umat Beragama or the Forum of Religious Harmony
Forum Externum	External dimension of religious freedom
Forum Internum	Freedom of thought or conscience itself
FPI	Front Pembela Islam or Islamic Defender Front
furu'iyya	Branches of the law or jurisprudence in Islam
Gotong Royong	Mutual cooperation or volunteerism in Indonesian society
Grundnorm	A basic legal norm in Kelsenian theory
GUI	Gerakan Umat Islam or Muslim People Movement
Habl min al-nas	A concept of humanitarian noble spirit in Islam
Habl min-Allah	Relationship between human beings and God in Islam
Haram	Any act forbidden by God in Islam
Himbauan	Appeals made by MUI
HRC	Human Rights Committee
HTI	Hizbut Tahrir Indonesia or Indonesian Party Liberation
ICCPR	International Covenant on Civil and Political Rights
Ijma	Independent agreement among Muslim scholars
Ijtihad	Independent legal reasoning
Ikhtilaf	Differences of opinion among Muslim scholars on religious matters
ILRC	The Indonesian Legal Resource Center
Imamiyah	The concept of leadership in Shi'ah

Inter alia	A term which means "among other things"
Islah	The concept of improvement in Islam
Islam Jamaah	A Messianic Islamic group which renamed itself as Lembaga Dakwah Islam Indonesia (LDII)
Ius non scriptum	Unwritten law
Ius scriptum	Written law
JaksaAgung	Attorney General
Jalan Tengah	Margin of appreciation in the Indonesian socio-legal system to bridge the interest between the parties in order to achieve the right balance
Jam'iyyatul Islamiyah	A religious minority group in Islam in Indonesia accused by the MUI as deviant
JI	Jamaah Islamiyah or Islamic Congregation
JIL	Jaringan Islam Liberal or Liberal Islamic Network
Joint Ministerial Decree	A decree made by two or more ministers to administer a particular matter
Jural Community	Informal tribunal which is run by consensus and consists of community leaders such as the head of a village, the local police officer, religious leaders and community elders
Kades	Kepala Desa or head of a village
Kafir	An Islamic doctrine which refers to disbelievers or infidels
Kafir Londo	Nickname which refers to the Dutch in the era of colonisation
Kebatinan	Javanese religious tradition
Kecamatan	District
Kepercayaan	Non-organised religious belief
Kharijites	The first groups of Muslims who split away from Mainstream Islamic groups in the Caliphate Era
Khurafat	Non-Islamic beliefs
KLI	Komando Laskar Islam or Commando of the Islamic Army
Komnas HAM	Komisi Nasional Hak Asasi Manusia or National Human Rights Commission
KUHP	Kitab Undang-Undang Hukum Pidana or Indonesian Criminal Code
Kyai	A traditional Islamic scholar and this term is particularly used within the NU community
LDII	Lembaga Dakwah Islam Indonesia or Indonesian Islamic Propagation Board, an Indonesian-Sunni dominant minority
Lex specialis	A legal doctrine which states that if there are two laws governing the same factual situation, a law

	governing a special subject (*lex specialis*) overrides laws which only govern general matters (*lex generalis*)
MA	Mahkamah Agung or Supreme Court
Mahesa Kurung	A Sufi-Sunni Islam in Bogor West Java
Maslaha umma	A principle of public interest in Islamic law
Maslahah Mursalah	An Islamic concept of greater public interest for the Islamic community
Membumikan Islam	Indigenising Islam based on the Indonesian context
Menteri Dalam Negeri	Ministry of the Interior
MK	Mahkamah Konstitusi or Constitutional Court of the Republic of Indonesia
MMI	*Majelis Mujahidin Indonesia* or the Holy Warriors Council
MORA	Ministry of Religious Affairs
MPR	Majelis Permusyawaratan Rakyat or People's Consultative Assembly
Mu'amalat	Islamic concept of inter-human relations
Mufti	fatwa giver
Muhammadiyah	An Indonesian Islamic organisation founded by Ahmad Dahlan in 1912
MUI	Majelis Ulama Indonesia or Indonesian Ulema Council
Mujtahid	Islamic jurist
Munafiqun	A group of hypocrites in Islamic doctrine
Munas	*Musyawarah Nasional* or National Summit
Musyawarah	Consensus or informal litigation process held to overcome a particular dispute among people
Mutazilite	A school of thought in Islamic theology which is based on reason and rationalism
Nasakom	*Nasionalisme, Agama dan Komunisme* or Nationalism, Religionalism and Communism
NKRI	Negara Kesatuan Republik Indonesia or the Unitary State of the Republic of Indonesia
NTB	West Nusa Tenggara
NU	An Islamic organisation in Indonesia founded by Hasyim Asyarie in 1926
OHCHR	Office of the High Commissioner of Human Rights
OIC	Organisation of the Islamic Conference is an international organisation founded in 1969
Pancasila	Ideology of the state and the supreme source of law in the Indonesian legal system
Perda	*Peraturan Daerah* or bylaw
Peremptory norm	A fundamental principle of international law that is accepted by the international community of states

Pernyataan Sikap	Position Statements
Persis	Persatuan Islam or the Islamic Unity
Pesantren	A traditional Islamic school
PKS	Partai Keadilan Sejahtera or Prosperous Justice Party
PN	Pengadilan Negeri or Public Court
PP	*Peraturan Pemerintah* or Government Regulation
PT	Pengadilan Tinggi or Appeal Court
Qiblah	Direction that Muslims should face when Muslims do prayers
raison d'être	The most important reason
Rechtsstaat	Legal State or a state based on a constitution
Reformasi	A reformation movement in 1998 brought about by students, activists, scholars and politicians to overthrow the Soeharto Authoritarian regime and change it to democracy
Ridda	Apostasy or act of rejection of faith committed by Muslims
RT	Rukun Tetangga or Neighbourhood Harmony
Rukn Iman	Islamic faith
Sabb	Concept of blasphemy in Islam
Salafi	A religious minority within Islam which is based on strict literalism and Puritanism
Salam	The utterance which means peace
Salamullah	Religious sect led by Lia Aminudin, who claims herself as the archangel Gabriel and founded a new religion
Sati	A custom of Hindus in the Moghul era in which the widow is burned with the body of her late husband
Special Rapporteur	Special representative of the Secretary General and independent expert of the United Nations
Staatsfundamentalnorm	Basic constitutional norm
Sufi	A concept of mystical dimension in Islam
Sumbangan Pikiran	Thought contributions made by MUI
Sunni	The largest denomination of Islam
Syi'ar	To proselytise religious belief to other people
Syiah	An Indonesian term which refers to Shiite and the second largest denomination of Islam
Syirik	The concept of polytheism in Islam
Tadzkirah	Admonitions made by MUI
Tahayul	The concept of superstitions in Islam
Tahlilan	Reciting Qur'anic verses and other forms of Islamic rituals for persons who have passed away
Tajdid	The concept of reformation or renewal in Islam

Talaq	A term which refers to divorce in Islam
Taqlid	A follower of an Islamic jurist
Tarekat At-Tijani	A religious sect which believed that there would be a tsunami in Jakarta and that the Day of Judgement would occur on 17 August 2012
Tauhid	The concept of monotheism in Islam
Tausiyahs	Recommendation made by MUI
UDHR	Universal Declaration of Human Rights adopted by the UN General Assembly on 10 December 1948
UIDHR	Universal Islamic Declaration of Human Rights adopted by Islamic Councils in Paris and London
Ulama	Islamic scholars
Ulil Absar Abdalla	A founder of the Liberal Islamic Network
Umma	Islamic community in Islamic doctrine
Ummah	The concept of community in Islam
UN	United Nations
Wahdatul wujud	Idea of the unity of existence proposed by an Indonesian sufi, Siti Jenar
YKNCA	Yayasan Kanker dan Narkoba Cahaya Alam or Narcotic and Cancer Rehabilitation Centre
Zandaqah	Heresy or religious dissidence in Islam

1 Introduction

Indonesia is well known as a country with diverse ethnicities, cultures and religions. Despite being the largest Muslim populated country in the world – over 80% from an estimated 250 million are Muslims – Indonesia is not an "Islamic state"[1], but a Republic-Pancasila state.[2] Besides being the ideology of the state, Pancasila has also become a supreme source of law in the Indonesian legal system, as well as the philosophical foundation of the state polity.[3] The acknowledgement of Pancasila as a state ideology was designed by Indonesia's founders to build a collective awareness of the Indonesian socio-religious pluralistic character. Thus, apart from some criticisms of its vagueness and meaninglessness, Pancasila undoubtedly plays a significant role in Indonesia's legal discourse, a development seen most prominently after the establishment of the Indonesian Constitutional Court (Mahkamah Konstitusi, MK) in 2003.

Religious pluralism is also acknowledged in article 29 (1) of the 1945 Indonesian Constitution, by which the country believes in One Supreme God without referring to a specific name of God, leaving an open interpretation of this concept to all Indonesians. Thus, the 1945 Constitution makes provisions for all monotheistic religions and asserts that this supreme theistic canopy in the Indonesian legal system respects all believers equally, no matter which religious denomination they follow. This constitutional provision can be interpreted as

1 According to Nasim Hasan Shah, a state which is inhabited entirely by Muslims or predominantly Muslims is not synonymous with an Islamic state. What I mean by "Islamic state" in this book is a state which applies Islamic law as a supreme source of law in the constitution and national legislation. On the concept of Islamic state, see Nasim Hasan Shah, 'Islamic Concept of State' (1987) 26 *Islamic Studies* 97, 97–155.

2 "Pancasila", derived from Javanese philosophy, means five principles (*Panca* – five and *Sila* – principle); (1) belief in One Supreme God or monotheism, (2) just and civilised humanitarianism, (3) Indonesian unity, (4) democracy, and (5) social justice. See Howard M Federspiel, *A Dictionary of Indonesian Islam* (Ohio University, Center for International Studies 1995) 97. For further discussion on Pancasila, see Chapter 5 of this book.

3 See *e.g. Blasphemy Law* (2010) Mahkamah Konstitusi 140/PUU-VII/2009 305. and *Decree of the Indonesian Consultative Assembly on Legal Sources and Hierarchy of Indonesian Legal System 2000 (NO III/MPR/2000).*

saying that religion, under Pancasila and the 1945 Constitution, is a fundamental part of the legal and human rights system, as well as all aspects of national development in Indonesia. It is generally accepted that religion is one of the main elements of the democratic system adopted by Indonesia and must be applied as a necessary filter for all ideas, doctrines and any other forms of thoughts alien to Indonesian society. This means that religion must be interpreted by all Indonesians as a tool to boost human rights application in Indonesia, including the state's approach to complying with binding obligations of human rights instruments that have been ratified by the country.

Apart from the acknowledgement of the importance of religion, article 29 (2) of the 1945 Constitution further asserts that Indonesia acknowledges far-reaching religious freedom by guaranteeing the right of every person to embrace and practise his/her own religion. These two constitutional provisions signify that Indonesia, despite having asserted the significant influence of theistic religions in all aspects of development, has normatively acknowledged equal rights for all believers to embrace their religions or beliefs. This recognition was written into the constitution three years before the enactment of the Universal Declaration of Human Rights (UDHR) in 1948. Thus, it is argued that the basic acknowledgement of religious freedoms in Indonesia has historically not been influenced by international human rights doctrines, but instead derives from the Indonesian culture, which perceives religion as a significant element of life that should be enjoyed equally by every person. The religious principle of Pancasila and the 1945 constitutional religious rights clauses have become precepts of religious tolerance in Indonesia, especially in the early phase of modern (post-colonial) Indonesia and have partially inspired Indonesians to preserve religious tolerance in a form of dynamic religious pluralism.

As the world's largest Muslim populated country, Indonesia has basically been recognised as tolerant and pluralist.[4] Some say that Indonesians practise a more moderate and peaceful form of Islam than their counterparts in the Middle East, specifically on the issue of minority rights.[5] Since gaining independence in 1945 until the middle of 1998, when Soeharto, the leader of the New Order regime fell from power, religious conversion and proselytism tended to be unrestricted within the atmosphere and general provisions of a secular society.[6] Religious minorities also experienced less discriminatory treatment than they have faced more recently, because the New Order regime had established a monolithic harmonious relationship among religions. Religious minorities within Islam, such as the Shiite (hereafter Shi'ah) and Ahmadiyah, two of the largest religious

4 Andy Fuller, 'Religious Freedom in Indonesia: Curious Cases of Dialogues, Fatwas and Laws' (2011) 5 *Journal of Indonesian Islam* 1, 3.

5 James B Hoesterey, 'Is Indonesia a Model for the Arab Spring? Islam, Democracy, and Diplomacy' (2013) 47 *Review of Middle East Studies* 56, 3.

6 Murray Hunter, 'A Critical Essay on Islamic Freedom in ASEAN' (2014) 6 *Contemporary Readings in Law and Social Science* 3.

minorities within Islam in Indonesia,[7] lived side by side with the Muslim majority even though they had historically experienced some tensions.

The traditionally tolerant behaviour of the Indonesian Muslim majority towards their fellow religious minorities reflected that religious tolerance in Indonesia is not unfamiliar in the nation's history. Since its first inception in this archipelagic country, Islam has been thought of positively and equally as a facilitator of trade and, in affirmative ways, as a result of doctrinal adherence.[8] Religious tolerance among Muslims in Indonesia derives not only from Islamic theological approaches, but also from older, pre-Islamic traditional and customary norms of Indonesian society. Most Indonesian Muslims believe that Islam is a religion that should give peace and prosperity to all human beings.[9] Religious tolerance could be maintained because Islam is normally perceived by Indonesian Muslims as an umbrella term, which covers multiple groups and differences within the religion. While Muslims hold similar beliefs concerning God, the Prophet Muhammad and the holy Qur'an, a wide diversity exists when it comes to the details and interpretation of religious doctrines.[10] Thus, in most parts of Indonesia, Muslims can be generally divided into three main categories. The first are Muslims oriented towards mainstream orthodox Islamic teachings. The second are Muslims who self-define as Muslims, but do not practise Islamic teaching in the traditional manner.[11] The third are Muslims who practise non-mainstream Islamic beliefs, or religious minorities within Islam.

During its development, Islam in Indonesia has also shown a high degree of intellectual activity, which has promoted tolerant theological thought, civil pluralism and legal development. This proposition is emphasised by some scholars, who envisage that the future progress of Islam will not occur in the Middle East, but rather in Indonesia.[12] The phrase "future progress of Islam" means Islam as religion being used as a progressive tool to promote religious pluralism and boost human rights fulfilment, including the implementation of religious freedom for the adherents of all religions. Even though most religious

7 There are some sources which provide different data on the precise number of Shi'ah and Ahmadiyah members. Yet, each of these religious minorities within Islam is assumed to have less than 100,000 active members around Indonesia. See *e.g.* Human Rights Watch, 'In Religion's Name | Abuses against Religious Minorities in Indonesia' (*Human Rights Watch* 28 February 2013) www.hrw.org/report/2013/02/28/religions-name/abuses-against-religious-minorities-indonesia accessed 21 May 2019.

8 Fauzan Saleh, *Modern Trends in Islamic Theological Discourse in 20th Century Indonesia: A Critical Survey* (Brill 2001) 1.

9 Said Agil Siradj, 'The Sunni-Shi'ah Conflict and the Search for Peace in Indonesia' (2013) 7 *Journal of Indonesian Islam* 145, 5.

10 Ali Mamouri, 'Islam's Silent Majority: Moderate Voices Drowned Out by Extremists' (*The Conversation* 22 August 2014).

11 People who practise non-standard Islamic teaching are often associated with 'Islam KTP'. The KTP stands for *Kartu Tanda Penduduk* or Identity Card.

12 Carool Kersten, *Cosmopolitans and Heretics: New Muslim Intellectuals and the Study of Islam* (Columbia University Press 2011) 4.

persecutions against minority religions in Indonesia occurred in Muslim societies, it must be noted that the main cause of the persecution is the discontent of majority and minority relations in a fragile democratic environment and the communal character of religion in the country. This argument is drawn from the fact that even though Islam is the majority religion, Muslims can become victims when they are minorities in a particular society. On the other hand, in regions that are predominantly Muslim, Christians and other religious minorities are usually the victims.

The high degree of intellectual activity in Islam can also be seen from some Muslims who have promoted human rights norms in the country. Thus, even though some traditional Muslim scholars promote orthodox Islam to counter Islamic syncretism and reject heterodox Islam,[13] many open-minded Muslim scholars like the late Abdurrahman Wahid, the former president of Indonesia, frequently sought to defend the rights of religious minorities within Islam. Consequently, many Indonesian Muslims still subscribe to different Islamic schools of thought within the growing ascendance of Islamic reform.[14]

After the decline of the New Order, Indonesia has generally still maintained fluctuating peaceful relations among religions, apart from a bloody conflict between Christians and Muslims in 1999, as a consequence of the fragile democratic transition.[15] The government has also been able to ensure the protection of basic rights, especially civil and political rights for non-Muslim minorities, but not the rights of non-mainstream religious groups such as religious minorities within Islam. Since the fall of the New Order in 1998, the situation of religious minorities within Islam, especially the Shi'ah and Ahmadiyah, seems to be getting worse. Violations of religious rights have not only occurred in the regions where hard-line Islamic groups[16] such as the Islamic Defenders Front (FPI) dominate the public sphere, such as in Jakarta and most parts of West Java, but have also spread all over Indonesia. Besides living in fear, the Shi'ah and

13 The term heterodox Islam occurs as a consequence of the recognition of Islam as one of the official religions in Indonesia and the term official Islam is always determined by the state. On the recognition of six official religions, namely: Islam, Hinduism, Buddhism, Christian Protestants, Catholics and Confucianism, see the elucidation of article 1 of the *Presidential Decree on Blasphemy Law 1965 (No1/PNPS/1965)* and *Presidential Decree on the Revocation of Presidential Instruction No. 14 1967 2000 (No 6/2000)* on the Recognition of Confucianism.

14 Robert W Hefner, 'Islamization and the Changing Ethical Imagination in Java' (2013) 96 *Indonesia* 187, 4.

15 See *e.g.* Jon Goss, 'Understanding the "Maluku Wars": An Overview of the Sources of Communal Conflict and Prospects for Peace' (2004) 11 *Cakalele: Maluku Research Journal* 7, 88–89; Badrus Sholeh, 'The Dynamics of Muslim and Christian Relations in Ambon, Eastern Indonesia' (2013) 4 *International Journal of Business and Social Science* 9.

16 "Hardline" Islamic organisations refer to puritan-fundamentalist groups which believe that Islam has a separate and distinct system of rights and duties and hence take the position that international human rights law is not applicable or is only partly applicable in their domestic jurisdictions. See Niaz a Shah, *Women, the Koran and International Human Rights Law* (Brill 2006) 3.

Ahmadiyah also face discriminatory treatment from central and local governments, either from general government policies or from regulations that restrict the rights of religious minorities within Islam to embrace and practise their religious beliefs.[17] In 2010, the National Human Rights Commission (Komisi Nasional Hak Asasi Manusia, Komnas HAM) identified approximately 3,200 local laws as breaching the human rights of minorities, particularly those related to freedom from discrimination.[18]

Some members of religious minorities within Islam are persecuted and jailed by public courts due to their non-mainstream religious practices or are accused of causing conflicts among religious believers.[19] Perpetrators of the violence against such minorities generally receive light imprisonments or are exempt from any prison sentences.[20] Some human rights defenders have observed that decisions in cases of violations against religious minorities within Islam brought before the courts are often reached unfairly, due to the intervention of some Islamic majority groups, and thereby compromise the principle of judicial independence.[21] Thus, human rights defenders perceive that legal institutions have lost their autonomy in upholding laws relating to human rights, which has brought about a sharp decline in religious tolerance in Indonesia.

The contentious evaluation of human rights fulfilment for religious minorities within Islam has in fact become an anomaly within the spirit of the "*Reformasi*", or reformation era, which began in 1998. As a transition era from authoritarianism to democracy, *Reformasi* was followed by significant legislative reform. Within a very short time, the *Reformasi* government adopted a wide range of constitutional human rights provisions, enacted a Human Rights Act and ratified different international human rights instruments to enhance the fulfilment of human rights in the country.[22] Also, the far-reaching acknowledgement of monotheistic religious freedom has been upheld as one of the national agendas

17 Setara Institute reported that there were approximately 367 cases of violations against religious minorities in 2009 and only one case brought before the court, a case which successfully imprisoned Habieb Rizieq Shihab, a perpetrator of the Monas Incident. See generally Ismail Hasani, *Berpihak dan bertindak intoleran: intoleransi masyarakat dan restriksi negara dalam kebebasan beragama/berkeyakinan di Indonesia: laporan kondisi kebebasan beragama/berkeyakinan di Indonesia, 2008* (Setara Institute 2009) 3.

18 See Simon Butt and Nicholas Parsons, 'Judicial Review and the Supreme Court in Indonesia: A New Space for Law?' (2014) *Indonesia* 55, 3.

19 See verdict of Sampang Court on *Tajul Muluk Als H Ali Murtadha* (2012) Sampang 69/PID.B/2012/PN.Spg., which jailed Tajul Muluk, leader of Shi'ah, for four years.

20 See verdict of Serang Court on *Yusri bin Bisri* (2011) Serang No. 314/Pid.B/2011/PN.SRG.

21 Uli Parulian Sihombing and Indonesian Legal Resource Center (eds), *Injustice in Belief: Monitoring the Results of Cases on Blasphemy of Religion and Religious Hate Speech in Indonesia* (Indonesian Legal Resource Center 2012) 3.

22 Melissa Crouch, *Law and Religion in Indonesia: Conflict and the Courts in West Java* (Routledge 2014) 4. This includes ratification of several human rights instruments; *i.e.* CERD in 1999, Additional Protocol of the CEDAW in 2000, Additional Protocol of the CRC in 2001, International Convention of the Protection of the Rights of Migrant Workers and Members

of the *Reformasi* government even though this broad legal reform still did not improve issues of minority rights significantly.[23] The long history of rebellion by religious and ethnic groups, since the early period of Indonesia's modern history until the present day, has caused the central government to place trust in and emphasise the concept of the Indonesian unitary state, also known as NKRI, within a series of still-infant legal and human rights reforms.[24]

The recognition and protection of a monotheistic religious freedom have been greatly reaffirmed through the enactment of the Indonesian Human Rights Act in 1999[25] and the second amendment of the 1945 Constitution in 2000.[26] Article 28E of the 1945 Constitution provides, inter alia, that "every person shall be free to choose and to practise the religion of his/her choice". The same article further states that "every person shall have the right of freedom to believe his/her faith (*kepercayaan*), and to express his/her views and thoughts, in accordance with his/her conscience". A similar provision has also been written into article 22 of the Indonesian Human Rights Act 1999, stating that every person shall be free to hold and practise their religions or beliefs.

These achievements are, however, critiqued for failing to protect vulnerable groups such as non-mainstream religious minorities, including religious minorities within Islam. *Reformasi* theoretically meant to establish a more open and democratic society but has in fact seen vulnerable groups of people excluded. Persecutions of religious minorities within Islam have become an anomaly in the process of legal reform in Indonesia and have shown a lack of legal cohesion between legal reform in the theoretical realm and the realities of human rights protection. Based on the high number of persecutions of non-mainstream religious groups, including religious minorities within Islam, Indonesia has now been associated with states that have high restrictions on religious freedom or insufficient legal enforcement to protect religious minority groups. In 2011, the Pew Forum on Religion and Public Life, for example, reported that Indonesia had very high restrictions on religious freedom, indicated by the government's restrictions and social hostilities, especially towards the non-official minority

of their Families in 2004, ICCPR and ICESCR in 2006 and Convention on the Rights of Persons with Disabilities in 2007.

23 The concept of monotheistic religious freedom means such rights and freedoms must be in accordance with the first principle of Pancasila, namely Belief in One Supreme God as a supreme source of religious freedom in Indonesian human rights law.

24 The concept of NKRI is still significant in Indonesia even though in 2013 the Constitutional Court of Indonesia (Mahkamah Konstitusi, MK) adopted a verdict to review and rejected the idea of NKRI as one of four pillars of Indonesian polity. See the verdict of MK at *Revocation of Four Pillars on National and State Life* (2014) Mahkamah Konstitusi No. 100/PUU-XI/2013.

25 *Law Concerning Human Rights 1999.*

26 What I mean by monotheistic religious freedom is that all concepts of human rights including religious freedom must not contravene the first principle of Pancasila and article 29 of the 1945 Constitution which declares that Indonesia believes in One Supreme God.

religions in the state.[27] The restrictions were still high in 2013, when both the government and society at large imposed numerous limits on religious beliefs and practices for non-mainstream religions, including religious minorities within Islam.[28] The restriction on the rights of religious minorities within Islam is not only imposed by the Indonesian Ulema Council (Majelis Ulama Indonesia, MUI),[29] but also by the central and local governments,[30] a collaboration of the state and non-state actors and judicial institutions.

The Wahid Institute similarly reported that there were 93 cases related to the violation of religious freedom in Indonesia in 2011 with various kinds of violations, such as religious intolerance, vandalism, physical assault, intimidation, discrimination, hatred, killing and deviant accusations.[31] Most known cases are directed towards religious minorities within Islam that are seen to deviate from the Islamic orthodoxy officially recognised by the state. The most troubled religious minority group in this regard is Ahmadiyah, an Islamic religious minority marked as deviant to Islamic orthodoxy, which accounts for 47 of the 93 cases, approximately 50% of the total violations.[32] There are various kinds of perpetrators, such as organised and unorganised mobs affiliated with radical Islamic groups, the police, government officials, members of parliament, the Supreme Court[33] and local governments, as well as individuals. It should be noted that there are some other forms of violations unreported due to limited media coverage.

The Indonesian government's restrictions are indicated by the enactment of discriminatory laws, government policies and actions that ban particular faiths, especially unofficial religious minorities, or give preferential treatment to one or more religious groups.[34] Local governments in some regions are also accused of collaborating with hard-line religious groups to restrict religious minorities

27 Pew Research Center, 'Rising Restrictions on Religion – One-Third of the World's Population Experiences an Increase' (Pew Research Center 2011).

28 Pew Research Center, 'Latest Trends in Religious Restrictions and Hostilities' (Pew Research Center 2015).

29 See *e.g. Fatwa* of MUI dated 7 May 2005 concerning Bilingual Prayer, *Fatwa* of MUI East Java No. Kep-01/SKF-MUI/JTM/I/2012 concerning Shi'ah, *Fatwa* of MUI No. 11/MUNAS VII/MUI/15/2005 concerning Ahmadiyah & *Fatwa* of MUI Sampang East Java No. 0-35/MUI/SPG/1/2012 concerning Shi'ah.

30 See *e.g.* Decree of East Java Governor No. 188/94/KPTS/013/2012 concerning the restriction of Ahmadiyah activities & Decree of East Java Governor No. 55/2012 concerning the restriction of the spread of so-called "deviant" religious teaching.

31 See generally Yenny Zannuba Wahid, 'Lampu Merah Kebebasan Beragama, Laporan Kebebasan Beragama Dan Toleransi Di Indonesia 2011' (The Wahid Institute 2011).

32 ibid 3.

33 In an appeal on the prohibition of Ahmadiyah in Bogor West Java by local government in 2007, the Supreme Court refused to repeal the policy and confirmed that the prohibition by collective government offices is not illegal. This verdict signifies that Ahmadiyah in West Java are still prohibited from practising their religious freedom. See *Cassation of the Prohibition of Ahmadiyah* (2009) Supreme Court of the Republic of Indonesia No. 182 K/TUN/2007.

34 ibid 9–10.

within Islam. One reason often adduced is that the local government is authorised by law to ensure and protect social and religious harmony among religious adherents.[35] Central and local governments generally prefer to restrict the rights of religious minorities within Islam to achieve religious harmony within society because most Muslims believe that non-mainstream groups, such as the Shi'ah and Ahmadiyah, uphold deviant Islamic beliefs. In fact, under article 18 of the International Covenant on Civil and Political Rights (ICCPR) and General Comment No. 22 of the Human Rights Committee, embracing a certain religious belief is protected unconditionally so that no one can be compelled to reveal his adherence to a certain religion or belief.[36] Thus, Indonesia, as a state party to the ICCPR, must ensure that all individuals can enjoy their freedom of religion or belief on the basis of respect for their inherent human dignity.

On a domestic level, even though there are several Indonesian laws, such as the first principle of Pancasila, the 1945 Constitution and the Human Rights Act 1999, that recognise human rights comprehensively, especially the rights of non-mainstream religions, there are other ordinances that contain discriminative provisions and are still currently applied. For instance, article 156 (a) of the Indonesian Criminal Code (Kitab Undang-Undang Hukum Pidana, KUHP) asserts that spreading heresy, blasphemy or defamation of religion is punishable by up to five years in prison. This law is hereafter referred to as the KUHP Blasphemy Law. These articles of the KUHP Blasphemy Law refer to the content of article 1 of the Presidential Decree No. 1/PNPS/1965, which asserts that nobody can intentionally and publicly persuade people to reinterpret religion (which automatically refers to the six official religions) in Indonesia or conduct deviant religious activities.[37] This Presidential Decree is hereafter referred to as the 1965 Blasphemy Law.

Until recently, many of those sectarian groups were not officially recognised as religions by the state, thus the government may be forced to choose conversion as a refuge from potential accusations, imprisonment and discrimination, as well as suspicion of communism.[38] For instance, in order to get basic rights, members of religious minorities are also forced to identify themselves on their national identity cards as followers of a religion that is different from their actual religion.[39] This policy would clearly go against the universalistic spirit of human

35 See article 10 of the *Regional Autonomy Law 2004.*

36 See *Compilation of General Comments and General Recommendations Adopted by Human Rights Treaty Bodies 2008 (Human Rights Instrument) 156.*

37 See Ota Atsushi, Okamoto Masaaki and Ahmad Suaedy, *Islam in Contention: Rethinking Islam and State in Indonesia* (Wahid Institute 2010) 158–159. Phrase in brackets was added by the writer.

38 Jacques Bertrand, *Nationalism and Ethnic Conflict in Indonesia* (Cambridge University Press 2004) 74.

39 Religion is written in people's national identity cards (KTP) and the adherents of unofficial religious minorities or religious sects are required to write one of the six official religions in their KTP. See Luthfi Assyaukanie, *Islam and the Secular State in Indonesia* (Institute of Southeast Asian Studies 2009) 156.

rights, based on respect for everyone's human dignity, because it often negatively affects members of minority religions, as well as religious minorities within Islam. This policy can be classified as an administrative force or a sanction that is not in accordance with General Comment No. 22, which says that all sanctions that would impair the right to have or adopt a religion or belief are prohibited under international human rights law.[40]

International human rights law theoretically does not restrict states or parties to recognise a certain religion as a state religion. Yet, when a particular religion is established as an official religion of the state, this shall not discriminate against adherents of other religions or non-believers.[41] It implies that the state recognition of six official religions is often used by government and mass organisations to justify discrimination and restrictions against religious minorities, or those marked as threats against national and communal security interests. In some cases, state and non-state actors have often collaborated to systematically exclude religious minorities from the concept of Indonesian unity and religious harmony.

Those two discriminative laws, the 1965 Blasphemy Law and the KUHP Blasphemy Law, are intended to protect religious orthodoxy and the religious interpretation of majorities, all of whom occupy the upper hierarchy in society and determine the proper rights for the lower minority groups. The enactment of those two laws asserts that the strong religious belief of the majority is incorporated into the national legal system, which brings about the unshakable religious rights of the majority. Recognition of official religions by the state and discriminatory treatment toward "non-official" religious minorities, stipulated in the Indonesian legal system, illustrates that the higher religions in Indonesia (official religions) are marked as orthodox, authoritative and supreme, while the lower (non-official) religions are marked as deviant, misleading or even enemies of official religions.

This has resulted in different social hostility measures, such as acts of religious hostility by private individuals, organisations and social groups, including mob or sectarian violence against the non-official religions.[42] The mobs, usually affiliated with Islamic majority or radical groups, often take advantage of the government restrictions and rely on *fatwas* from the Indonesian Ulama Council (MUI)[43] to justify their restrictions, even though *fatwas* are not legally binding

40 *Compilation of General Comments and General Recommendations Adopted by Human Rights Treaty Bodies 156.*

41 ibid 157.

42 Pew Forum on Religion and Public Life, 'Rising Restrictions on Religion – One-Third of the World's Population Experiences an Increase' (*Pew Research Center's Religion & Public Life Project* 9 August 2011) 10 www.pewforum.org/2011/08/09/rising-restrictions-on-religion2/ accessed 8 June 2017.

43 The MUI was established in 1975 at the initiative of the government to control public expression of Islam under state auspices. The MUI is authorised to issue *fatwa*, which means an Islamic religious ruling, a scholarly opinion on a matter of Islamic law and non-*fatwa* discourses. To obtain an explanation of the *fatwa* discourse in Indonesia, see Piers Gillespie, 'Current Issues in Indonesian Islam: Analysing the 2005 Council of Indonesian Ulama Fatwa

in the Indonesian legal system. The religious majorities, who have special access to the government through the legalisation of their religions and their representation in religious institutions, have frequently abused the rights of religious minorities in the country. It must be noted that even though Islam is the majority in Indonesia, it can become the minority in other regions due to the implementation of regional autonomy in 1999. Islam is not the majority in Bali, nor is it in other parts of Eastern Indonesia. In this matter, generally, government policies substantiate social hostilities against the rights of religious minorities, putting the religious minorities on the ground as groups of people who are unable to live peacefully and who suffer frequent economic, political and social discrimination, occasionally facing personal and/or group-based violence.[44]

The persecution of religious minorities within Islam has increased since the fall of the New Order Regime and the beginning of the "Reformation era" in 1998. Consequently, there has been a decline in the implementation of the ideology of tolerance in Pancasila, the spirit of religious diversity as a genuine feature of Indonesia and the protection of freedom of religion or belief guaranteed in the 1945 Constitution and the ICCPR[45] (ratified by Indonesia in 2006). This situation has apparently been facilitated by the government's special treatment of particular religions, which has significantly discriminated against religious minorities, especially when the state acted as the guardian of religions and, consequently, could not successfully release itself from partial religious interference. This is reflected in the religious institutions, such as the Ministry of Religious Affairs (MORA), the MUI and Islamic mass organisations that significantly control people's religious life in the country. They habitually refer to article 28J (2) of the 1945 Constitution, which recognises "religious values"[46] and the KUHP and 1965 Blasphemy Laws as legitimate and legal grounds to limit rights and freedoms. It may be assumed that even though religion in Indonesia is theoretically subordinated by secular law due to the absence of a constitutional status for particular religions,[47] most Indonesian people in

No. 7 Opposing Pluralism, Liberalism and Secularism' (2007) 18 *Journal of Islamic Studies* 202, 207–208.

44 Mary Gardiner Jones, 'National Minorities: A Case Study in International Protection' (1949) 14 *Law and Contemporary Problems* 599, 602.

45 See article 18 of the ICCPR.

46 Article 28J (2) of the 1945 Constitution says

> in exercising his/her rights and freedoms, every person shall have the duty to accept the restrictions established by law for the sole purposes of guaranteeing the recognition and respect of the rights and freedoms of others and of satisfying just demands based upon considerations of morality, *religious values*, security and public order in a democratic society.

47 The recognition of the six official religions, namely: Islam, Hinduism, Buddhism, Christian Protestants, Catholics and Confucianism, is based on the elucidation of article 1 of the *Law on Blasphemy 1965* and the *Presidential Decree on the Recognition of Confucianism 2000.*

practice still consider religion as higher than the law, as collectively formulated within the secular context of the state.[48]

Based on the "secular" character of the 1945 Constitution and Pancasila, it is submitted that the recognition of six official religions, including Islam, by the government does not mean that these recognised religions have the right to restrict any unofficial religions in Indonesia. Additionally, the recognition of a strict orthodox version of a particular religion cannot be used to justify discrimination against non-mainstream religious teachings within the religion. Regrettably, empirical studies show that the rights of religious minorities are not based upon the individual rights of the people, as stipulated in the state ideology and constitution, because the right to embrace particular religions has theoretically been taken over by the state and the majority population. The MUI, the MORA, some Islamic mass organisations and the government routinely use the KUHP and 1965 Blasphemy Laws to restrict non-mainstream religions and argue that these laws are a legal elucidation of the constitution and the state ideology.

The other reason for the rise of persecutions against religious minorities appears to be that the fall of the New Order regime has also led to the birth of vocal and anti-democratic religious groups, which often resort to violence. These groups argue that laws, such as Pancasila, the 1945 Constitution and the international human rights instruments, which protect religious beliefs in a wider context, not only disturb religious harmony but also would change the character or identity of the country's religious community. Thus, some Muslim groups have pushed to introduce an "Islamic standard" into the Indonesian legal system or try to interpret all regulations on religious freedom based on their version of Islamic law.[49] Some other Muslims also interpret the first principle of Pancasila as only referring to their God and believe that the provision of religious freedom in the 1945 Constitution should be properly determined by their own community and that the broad dimension of the rights of religious minorities in international human rights law can be voided if it disturbs their rights. For example, some Islamic organisations such as FPI have frequently subordinated Pancasila and the 1945 Constitution by referring to their traditional religious orthodoxy for an understanding of the scope of religious freedom.

The previous analysis demonstrates that the entitlement to the rights of religious minorities within Islam in Indonesia is generally based, not on the writing of legal instruments, but on a perceived consensus of the majority. The consensus can occur both in a courtroom as well as in a non-litigation process by a rural community. Additionally, the majority also uses blasphemy laws to

48 'Wahid Institute › Programs › Annual Report on Religious Freedom and Religious Life in Indonesia' (The Wahid Institute 2009).

49 On the effort of some Muslim groups to incorporate Islamic values into the 1945 Constitution, see Simon Butt, 'Islam, the State and the Constitutional Court in Indonesia' (2010) 19 *Pacific Rim Law & Policy Journal* 279, 283.

discriminate against every person who performs or promotes non-mainstream Islamic religious teachings. Based on this complexity, the issue of religious minorities within Islam in Indonesia cannot be solved from one single legal perspective, such as international human rights law or Islamic law respectively, but must also consider other socio-legal traditions and customs operating within the society. Therefore, this study will explore the contentious interaction between international human rights law and Islamic law as well as other Indonesian socio-legal traditions and customs relating to the protection of religious minorities within Islam.

1. The significance of the book

Based on the preceding background analysis, the main purpose of this book is to examine the complexity of the legal and human rights discourses in Indonesia to protect the rights of religious minorities within Islam in the country. There is a legal conundrum between the protection of religious freedom in international and national written documents, the differences of opinion (*ikhtilaf*) on the protection of theological differences in Islamic law and the practice of non-litigation or "consensus" as part of the Indonesian legal tradition. As a state that still absorbs cultural and religious values in its legislation, the Indonesian secular legal system generates a great bulk of human rights discourse. On the one hand, Indonesian law is generally characterised secularly, but on the other hand it also accommodates religious values to set the standard of permissible rights and freedoms for individuals and groups. Thus, the effective protection of the rights of religious minorities within Islam in Indonesia requires, as a matter of necessity, a consideration of the full spectrum of Indonesian law, society and culture.

In exploring these purposes, the book focuses specifically on interactions and processes in a socio-legal context about the protection of religious minorities within Islam which are seen as deviant or heretic by the official Islamic religious orthodoxy recognised in Indonesia. This discussion provides a critical analysis of the issues, covering the relevant legal, political, social and religious perspectives. This is because discussing the rights of religious minorities, especially religious minorities within particular religions, cannot be separated from the critical examination of issues relating to religious orthodoxy, the concept of the nation-state and the legal scope of the right to freedom of religion in international human rights law.

Firstly, the book examines how international human rights law regulates the legal position of religious minorities, especially their religious freedom. It generally explores the concept and the scope of the right to freedom of religion. This is aimed at laying the necessary foundation of the scope and limitations of the right to freedom of religion under international human rights law, within which the engagement and discourse of the rights of religious minorities within Islam in Indonesia will consequently be explored. It is important, in that regard, to also examine the contentious debate about the universality of human rights in relation to the rights of religious minorities within Islam in the Indonesian context.

Secondly, it interrogates how Islamic law defines and treats religious minorities generally. It then seeks to identify the formulation of Islamic law regarding the rights of religious minorities within Islam specifically. This necessarily engages with the role of Islam in Indonesia and explores the different legal arguments from egalitarian and conservative Islamic scholars on the issue of minority rights. It then determines which view is currently prevailing in Indonesia and proposes the most appropriate human rights friendly view to be applied in Indonesia, based on the social and legal contexts. This process is important because the influence of Islamic orthodoxy has immensely shaped the history and level of persecution of minorities in the country, even though Indonesia has ratified different international human rights instruments and has denounced the establishment of an Islamic state.

Thirdly, the examination of the Indonesian social context is concerned with the concept of theocratic society in relation to the presence of religious minorities within Islam, who are seen as aliens to the inner official religious-cultural orthodoxy. This is to evaluate how Islamic clerics play a significant role in pressuring state policy and influencing the scope and implementation of the right to freedom of religion in Indonesia. Additionally, it also examines the relationship between different social-legal concepts such as: the quasi-theistic secular state, religious harmony within society, Indonesian unity and the impact of the protection of religious minorities within Islam in the country.

Another important discussion includes engaging with how Pancasila, as the supreme source of law, and the 1945 Constitution protect religious minorities within Islam. It evaluates the framework of Indonesia's national human rights scheme and the country's international obligation to protect religious minorities within Islam. At first, it engages with the different treatment of religious minorities, in general, within the human rights framework of the Indonesian Constitution and other relevant Indonesian rights legislation and policies. Essentially, this discussion is aimed at examining the plight of religious minorities within the hierarchical structure of Indonesian law and evaluates to what extent the rights of religious minorities in Indonesian legislation are influenced by Islamic law and international human rights law.

With regard to the role of the Indonesian judiciary in protecting the rights of religious minorities within Islam in the country, the research also critically examines the judicial review of the 1965 Blasphemy Law KUHP Blasphemy Law, brought before the Indonesian Constitutional Court by several human rights organisations, Islamic scholars and human rights activists in 2009. This part specifically examines the distinctive concept of Indonesian law adopted by judges of the Constitutional Court to examine blasphemy law. It analyses the legal trajectory and implementation of the provisions on religious freedom in international human rights law, Islamic law and Indonesian law – especially unwritten rules.

The relevance of Indonesian customary law is also explored because the Indonesian Muslim society generally perceives the presence of religious minorities within Islam as alien to the inner religious and cultural norms of Indonesian society. The book goes on to evaluate how Indonesian customary law tries to resolve conflicts between mainstream Islamic groups and religious minorities within Islam. It then discusses how the norms of international human rights law on religious freedom, and the rights of religious minorities, encounter various local values such as religion and tradition within Indonesian society, which generally privileges community and religious harmony over individual religious rights.

This book does not repudiate that religious minorities have the right to embrace and practise their religion or beliefs. Besides being protected to enjoy their own culture and speak their own language, the rights of minorities to embrace and practise their religion or beliefs should not be denied.[50] In Indonesia for example, some communities constituting a minority speak their own language, share their own culture among members and profess and practise their own religion or beliefs.[51] Yet, it must be emphasised that the Ahmadiyah and Shi'ah, as two religious minorities within Islam studied in this book, speak the same language, share the same culture and belong to the same race as the Muslim majorities in a particular society where they reside together.

The Ahmadiyah and Shi'ah are categorised as "religious minorities" due to their different understanding of Islamic teachings from the Muslim majority. Thus, the protection of their rights is closely related to religious freedom, stipulated in article 18 of the ICCPR. In the context of international human rights law, even though the ICCPR and General Comment of the HRC do not explicitly explain the internal pluralism within a certain religion, the protection of the right of religious minorities within Islam to embrace different Islamic teachings must fall within the framework of articles 18 and 27 of the ICCPR.[52] On the other hand, the significance of Islamic law on this matter is due to the fact that most Muslims in Indonesia, and in the Muslim world, perceive Islam as an integral part of the legal system that must be obeyed by all Muslims. Thus, besides promoting international human rights law, this book is also aimed at promoting the internal reformation of Muslims' thoughts to protect the rights of religious minorities within Islam.

Based on the examination above, the contribution of this research is significant in terms of the knowledge, theory and practice of minority rights generally, but specifically in relation to the understanding of the challenges to, and possible remedies for, the protection of religious minorities within Islam in

50 *Compilation of General Comments and General Recommendations Adopted by Human Rights Treaty Bodies 159.*

51 See for example discussion on a syncretistic religion practised by the Sasak Tribe in Lombok West Nusa Tenggara in Erni Budiwanti, *Islam Sasak: Wetu Telu versus Waktu Lima* (LKiS 2000).

52 See for example Nazila Ghanea-Hercock, 'A Human Rights Framework for Defining and Understanding Intra-Religious Persecution in Muslim Countries', in Nazila Ghanea-Hercock, *The Challenge of Religious Discrimination at the Dawn of the New Millennium* (Springer 2013) 87.

Indonesia. It is therefore expected to enrich the study of human rights generally in Indonesia, but especially with regard to the protection of religious minorities within Islam. This research may also be used to expand or test the existing theories to find new propositions on the topic, so that Indonesians and other scholars can have a new general legal paradigm of the protection of religious minorities in Indonesia.

2. The book's structure

This book is divided into eight chapters. The first is this Introductory Chapter, which provides the necessary background of the book. This chapter also illustrates the significant issues and questions of the book.

The second chapter provides an analysis of the universal concept of the rights of religious minorities and how their definition, provision and protection are regulated by international human rights instruments. It also provides an analysis of the rights of religious minorities within Islam, under Islamic law. This chapter specifically examines the differences and similarities in human rights protection under international human rights law and Islamic law respectively, with particular emphasis on the standard of recognition and protection of the rights of religious minorities within Islam. It also analyses the potential challenges and obstacles in the application of international human rights and Islamic norms in the Muslim world, including Indonesia.

The third chapter engages with the discourse of religion and its relationship with the complex protection of religious minorities in Indonesia. This chapter discusses the history of Islam, the existence of religious institutions, the position of Islam as a public religion within the Indonesian legal spectrum and the debate of secularisation in Indonesia. It also examines the complex role of religion in Indonesia as a quasi-theistic secular state, a state which provides equal opportunity for all monotheistic religions to exist but at the same time does not explicitly declare itself as a theocratic state. It will then interrogate the existence of religious institutions and Islamic organisations, which frequently create complexities in the protection of religious minorities within Islam in Indonesia. The close relation of state and religion in Indonesia is also examined, together with the challenges that it poses for international human rights law to effectively implement a universal standard of religious freedom for non-mainstream religious beliefs.

Chapter 4 discusses three types of persecutions for religious minorities within Islam in Indonesia, specifically the persecution of the right to embrace and practise non-mainstream religious beliefs. The first section of this chapter uses examples of persecutions from other countries, especially cases of persecutions of religious minorities within Islam in other parts of the Muslim world. It critically examines state-sanctioned enforcement actions, extra-legal enforcement and mixed cases of persecution of non-mainstream Islamic groups.

Chapter 5 then analyses the challenges to protect the "*forum internum*" or the internal right to profess religion for religious minorities within Islam in

Indonesia. This chapter examines the scope of religious freedom under the principle of Pancasila, the 1945 constitutional provisions of religious freedom and human rights law enacted in 1999, to understand the status of religious minorities within Islam in the Indonesian human rights scheme. The last section then evaluates the recognition of "religious values" in the constitution as a restriction on certain freedoms and rights, including the rights of religious minorities within Islam.

The sixth chapter examines the challenges in protecting the "*forum externum*", that is the external right to practise religion for religious minorities within Islam in Indonesia. This chapter examines the challenges for religious minorities within Islam to build religious places of worship, to openly propagate their religious beliefs, to receive administrative services and other practical rights. It also examines a case of religious-inspired hate speech brought before the Central Jakarta Court in 2008.

Chapter 7 follows the analysis of the case about judicial review of the blasphemy law, brought before the Constitutional Court of the Republic of Indonesia in 2009. This judicial review action was meant to repeal the blasphemy law, which triggered many religious persecutions of religious minorities within Islam in Indonesia. It is intended to provide an understanding of the character of judicial interpretation of Indonesian law and its impact on the individualism of human rights, as well as the influence of Islamic law in Indonesia. Chapter 8, as the concluding chapter, provides the overall conclusions and recommendations of the study. The recommendation of the research will provide a midway alternative approach for the protection of religious minorities within Islam through the integration of legal and human rights discourse in Indonesia.

Bibliography

Assyaukanie L, *Islam and the Secular State in Indonesia* (Institute of Southeast Asian Studies 2009).

Atsushi O, Masaaki O and Suaedy A, *Islam in Contention: Rethinking Islam and State in Indonesia* (The Wahid Institute 2010).

Bertrand J, *Nationalism and Ethnic Conflict in Indonesia* (Cambridge University Press 2004).

Budiwanti E, *Islam Sasak: Wetu Telu versus Waktu Lima* (LKiS Pelangi Aksara 2000).

Butt S, 'Islam, the State and the Constitutional Court in Indonesia' (2010) 19 *Pacific Rim Law & Policy Journal* 279.

Butt S and Parsons N, 'Judicial Review and the Supreme Court in Indonesia: A New Space for Law?' (2014) 97 *Indonesia* 55.

Cassation Verdict of the Prohibition of Ahmadiyah (2009) Supreme Court of the Republic of Indonesia No. 182 K/TUN/2007.

Compilation of General Comments and General Recommendations Adopted by Human Rights Treaty Bodies 2008 (United Nations International Human Rights Instruments).

Crouch M, *Law and Religion in Indonesia: Conflict and the Courts in West Java* (Routledge 2014).

Decree of the Indonesian Consultative Assembly on Legal Sources and Hierarchy of Indonesian Legal System 2000 (NO III/MPR/2000).

Federspiel HM, *A Dictionary of Indonesian Islam* (Ohio University, Center for International Studies 1995).

Fuller A, 'Religious Freedom in Indonesia: Curious Cases of Dialogues, Fatwas and Laws' (2011) 5 *Journal of Indonesian Islam* 1.

Ghanea-Hercock N, 'A Human Rights Framework for Defining and Understanding Intra-Religious Persecution in Muslim Countries', in Nazila Ghanea-Hercock, *The Challenge of Religious Discrimination at the Dawn of the New Millennium* (Springer 2013).

Gillespie P, 'Current Issues in Indonesian Islam: Analysing the 2005 Council of Indonesian Ulama Fatwa No. 7 Opposing Pluralism, Liberalism and Secularism' (2007) 18 *Journal of Islamic Studies* 202.

Goss J, 'Understanding the "Maluku Wars": An Overview of the Sources of Communal Conflict and Prospects for Peace' (2004) 11 *Cakalele: Maluku Research Journal* 7.

Hasani I, *Berpihak dan bertindak intoleran: intoleransi masyarakat dan restriksi negara dalam kebebasan beragama/berkeyakinan di Indonesia: laporan kondisi kebebasan beragama/berkeyakinan di Indonesia, 2008* (Setara Institute 2009).

Hefner RW, 'Islamization and the Changing Ethical Imagination in Java' (2013) 96 *Indonesia* 187.

Hoesterey JB, 'Is Indonesia a Model for the Arab Spring? Islam, Democracy, and Diplomacy' (2013) 47 *Review of Middle East Studies* 56.

Human Rights Watch, 'In Religion's Name | Abuses against Religious Minorities in Indonesia' (*Human Rights Watch* 28 February 2013) www.hrw.org/report/2013/02/28/religions-name/abuses-against-religious-minorities-indonesia accessed 21 May 2019.

Hunter M, 'A Critical Essay on Islamic Freedom in ASEAN' (2014) 6 *Contemporary Readings in Law and Social Science* 82.

Jones MG, 'National Minorities: A Case Study in International Protection' (1949) 14 *Law and Contemporary Problems* 599.

Kersten C, *Cosmopolitans and Heretics: New Muslim Intellectuals and the Study of Islam* (Columbia University Press 2011).

Law Concerning Human Rights No. 39/1999.

Law on Blasphemy No. 1/PNPS 1965.

Mamouri A, 'Islam's Silent Majority: Moderate Voices Drowned Out by Extremists' (*The Conversation* 22 August 2014).

Pew Forum on Religion and Public Life, 'Rising Restrictions on Religion – One-Third of the World's Population Experiences an Increase' (Pew Research Center's Religion & Public Life Project 9 August 2011) www.pewforum.org/2011/08/09/rising-restrictions-on-religion2/ accessed 8 June 2017.

Pew Research Center, 'Rising Restrictions on Religion – One-Third of the World's Population Experiences an Increase' (Pew Research Center 2011).

———, 'Latest Trends in Religious Restrictions and Hostilities' (Pew Research Center 2015).

Presidential Decree No. 1/PNPS/1965 on the Prevention of Blasphemy and Abuse of Religions.

Presidential Decree on the Recognition of Confucianism 2000.

Presidential Decree No. 6/2000 on the Revocation of Presidential Instruction No. 14/1967.

Regional Autonomy Law No. 32/2004.

Saleh F, *Modern Trends in Islamic Theological Discourse in 20th Century Indonesia: A Critical Survey* (Brill 2001).

Shah NA, *Women, the Koran and International Human Rights Law* (Brill 2006).

Shah NH, 'Islamic Concept of State' (1987) 26 *Islamic Studies* 97.

Sholeh B, 'The Dynamics of Muslim and Christian Relations in Ambon, Eastern Indonesia' (2013) 4 *International Journal of Business and Social Science* 9.

Sihombing UP and Indonesian Legal Resource Center (eds), *Injustice in Belief: Monitoring the Results of Cases on Blasphemy of Religion and Religious Hate Speech in Indonesia* (Indonesian Legal Resource Center 2012).

Siradj SA, 'The Sunni-Shi'ah Conflict and the Search for Peace in Indonesia' (2013) 7 *Journal of Indonesian Islam* 145.

Verdict on Judicial Review of Blasphemy Law No. 1/PNPS/1965 (2010) Mahkamah Konstitusi 140/PUU-VII/2009.

Verdict on the Revocation of Four Pillar on National and State Life (2014) Mahkamah Konstitusi No. 100/PUU-XI/2013.

Verdict of Tajul Muluk Als H Ali Murtadha (2012) Sampang 69/PID.B/2012/PN.Spg.

Verdict of Yusri bin Bisri (2011) Serang No. 314/Pid.B/2011/PN.SRG.

'Wahid Institute › Programs › Annual Report on Religious Freedom and Religious Life in Indonesia' (The Wahid Institute 2009).

Wahid YZ, 'Lampu Merah Kebebasan Beragama, Laporan Kebebasan Beragama Dan Toleransi Di Indonesia 2011' (The Wahid Institute 2011).

2 Religious minorities under international human rights law and Islamic law

1. The scope of human rights law

It is necessary to discuss the rights of religious minorities as a human right within Islam in a wider context. This is to show that the fundamental reason for the protection of the rights of religious minorities is not based on their religious status but is related to their status as dignified human beings. International human rights instruments comprehensively honour human beings by asserting that all humans are born free with equal rights and dignity. Therefore, everyone should be entitled to human rights without any kind of distinction such as race, colour, sex, language, religion, political or other opinion, national or social origin, property, birth or other status.[1] The instruments further assert: "each state party must ensure that all individuals are granted their rights equally without distinction based on, *inter alia*, religion".[2] The instruments also require that all persons should be entitled to their rights equally and the state should prohibit any discrimination which impairs the equal enjoyment of rights and provide effective protection against discrimination on any ground such as, inter alia, religion.[3]

The principles of equality and non-discrimination have become fundamental to the peremptory nature of international human rights law.[4] The two principles affirm the character of human rights as universal because the entitlement of these rights is not according to membership of a particular group but according

1 See *e.g.* the preamble and article 1 and 2 of the UDHR, the preamble of the CEDAW, the CERD and the Convention on the Rights of Persons with Disabilities and article 55 of the UN Charter.

2 See *e.g.* article 2 (1) of the ICCPR. The regulation of "equal treatment" is also stipulated in the preambles of the Convention against Torture and Other Cruel, Inhuman and Degrading Treatment or Punishment (CAT) and the Convention on the Rights of the Child (CRC), which say that equal and inalienable rights are the foundation of freedom and justice in the world.

3 See article 26 of the ICCPR and Compilation of General Comments and General Recommendations Adopted by Human Rights Treaty Bodies 2006 167.

4 See Olivier De Schutter, *International Human Rights Law: Cases, Materials, Commentary* (Cambridge University Press 2014) 123.

to the character of the right.[5] Therefore, the entitlement to human rights is generally not due to the status of a person as a member of a minority or majority group, religious affiliation, political party or other organisations or his status as a person who has a different religion or belief.[6] Thus, it may be noted that the principles of equality and non-discrimination are two fundamental aspects of international human rights architecture because all international human rights instruments recognise those two principles. Additionally, the equality principle has been placed at the forefront of the human rights agenda for many years in response to the culture of inequality stubbornly entrenched in all societies.[7] The provision of "born free with equal rights and dignity" in Article 1 of the UDHR and Article 26 of the ICCPR also reaffirms that human rights are rights characterised as universal, not benefits, duties, privileges, or some other perhaps related practice as the result of the dignity of being human. To be entitled to those rights, someone should not be anything other than human,[8] because the universality of rights is rooted in the inherent dignity and the inherent character of these rights.[9] International human rights instruments concern the right of individuals to enjoy equal human rights in all situations because rights and freedoms should be possessed by all human beings equally.[10] This establishes that the instruments put human beings as the subjects of human rights and every discussion of human rights should refer to the human being as the holder of these rights.

The enactment of the Charter of the United Nations (UN) and, subsequently, the international bill of rights was not simply to regulate the relations between states for the prevention of war but also to establish a new world order based on the recognition and protection of the rights and dignity of human beings. The enactment of international human rights instruments is meant to protect human dignity by limiting the intervention of states on all individual rights. For instance, states are not to use coercion to impose beliefs and attitudes on the areas of human life that are essentially personal and in a manner incompatible with due respect for the dignity of persons.[11] As recognised by peoples of diverse backgrounds, "human dignity" appears to have been taken as

5 Guy S Goodwin-Gill, RK Jenny and Richard Perruchoud, 'Basic Humanitarian Principles Applicable to Non-Nationals' (1985) 19 *International Migration Review* 556, 4.

6 However, minority rights under Article 27 of the ICCPR can, specifically, only be claimed by an individual as a member of a minority group. See further Section 2.1.1 below.

7 See Evadné Grant, 'Dignity and Equality' (2007) 7 *Human Rights Law* Review 299, 4.

8 Jack Donnelly, 'Human Rights and Human Dignity: An Analytic Critique of Non-Western Conceptions of Human Rights' (1982) 76 *The American Political Science Review* 303, 4.

9 Raija Hanski and Markku Suksi, 'What Are Human Rights?', in Raija Hanski and Markku Suksi (eds), *An Introduction to the International Protection of Human Rights: A Textbook* (Institute for Human Rights, Åbo Akademi University 1999) 4.

10 Martin Dixon, Robert McCorquodale and Sarah Williams, *Cases & Materials on International Law* (Oxford University Press 2016) 4.

11 Oscar Schachter, 'Human Dignity as a Normative Concept' (1983) 77 *American Journal of International Law* 848, 5.

a self-explanatory justification for human rights protection. Additionally, the recognition of dignity is important not only to protect individuals but also to integrate society within a particular nation.[12] It signifies that human rights principles are required by every society to establish a democratic state based on equal protection towards every individual in its jurisdiction.

1.1. The status of minorities in international human rights law

Before the enactment of the UN Charter, several documents on the protection of minorities were partially international and focused on specific regions. Regrettably, after the adoption of the Charter, the questionable status of minorities has not been fully addressed on the UN main agenda because neither the UN Charter nor the Universal Declaration of Human Rights (UDHR) contains provisions on minority groups.[13] The first binding international human rights instrument that explicitly regulates the rights of minorities is the International Covenant on Civil and Political Rights (ICCPR), which specifically mentions the rights of minorities in Article 27. This became the first international standard-setting instrument and was a way of integrating minority provisions into the international framework of human rights.[14] Additionally, this Covenant serves as the starting point for all subsequent changes in the international regime of minority rights.[15] The provision on the rights of minorities in Article 27 of the ICCPR says:

> In those States in which ethnic, religious or linguistic minorities exist, persons belonging to such minorities shall not be denied the right, in community with the other members of their group, to enjoy their own culture, to profess and practise their own religion, or to use their own language.

This provision generally regulates that the one criterion for identifying minority status is the existence of objective characteristics which distinguish the group from the rest of the population within a particular state. Examples of this could be the distinctive characteristics of ethnicity, language and religion. The Human Rights Committee (HRC) has observed that the article also indicates that: "the individuals designed to be protected need not be citizens of the State party".[16]

12 Man Yee Karen Lee, 'Universal Human Dignity: Some Reflections in the Asian Context' (2008) 3 *Asian Journal of Comparative Law* 1, 4.
13 Gaetano Pentassuglia, 'Evolving Protection of Minority Groups: Global Challenges and the Role of International Jurisprudence' (2009) 11 *International Community Law Review* 185, 5.
14 ibid 4.
15 Miodrag Jovanovic, 'Recognizing Minority Identities through Collective Rights' (2005) 27 *Human Rights Quarterly* 625, 5.
16 Compilation of General Comments and General Recommendations Adopted by Human Rights Treaty Bodies 123.

It signifies that the essence of this article is relevantly associated with the principle of all human beings within a state party as stipulated in Article 2 (1) of the Covenant, which obligates a state party to respect and ensure the entitlement of human rights for individuals in its jurisdiction.

However, there has been no single reference to the definition of minority status in international human rights instruments until recently.[17] The absence of a definition is intended to avoid the reduction of the scope and category of minorities and their rights due to their distinctive character, which differs from one country to another. It is because naturally ethnic, religious and linguistic differences within states may be of startling complexity; languages branch into dialects, cultures flourish in diverse forms[18] and religions and particular beliefs, which have unique features distinguishing members of minorities from the majority, divide into sects and denominations. Thus, in contrast to other human rights generally, it is important to note that minority rights under Article 27 of the ICCPR can, specifically, only be claimed by an individual as a member of a minority group. The HRC has noted in its General Comment 23 that Article 27

> establishes and recognises a right which is conferred on individuals belonging to minority groups and which is distinct from, and additional to, all the other rights which, as individuals in common with everyone else, they are already entitled to enjoy under the Covenant.[19]

In the case of religious minorities it is not possible to explain religion in a definitive manner and consequently a consensus on the definition of religious minorities is an even harder task.[20] Even the category of religious minority may at the same time be equally regarded as an ethnic and/or a linguistic minority. For instance, it is not fully clear whether European Jews are a religious or an ethnic minority, or incorporate elements of both.[21] In principle, all Jews define membership of their religion by descent or conversion but it is also unquestionably true that all Jews, whether they are Orthodox, Liberal, Progressive or Masorti, constitute an ethnic group.[22] Based on this case, the main objective in

17 Kristin Henrard, 'Charting the Gradual Emergence of a More Robust Level of Minority Protection: Minority Specific Instruments and the European Union' (2017) 22 *Netherlands Quarterly of Human Rights* 4.

18 Patrick Thornberry, *International Law and the Rights of Minorities* (Clarendon Press 2001) 5.

19 Compilation of General Comments and General Recommendations Adopted by Human Rights Treaty Bodies 197.

20 Kamran Hashemi, 'The Right of Minorities to Identity and the Challenge of Non-Discrimination: A Study on the Effects of Traditional Muslims' "Dhimmah" on Current State Practices' (2006) 13 *International Journal on Minority and Group Rights* 1, 4.

21 ibid 6.

22 See *R (E) v Governing Body of JFS* (2009) UK Supreme Court UKSC 2009/0105 45–46.

providing a definition of minorities in this research is not to give a static definition but to illustrate their common character. The types of recognised minorities are a useful way of defining the scope of the law, but they should not be used to define particular minorities in a singular and exclusive manner.[23]

There are many definitions of minorities proposed by scholars but the most widely accepted definition, which is adopted in this thesis, is the one proposed by Francesco Capotorti, a former Special Rapporteur of the UN on Prevention of Discrimination and Protection of Minorities. In his study submitted to the Sub-Commission of the Prevention of Discrimination and the Protection on Minorities in 1979, Capotorti noted that:

> Minority is a group numerically inferior to the rest of the population of a State, in a non-dominant position, whose members being nationals of the State possess ethnic, religious or linguistic characteristics differing from those of the rest of the population and show, if only implicitly, a sense of solidarity, directed towards preserving their culture, traditions, religion or language.[24]

This proposition differs slightly from the HRC's interpretation of Article 27, which indicates that minorities are not restricted to nationals of the state. However, both definitions emphasise that groups of people can be considered minority groups if they are numerically inferior to the rest of the population of a state and possess ethnic, religious or linguistic characteristics differing from those of the rest of the population and show, if only implicitly, a sense of solidarity directed towards preserving their culture, tradition, religion or language.[25] The sense of solidarity refers to minorities' preservation of their own cultural, religious or linguistic identity to strengthen their social cohesion and to take pride in their cultural or religious distinctiveness through a revival of their own traditional identity.

1.2. The rights of religious minorities in international human rights law

Minority groups are likely to need greater protection than majority groups under a constitutional democracy in that they may not be able to gain protection through the normal channels such as non-discrimination and equality principles. This is especially true if such a democracy coexists with a society that has a communal character, where its members share a certain value that binds them.

23 Geoff Gilbert, 'Religious Minorities and Their Rights: A Problem of Approach' (1997) 5 *International Journal on Minority and Group Rights* 97, 25.

24 See Manoj Kumar Sinha, 'Minority Rights: A Case Study of India' (2005) 12 *International Journal on Minority and Group Rights* 355, 56. See also Office of the High Commissioner, *Minority Rights: International Standard and Guidance for Implementation* (United Nations 2010) 2.

25 See Thornberry (n 18) 67.

Minorities generally face severer conditions under authoritarian regimes because their rights are sidelined or excluded entirely from the list of political priorities.[26] Their non-dominant position and numerical inferiority usually causes minorities to become vulnerable, with a likelihood of being suppressed by the majority.[27] Non-discrimination and equality principles seem insufficient to protect persons belonging to minorities and to quell tension between minorities and majority groups.[28] Thus, besides enacting Article 27 of the ICCPR, the UN General Assembly also enacted the 1992 Declaration on the Rights of Persons belonging to National or Ethnic, Religious and Linguistic Minorities (hereafter Minorities Declaration) as one of the ways to develop standard protection for persons belonging to a minority group. According to this Declaration, states shall provide appropriate legislative and other measures to protect the existence and identity of minorities and the right to participate effectively in decisions concerning that identity.[29] The enactment of the Declaration and a special article on the rights of minorities show that the international human rights regime tends to emphasise the importance of extraordinary channels to protect minorities.

Minorities require special measures or affirmative protection because their specific views may be considered by the majority as conflicting directly with democratic values. The majority usually argues that no recognition should be given to these views to avoid tension in society.[30] The obligation of the state in such situations is not to remove the cause of the tension, such as eliminating non-mainstream views advanced by minorities, but to regulate that every non-mainstream view is also equally protected. In the case of conflict between or within religious groups, the state should not aim to eliminate one group but ensure that the competing groups tolerate each other.[31] The state cannot restrict minority groups as they, like any other group, are keen to preserve and promote their identity within the general recognition of minority rights.[32]

26 Nazila Ghanea-Hercock, Alexandra Xanthaki and Patrick Thornberry, 'The African Union and the Prospects for Minority Protection', in Nazila Ghanea-Hercock and Alexandra Xanthaki (eds), *Minorities, Peoples and Self-determination: Essays in Honour of Patrick Thornberry* (Martinus Nijhoff Publishers 2005) 345.

27 Marie-Luisa Frick and Andreas Th Muller, 'Islamic Law and International Protection of Minority Rights in Context', in Marie-Luisa Frick and Andreas Th Muller, *Islam and International Law: Engaging Self-Centrism from a Plurality of Perspectives* (Martinus Nijhoff Publishers 2013) 34.

28 Yousef T Jabareen, 'Toward Participatory Equality: Protecting Minority Rights under International Law' (2008) 41 *Israel Law Review* 635, 34.

29 See *e.g.* article 1, 2, 4 and 5 of the Declaration.

30 Samantha Knights, *Freedom of Religion, Minorities, and the Law* (Oxford University Press 2007) 85.

31 ibid 87.

32 Kristin Henrard, 'The Protection of Minorities through the Equality Provisions in the UN Human Rights Treaties: The UN Treaty Bodies Reforming the UN Human Rights

In this sense, every minority has the right to be different in a wide range of ways, varying from group to group, according to its nature and cohesive social components. For instance, the rights of religious minorities will not be the same as the rights of linguistic, cultural and ethnic minorities.[33] Clearly, Article 27 of the ICCPR links ethnic minorities to cultural rights, linguistic minorities to language rights and religious minorities to religious rights. Even the reality of religious rights for religious minorities is sometimes different, even though international human rights instruments assert that there should not be discrimination against a particular group of people. For instance, in an Islamic state or a Muslim society,[34] the rights of religious minorities within Islam and non-Muslims are firmly different and therefore the approach and scope of the protection is also fundamentally different.[35]

The right of dissent within Islam, which is part of the nature of the religion, may result in intra-religious persecution especially against religious minorities within Islam. Protecting the rights of religious minorities within Islam, based on international human rights law, seems to be lacking support from most Muslims because of the significant influence of their interpretation of Islamic law. Thus, this religious persecution needs a greater understanding of Islamic law from Muslims since the persecuted and the persecuting groups are from the same religion.[36] The similarity of standard protection between intra- and inter-religious persecution is reflected in the state obligations deriving from international norms and this protection must be equally applicable to violations resulting from the repression of religious minorities by the majorities.[37]

It may be noted that the basic rights of religious minorities are mostly related to their survival and existence as such,[38] not only to establish communities but also to perform their beliefs. The most basic sense of existence is existence

Machinery: What Does the Future Hold for the Protection of Minorities and Indigenous Peoples' (2007) 14 *International Journal on Minority and Group Rights* 141, 45.

33 Nātān Lerner, *Group Rights and Discrimination in International Law* (Martinus Nijhoff Publishers 2003) 4.

34 A state which is inhabited predominantly or even entirely by Muslims is not necessarily synonymous with an Islamic state because a state can become truly Islamic only by the conscious application of the socio-political tenets of Islam to the life of the nation and by the incorporation of those tenets in the basic constitution of the country. See Nasim Hasan Shah, 'Islamic Concept of State' (1987) 26 *Islamic Studies* 97, 12.

35 Christians and Jews are usually regulated by the various compacts or charters that granted them a certain degree of communal autonomy, which brought about the inferior status of *dhimmis*. See Abdullahi Ahmed An-Na'im, 'Constitutionalism and Islamization in the Sudan' (1989) *Africa Today* 11, 4.

36 See generally Nazila Ghanea-Hercock, 'A Human Rights Framework for Defining and Understanding Intra-Religious Persecution in Muslim Countries', in Nazila Ghanea-Hercock, *The Challenge of Religious Discrimination at the Dawn of the New Millennium* (Springer 2013) 5.

37 ibid 85.

38 Office of the High Commissioner (n 24) 456.

through the lives of members, or physical existence.[39] The right of existence and survival is associated with the prohibition of genocide and crimes against humanity, while the rights to non-discrimination and meaningful participation are to protect minorities from being legally excluded by the government and/or socially alienated from their society. Meaningful participation is usually correlated with government policy to integrate or assimilate certain minorities into social uniformity and national unity. In the case of religious minorities, their rights are related to their socio-religious existence, whose sole interest is their religious identity and its preservation. However, if someone's rights were violated or restricted because of a group's characteristic such as "deviant belief", which contrasts with the teachings or tenets of a particular orthodox religion, the matter could, or rather should, be taken care of by protecting the rights of the individual on a purely individual basis, mainly by the principle of non-discrimination.[40]

The right to the promotion and protection of the identity of religious minorities is related to the right to special measures to maintain a group's identity, even though the nature of such measures may depend on the degree of discrimination or disadvantage suffered by the respective group.[41] They require a broader range of rights, such as special measures of the rights as a consequence of the distinguishing feature of their religions or beliefs against the religious majorities. This proposition is related to the HRC's observation that a state party may also be required to take positive measures to protect the rights of minority members asserted in Article 27 of the ICCPR by respecting the principles of non-discrimination equality stipulated in Article 2 (1) and 26 of the same instrument.[42] The term positive measures here can be interpreted as affirmative treatment for religious minorities, in order that they can experience real or substantively equal treatment in comparison with the rest of the population.[43]

Such substantive equality is required because minority rights, as a sub-category of human rights, should be seen as a form of added protection to universal human rights. These rights should be deemed necessary in order to secure human rights for those persons in a minority situation.[44] Minority rights are legal rights, a part of the general body of human rights, and add a further element of specificity in relation to minority communities and individuals. They are

39 See Thornberry (n 18) 67.
40 Lerner (n 33) 45.
41 ibid 46.
42 Compilation of General Comments and General Recommendations Adopted by Human Rights Treaty Bodies 156.
43 Henrard (n 32) 58.
44 Marc Weller, 'Legal Nature of Minority Rights as Part of Human Rights, Limitations, Derogations, Reservations, and Interpretative Statements', in Marc Weller (ed.), *Universal Minority Rights: A Commentary on the Jurisprudence of International Courts and Treaty Bodies* (Oxford University Press 2007) 45.

a sub-category in the body of general human rights, with the purpose of ensuring the de facto equality of minorities with the majority and/or the survival of minorities. Therefore, these rights may contain supportive features, such as affirmative action or special protection, to ensure de facto equality or to ensure the survival of minorities.[45] The problem is that some states seem reluctant to apply affirmative action to protect minorities because of the issue of self-determination and fragmentation or separatism, even though international law has insisted that minorities do not have rights to external self-determination.[46] Some other states also argue that affirmative action to protect minorities can disturb socio-political stability in their jurisdiction if the majority challenges the special protection given to minorities.

In the case of religious minorities, their members normally seek equality in law and in everyday life with the religious majority to maintain their religious traditions and characteristics, rather than being assimilated into the majority of the population as represented by the state.[47] Additionally, the persons belonging to religious minorities should also have access to the necessary socio-political life in their state of residence, thus achieving de facto parity with the dominant religious majority population, who may control various matters affecting the rights of religious minorities.[48] This indicates that, besides having a socio-cultural life equal to the majority, religious minorities should be guaranteed effective participation in decision-making on issues concerning minorities, not only at the national level but also at the regional level.[49] It signifies that in the context of religious minority rights, the architectural principles of equality and non-discrimination can also be applied to protect collective human rights as well as individual human rights.[50] Collective human rights are required to protect all members of religious minorities who generally share particular religious beliefs within their own groups.

International human rights instruments set up comprehensive provisions on freedom of religion or belief for religious minorities which are not limited to a certain religion or a particular adherent of religion. Article 18 of the UDHR, for instance, stipulates that: "everyone has the right to freedom of thought, conscience and religion" in a wider dimension, due to the absence of a definition of religion. Article 18 (1) of the ICCPR similarly provides for "the right to freedom of thought, conscience and religion", which "shall include freedom to have or adopt a religion or belief of [one's] choice". The HRC emphasises that

45 ibid 89.
46 ibid 67.
47 Gilbert (n 23) 45.
48 See Jungwon Park, 'Integration of Peoples and Minorities: An Approach to the Conceptual Problem of Peoples and Minorities with Reference to Self-Determination under International Law' (2006) 13 *International Journal on Minority and Group Rights* 69, 34.
49 See Saeko Kawashima, 'The Right to Effective Participation and the Ainu People' (2004) 11 *International Journal on Minority and Group Rights* 21, 34.
50 See Thornberry (n 18) 78.

the terms belief and religion are to be broadly construed and that Article 18 protects theistic, non-theistic and atheistic beliefs and is "not limited in its application to traditional religions or to religions and beliefs with institutional characteristics or practices analogous to those of traditional religions".[51] The right to freedom of religion or belief implies that no one can be compelled to reveal his or her thoughts or adherence to a religion or belief because the instruments recognise broadly construed religion and the far-reaching and profound provision of religious freedom.[52] This provision becomes the most essential element of human rights protection for religious minorities because the absence of an explicit definition of religion can protect the distinctive character of religious beliefs practised by religious minorities, specifically religious minorities within a certain religion.[53]

Besides the aforementioned rights, one of the most essential rights for religious minorities in Article 18 of the UDHR and ICCPR is their right to profess their religion or belief (*forum internum*) and to manifest their religion or belief (*forum externum*).[54] The *forum internum* encompasses the internal and private realm of the individual to embrace, to change and to replace one's religion or belief against which no interference is justified in any circumstances.[55] The *forum externum* comprises all kinds of manifestations of beliefs, either alone/individually or in community with others and in private or public, although those manifestations may be limited by law to protect public safety, order, health or morals or the fundamental rights and freedoms of others.[56] If the purposive application of limitation is mainly to protect other rights, the application of restriction generally affects the broader scope of religious freedom in relation to a certain individual or community. It can be concluded that restriction is an illegitimate limitation because it is applied discriminatorily generally against religious minorities.

In response to the rights of minorities, the HRC indicated that the rights in Article 27 of the ICCPR are distinct from, and additional to, all the other rights which individual minorities have in common with everyone else stipulated in the

51 Compilation of General Comments and General Recommendations Adopted by Human Rights Treaty Bodies 195.

52 Jeroen Temperman, *State–Religion Relationships and Human Rights Law: Towards a Right to Religiously Neutral Governance* (Brill 2010) 56.

53 In fact, the major reason for the absence of a definition of religion in international human rights law is to avoid ideological confrontation among states and cultures as reflected in the drafting of some human rights instruments. See Natan Lerner, 'The Nature and Minimum Standards of Freedom of Religion or Belief' (2000) *BYU Law Review* 905, 56.

54 The terms *forum internum* and *forum externum* were proposed by Special Rapporteur Asma Jahangir; see Michael Wiener, 'The Mandate of the Special Rapporteur on Freedom of Religion or Belief – Institutional, Procedural and Substantive Legal Issues' (2007) 2 *Religion and Human Rights* 3, 45.

55 Paul M Taylor, *Freedom of Religion: UN and European Human Rights Law and Practice* (Cambridge University Press 2005) 115.

56 ibid 203.

Covenant.[57] However, this article signifies that the protection of religious minorities is related to the scope of Article 18 because the HRC does not distinguish the scope of those two articles.[58] The correlation between those two articles is significant in reinforcing the equality principle among major religious adherents and protecting religious minorities' right to adopt a particular religion or belief. This is because the majorities often justify their rule over the minorities based on their religious orthodoxy. The persecution of religious minorities within Islam is drawn from the fact that the Muslim majorities usually do not welcome competitors, who are accused of threatening the majority's well-established domination in a Muslim society. For instance, even though the Qur'an does not clearly stipulate apostasy, it has been imputed to Muslims who deviate from Islamic orthodoxy, such as the case of religious minorities within Islam in Pakistan, Indonesia and in other Muslim countries.[59]

Based on international human rights law and the universalistic nature of human rights, all religious minorities deserve respect for their self-understanding of religion or belief.[60] Yet, in the context of religious minorities within Islam, it is not only international human rights law that must be interpreted inclusively to protect these minorities but Islam as well, because the broad and exclusive understanding of the two will potentially establish stronger protection of religious minorities within Islam. For example, all Muslims must understand that the term religious minorities in international human rights law should cover all relevant groups of persons, including non-Islamic communities.[61]

It can be said that religious minorities should enjoy all human rights, especially equal rights to embrace a religion or belief as religious majorities do, because such rights are part of unconditional religious freedom under Article 18 of the ICCPR. Indonesia as a state party must ensure that persons belonging to religious minorities have the right to profess and practise their own religion.[62] Thus, the right to embrace a certain religion or belief is primarily a matter of individual conscience and it is their freedom to practise their beliefs.[63] This implies that the rights of religious minorities are theoretically individual but the distinctive character of religious minorities requires special recognition in order to be accepted as a part of the community. Therefore, the standard provision of

57 Compilation of General Comments and General Recommendations Adopted by Human Rights Treaty Bodies 199.

58 Compilation of General Comments and General Recommendations Adopted by Human Rights Treaty Bodies 2008 (Human Rights Instrument) 157.

59 For further illustration, see Jeroen Temperman, *State-Religion Relationships and Human Rights Law: Towards a Right to Religiously Neutral Governance* (Brill 2010) 67.

60 HRC, 'Report of the Special Rapporteur on Freedom of Religion or Belief, Heiner Bielefeldt' (2012) A/HRC/22/51, 9.

61 ibid 9.

62 Compilation of General Comments and General Recommendations Adopted by Human Rights Treaty Bodies 158.

63 Gilbert (n 23) 112.

religious freedom which basically enables every individual to hold, practise and manifest the religion or belief of her/his choice has two implications for the rights of religious minorities. The first is the rights of religious minorities as distinct communities or religious communities and the second is their rights as the individual members that compose them.[64] All countries are mandated not only to protect the rights of all individuals as members of minorities but also to acknowledge that all minority groups must have equal status with the majority.

1.3. The significance of protecting religious minorities

Even though many states have become parties to the ICCPR and other human rights instruments, it may be contended that there is no nation that has a perfect record on religious freedom,[65] especially in relation to the rights of religious minorities. Socio-legal and political issues such as national integrity, religious harmony, loopholes within national law, as well as religious matters, have perpetrated violations of the rights of religious minorities over time. Besides exploring exhaustive grounds of limitation to the application of human rights, many states also apply a broad range of limitations in the interest of state defence, national security, national unity and public nuisance,[66] as well as orthodox religious values.[67] These limitations sometimes put non-dominant or non-traditional religions at a disadvantage.[68]

The issue of orthodox religious values can be noted from the case of Saudi Arabia abstaining from ratifying the UDHR in 1948 due to the provision of "the right to change religion". Al Baroody, the Saudi Arabian representative to the UN Commission on Human Rights, on behalf of his state, opposed the inclusion of the clause and argued that this right violates the Qur'an.[69] He argued that the right to change religion did not acknowledge such a right to be a gift of God even though his Islamic counterpart, the representative of Pakistan, defended his country's support for the declaration on the grounds that the Qur'an permits one to believe or disbelieve.[70] The contention also occurred in the drafting of the ICCPR, where some representatives of Islamic states did not agree to put the right "to change one's religion" in the Covenant.[71] The debate

64 See Nazila Ghanea, 'Human Rights of Religious Minorities and of Women in the Middle East' (2004) 26 *Human Rights Quarterly* 705, 34.

65 See David R Hodge, 'Advocating for the Forgotten Human Right: Article 18 of the Universal Declaration of Human Rights – Religious Freedom' (2006) 49 *International Social Work* 431, 34.

66 See Temperman (n 59) 222.

67 Article 28J (2) of the Indonesian Constitution (2nd Amendment).

68 Temperman (n 59) 223.

69 Paul Sieghart, *The International Law of Human Rights* (Clarendon Press 1983) 24.

70 Robert Traer, *Faith in Human Rights: Support in Religious Traditions for a Global Struggle* (Georgetown University Press 1991) 56.

71 Katarzyna Wazynska-Finck and Francois Finck, 'The Right to Change One's Religion According to Article 18 of ICCPR and the Universality of Human Rights' (2013) 9 *Journal of Islamic State Practices in International Law* 36.

over the right to change one's religion or belief still occurred in the drafting of the preamble of the Declaration on the Elimination of All Forms of Intolerance and of Discrimination Based on Religion or Belief in 1981 (1981 Declaration), which some Muslim states insisted on omitting from the draft; "including the right to choose, manifest and change one's religion or belief".[72] Therefore, Article 1 (1) of the 1981 Declaration uses a more moderate phrase; "... to have a religion or whatever belief of one's choice". This signifies that the critical issue of religious freedom has been ongoing since six decades ago and religious minorities were the groups that have mostly been discriminated against.

Religious freedom principles in international human rights law actually began as an attempt to protect marginalised groups, particularly religious minorities, through an initial emphasis on tolerance more than on rights.[73] Religious minorities frequently find themselves in a disadvantageous position, particularly in states or communities professing an orthodox or traditionally established religion. Therefore, protection against discrimination is one of the most important safeguards for religious minorities in the enjoyment of their religious rights because many states, including Indonesia, acknowledge some religious denominations but are not neutral in respect of the different religious communities living within the states.[74] Principles of non-discrimination and equality can be found in article 26 of the ICCPR, which assert that everyone has the right to be equal before the law and enjoy rights and freedoms without discrimination. The principles also prohibit any discrimination under the law and guarantee to all persons equal and effective protection against discrimination on any ground, including religion.

Regarding state duties, Article 1(1) of the 1981 Declaration spells out that: "states shall protect the existence and the national or ethnic, cultural, religious and linguistic identity of minorities within their respective territories and shall encourage conditions for the promotion of that identity". This article continues by stating that: "states shall adopt appropriate legislative and other measures to achieve those ends". Meanwhile, Article 27 of the ICCPR also relates to rights whose protection imposes specific obligations on state parties. The HRC has indicated that there is a need for positive measures to be undertaken by states to protect the identity of a minority and the rights of its members to enjoy and develop their culture and language and to practise their religion in a community with other members of the group.[75]

72 See Bahiyyih G Tahzib, *Freedom of Religion or Belief: Ensuring Effective International Legal Protection* (Martinus Nijhoff Publishers 1996) 45.

73 Lerner (n 33) 6.

74 See Marc Weller, 'Religious Rights', in Marc Weller (ed.), *Universal Minority Rights: A Commentary on the Jurisprudence of International Courts and Treaty Bodies* (Oxford University Press 2007) 34.

75 Compilation of General Comments and General Recommendations Adopted by Human Rights Treaty Bodies 197.

Protection of religious and other minorities is significant because, in society, the problem of minorities appears "to be part of the general setting of us-them divides, manifesting itself in three distinct ways: collective prejudice against people associated with certain constructed categories, discrimination against members of such groups, and systemic inequalities".[76] It may be assumed that to successfully defend religious minority protection, including religious minorities within a particular religion, we must also recognise the breadth of religious pluralism or more precisely internal religious pluralism and the cultural identity of the members of religious minorities.

1.4. The liberal character of international human rights law

The UDHR is a historic document expressing an unprecedented faith in human dignity and optimism about the prospect of improving the human condition in the global world.[77] Since 1948 there have been hundreds of binding and non-binding human rights instruments enacted by the international human rights regime. These instruments attempt to mainstream liberal human rights, including strengthening the rights of individuals within minority groups around the world.[78] As a consequence, even though human rights norms in the UDHR are theoretically not binding, human rights regimes and most states have acknowledged that the UDHR was a common standard of achievement of human rights for all peoples in all nations.[79] One of the common standards is that all individuals are entitled to rights and freedom as a consequence of being human.[80] This equal entitlement of human rights for all individuals includes the accommodation of non-mainstream thought, practice and other forms of rights and freedoms within a particular society.

Human rights instruments advocate liberal principles and standards of human rights protection across nations and hence the protection of the rights of individuals is believed to be one of the significant elements of a democratic state. The liberal principle asserts that individuals have a right to moral independence and a legally secured possibility of living their own self-determined

76 Bas de Gaay Fortman, 'Minority Rights: A Major Misconception?' (2011) 33 *Human Rights Quarterly* 265, 344.

77 Koen De Feyter and George Pavlakos, 'Introduction: Groups Rights and Human Rights', in Koen De Feyter and George Pavlakos (eds), *The Tension Between Group Rights and Human Rights: A Multidisciplinary Approach* (Hart Publishing 2008) 34.

78 See Christopher McCrudden, 'Mainstreaming Human Rights', in Colin Harvey (ed.), *Human Rights in the Community: Rights as Agents for Change* (Bloomsbury Publishing 2005) 9.

79 Carol Anderson, 'Roland Burke. Decolonization and the Evolution of International Human Rights' (2010) 115 *The American Historical Review* 1113.

80 This proposition is commonly advocated by liberal theorists such as Jack Donnelly. See for instance his argument at Jack Donnelly, 'The Relative Universality of Human Rights' (2007) 29 *Human Rights Quarterly* 281, 281–306.

life.[81] The liberal character of human rights elevates non-mainstream groups of people and individuals to enjoy equality with others, evidently because their status as human beings is equally protected. Based on this principle, it would be wrong for any state to deny the rights of individuals as well as non-mainstream groups, even though it would be in the general interest to do so, because when rights and general interest collide, the former trumps.[82] States must respect the rights of individuals even though this practice may trigger mass demonstrations from the majority, which in the end disturbs economic development and political stability in the country.

The liberal concept emphasises rights and freedoms, which are fundamental to the realisation of human rights globally. It is submitted that the liberal concept of human rights may be considered as a customary law of human rights because the concept is well established by *opinio juris*.[83] The blueprint of the liberalistic character of international human rights started with the enactment of the UDHR because it established the very foundation of the supremacy of individual rights over group or communitarian rights. This individualism is mostly advocated by liberal theorists who believe that all individuals should have equal rights, including the right to do whatever they think fit to preserve themselves, as far as this right does not violate the rights of others.[84] Another argument also asserts that the construction of a human rights system under the UN, which promotes the protection of members of minority groups as individuals, was one of the greatest moral achievements of the modern era.[85]

Even though the development of liberal human rights has become a global phenomenon since the enactment of the UDHR, the contentious debate about the scope of human rights, especially its individualistic character, cannot be ignored. The debates about individualism had also started from the drafting stage of the UDHR, especially due to the challenge from socialist and less developed countries; mainly South America, Asia and Africa. The delegation of the Soviet Union (now Russia) in responding to the relationship of individuals and the state, for instance, argued that human rights cannot be conceived outside the state because the government was in fact the collective of individuals and where the state and the individual were in harmony with each other, their interests would coincide.[86] In

81 Rainer Forst and Professor Rainer Forst, *Contexts of Justice: Political Philosophy beyond Liberalism and Communitarianism* (University of California Press 2002) 32–33.

82 Stephen Angle, *Human Rights in Chinese Thought: A Cross-Cultural Inquiry* (Cambridge University Press 2002) 209–210.

83 Theodor Meron, *Human Rights and Humanitarian Norms as Customary Law* (Clarendon Press 1991) 87.

84 John Charvet, *The Liberal Project and Human Rights: The Theory and Practice of a New World Order* (Cambridge University Press 2008) 3.

85 David Boucher, *The Limits of Ethics in International Relations: Natural Law, Natural Rights, and Human Rights in Transition* (Oxford University Press Oxford 2011) 287.

86 Johannes Morsink, *The Universal Declaration of Human Rights: Origins, Drafting, and Intent* (University of Pennsylvania Press 1999) 21–22.

responding to the individualistic character of religious freedom, Guy Perez Cisneros, the delegate from Cuba, thought the article "placed too much emphasis on the individual's right to change his religion, and thus weakened the absolute value of the ideas expressed".[87]

In the debate on the realisation of human rights around the world, Danilo Turk similarly emphasised that:

> One of the most fundamental issues in the process of realisation of human rights is expressed in relationships between the individual and the community and between the individual and a variety of social groups in which the individual exists. But no individual lives in a vacuum, every-one belongs to more than one social group and to the society as a whole. It is axiomatic that the "full realisation" of human rights requires careful balancing of the rights of the individual and the social and cultural norms existing within the relevant groups.[88]

Based on this complexity, religious minority groups at the domestic level face external and internal dimensional problems. The external problems are caused by the liberal nature of international human rights, which stress the importance of supplementing individuals within minority groups, such as expressing and exercising their distinctive characters. In many cases, states are apprehensive that this can undermine national stability and hence place the minority rights issue in complex settings.[89] In this context, minority rights become a matter of power sharing and a challenge to the status quo that favours the majority to the detriment of minority groups.[90] The internal problem is drawn from the fact that a minority group, especially a religious group, can stand in conflict not only with non-members but also with its members and its own dissenting subgroups, due to the communal normative systems of religions.[91]

In the context of freedom of religion or belief and the rights of religious minority groups, the liberal nature of human rights can be appreciated by the fact that international human rights law ensures the protection of individual human beings as the believers of religion.[92] This inadvertently challenges the powerful influence of religion in certain states, like Indonesia, due to the

87 ibid 25.
88 Hanski and Suksi (n 9) 2.
89 Koen De Feyter and George Pavlakos, 'Supporting Minority Rights: Inter-Group Determinants and Consequences', in Koen De Feyter and George Pavlakos, *The Tension Between Group Rights and Human Rights: A Multidisciplinary Approach* (Bloomsbury Publishing 2008) 221.
90 ibid 222.
91 Anat Scolnicov, *The Right to Religious Freedom in International Law: Between Group Rights and Individual Rights* (Routledge 2010) 1.
92 Irene Oh, *The Rights of God: Islam, Human Rights, and Comparative Ethics* (Georgetown University Press 2007) 1.

privilege given by the state authority to the majority religion over the protection of all citizens, because the term "religion" is broadly construed in international human rights instruments. The HRC affirms that Article 18 is not limited in its application to "traditional religions" or "official religions" of a particular state, so the Committee views with concern any tendency to discriminate against any religion or belief that represents religious minorities that may be the subject of hostility on the part of a predominant religious community.[93]

Therefore, the international human rights regime encourages states to ensure that all domestic laws must be independent of sectarian considerations. Thus, the HRC asserts that a state which officially recognises a certain number of religions due to their followers comprising the majority population, like Indonesia, must ensure that religious minorities within a particular official religion can enjoy their rights to religious freedom.[94] This argument was meant to expand the implementation of religious freedom in states that acknowledge a particular religion, as the religion of the state like Pakistan and most Muslim-majority states in the Middle East.

In the Indonesian context, the country ratified the ICCPR in 2006 and did not enter any reservations to Article 18 and 27. This ratification is emphasised further by Law No. 12/2005 on Civil and Political Rights, which clearly states that all human rights norms in the Covenant are in accordance with the norms of Pancasila and the Indonesian Constitution. The country only made a reservation to Article 1 of the ICCPR due to socio-political reasons. If Article 1 is applicable in the country's jurisdiction it might affect the unity of Indonesia, because Indonesia comprises thousands of islands with different cultures, religions, languages and ethnicities. Previously, Indonesia also signed the Convention on the Elimination of All Forms of Discrimination against Women (CEDAW) in 1984 and the Convention on the Protection of the Rights of the Child in 1990. Both instruments also regulate the protection of women and children to embrace and practise their religion or belief.

Accordingly, in general, the state accepts the legal obligation to protect the rights of religious minorities to enjoy the freedom to embrace, practise and manifest their religion or beliefs. According to Article 3 and 4 of the ICCPR, Indonesia as a state party is obligated to ensure equal rights for every person and is only permitted to derogate from certain obligations under the Covenant in times of public emergency.[95]

As already highlighted, even though religious freedom in international human rights law is characterised as individual, this brings about two implications for the protection of religious minorities within Islam in Indonesia. Firstly, this has implications for the religious freedom of religious minorities within Islam as

93 General Comment No. 22, Compilation of General Comments and General Recommendations Adopted by Human Rights Treaty Bodies 344.

94 General Comment No. 23, ibid 157.

95 General Comment No. 18, ibid 146.

distinctive communities. Secondly, it has implications for individual Muslims within a particular group of religious minorities within Islam.[96] It means Indonesia should protect religious minorities within Islam as a group as well as ensuring that Muslims within the group receive equal enjoyment of human rights.

2. Islam and human rights discourse

Protection of religious minorities within Islam in Indonesia must consider all the legal spectrums experienced by Indonesians because Indonesia still struggles to reinforce state law within the shadow of various kinds of living laws practised in society. Besides recognising the Indonesian customary law generally practised by different sectors of Indonesian society,[97] the country also applies Islamic law in the area of family law. However, some puritan-traditionalist Muslims are attempting to expand the application of Islamic law to Indonesian human rights discourse. Even though it is clearly stated in the constitution that Indonesia does not recognise "theocratic constitutionalism",[98] the influence of Islamic law on the issue of the protection of religious minorities within Islam cannot be neglected.

Discussion of the rights of either Muslim or non-Muslim religious minorities has been very critical in Islamic law.[99] Within that discourse, terms such as heretic, apostasy, infidel and jihad, intended to maintain the purity of Islam, have been utilised and exploited as a legitimating tool behind the persecution of religious minorities within Islam, leading to their unequal treatment in different Muslim-majority states including Indonesia. This illustrates that the tension between minorities and majorities, especially when it involves the exercise of personal freedom and the establishment of community, is one of the principal ongoing problems in many Muslim-majority states.[100] The problem becomes more pronounced when the

96 Ghanea (n 64) 708.

97 Article 18B (2) of the 1945 Constitution asserts that "the State shall recognise and respect, to be regulated by law, the homogeneity of societies with customary law along with their traditional rights for as long as they remain in existence and in agreement with societal development".

98 The very basic definition of theocratic constitutionalism means a certain religion is used by a certain state as the basis of ordering. On the explanation of theocratic constitutionalism, see generally Larry Backer, 'Theocratic Constitutionalism: An Introduction to a New Global Legal Ordering' (2006) 16 *Indiana Journal of Global Legal Studies* 85 (2009) 85–172.

99 This article uses the term Islamic law rather than Sharia because those two terms are different. Sharia refers to the fundamental sources of Islam, namely the Qur'an and the authentic traditions (*Sunnah*) and therefore it is "law plus", while Islamic law is derived from the Sharia by Muslim jurists and is applied by judges. For further discussion, see Manisuli Ssenyonjo and Mashood A Baderin, *International Human Rights Law: Six Decades after the UDHR and Beyond* (Ashgate Publishing 2013) 340.

100 Mohamed Berween, 'Non-Muslims in the Islamic State: Majority Rule and Minority Rights' (2006) 10 *The International Journal of Human Rights* 91, 91.

Muslim ruling majority applies conservative-sectarian religious doctrines to determine the lawful rights of religious minorities.

Many traditionalist Muslim scholars, along with some Muslim governments, argue that Islam should not adhere to Western notions of human rights because it has its own distinct system of rights and duties. This argument seems to neglect the large part of international human rights law which is, in fact, in accordance with protections granted in Islam.[101] For instance, the Universal Islamic Declaration of Human Rights (UIDHR), which claims to represent the voices of Muslims on human rights,[102] asserts that Islam recognises and protects every person who embraces religion and worship in accordance with her or his religious belief. On a regional level, the discourse of Islam and human rights can be examined from the Arab Charter on Human Rights adopted by the League of Arab States in 2004. The preamble of this Charter similarly emphasises the principles of fraternity, equality and tolerance among human beings consecrated by the noble Islamic religion and the other monotheistic religions.[103] The brotherhood, tolerance, and equality principles basically demonstrate that the Charter aims to accommodate the principles of international human rights law and Islamic law. In Islam, tolerance towards different opinions among members of the community is highly encouraged; differences of opinion among the Companions of the Prophet are recognised as a mercy of God.[104]

Regrettably, the practical aspect of religious freedom in the Muslim world demonstrates divergences from this ideal because, up to the present day, many religious minorities within Islam have been discriminated against. In this context, Islam continues to be utilised and exploited by certain Muslim states as a legitimating factor behind repressive policies against non-Muslim religious minorities, as well as religious minorities within Islam.[105] Consequently, it is submitted that the discrimination against religious minorities within Islam is due to the fact that the values of egalitarian Islamic principles have been wrongly conflated not only with old customs and traditions but also with political reasons that are incompatible with human rights in Islam.[106]

Additionally, the discourse of human rights in the Muslim world is also influenced by the dynamic legal and human rights paradigms among Muslims. Some

101 Fait A Muedini, 'Examining Islam and Human Rights from the Perspective of Sufism' (2010) 7 *Muslim World Journal of Human Rights* 3–4.

102 The UIDHR was not adopted by states but by private individuals and was not binding on Muslim states. Rather it is the Cairo Declaration that was adopted by member states of the Organisation of the Islamic Conference (now Cooperation) in 1990.

103 The Charter has been ratified by several Arab Muslim-majority states such as Algeria, Iraq, Jordan, Kuwait, Lebanon, Libya, Palestine, Qatar, Syria, the UAE and Yemen.

104 Israel Friedlaender, 'The Heterodoxies of the Shiites in the Presentation of Ibn Ḥazm' (1907) 28 *Journal of the American Oriental Society* 1, 7.

105 Ghanea (n 64) 707.

106 Anne Orford, 'The Perplexities of Modern International Law' (2005) 99 *American Journal of International Law* 274, 304.

Muslims have uncompromisingly associated loyalty to Islam and religious institutions with strong resistance to the encroachments of international human rights principles; in contrast, others are linked to the secularisation of human rights.[107] In a state like Indonesia, whose majority population is Muslim and there is a close relationship between law and religion (particularly Islam), it is inescapable for the government to consider Islamic religious values in determining particular rights and freedoms that can be enjoyed by individuals or groups. The discourse of Islam and human rights is even more complicated in Muslim-majority states that constitutionally acknowledge Islam as a sole state religion because many rulers from such Muslim states generally uphold Islamic orthodoxy to oppress religious minorities within Islam.

In addressing that problem, some Muslim scholars like Baderin argue: "the implementation of all rights and freedoms of international human rights principles must consider a multicultural approach to realise an inclusive theory of universalism".[108] International human rights instruments cannot be successfully implemented in the Muslim world if the international human rights regime still uses a strict anthropocentric approach and, at the same time, eliminates the theocentric approach of Islamic law on human rights.[109] There must be a complementary approach to implementing human rights principles in the Muslim world because the reliance on divine revelation is central to many Muslim scholars, for whom the philosophy of law and the legal sovereignty of God are all-embracing.[110] As asserted by An-Naim: "Muslims often perceive Islamic law as a sacred law and seem reluctant to re-formulate it even though naturally it is not divine because it is the product of human interpretation of Qur'an and hadith".[111] Based on this perspective, it can be noted that there is the need to depart from an exclusive approach in the interpretation of international human rights principles to encourage the promotion and realisation of the provisions of international human rights in the Muslim world.[112]

Regarding the discourse of the anthropocentric and theocentric differences, Baderin argues:

107 Ann Elizabeth Mayer, 'Law and Religion in the Muslim Middle East' (1987) 35 *The American Journal of Comparative Law* 127, 128.

108 Mashood Baderin, 'Dialogue among Civilisations as a Paradigm for Achieving Universalism in International Human Rights: A Case Study with Islamic Law' (2001) 2 *Asia Pacific Journal on Human Rights and the Law* 1, 8.

109 Baderin defines "anthropocentric as having Man (*i.e.* human being) as the central point of focus while theocentric means having God as the central point of focus". For the analyses on anthropocentric and theocentric approaches of human rights see Baderin above.

110 For the work of Baderin, see generally Baderin, 'Dialogue among Civilisations as a Paradigm for Achieving Universalism in International Human Rights: A Case Study with Islamic Law' (n 108).

111 Charles Kurzman, *Liberal Islam: A Source Book* (Oxford University Press 1998) 237.

112 Mashood A Baderin, *International Human Rights and Islamic Law* (Oxford University Press Oxford 2003) 8.

> ...the dialogical approach demands a bilateral harmonisation of the theocentric and anthropocentric differences. The divine and the secular need not be imperatively conflicting or reproaching. There cannot be a total separation between Man and God, especially in matters of human welfare. This is because of the strong influence which religion has on a great population of the world's people.[113]

Baderin further argues: "where the door is shut completely against the Islamic theocentric perspective, it will be difficult if not impossible to interpret the Sharia in the language of international human rights".[114] The reason is that most Muslims generally feel obligated to conduct their lives in conformity with the precepts of the Qur'an and *Sunnah* as well as historically formulated interpretations of those two supreme laws produced by earlier Islamic jurists.[115] According to this proposition, the purely secular approach to human rights will fail to answer the problem of religious minorities within Islam in the Muslim world, including Indonesia, since it requires Muslims to subordinate their religious doctrines to merely human and arguably "non-Islamic" criteria.

These propositions demonstrate that a secular approach to international human rights principles would not only have to encounter doctrinal questions emanating from Islamic beliefs but also legal traditions. The implementation of human rights in the Muslim world, particularly rights closely associated with religious doctrines such as freedom of religion, requires a legal pluralistic approach. Therefore, it is not only international human rights law that encounters a socio-legal context. Islamic law must also deal with localities of Indonesian legal tradition, or the existence of *adat* law (customary law) practised by some societies, on the issue of religious minorities within Islam. Some Indonesian Muslims have attempted to "indigenise" Islam in order to accommodate cultural and legal traditions, to promote moderate Islam and to respond to contemporary problems including the issue of religious minorities within Islam.[116]

Based on that, the international human rights regimes and Muslims must be able to navigate all legal possibilities in order to successfully implement international human rights principles, because the dynamic discourse of human rights in the Muslim world is based on many legal factors. For example, some Muslim majority states like Indonesia still recognise customary law, which emanates from Indonesian legal cultures and is frequently in conflict with Islamic law

113 Baderin, 'Dialogue among Civilisations as a Paradigm for Achieving Universalism in International Human Rights: A Case Study with Islamic Law' (n 108) 25.
114 ibid 27.
115 David Little, 'Religion, Catalyst or Impediment to International Law? The Case of Hugo Grotius' (1993) 87 *Proceedings of the Annual Meeting (American Society of International Law)* 322, 327.
116 Al Khanif, 'NU Must Deal with Members Persecution of Minorities' (*The Jakarta Post* 5 August 2015).

and international human rights law.[117] This brings about a complex legal reality of human rights discourse because the executive and adjudicative bodies must be able to negotiate the tensions arising from multiple and sometimes conflicting judicial systems on certain rights and freedoms.[118]

It may be argued that using only a Western-centric or Islamic approach to implement international human rights principles in Muslim-majority states would not solve the complex problem. In the post-colonial era, many states, especially in Asia and Africa and including Indonesia, have very complex legal systems due to the mixture of Western legal positivism transplanted by colonialists and local legal traditions in the form of customary law practised by society. Thus it is better, as asserted by Menski, "to turn towards recognition of legal pluralism as an admittedly difficult but reality-focused tool kit for making appropriate decisions and seeking better forms of justice".[119] It is due to the fact that customary law is often perceived by its society as a fundamental structural system, which forms the basis of all ethical and legal judgements and is the source of social expectations.[120] In some Indonesian communities, the role of customary law is even greater than religious (Islamic) law and international human rights law, making the enforcement of human rights more complex.

It is agreed by all Muslims that the Islamic creed (*aqidah*) does not accept alteration, but inter-human relations (*mu'amalat*) accept alterations because societies evolve and undergo change over time.[121] The sources of Islamic law should be examined from a strictly historical perspective for the contextualisation of the literal interpretation of Qur'anic scripture, to achieve a fair assessment of its treatment of human rights.[122] For instance, Amr ibn As allowed Egyptians to practise their conventional laws except for the custom of sacrificing a girl to the Nile for more water. Furthermore, at the time of the Mogul rulers, the Hindus in India were allowed to practise their law except for the custom of *sati*; burning the widow with the body of her late husband.[123]

117 More examination on the impact of customary law against human rights discourse in Indonesia is discussed in Chapters 7 and 8.

118 William R Roff, 'Customary Law, Islamic Law, and Colonial Authority: Three Contrasting Case Studies and Their Aftermath' (2010) 49 *Islamic Studies* 455, 461.

119 Werner Menski, 'Flying Kites in a Global Sky: New Models of Jurisprudence' (2011) *Socio-Legal Review* 22, 13.

120 Jamie Davidson and David Henley, 'The Many Roles of Adat in West Sumatera', in Jamie Davidson and David Henley (eds), *The Revival of Tradition in Indonesian Politics: The Deployment of Adat from Colonialism to Indigenism* (Routledge 2007) 204.

121 Recep Senturk, 'Sociology of Rights: "I Am Therefore I Have Rights": Human Rights in Islam between Universalistic and Communalistic Perspectives' (2005) 2 *Muslim World Journal of Human Rights*, in Mashood A Baderin, Mahmood Monshipouri, Shadi Mokhtari and Lynn Welchman (eds), *Islam and Human Rights: Advocacy for Social Change in Local Contexts* (Global Media Publications 2006) 33.

122 Isha Khan, 'Islamic Human Rights: Islamic Law and International Human Rights Standards' (1999) 5 *Appeal: Review of Current Law and Law Reform* 74, 80.

123 Senturk (n 121) 389.

These examples illustrate that Muslim rulers acknowledged that Islam was revealed to enhance religious morality by limiting particular religious beliefs that may threaten public order and safety. If two similar cases occurred nowadays, the limitations would be justified under international human rights law because the practice of burning or sacrificing human beings is incompatible with the concept of respecting human dignity as a fundamental element of human rights.

2.1. *Towards an egalitarian Islamic law on religious freedom*

According to some Muslim scholars, the second Caliph, Umar b. al-Khattab, granted the people of the book (*ahlul kitab*) protection, as well as Christians and Jews as "*dhimmis*", under the shelter of Islam in exchange for their acceptance of certain conditions. These conditions demonstrated their submission to a Muslim ruler and their recognition of Islam's superiority.[124] In relation to their religious rights, classical Islamic jurists argued that the rights of *dhimmis* must be protected due to their pledged loyalty to the Islamic state by giving *jizyah* (tax).[125] The status of *dhimmis* is significant in that, traditionally, the concept theoretically referred to the adherents of religions revealed before Islam and, consequently, the status of *dhimmi* did not apply to post-Islamic religions,[126] or to religious minorities within Islam. However, as Islam expanded eastwards, the pre-modern doctrines of Islamic law concerning the status of *dhimmi* have had to be adjusted and Muslims have learned to co-exist with adherents of Hinduism, Buddhism, Confucianism, Zoroastrianism and other polytheists.[127] It must be noted that in modern times all Muslims must acknowledge religious pluralism even though they believe that Islam is the only true religion recognised by God, because accepting the faith is a matter of choice.[128]

Despite historical incidents of mistreatment of non-Muslim religious minorities and religious minorities within Islam, the rise of secular nationalism in the Muslim world seemed to diminish the status differences between Muslims and non-Muslim religious minorities. The proponents of egalitarian human rights schemes in Islam, such as Subhi Mahmassani, have argued that there can be no discrimination based on religion in an Islamic system and therefore there should be harmony between Islam and international law.[129] Similarly, Mahmud Muhammad Taha also asserted that the applicability of legal rules in various

124 Daniel Tsadik, 'The Legal Status of Religious Minorities: Imāmī Shīʿī Law and Iran's Constitutional Revolution' (2003) 10 *Islamic Law and Society* 376, 380.

125 Mashood A Baderin, 'Islamic Law and International Protection of Minority Rights in Context', in Marie-Luisa Frick and Andreas Th Muller, *Islam and International Law: Engaging Self-Centrism from a Plurality of Perspectives* (Martinus Nijhoff Publishers 2013) 326.

126 Baderin and others (n 121) 222.

127 Ann Mayer, *Islam and Human Rights: Tradition and Politics* (Avalon Publishing 2006) 152.

128 Baderin (n 125) 322.

129 Mayer (n 127) 152–153.

Qur'anic verses must be rethought. By distinguishing verses that were meant to govern the early Islamic community from those that were meant to have enduring validity, Taha identified Islamic principles that abolish the status of *dhimmis* and mandate an end to all discrimination on the basis of religion.[130]

The foundation for an egalitarian human rights scheme in Islam had also been proposed by Imam Abu Hanifa, the founder of the Hanafi School of Islamic law. Abu Hanifa and his followers advanced the cause of universal human rights by unconditionally granting equal dignity to all by birth, on a permanent and equal basis, by virtue of being a human – which cannot be taken away by any authority.[131] He established the concept of *adamiyyah* (personhood or humanity) and the concept of *ismah* (inviolability) which means that every human being, whether Muslim or not, serves as the legal ground for possessing basic rights (*al-ismah bi al-adamiyyah*). Basic human rights in this concept are such that the rights to inviolability of life, property, religion, reason, family and honour should be granted to all human beings for the sake of their humanity.[132] The concept of *al-ismah bi al-adamiyyah* recognises the "universality of human rights"[133] because all human beings are entitled to fundamental rights and freedoms and they must be equally protected because their dignity cannot be protected unless they are granted sanctity and freedom. Additionally, human beings should be protected because God in the Qur'an and the Prophet Muhammad in his Traditions strictly prohibited assaulting and slaying the honour of any human being.[134] Freedom is fundamentally and ultimately an act of respect for God's sovereignty and for the mystery of His plan for man. To respect man's freedom is to respect God's plan.[135]

The concept of *al-ismah bi al-adamiyah* emanates from the principle of human dignity stipulated in Qur'an 95:4. The verse says that God created human beings of the best stature and bestowed great dignity and honour on them. Qur'an 49:13 further emphasises that all human beings are equal according to the revealed Book of Islam. The superiority of one over the other in the sight of God is due to one's virtues and merits.[136] This means that human rights in Islam are sacred and inviolable, as these rights have been granted by God and cannot be violated by any human authority, even by an Islamic state, under any pretext and in any circumstance.[137] The degree of treatment, which

130 ibid 153.
131 Senturk (n 121) 387.
132 ibid 387–388.
133 ibid 385.
134 ibid 388.
135 Heiner Bielefeldt, 'Muslim Voices in the Human Rights Debate' (1995) 17 *Human Rights Quarterly* 609.
136 Muhammad Sharif Chaudhry, *Islam's Charter of Fundamental Rights and Civil Liberties* (Al Matbaat Ul Arabia 1995) 22.
137 Muhammad Sharif Chaudhry, *Human Rights in Islam* (All Pakistan Islamic Education Congress 1993) 20–21.

may cause inequality against human beings, belongs to God on the Day of Resurrection, due to each human being's virtues and merits based on her/his piety and righteousness.

These arguments are all based on the notion of a universal human being and aim to establish peaceful relations between Muslims and non-Muslims and among religious adherents from different religions.[138] Thus, it is submitted that the concept of *al-ismah bi al-adamiyyah* should apply to all non-Muslims or other religious minorities within Islam that are numerically inferior and live among a Muslim ruling majority. Religious minorities within Islam should be treated equally because they possess a dignified character of humanity, irrespective of social status, treaty or any other kind of agreement with Muslims.

In Islam, the concept of sovereignty, which belongs to God and His commandments, is the supreme law.[139] No one is allowed to force human beings to follow his or her way, including forcing them to believe in God. It is God who has the right to determine reward and punishment for human piety. This proposition is related to the saying of the Prophet Muhammad that there should not be a distinction of treatment for all human beings except on the basis of *taqwa* (piety).[140] These arguments affirm that human rights are sacredly protected, because these rights are bestowed by God on all human beings.

Another verse that promotes the universality of human rights in Islam is Qur'an 16:90, which regulates that: "Surely, God commands justice".[141] The premise of "justice", which belongs to God, essentially shows that Islamic doctrines speak about the equal creation of human beings, sharing their parentage and endowed with honour and dignity as the children of Adam.[142] The word Adam in the Qur'an refers to a human being as a perfect creation of God. Granting freedom and rights in an Islamic concept should solely refer to the status of Adam as God's creation. Therefore, the Hanafi school argues that the *dhimmah* treaty between Muslim rulers and non-Muslim religious minorities is not essential for the inviolability of the rights of *dhimmis*; rather, it is an alliance against third parties and allegiance to the state.[143] It signifies that non-Muslims and religious minorities within Islam should also have equal rights as a consequence of being Adamic.

138 Senturk (n 121) 388.
139 ibid 14.
140 ibid 32–33.
141 Mashood A Baderin, Mahmood Monshipouri, Shadi Mokhtari and Lynn Welchman, 'Extension of Shari'ah in Northern Nigeria: Human Rights Implementations for Non-Muslim Minorities', in Mashood A. Baderin, Mahmood Monshipouri, Shadi Mokhtari and Lynn Welchman (eds), *Islam and Human Rights, Advocacy for Social Change in Local Contexts* (Global Media Publications 2006) 160.
142 Abdulaziz Sachedina, *Islam and the Challenge of Human Rights* (Oxford University Press 2009) 12.
143 Senturk (n 121) 393.

A universalistic view of human rights, particularly the right to freedom of religion in Islam, can also be found in Qur'an 10:99–100, which says:

> And if thy Lord had willed, whoever is in the earth would have believed, all of them, all together, wouldst thou then constrain the people, until they are believers? It is not for any soul to believe save by the leave of God; and He lays abomination upon those who have no understanding.[144]

This verse seeks to convince the Prophet Muhammad that matters of religious belief are in the hands of God, and that any attempt to spread his faith by coercion would be a futile exercise. Qur'an 5:92 and 5:99 also declare that the Prophet can only deliver the divine message and it is not within his power to assure its acceptance or implementation. He is clearly and firmly warned to respect human freedom and God's mystery.[145] All these indicate that in Islam, compelling people to embrace religion not only nullifies people's faith but also humiliates God's plan. Even though the Qur'an affirms that Islam is the only true religion, it also acknowledges religious pluralism because Qur'an 109 asserts that accepting the faith is a matter of choice.[146] For instance, a *dhimmi* compelled to embrace Islam is not considered a Muslim unless he retains his new faith after compelling force is no longer applied to him. If he dies while still under compulsion, his conversion is not valid.[147]

The acknowledgement of religious pluralism and respect for other beliefs in Islam is regulated in various verses of the Qur'an.[148] However, state practices in some Muslim-majority states show divergent points of view between the normative foundation of religious pluralism in the Qur'an and practical requirements for religious minorities. Religious freedom and the rights of religious minorities in Islam are still very relevant questions in the Muslim world because state practices in the Muslim world habitually discriminate against religious minorities. Nazila Ghanea, for example, reported that there are various kinds of discrimination faced by non-Muslim religious minorities in Muslim countries, particularly in the Middle East. She notes that the challenges that affect religious minorities as individuals include inter alia severe restrictions on missionary activities.[149] It is regrettable that the aforesaid egalitarian and universalistic ideas that preserve equality and egalitarian and tolerant principles in Islamic law have, however, not been fully developed and in some cases have been rejected by some Muslims.

144 ibid.
145 See Kurzman (n 111) 163.
146 Baderin, 'Dialogue Among Civilisations as a Paradigm for Achieving Universalism in International Human Rights: A Case Study with Islamic Law' (n 108) 326.
147 Yohanan Friedmann, *Tolerance and Coercion in Islam: Interfaith Relations in the Muslim Tradition* (Cambridge University Press 2003) 144–145.
148 See further observation of the Qur'anic verses at Hirji Zulfikar, *Diversity and Pluralism in Islam: Historical and Contemporary Discourses amongst Muslims* (2012) 5–6.
149 Ghanea (n 64) 709–710.

Some Muslims have restricted particular rights of religious minorities, whereby different religious minorities within Islam have been subjected to differing degrees of discrimination in terms of social privilege.[150]

Some have argued that the concept of *dhimmi* in Islamic law, even though it has been reformulated or abolished by some Muslim-majority states like Turkey since the Ottoman Empire in 1856,[151] still holds the key to establishing equal rights for non-Muslims.[152] However, other contemporary Muslim scholars argue that the traditional concept of *dhimmi* needs to be abandoned for a more egalitarian concept to ensure equal treatment of minorities. There is no doubt that the reform of a particular practice of Islamic law like *dhimmi* is inevitable and, whether Muslims are reform-minded or not, they will have to confront the reality of reform and respond to it.[153] Certainly, the classical *dhimmi* rules are not immutable because there are relevant provisions of the Qur'an and the *Sunnah*, as well as legitimate jurisprudential methods and principles of Islamic law, that can facilitate the modification of the classical rules to meet the contemporary challenges of minority rights protection in the Muslim world today.[154]

Yet history and the recent situation of human rights application, especially in respect of the protection of religious minorities within Islam in the Muslim world, seems to have been neglected, and the position could even be deteriorating. The egalitarian Islamic law on human rights, especially the concept of *al-ismah bi al-adamiyah*, does not receive consensus in Islam because most Muslims prefer to keep the monolithic interpretation of Islamic jurisprudences, which are commonly resistant to human rights. In fact, consensus as the most authoritative source of Islamic law played a very significant role in shaping Muslims' perspective on the Muslim world.[155] Consensus guarantees the correct interpretation of the Qur'an and the faithful transmission of the Hadith, including the recognised differences of the several Islamic jurisprudences produced by four schools of Islamic law.[156] This means "community" in Islam has a privilege so that any jurisprudences produced by a certain jurist need to be accepted by Muslims and recognised by the community. In an Indonesian context, consensus is held not only to accept a certain Islamic jurisprudence but also to resolve issues in a particular society through a deliberation process.

150 Marshall GS Hodgson, *The Venture of Islam: The Classical Age of Islam* (University of Chicago Press 1974) 242–243.

151 Maurits Berger, 'Public Policy and Islamic Law: The Modern Dhimmī in Contemporary Egyptian Family Law' (2001) 8 *Islamic Law and Society* 88, 92.

152 For an illustration of the different application of Islamic law in Nigeria, see Baderin and others (n 141) 555.

153 ibid 163.

154 Baderin (n 125) 312.

155 Baber Johansen, *Contingency in a Sacred Law: Legal and Ethical Norms in the Muslim Fiqh* (Brill 1999) 48.

156 Ahmad Hasan, 'Ijma' in the Early Schools' 125.

2.2. *The contested concepts of apostasy and heresy in Islamic law*

In some recent cases, the protection of religious minorities within Islam in the Muslim world has become one of the most contentious human rights discourses. The expression of unorthodox Islamic views is seen by majority orthodox Muslims as cause to often refer to their minority counterparts as "infidels" or even as "apostates", leading the majority to discriminate against them. The Muslim world has endeavoured to take some steps to reform classical concepts of religious freedom in order to respect theological differences which, for example, can be noted from the provision on religious freedom and the rights of minorities in the UIDHR adopted in 1981. Article 10 of the UIDHR asserts that the rights of non-Muslim minorities to embrace and practise their religion and their own laws are protected by Qur'anic principles, while Article 13 further provides that everyone has the right to freedom of conscience and worship in accordance with her/his beliefs.[157] On the face of it, these provisions appear to reflect egalitarian principles of human rights in Islam. In practice however, there is often a departure from these principles because many Muslims still rely on traditional Islamic law as interpreted by the classical Islamic jurists in the first century of Islam, reflecting the circumstances of a particular historical period to resolve contemporary human rights problems.[158]

Some cases related to this may be seen from the case of religious minorities in Iran and Pakistan. Iranian law, which is based on Shi'ah jurisprudence, asserts that heretical books and matters hurtful to Islam are forbidden, while societies and associations are permissible so long as they do not threaten inter alia the religion or the state.[159] The term Islam here should be understood as referring to Shi'ah Islam while Sunni and other religious minorities within Islam are in practice seen as heretical. Iran's constitution provides that the (*Twelver*) Shi'ah Muslims are adherents of the official religion and are held in the highest regard before the law, other Muslims (*Sunni*) are *de jure* recognised and respected, *dhimmis* are *de jure* tolerated, and non-Muslims are adherents of non-Abrahamic religions and not granted rights.[160] Another case relates to the Ahmadis in Pakistan, an Islamic minority sect and school of thought that is subject to official discrimination by government policy, which regards Ahmadis as

157 See UIDHR.

158 Mayer (n 127) 151.

159 Tsadik (n 124) 378.

160 See Temperman (n 52) 224. Article 12 of Iran's Constitution provides that the official religion of Iran is Islam and the Twelver Ja'fari school [in usul al-Din and fiqh], and this principle will remain eternally immutable. Other Islamic schools, including the Hanafi, Shafi'i, Maliki, Hanbali and Zaydi, are to be accorded full respect, and their followers are free to act in accordance with their own jurisprudence in performing their religious rites. Article 13 further says that Zoroastrian, Jewish and Christian Iranians are the only recognised religious minorities, who, within the limits of the law, are free to perform their religious rites and ceremonies and to act according to their own canon in matters of personal affairs and religious education.

"non-Muslims". The government, on behalf of the Islamic ruling majority, perceive Ahmadis as heretics, threatening Islamic belief, because they believe that Mirza Ghulam, the founder of Ahmadiyah, is a prophet,[161] contrary to the beliefs of the orthodox Muslim majority.

The Iranian and Pakistani cases illustrate that, to examine the rights of religious minorities, religious freedom should be considered because the rights of non-Muslims and religious minorities within Islam are often curtailed through the operation of Islamic law. This occurs especially when concerning the equal right to embrace religion and perform religious rituals. The cases also signify that the Islamic state, as a model of theocracy in which an official Islam exists as state policy and which forms the social framework in civil society,[162] is premised upon a state ruling on behalf of a specific religious community. This raises difficult questions about the position of religious minorities.[163] Thus, the Islamic and international human rights concepts of religious freedom are pertinent not only to non-Muslims who live in Muslim states but also to Muslims who deviate from beliefs considered orthodox by the religious establishment of their time and place.[164] In the case of religious minorities within Islam, the concept of heresy is essentially an internal Islamic theological discourse and could be resolved through internal intellectual theological discourse among Muslims. However, when there is criminalisation of a belief considered as heretical, international human rights law can intervene to protect all individuals without discrimination.[165]

Essentially, the persecution of religious minorities within Islam has become controversial in the Muslim world, even though it is apparent that Islam clearly states that compulsion in religion is forbidden and incompatible with Islam (Qur'an 2:256) because religion is a matter of free will (Qur'an 18:29).[166] Hence, everyone is responsible for her/his own actions before God. The term apostasy fits with the history of early Islam when Muslims, small in number, were under constant pressure from their powerful adversaries to revert to their former faith. There is no single verse in the Qur'an which justifies killing apostates except in time of war. For example, the Qur'an enjoins Muslims to fight infidels and weaken them but, if they cease, let there be no transgression.[167] The first Caliph, Abu Bakr, commanded the rebellious tribes to conform not only in the purely religious sense but also to pay their share in financing the nascent Muslim state.[168]

161 Mayer (n 127) 162.
162 Nalini Rajan, *Democracy and the Limits of Minority Rights* (Sage Publications 2002) 87.
163 Maya Shatzmiller, *Nationalism and Minority Identities in Islamic Societies* (McGill-Queen's Press – MQUP 2005) 127.
164 Friedmann (n 147) 9.
165 Baderin (n 125) 333.
166 Baderin and others (n 141) 166.
167 Qur'an 2:193.
168 Scolnicov (n 91) 80–83.

Up to the present day, the issue of apostasy has been very critical in Islamic law. The Arabic equivalent term of apostasy is *ridda*,[169] defined as an act of rejection of faith committed by Muslims to the *shahadah* and a Muslim who insults Islam by desecrating the Qur'an or humiliating the Prophet.[170] Apostasy can also be defined as turning away from Islam or severing ties with Islam.[171] Every Muslim must pronounce *shahadah* wholeheartedly, affirming the oneness of God and the Prophethood of Muhammad and therefore the Islamic jurists maintain that the denial of the *shahadah* is the foremost indication of apostasy. Thus, whoever claims prophethood after the Prophet Muhammad, or gives support to such a claimant, also becomes an apostate and contradicts the idea of the finality of Muhammad's prophethood, which is absolutely central to the Islamic creed.[172]

Al-Samarra'i argues that even though the Qur'an sometimes provides the term *al-ridda*, the punishment of the apostate is not to be found within it but in the *Sunnah* only.[173] Some Islamic scholars hence use cases on apostasy in the era of the Prophet Muhammad as a prophetic precedent substantiating the legality of capital punishment for apostates. The prophetic traditions that are always cited as the basis of the law of apostasy are: "the blood of a fellow Muslim should never be shed except in three cases; that of the adulterer, the murderer, and whoever forsakes the religion of Islam and separates himself from the (Muslim) community",[174] and "whoever changes his religion kill him".[175] One of the traditional Islamic scholars who rely on these prophetic traditions is Ibn Taymiyya, who argues that the apostate is cruder in her/his infidelity than an original unbeliever and therefore killing the unrepentant apostate is mandatory while an original unbeliever is killed only if she or he is a combatant.[176]

The second Caliph, Umar Ibn Khattab, chose a different treatment of imprisonment, rather than executions, as the punishment of choice. Some other jurists, such as Sufyan al-Thawri and Ibrahim al-Nakha'i, preferred to give the apostate an opportunity to repent forever as long as there is hope for her/his repentance.[177] The Hanafis argue differently that apostasy has two aspects. It is a religious transgression to be punished by God in the hereafter and it is also

169 Mohamed Mohamed Adil, 'Law of Apostasy and Freedom of Religion in Malaysia' (2007) 2 *Asian Journal of Comparative Law* 1.

170 ibid 2.

171 Gert JJ De Vries and Rudolph Peters, 'Apostasy in Islam' (1976) 17 *Die Welt des Islams* 1, 2.

172 Friedmann (n 147) 121–122.

173 Mohamed SM Eltayeb, *A Human Rights Approach to Combating Religious Persecution: Cases from Pakistan, Saudi Arabia, and Sudan* (Intersentia 2001); JEJ Prins, PMA Ribbers and Henk CA Van Tilborg, *Trust in Electronic Commerce: The Role of Trust from a Legal, an Organizational, and a Technical Point of View* (Kluwer Law International BV 2002) 49.

174 Shahih Bukhari, 83:37.

175 ibid, 84:57.

176 Friedmann (n 147) 123. For cases of apostasy in the era of Prophet Muhammad, see at 125.

177 ibid 128.

a political crime likely to be followed by rebellion. Only this latter aspect of apostasy is punished here and now.[178] It can be asserted that most Islamic scholars argue that apostasy is a crime under Islamic law. Yet, their different opinions on the punishment of apostasy confirm that apostasy is also differently understood by Muslims. For those who perceive apostasy as a crime that causes tensions in Muslim society and disruption to a status quo of Islamic orthodoxy, the harsh punishment of apostasy must be enforced. For those who believe that changing religion from Islam to another religion is a human responsibility to his/her God, apostasy is solely located within the right to have freedom of religion that must be respected.[179]

In practical Islam, since the death of the Prophet until recently, there is considerable overlap between the crimes of apostasy, heresy and blasphemy. Anti-blasphemy laws in several Muslim states, including Indonesia, have been enacted or used to crack down on specific religious minorities that deviate from state-sanctioned religious orthodoxy. For example, the Pakistan anti-Ahmadi laws of 1984 criminalised a range of specific deviations from Islamic orthodox doctrine and are designed to make it impossible for Ahmadis to openly practise and propagate their faith.[180]

Blasphemy laws and other laws that stand for religious orthodoxy are used to prohibit freedom of religious expression, seen to deviate from Islamic religious orthodoxy. Punishment of heretical or deviant Muslims often even extends to execution and other severe treatments. For example, An-Naim was denounced as a heretic by Muslims in Mauritius after he said that the historical formulations of Islamic law discriminate against women and called for the reinterpretation of Islamic sources to secure equality between men and women.[181] Another example is the killing of Farag Foda in 1992, an Egyptian Muslim thinker declared an apostate and insulter of Islam because of his critique of Islamic fundamentalism.[182]

It may be concluded that the historical evidence indicates that the issue of humanity in Islamic law has actually never been static; rather it has been evolutionary and has responded in the past to changes in most Muslim societies in Muslim states.[183] Moreover, different legal arguments have been put forward

178 ibid 137.

179 Ghanea N, 'Apostasy and Freedom to Change Religion or Belief', in Tore Lindholm, W. Cole Durham, Jr. and Bahia G. Tahzib-Lie, *Facilitating Freedom of Religion or Belief: A Deskbook* (Springer 2013) 671.

180 Temperman (n 59) 241.

181 Abdullahi A An-Na'im and Louis Henkin, 'Islam and Human Rights: Beyond the Universality Debate' (2000) 94 *Proceedings of the Annual Meeting (American Society of International Law)* 95, 100.

182 Sita Ram Goel, 'Was Mohammed a Liar?', in Sita Ram Goel, *Freedom of Expression: Secular Theocracy versus Liberal Democracy* (Voice of India 1998) 139.

183 Mashood Baderin, 'Islam and the Realization of Human Rights in the Muslim World: A Reflection on Two Essential Approaches and Two Divergent Perspectives' (2007) 4 *Muslim World Journal of Human Rights* 15–16.

since the era of the four prominent Islamic schools of thought,[184] producing immensely complex jurisprudence (*fiqh*) on various matters, including human rights. Until recently, there have been different rulings on the subject based on Islamic jurisprudence (*fiqh*) by Islamic jurists, which are not absolute opinions in Islam. Islamic jurisprudence is the process of extrapolation by a jurist which is open to change and revision depending on time and place.[185] For this reason, legal discourse in Islam is open to various interpretations which comprise all facets of life that should be applied universally to all human beings without regard to difference.

This perspective is important to the development of a thesis about natural law in Islam and its connection with the natural, inalienable rights of human beings based on human equality.[186] It is submitted that the egalitarian principles of Islamic law are compatible with the norms of international human rights law, especially the concept of equality and dignity. Essentially, Islamic law seeks to diminish the discriminatory treatment against particular groups of people and avoid using religious sectarianism in matters of human rights. However, through human interpretation, the rights of religious minorities encounter very pronounced difficulties because, in an Islamic theocratic state, a ruling Muslim majority usually serves the interests of both state and religion. Therefore, the idea of equal religious freedom becomes difficult to achieve for religious minorities because the majority manipulates the religion (Islam) and acts as the shadow of God to justify their religious interpretation of rights and freedom. For instance, a Shi'ah minority will be viewed as a heretical group by a Sunni majority in power while the situation changes when a Shi'ah majority is in power. This example portrays that the history and future of Islam regarding the execution of "heretics" is solely about who posed or will pose a threat to an Islamic ruling majority, which is more of a political issue and openly dissents from the official majority view of Islam and under Islamic law.[187]

2.3. Communitarian Islamic law and religious minorities within Islam

Unlike Western legal traditions, which posit the existence of a higher law grounded in human reason and a relatively weak idea of divine law, many Muslims believe the theoretical foundation of Islamic law is, by contrast, a robust notion of divine law with a relatively weak conception of natural law.[188] Even though conservative-traditionalist and modern-reformist Muslims generally have different opinions regarding relations between Islam and human rights and how

184 Werner F Menski, *Comparative Law in a Global Context: The Legal Systems of Asia and Africa* (Cambridge University Press 2006) 315.
185 Sachedina (n 142) 28.
186 ibid 87.
187 Ali Reza Abootalebi, *Islam and Democracy: State-Society Relations in Developing Countries, 1980–1994* (Psychology Press 2000) 215.
188 Sohail Hashmi, 'Islam and Constitutionalism' *Law & Liberty* (2013).

human rights are sensitive to Islamic beliefs in particular, they are universally keen to argue that Islamic law reflects, above all, immutable-divine law. Muslim jurists in Islamic jurisprudence were generally guided not by intuition but by textual evidence and hence Islamic jurisprudence becomes conceptual knowledge rather than intuitive perception.[189] Most Muslims believe that any type of law and justice, including human rights discourses in Islam, should unquestionably be framed as theological matters.

In Islamic jurisprudence, as asserted by Weiss:

> Legal knowledge can only be acquired pursuant to the ascertainment of the existence of God, the reality of revelation, and the authenticity and meaning of those texts in which revelation is contained. Thus, legal knowledge depends upon the results of theological reflection and textual criticism and interpretation.[190]

This does not mean that in Muslim states Islamic law applies as a single source of law; autonomous and government-supported religious institutions generally have authority to interpret sources when the language of a source text is not clear.[191] As a consequence, man-made regulations in the Muslim world have the potential to clash with Islamic law, as Islamic law is understood to also contain specific and immutable legal rulings. This potential clash often limits the ability of Muslim reformers to revise Islamic law according to their understanding of what liberal human rights require.[192]

Besides the influence of external legal systems in other countries, the clash of human rights discourse in the Muslim world has not been caused by Islam as a religion, but generally triggered by the divergent jurisprudences from the Islamic schools of law. The conservative-traditionalists, for example, use Islamic criteria to evaluate international human rights law because Islam, as the unconditional surrender to the will of God, constitutes ideas and thought rendered through the Qur'an and Hadith. For them, human rights are the privilege of God because authority ultimately belongs to him.[193] They further argue that human rights outside the Islamic faith are based on man-made reasoning and are thus inferior. Consequently, they generally establish a minimum standard of human rights entitlement for a certain people based on their interpretation of

189 Bernard Weiss, 'Interpretation in Islamic Law: The Theory of Ijtihād' (1978) 26 *The American Journal of Comparative Law* 199, 202.
190 ibid 204.
191 Anver M Emon, *Religious Pluralism and Islamic Law: Dhimmis and Others in the Empire of Law* (Oxford University Press Oxford 2012) 174–175.
192 Hashmi (n 188).
193 See Javaid Rehman and Susan Carolyn Breau, 'Some Arguments on the Universality of Human Rights in Islam', in Javaid Rehman and Susan Carolyn Breau, *Religion, Human Rights and International Law: A Critical Examination of Islamic State Practices* (Martinus Nijhoff Publishers 2007) 170.

the Qur'an and Hadith. For instance, religious freedom should be granted to everyone as long as they do not insult any element of the orthodoxy of Islam.[194] This conservative interpretation of religious texts unfortunately still overwhelmingly inspires Muslims' views on human rights in Islam and affects the implementation of human rights and the protection of religious minorities within Islam in the Muslim world.

The modern reformists, on the other hand, have attempted to search for a common ground between Islam and human rights. They believe that Muslims should acknowledge the difference between being believers and being citizens – who have different duties. While obedience and submission are the decisive principle for religious belief, equality and the right to make decisions are the determinants of citizenship.[195] Some other modern-reformist Muslims also propose that human rights in Islam are basically compatible with international human rights standards, but where they are in conflict those areas could be reformulated and reconciled with international standards.[196] The advocates of Islam and human rights reconciliation suggest that Muslims should use *ijtihad* to reinterpret Islamic law by considering its historical, social and theological perspectives in relation to which verses of the Qur'an or Hadith were revealed. Thus, *ijtihad* means the endeavour of a jurist who has juristic abilities to interpret the Qur'an and Hadith as the supreme source of Islamic law in order to formulate the rule of law on the basis of evidence (*dalil*) in the sources.[197] Islamic jurisprudence affirms that the product of *ijtihad* is classified as "opinion" rather than knowledge, but the opinion is binding when knowledge is lacking.[198]

Regrettably, since the third and fourth century until recently, most Muslims have believed that they were incapable of interpreting the sacred texts, even though after that time *ijtihad* still remained an integral part of Islamic legal doctrine.[199] Most Muslims prefer to follow (*taqlid*) Islamic jurisprudences produced by early Muslim scholars rather than undertaking *ijtihad*, even though the early jurisprudences seem to fail to tackle contemporary human rights issues. Thus, even though some Muslim scholars have argued that *ijtihad* is already closed, *ijtihad* was indispensable in Islamic law because it constituted the only means by which *mujtahid*, a person entitled to *ijtihad*, were able to reach the law of God in the sacred texts.[200] Abd al-Barr, for example, argues that Islamic law must deal with contemporary issues including human rights issues and Muslim society needs *ijtihad* to deal with such issues.[201]

194 Zainal Fikri, 'The Rule of Bad Law' (*The Jakarta Post* 2 May 2008).
195 Rehman and Breau (n 193) 8.
196 Niaz A Shah, *Women, the Koran and International Human Rights Law: The Experience of Pakistan* (Martinus Nijhoff Publishers 2006) 8.
197 Weiss (n 189) 200.
198 ibid 202–204.
199 Wael B Hallaq, 'Was the Gate of Ijtihad Closed?' (1984) 16 *International Journal of Middle East Studies* 3, 7.
200 ibid 4.
201 ibid 12.

Unlike the conservative readings of the Qur'an still practised by most Muslims today, this reform is still advocated by a small number of Muslim scholars and hence is intended to bring about a deliberate development of human rights in the Muslim world. This is because clashes between "conservative-traditionalists'" and "modern-reformists'" ideas of human rights, particularly regarding religious freedom, frequently bring about tensions related to the protection of religious minorities within Islam. These clashes of theological, social and legal discourses have in fact become a continuation of historical-theological contestations, which have mainly ancient roots in the Islamic intellectual tradition. Coulson recorded that: "since the nineteenth century, the conflict of juristic principles influenced a polemical and intolerant attitude among the followers of the Sunni school of Islamic law as they vied for recognition as the superior expression of God's law".[202] In the present day, many Muslim reformers are frequently accused by conservative-traditionalists as heterodox Muslims and hence deemed not credible to do *ijtihad*.

The intolerant attitude of the earlier Wahhabis towards their fellow Muslims, for example, caused them for a long time to be suspected as heretics, and they have come to be generally considered orthodox only since their political successes in the present generation.[203] Another conflict also occurred between rationalists and traditionalists. The rationalist Mu'tazili faith in reason was vociferously challenged by the Maturidi school, which accepted reason as a source of moral knowledge but held that the Mu'tazili position relied excessively on reason over revelation.[204] Apart from their different interpretations of Islamic law, it can be assumed that their concept of justice is nonetheless theological in nature because all of them believe that justice should be in accordance with the doctrines laid down by the theologians concerning God's will and essence.[205]

After the Caliphate of Ali ibn Abi Talib (656–661), Islamic jurisprudence was generally intolerant of individual legal reasoning. Besides being influenced by the discourse of the closure of *ijtihad* and some highly restricted requirements to become a *mujtahid* (jurist), many Muslims believe that Islamic law contains divine legal elements that should not be revised or easily interpreted by all Muslims.[206] History in Islam has demonstrated that individual legal reasoning or any form of *ijtihad* which produced non-mainstream legal perspectives had been often considered as a deviation, apostasy or even rebellion against the long and well-established schools of law.[207] This shows that most Muslims believe

202 NJ Coulson, *A History of Islamic Law* (AldineTransaction 2011) 87.
203 Joseph Schacht, *An Introduction to Islamic Law* (Clarendon Press 1966) 66.
204 About the conflict between rationalists and traditionalists regarding *ijtihad* in the early period of Islam, see Hallaq (n 199) 8–10.
205 Majid Khadduri and Wael B Hallaq, 'The Islamic Conception of Justice' (1986) 20 *Middle East Studies Association Bulletin* 305, 306.
206 This argument was endorsed mainly by traditionalists. See Hallaq (n 199) 215.
207 See the description of Islamic schism in Soualhi Younes, 'Islamic Legal Hermeneutics: The Context and Adequacy of Interpretation in Modern Islamic Discourse' (2002) 41 *Islamic Studies* 585, 585–615.

the authority to determine true *ijtihad* rests upon majority groups. Non-mainstream *ijtihad* is not recognised as legitimate independent legal reasoning until the majority permits it. Also, the majority generally also does not accept *ijtihad* if the result is considered as confronting their interests.

A moral epistemology rooted in revelation is intrinsically conservative and can be modernised to respond to human rights issues through a combination of theological reflection and human reasoning. The former is required by Muslims to preserve the distinctive character of Islamic law which posits a divine dimension, while the latter is needed to contextualise God's command written in revelation. The distinctiveness of Islamic law and human rights realities should be peacefully reconciled by Muslims because the Qur'an and the Hadith as two fundamental sources of Islamic law basically recognise the importance of reflection and reason in the pursuit and fulfilment of justice. Muslim scholars, when they discuss justice, generally adopt either the judicial or the moral sense to fulfil substantive justice because all human beings are created equal by God and hence there should not be any type of superiority, privilege and priority on the basis of social class.[208]

For many Muslim jurists, justice is also not a purely rational ideal; it was embedded between and among peoples living in a community.[209] This argument is based on the Qur'an, which asserts that all people should consider consultation among themselves to determine a particular issue, including human rights discourses.[210] There is no clear statement in the Qur'an and the Hadith to command Muslims to give priority to the community (*ummah*) over the individual, but practical realities demonstrate that whenever there is a conflict between individual and collective interests, the latter would be given priority.[211] Thus, ideal justice in Islam is often perceived by many Muslims not to protect the rights of individuals but more to preserve the public interest. It is submitted that most Muslims still hold that Islam is a religion that harmonises rights and duties as well as individualism and communalism.[212]

Regarding the privilege of the community in Islamic-cultural tradition, Guichon argues:

> The sacred nature of the *ummah* is fundamental to understanding that individuals are only its servants. Individual rights and freedoms are secondary, and the violation of those rights can be justified when it benefits the community.[213]

208 For further discussion about justice in Islam, see Tufail Ahmad Qureshi, 'Justice in Islam' (1982) 21 *Islamic Studies* 35, 33–51.
209 Emon (n 191) 177.
210 Qur'an, 42: 38.
211 Qureshi (n 208) 38–39.
212 Uriya Shavit, *Shari'a and Muslim Minorities: The Wasati and Salafi Approaches to Fiqh al-Aqalliyyat al-Muslima* (Oxford University Press 2015) 420.
213 Rehman and Breau (n 193) 43.

Guichon's proposition is beneficial for examining the practice of Muslim rulers towards the protection of human rights, which are frequently curbed by collective interest. However, strictly speaking this practice does not come from Islamic teaching because Islam basically advocates individual rights, including *ijtihad*. For example, Qur'an 17:15 explicitly recognises individualism by asserting that whoever is guided is only guided [for the benefit] of his own soul and whoever errs only errs against his own soul. Additionally, the fourth Caliph, Ali, made the statement that: "men and women speak for the Qur'an and so interpretation of its dictates is a part of applying Qur'anic injunctions to the lives of Muslims".[214] The Caliph Umar also did not follow Qur'an 59: 7–10 when he refused to distribute the lands of Syria and Iraq to Muslims after their conquest; he believed that doing so "would weaken the state and deprive it of valuable resources".[215] Related to this, Qureshi said that the "Qur'an basically wants to create a society in which individuals can become witnesses for justice even if the judgement goes against their own interest".[216]

There is no doubt that justice in Islam should include the protection of non-Muslims as well as individual rights. Islam was created to protect both individuals and the community because all of them are the basis of responsibility and honour, which are the pillars of Islamic society.[217]

Bibliography

Abootalebi AR, *Islam and Democracy: State-Society Relations in Developing Countries, 1980–1994* (Psychology Press 2000).

Anderson C, 'Roland Burke. Decolonization and the Evolution of International Human Rights' (2010) 115 *The American Historical Review* 1113.

Angle S, *Human Rights in Chinese Thought: A Cross-Cultural Inquiry* (Cambridge University Press 2002).

An-Na'im AA, 'Constitutionalism and Islamization in the Sudan' (1989) 36 *Africa Today* 11.

An-Na'im AA and Henkin L, 'Islam and Human Rights: Beyond the Universality Debate' (2000) 94 *Proceedings of the Annual Meeting (American Society of International Law)* 95.

Backer L, 'Theocratic Constitutionalism: An Introduction to a New Global Legal Ordering' (2006) 16 *Indiana Journal of Global Legal Studies* 85 (2009).

Baderin MA, 'Dialogue among Civilisations as a Paradigm for Achieving Universalism in International Human Rights: A Case Study with Islamic Law' (2001) 2 *Asia Pacific Journal on Human Rights and the Law* 1.

———, *International Human Rights and Islamic Law* (Oxford University Press Oxford 2003).

214 Rachel Anne Codd, 'A Critical Analysis of the Role of Ijtihad in Legal Reforms in the Muslim World' (1999) 14 *Arab Law Quarterly* 112, 114.

215 ibid 118.

216 Qureshi (n 208) 44.

217 Rehman and Breau (n 193) 173.

———, 'Islam and the Realization of Human Rights in the Muslim World: A Reflection on Two Essential Approaches and Two Divergent Perspectives' (2007) 4 *Muslim World Journal of Human Rights* 1.

———, 'Islamic Law and International Protection of Minority Rights in Context', in Marie-Luisa Frick and Andreas Th Muller, *Islam and International Law: Engaging Self-Centrism from a Plurality of Perspectives* (Martinus Nijhoff Publishers 2013) 326.

Baderin MA, Mahmood Monshipouri, Shadi Mokhtari and Lynn Welchman, 'Extension of Shari'ah in Northern Nigeria: Human Rights Implementations for Non-Muslim Minorities', in Mashood A Baderin, Mahmood Monshipouri, Shadi Mokhtari and Lynn Welchman (eds), *Islam and Human Rights, Advocacy for Social Change in Local Contexts* (Global Media Publications 2006a) 160.

Baderin MA, Mahmood Monshipouri, Shadi Mokhtari and Lynn Welchman (eds), *Islam and Human Rights: Advocacy for Social Change in Local Contexts* (Global Media Publications 2006b).

Berger M, 'Public Policy and Islamic Law: The Modern Dhimmī in Contemporary Egyptian Family Law' (2001) 8 *Islamic Law and Society* 88.

Berween M, 'Non-Muslims in the Islamic State: Majority Rule and Minority Rights' (2006) 10 *The International Journal of Human Rights* 91.

Bielefeldt H, 'Muslim Voices in the Human Rights Debate' (1995) 17 *Human Rights Quarterly* 4.

Boucher D, *The Limits of Ethics in International Relations: Natural Law, Natural Rights, and Human Rights in Transition* (Oxford University Press Oxford 2011).

Charvet J, *The Liberal Project and Human Rights: The Theory and Practice of a New World Order* (Cambridge University Press 2008).

Chaudhry MS, *Human Rights in Islam* (All Pakistan Islamic Education Congress 1993).

———, *Islam's Charter of Fundamental Rights and Civil Liberties* (Al Matbaat Ul Arabia 1995).

Codd RA, 'A Critical Analysis of the Role of Ijtihad in Legal Reforms in the Muslim World' (1999) 14 *Arab Law Quarterly* 112.

Compilation of General Comments and General Recommendations Adopted by Human Rights Treaty Bodies 2006 (United Nations International Human Rights Instrument) 2006, HRI/GEN/1/Rev.8.

Coulson NJ, *A History of Islamic Law* (AldineTransaction 2011).

Davidson J and Henley D, 'The Many Roles of Adat in West Sumatera', in Jamie S Davidson and David Henley (eds), *The Revival of Tradition in Indonesian Politics: The Deployment of Adat from Colonialism to Indigenism* (Routledge 2007) 204.

De Feyter K and Pavlakos G, 'Supporting Minority Rights: Inter-Group Determinants and Consequences', in Koen De Feyter and George Pavlakos (eds), *The Tension between Group Rights and Human Rights: A Multidisciplinary Approach* (Bloomsbury Publishing 2008) 221.

Dixon M, McCorquodale R and Williams S, *Cases & Materials on International Law* (Oxford University Press 2016).

Donnelly J, 'Human Rights and Human Dignity: An Analytic Critique of Non-Western Conceptions of Human Rights' (1982) 76 *The American Political Science Review* 303.

———, 'The Relative Universality of Human Rights' (2007) 29 *Human Rights Quarterly* 281.

Eltayeb MSM, *A Human Rights Approach to Combating Religious Persecution: Cases from Pakistan, Saudi Arabia, and Sudan* (Intersentia 2001).

Emon AM, *Religious Pluralism and Islamic Law: Dhimmis and Others in the Empire of Law* (Oxford University Press Oxford 2012).

Feyter KD and Pavlakos G, 'Introduction: Groups Rights and Human Rights', in Koen De Feyter and George Pavlakos (eds), *The Tension between Group Rights and Human Rights: A Multidisciplinary Approach* (Hart Publishing 2008).

Fikri Z, 'The Rule of Bad Law' (*The Jakarta Post* 2 May 2008).

Forst R and Forst PR, *Contexts of Justice: Political Philosophy beyond Liberalism and Communitarianism* (University of California Press 2002).

Fortman B de G, 'Minority Rights: A Major Misconception?' (2011) 33 *Human Rights Quarterly* 265.

Frick M-L and Muller A Th, 'Islamic Law and International Protection of Minority Rights in Context', in Marie-Luisa Frick and Andreas Th Muller, *Islam and International Law: Engaging Self-Centrism from a Plurality of Perspectives* (Martinus Nijhoff Publishers 2013).

Friedlaender I, 'The Heterodoxies of the Shiites in the Presentation of Ibn Ḥazm' (1907) 28 *Journal of the American Oriental Society* 1.

Friedmann Y, *Tolerance and Coercion in Islam: Interfaith Relations in the Muslim Tradition* (Cambridge University Press 2003).

Ghanea N, 'Human Rights of Religious Minorities and of Women in the Middle East' (2004) 26 *Human Rights Quarterly* 705.

———, 'Apostasy and Freedom to Change Religion or Belief', in Tore Lindholm, W. Cole Durham, Jr. and Bahia G. Tahzib-Lie, *Facilitating Freedom of Religion or Belief: A Deskbook* (Springer 2013) 671.

Ghanea-Hercock N, 'A Human Rights Framework for Defining and Understanding Intra-Religious Persecution in Muslim Countries', in Nazila Ghanea-Hercock, *The Challenge of Religious Discrimination at the Dawn of the New Millennium* (Springer 2013) 5.

Ghanea-Hercock N, Xanthaki A and Thornberry P, 'The African Union and the Prospects for Minority Protection', in Nazila Ghanea-Hercock and Alexandra Xanthaki (eds), *Minorities, Peoples and Self-determination: Essays in Honour of Patrick Thornberry* (Martinus Nijhoff Publishers 2005) 345.

Gilbert G, 'Religious Minorities and Their Rights: A Problem of Approach' (1997) 5 *International Journal on Minority and Group Rights* 97.

Goel SR, 'Was Mohammed a Liar?', in Sita Ram Goel, *Freedom of Expression: Secular Theocracy versus Liberal Democracy* (Voice of India 1998) 39.

Goodwin-Gill GS, Jenny RK and Perruchoud R, 'Basic Humanitarian Principles Applicable to Non-Nationals' (1985) 19 *International Migration Review* 556.

Grant E, 'Dignity and Equality' (2007) 7 *Human Rights Law Review* 299.

Hallaq WB, 'Was the Gate of Ijtihad Closed?' (1984) 16 *International Journal of Middle East Studies* 3.

Hanski R and Suksi M, 'What Are Human Rights?', in Raija Hanski and Markku Suksi (eds), *An Introduction to the International Protection of Human Rights: A Textbook* (Institute for Human Rights, Åbo Akademi University 1999) 4.

Harvey C, *Human Rights in the Community: Rights as Agents for Change* (Bloomsbury Publishing 2005).

Hasan A, 'Ijma' in the Early Schools' (1967) 6 *Islamic Studies* 121.

Hashemi K, 'The Right of Minorities to Identity and the Challenge of Non-Discrimination: A Study on the Effects of Traditional Muslims' "Dhimmah" on Current State Practices' (2006) 13 *International Journal on Minority and Group Rights* 1.

Hashmi S, 'Islam and Constitutionalism' (*Law & Liberty* 2013).

Henrard K, 'The Protection of Minorities through the Equality Provisions in the UN Human Rights Treaties: The UN Treaty Bodies Reforming the UN Human Rights Machinery: What Does the Future Hold for the Protection of Minorities and Indigenous Peoples' (2007) 14 *International Journal on Minority and Group Rights* 141.

———, 'Charting the Gradual Emergence of a More Robust Level of Minority Protection: Minority Specific Instruments and the European Union' (2017) 22 *Netherlands Quarterly of Human Rights* 4.

Hodge DR, 'Advocating for the Forgotten Human Right: Article 18 of the Universal Declaration of Human Rights – Religious Freedom' (2006) 49 *International Social Work* 431.

Jabareen YT, 'Toward Participatory Equality: Protecting Minority Rights under International Law' (2008) 41 *Israel Law Review* 635.

Johansen B, *Contingency in a Sacred Law: Legal and Ethical Norms in the Muslim Fiqh* (Brill 1999).

Jovanovic M, 'Recognizing Minority Identities through Collective Rights' (2005) 27 *Human Rights Quarterly* 625.

Kawashima S, 'The Right to Effective Participation and the Ainu People' (2004) 11 *International Journal on Minority and Group Rights* 21.

Khadduri M and Hallaq WB, 'The Islamic Conception of Justice' (1986) 20 *Middle East Studies Association Bulletin* 305.

Khan I, 'Islamic Human Rights: Islamic Law and International Human Rights Standards' (1999) 5 *Appeal: Review of Current Law and Law Reform* 74.

Khanif A, 'NU Must Deal with Members Persecution of Minorities' (*The Jakarta Post* 5 August 2015).

Knights S, *Freedom of Religion, Minorities, and the Law* (Oxford University Press 2007).

Kurzman C, *Liberal Islam: A Source Book* (Oxford University Press 1998).

Lee MYK, 'Universal Human Dignity: Some Reflections in the Asian Context' (2008) 3 *Asian Journal of Comparative Law* 1.

Lerner N, 'The Nature and Minimum Standards of Freedom of Religion or Belief' (2000) *BYU Law Review* 905.

———, *Group Rights and Discrimination in International Law* (Martinus Nijhoff Publishers 2003).

Little D, 'Religion, Catalyst or Impediment to International Law? The Case of Hugo Grotius' (1993) 87 *Proceedings of the Annual Meeting (American Society of International Law)* 322.

Mayer AE, 'Law and Religion in the Muslim Middle East' (1987) 35 *The American Journal of Comparative Law* 127.

Mayer AE, *Islam and Human Rights: Tradition and Politics* (Avalon Publishing 2006).

Menski WF, *Comparative Law in a Global Context: The Legal Systems of Asia and Africa* (Cambridge University Press 2006).

———, 'Flying Kites in a Global Sky: New Models of Jurisprudence' (2011) 22 *Socio-Legal Review*, 13.

Meron T, *Human Rights and Humanitarian Norms as Customary Law* (Clarendon Press 1991).

Mohamed Adil M, 'Law of Apostasy and Freedom of Religion in Malaysia' (2007) 2 *Asian Journal of Comparative Law* 1.

Morsink J, *The Universal Declaration of Human Rights: Origins, Drafting, and Intent* (University of Pennsylvania Press 1999).

Muedini FA, 'Examining Islam and Human Rights from the Perspective of Sufism' (2010) 7 *Muslim World Journal of Human Rights* 1.

Office of the High Commissioner, *Minority Rights: International Standard and Guidance for Implementation* (United Nations 2010).

Oh I, *The Rights of God: Islam, Human Rights, and Comparative Ethics* (Georgetown University Press 2007).

Orford A, 'The Perplexities of Modern International Law' (2005) 99 *American Journal of International Law* 274.

Park J, 'Integration of Peoples and Minorities: An Approach to the Conceptual Problem of Peoples and Minorities with Reference to Self-Determination under International Law' (2006) 13 *International Journal on Minority and Group Rights* 69.

Pentassuglia G, 'Evolving Protection of Minority Groups: Global Challenges and the Role of International Jurisprudence' (2009) 11 *International Community Law Review* 185.

Prins JEJ, Ribbers PMA and Tilborg HCAV, *Trust in Electronic Commerce: The Role of Trust from a Legal, an Organizational, and a Technical Point of View* (Kluwer Law International BV 2002).

Qureshi TA, 'Justice in Islam' (1982) 21 *Islamic Studies* 35.

Rajan N, *Democracy and the Limits of Minority Rights* (Sage Publications 2002).

Rehman J and Breau SC, 'Some Arguments on the Universality of Human Rights in Islam', in Javaid Rehman and Susan Carolyn Breau, *Religion, Human Rights and International Law: A Critical Examination of Islamic State Practices* (Martinus Nijhoff Publishers 2007).

R (E) v Governing Body of JFS (2009) UK Supreme Court UKSC 2009/0105.

Roff WR, 'Customary Law, Islamic Law, and Colonial Authority: Three Contrasting Case Studies and Their Aftermath' (2010) 49 *Islamic Studies* 455.

Sachedina A, *Islam and the Challenge of Human Rights* (Oxford University Press 2009).

Schacht J, *An Introduction to Islamic Law* (Clarendon Press 1966).

Schachter O, 'Human Dignity as a Normative Concept' (1983) 77 *American Journal of International Law* 848.

Schutter OD, *International Human Rights Law: Cases, Materials, Commentary* (Cambridge University Press 2014).

Scolnicov A, *The Right to Religious Freedom in International Law: Between Group Rights and Individual Rights* (Routledge 2010).

Senturk R, 'Sociology of Rights: "I Am Therefore I Have Rights": Human Rights in Islam between Universalistic and Communalistic Perspectives' (2005) 2 *Muslim World Journal of Human Rights* 1.

Shah NA, *Women, the Koran and International Human Rights Law: The Experience of Pakistan* (Martinus Nijhoff Publishers 2006).

Shah NH, 'Islamic Concept of State' (1987) 26 *Islamic Studies* 97.

Shatzmiller M, *Nationalism and Minority Identities in Islamic Societies* (McGill-Queen's Press – MQUP 2005).

Shavit U, *Shari'a and Muslim Minorities: The Wasati and Salafi Approaches to Fiqh al-Aqalliyyat al-Muslima* (Oxford University Press 2015).

Sieghart P, *The International Law of Human Rights* (Clarendon Press 1983).

Sinha MK, 'Minority Rights: A Case Study of India' (2005) 12 *International Journal on Minority and Group Rights* 355.

Ssenyonjo M and Baderin MA, *International Human Rights Law: Six Decades after the UDHR and Beyond* (Ashgate Publishing 2013).

Tahzib BG, *Freedom of Religion or Belief: Ensuring Effective International Legal Protection* (Martinus Nijhoff Publishers 1996).

Taylor PM, *Freedom of Religion: UN and European Human Rights Law and Practice* (Cambridge University Press 2005).

Temperman J, *State-Religion Relationships and Human Rights Law: Towards a Right to Religiously Neutral Governance* (Brill 2010).

Thornberry P, *International Law and the Rights of Minorities* (Clarendon Press 2001).

Traer R, *Faith in Human Rights: Support in Religious Traditions for a Global Struggle* (Georgetown University Press 1991).

Tsadik D, 'The Legal Status of Religious Minorities: Imāmī Shīʿī Law and Iran's Constitutional Revolution' (2003) 10 *Islamic Law and Society* 376.

Vries GJJD and Peters R, 'Apostasy in Islam' (1976) 17 *Die Welt Des Islams* 1.

Wazynska-Finck K and Finck F, 'The Right to Change One's Religion according to Article 18 of ICCPR and the Universality of Human Rights' (2013) 9 *Journal of Islamic State Practices in International Law* 36.

Weiss B, 'Interpretation in Islamic Law: The Theory of Ijtihād' (1978) 26 *The American Journal of Comparative Law* 199.

Weller M, 'Legal Nature of Minority Rights as Part of Human Rights, Limitations, Derogations, Reservations, and Interpretative Statements', in Marc Weller (ed.), *Universal Minority Rights: A Commentary on the Jurisprudence of International Courts and Treaty Bodies* (Oxford University Press 2007a) 45.

———, 'Religious Rights', in Marc Weller (ed.), *Universal Minority Rights: A Commentary on the Jurisprudence of International Courts and Treaty Bodies* (Oxford University Press 2007b) 34.

Wiener M, 'The Mandate of the Special Rapporteur on Freedom of Religion or Belief – Institutional, Procedural and Substantive Legal Issues' (2007) 2 *Religion and Human Rights* 3.

Younes S, 'Islamic Legal Hermeneutics: The Context and Adequacy of Interpretation in Modern Islamic Discourse' (2002) 41 *Islamic Studies* 585.

Zulfikar H, *Diversity and Pluralism in Islam: Historical and Contemporary Discourses Amongst Muslims* (I.B. Tauris 2012).

3 The discourse of religion and religious minorities within Islam in a "quasi-theistic secular" Indonesia[1]

1. The legal acknowledgement of pluralistic character

Indonesia is a republic politically and ideologically, but it is also not an Islamic state per se.[2] With a predominantly Muslim majority population, Indonesia does not deny a role for religion in relation to law and perceives itself as a religious-democratic state which does not hold onto a particular religion. Indonesia is built on the foundation that the nation is and will always be a religious-pluralistic country, as asserted in Pancasila as the ideology of the state.[3] As the supreme source of law in the Indonesian legal system, Pancasila also becomes the sole foundation of the polity which represents the supreme source of law of Indonesia. This basic framework is further emphasised by the preamble of the Indonesian Constitution (hereafter the 1945 Constitution), which declares that the independence of the nation was bestowed by God and therefore the structural form of the Republic of Indonesia is based upon the sovereignty of the people and shall be based upon belief in the One Supreme God.[4]

These two fundamental laws, Pancasila and the 1945 Constitution, assert that Indonesia is based on the rule of law, forming a state based on laws[5] which believes in monotheistic religions. This principle stipulates that Indonesians should respect their fellow citizens even if they have different religious beliefs, as a consequence of the observable fact that Indonesia is a religiously plural state

1 The term "quasi-theistic secular" state has been coined by the author to define Indonesia as a state that upholds secularism in its legislations but at the same time also considers the significant role of theistic religion in the public sphere.

2 Abdullah Saeed, 'Interpreting the Quranic Principle of Religious Pluralism', in Abdullah Saeed, *Approaches to the Qur'an in Contemporary Indonesia* (Oxford University Press 2005) 221.

3 Luthfi Assyaukanie, *Islam and the Secular State in Indonesia* (Institute of Southeast Asian Studies 2009) 16.

4 See Michael Barry Hooker, *Indonesian Islam: Social Change through Contemporary Fatåawåa* (University of Hawaii Press 2003) 17.

5 A state based on laws in Indonesian terms is known as "*negara hokum*". See Daniel S Lev, *Legal Evolution and Political Authority in Indonesia: Selected Essays* (Martinus Nijhoff Publishers 2000) 221.

and upholds the ideology of tolerance.[6] Hence, there should not be domination of the law by religion as religion cannot be enforced on people. The basic position seems to be rather that the laws should give freedom to people to find their own path to God.[7]

The establishment of Indonesia as a religious-democratic state is meant to preserve the diversity of Indonesia as an archipelago comprising thousands of islands and hundreds of different ethnicities, languages, cultures and religions. Every region has its own distinctive characteristics of tradition, customary law and ethical and moral values, creating a mixture of local culture and indigenous religion, combined with various imported religions. For years, Indonesia has been known as the largest Muslim nation in the world and roughly 88% of the 260 million population are Muslims.[8] The Pew Forum estimates that about 205 million Indonesians are Muslims, and the nation is home to about 13% of the world's Muslims.[9] The remaining population embraces many kinds of religions such as Christianity, Hinduism, Buddhism, Confucianism and various indigenous religions (dynamism, animism and mysticism). There is also religious syncretism within particular religions, as well as many different religious sects within the major religions such as Islam, Protestantism, Catholicism, Hinduism and Buddhism. This is truly a plurality of pluralities and is reflected in the Indonesian legal structures.[10]

The various kinds of religions and beliefs demonstrate that religion in Indonesia is very popular and an integral part of people's daily life, reflecting also the most prominent value system for most people. Notably, the numbers of new religions and beliefs as well as religious minorities within particular religions have greatly increased after the fall of the New Order regime of President Suharto in 1998,[11] due to the enactment of the second amendment of the 1945 Constitution in 2000, which acknowledged freedom of expression and broadly construed freedom of religion or belief.

The census of the Ministry of Religious Affairs in 2010 provides that the religious demography in Indonesia can be divided into three regions. The first is the eastern region, which predominantly contains non-Muslims such as Christians and Hindus. The second is the middle region, which, even though

6 Douglas E Ramage, *Politics in Indonesia: Democracy, Islam, and the Ideology of Tolerance* (Routledge 1995) 12 <http://search.ebscohost.com/login.aspx?direct=true&scope=site&db=nlebk&db=nlabk&AN=76332> accessed 14 July 2016.

7 See Ota Atsushi, Okamoto Masaaki and Ahmad Suaedy, *Islam in Contention: Rethinking Islam and State in Indonesia* (Wahid Institute 2010) 55.

8 Kevin Boyle and Juliet Sheen, *Freedom of Religion and Belief: A World Report* (Routledge 2013) 201.

9 Pew Forum on Religion and Public Life, 'Muslim Population of Indonesia | Pew Research Center' (4 November 2010) <www.pewforum.org/2010/11/04/muslim-population-of-indonesia/> accessed 15 May 2019.

10 About plurality of plurality concept, see Werner F Menski, *Comparative Law in a Global Context: The Legal Systems of Asia and Africa* (Cambridge University Press 2006).

11 The New Order Regime in office from 1967 until 1998.

predominantly Muslim, particularly "traditionalist Muslim", is considered more pluralist and diverse.[12] The term traditionalist refers to Islamic groups who generally hold to Islamic jurisprudence (*fiqh*).[13] They believe that the door of *ijtihad* has been closed since the establishment of the four Sunni schools of Islamic law and thus they are merely concerned with issues of creed and ritual.[14] The third is the western region, which is predominantly "puritan Muslims".[15] Some parts of this region have been significantly influenced by Islam from the Middle East. For instance, Aceh, one of the provinces in Sumatera, implements Islamic law and has become the only "Islamic Region"[16] in Indonesia. Historically, this is the first province in Indonesia to embrace Islam and to strongly view its identity as Islamic.[17]

Some Muslims are also influenced by the reformist ideas of Muhammad Abduh and Rashid Rida, who advocate independent legal reasoning (*ijtihad*) within the context of *ijtihad*.[18] Yet, Islamic reformism in Indonesia is not a rerun of Middle Eastern intellectualism but more an expression of local understanding of Islam.[19] The pursuit of *ijtihad* in Indonesia not only emerged within the context of Islamic modernisation but also as an attempt to respond to the growing number of syncretists in Islam.[20] Additionally, even though in early modern Indonesia *ijtihad* was mainly endorsed by modernist Muslims, some traditionalists, especially from the youth groups, have recently promoted *ijtihad* as a basis of internal transformation within their circle and as their attempt to respond to contemporary issues.[21]

Other Muslims also endorsed "radical *ijtihad*", calling for a return to the strict values and ideals of the Qur'an and *Sunna* to eliminate heretical Islamic

12 Timothy Lindsey, *Indonesia: Law and Society* (The Federation Press 1999) 341.
13 Rumadi, *Islamic Post-Traditionalism in Indonesia* (ISEAS – Yusof Ishak Institute 2015) 8.
14 Abdulkader Tayob, *Religion in Modern Islamic Discourse* (Hurst Publishers 2009) 39.
15 Western Indonesia has approximately 45 million Muslims and small numbers of Christian Catholics, Christian Protestants, Hindus, Buddhists, Confucianists and other religious adherents. The eastern part is predominantly non-Muslim, such as Bali is Hindu, Papua and the Moluccas Islands are Protestant and Southeast Nusa is mainly Catholic.
16 What I mean by "Islamic region" is that Aceh implements all aspects of Islamic law in its entire region based on Bylaw No. 5/2000 on the Implementation of Islamic Law. See Hasnil Basri Siregar, 'Islamic Law in a National Legal System: A Study on the Implementation of Shari'ah in Aceh, Indonesia' (2008) 3 *Asian Journal of Comparative Law* 1, 12–13.
17 Arskal Salim, '"Sharia from Below" in ACEH (1930s–1960s): Islamic Identity and the Right to Self-determination with Comparative Reference to the Moro Islamic Liberation Front (MILF)' (2004) 32 *Indonesia and the Malay World* 80, 82.
18 Jajat Burhanudin, 'Aspiring for Islamic Reform: Southeast Asian Requests for Fatwās in al-Manār' (2005) 12 *Islamic Law and Society* 9, 11.
19 Hooker (n 4) 19–20.
20 R Michael Feener and Mark E Cammack, 'Muslim Legal Thought in Modern Indonesia: Introduction and Overview', in R Michael Feener and Mark E Cammack (eds), *Islamic Law in Contemporary Indonesia: Ideas and Institutions* (Harvard University Press 2007) 14.
21 See about this internal transformation in Rumadi (n 13) 9.

practices.[22] This group argues that traditionalist Muslims and religious minorities within Islam are heretics and do not represent the "true Islam". For example, in the 1930s Ahmad Hasan from Islamic Unity (Persatuan Islam, Persis) introduced *ijtihad*, which urged Muslims to reach back into the Qur'an and *Sunna* in order to avoid dangerous human innovations (*bid'a*) in Islam.[23] On the other hand, some other Muslims like Moenawar Chalil and Hasbi Ash Shiddieqy also promoted moderate *ijtihad* but without rejecting the tradition of Islamic jurisprudence, in order to respond to the changing needs of Muslims in Indonesia.[24] This kind of *ijtihad* is an attempt from moderate Muslims to interpret Islam according to Indonesian conditions.[25] Some Muslim scholars call this *ijtihad* "Indonesian *fiqh*", "Islam *Nusantara*"[26] or "Progressive Islam".[27] This shows that since the beginning, the ongoing practice of *ijtihad* in Indonesia seems to be plural. These various kinds of Islamic practices by the different Islamic groupings signify that there is no uniformity of Islam in Indonesia because "Indonesian Islam" is "remarkably malleable, syncretistic, and multi-voiced".[28]

This heterogeneous Islamic demography means that Indonesian Islam has its own peculiar characteristic as a result of the reinterpretation of Islam in Indonesian local cultural terms.[29] Soekarno, a Muslim and one of the founding fathers of Indonesia, said that Islam means progress[30] and hence should not be understood as Islam "being" but more about Islam "becoming", because Islam exists in the present day, too.[31] It is new things that are simpler and higher in level than the old things. Progress means new products, new creations, not merely repeating old things, not just copying the past. This proposition signifies that Indonesian Islam should adapt and adjust to be more socially and culturally

22 Giora Eliraz, *Islam in Indonesia: Modernism, Radicalism, and the Middle East Dimension* (Sussex Academic Press 2004) 22.
23 Feener and Cammack (n 20) 15.
24 ibid 16–18.
25 ibid 19.
26 Al Khanif, 'NU Must Deal with Members' Persecution of Minorities' (*The Jakarta Post* 5 August 2015) <www.thejakartapost.com/news/2015/08/05/nu-must-deal-with-members-persecution-minorities.html> accessed 16 October 2017.
27 On the explanation of progressive Islam, see Ahmad Imam Mujadid Rais, 'Muhammadiyah's "Progressive Islam": Guideline or Tagline? – National – The Jakarta Post' (*Jakarta Post* Jakarta 3 August 2015) <www.thejakartapost.com/news/2015/08/03/muhammadiyah-s-progressive-islam-guideline-or-tagline.html> accessed 16 May 2019.
28 Clifford Geertz, *Islam Observed: Religious Development in Morocco and Indonesia* (University of Chicago Press 1971) 12.
29 Hooker (n 4) 11.
30 Clifford Geertz, 'The Javanese Kijaji: The Changing Role of a Cultural Broker' (1960) 2 *Comparative Studies in Society and History* 228, 240.
31 Plato made the philosophical distinction between "being" and "becoming", with "being" consisting of things which never change in any way, and "becoming" consisting of things which are never stable in any way. *See e.g.*, Robert Bolton, 'Plato's Distinction between Being and Becoming' (1975) 29 *The Review of Metaphysics* 66, 66–95.

engaged with its new society. Therefore, characterisations of Indonesian Islam are seen as a thin and flaking glaze or as thoroughly syncretistic, because they have tended to suggest that religious diversity as the Indonesian genuine reality cannot be adequately appreciated if people still hold on to the uniformity of interpretation of Islam.[32]

Based on such observations, the founders of Indonesia tried to compromise by making Indonesia neither an Islamic state nor a secular state. They wanted a state which would have a plurality-sensitive religious state philosophy so that the ideals of every religious denomination could be realised,[33] in the sense that the state allowed and assisted its citizens to enjoy their respective religious freedom.[34] Soekarno, a secular nationalist, believed that Islamic values could be beneficial in the quest for development because the majority of the Indonesian population was Muslim. However, as a statesman, he believed that preservation of Indonesian unity was more valuable and hence he preferred to give precedence to the history of Indonesia as a "deeply diverse-religious society".[35] Meanwhile, however, the element of religions in the development process in post-independence Indonesia could not be ignored. Therefore, a religious-democratic state based upon Pancasila was established to accommodate the diversity of religious groups and served to designate the state as broadly religious rather than having a specifically Islamic religious nature.[36]

Pancasila was thus designed as a statement of universal values, brilliantly couched by Soekarno and other founders in indigenous terms, upon which all Indonesians could agree.[37] Therefore, many Indonesians assume that Pancasila is the living ideology because it does not only successfully manage political matters in the higher echelons but also successfully embeds Indonesian social-cultural life to bridge the gaps between religious beliefs, customary laws and political ideology. It is a philosophical basis to the Indonesian legal system, a kind of glue, comprising essential social values based on the ideology of tolerance, particularly in matters of religion, suggesting that the state will not prioritise Islam over other religions. Based on the Pancasila doctrine, Indonesia is an "integralist state", which should preserve the Indonesian culture of harmony and consensus to achieve public good as the spirit of the nation.[38] The

32 See Sven Kosel, 'The History of Islam in Bolaang Mongondow, North Sulawesi' (2010) 38 *Indonesia and the Malay World* 43, 44–45.

33 See Alfitri, 'Religious Liberty in Indonesia and the Rights of "Deviant" Sects' (2008) 3 *Asian Journal of Comparative Law* 1, 5.

34 Bahtiar Effendy, *Islam in the Contemporary Indonesian Politics* (Ushul Press 2006) 180.

35 Abdullah Saeed, 'Towards Religious Tolerance through Reform in Islamic Education: The Case of the State Institute of Islamic Studies of Indonesia' (1999) 27 *Indonesia and the Malay World* 177, 181.

36 Al Khanif, 'Questioning a Theistic, Secular Pancasila to Protect Religions' (*The Jakarta Post* 6 January 2015).

37 Ramage (n 6) 2.

38 Timothy Lindsey, 'The State and Syariah in Indonesia 1945–1995', *Indonesia: Law and Society* (Federation Press 2008) 186.

government should respect the religious diversity of its citizens[39] by equally protecting all kinds of ethnicities, languages, cultures and religions spread over the archipelagos, within the framework of Indonesian unity, as a common good for Indonesians.

Indonesia also adopted an intermingling of religions and cultures as its national symbol, which illustrates that Indonesia is a culturally and religiously heterogeneous country, not only within Islam but also within the minority religions of the country. The anonymous name of God in state ideology signifies that Indonesia believes in a "multi-faith God".[40] This term means that God in Indonesian law is inclusive. The term also leaves God open to interpretation, allowing individuals to decide which God accommodates the belief systems present in Indonesia. Thus, all Indonesians have an equal right to interpret God and religion as long as it is in accordance with international human rights law and the spirit of pluralism as one significant foundation of the state.[41]

Based on that principle there should be no domination of religion, while at the same time the nation should also ensure and protect religious national identity. The legal recognition of religion is not only vital for Indonesian society but is also important in view of legalising the general religious identity of the nation and preserving the survival of religious-pluralistic societies. People must understand the deep differences between religious values and forms of religious life and endeavour to tolerate and accept those differences in Indonesia.[42] They should know that the greater concept of Indonesia in the frame of Pancasila, which covers Humanitarianism, Indonesian Unity, Democracy and Social Justice, is as sacred as God or religion and thus protects the rights of people to embrace religions. It is also as sacred as protecting the sustainability of Indonesia as a nation-state.

2. The discourse of Indonesian Islam

Religion in Bahasa Indonesia is called *agama*[43] and is perceived as an organised system of beliefs with a basis in authoritative written sources. Most Indonesians believe that *agama* is different from *kepercayaan* (non-organised religious belief) as part of Indonesian culture.[44] The first stream of *agama* is perceived as "purist or religious", while the second stream can be identified as "cultural syncretist". The purist and religious are represented by mainstream religions and this stream is perceived as more authoritative than cultural syncretist, generally practised by

39 ibid 2.

40 Another term is "secular God" as proposed by Hooker. See Hooker (n 4) 17.

41 Khanif (n 36).

42 John Richard Bowen, *Islam, Law, and Equality in Indonesia: An Anthropology of Public Reasoning* (Cambridge University Press 2003) 3.

43 The term itself comes from Sanskrit, where it refers to a particular class of philosophical/religious literature or cultural text.

44 Timothy Daniels, *Islamic Spectrum in Java* (Routledge 2016) 29.

the followers of various kinds of mysticism and local religions.[45] The government and society have used the two streams to determine which belief should be classified as religion and which one should be excluded.

After the government enacted Presidential Decree No. 6/2000 on the Withdrawal of the Regulation on Chinese Culture, Belief, and Religion No. 14/1967, Indonesia recognised Confucianism, adding it to the previous five official religions (Islam, Christian Protestant, Christian Catholic, Hinduism and Buddhism).[46] Lukman Hakim Syaifuddin, appointed as Minister of Religious Affairs in 2014, said that even though Indonesia has not recognised Baha'i as a religion, he personally argued that Baha'i should be recognised as a new religion in Indonesia.[47] It implies that not all religions and customary non-religious beliefs are recognised as official religions, even though people can embrace them practically. However, people who lack an officially recognised religion are generally referred to in Indonesia as people who do not possess a religion. The negative sense is significant here for it implies that eventual conversion into a recognised religion is inevitable.[48] It means that those who embrace "*kepercayaan*" and non-mainstream religions should convert to one of the six religions in order to be entitled to the relevant freedoms and rights that are guaranteed by the constitution.

Islam, as one of the mainstream religions, was probably first brought to Indonesia by Muslim traders and priests from Gujarat, India. These traders followed a mystical form of Islam that had been subject to Hindu and Isma'ili Shi'ah influences and local animisms of the Indian coastal areas.[49] Some other reports state that Islam was directly brought by Arab traders from Hadramawt, a province of modern-day Yemen and from Hijaz, a region in Saudi Arabia.[50] Due to these different historical versions, the precise date of Islam's arrival in the archipelago is not clear and it has never been agreed, but it is clear that a large number of conversions to Islam occurred from the thirteenth century onwards.[51]

Besides traders, Islamic preachers, known as *wali songo* or "nine saints", also contributed to the larger conversions of Indonesians to Islam because their

45 See James L Peacock, 'The Creativity of Tradition in Indonesian Religion' (1986) 25 *History of Religions* 341, 344.

46 Before 1967 Confucianism had been recognised as an official religion but during the New Era regime it had been denied as a religion due to the alleged involvement of communism in the 1965 Coup d'État.

47 'Menag: Resmi Atau Tidak Agama Bukan Otoritas Saya – Nasional Tempo.Co' <https://nasional.tempo.co/read/596011/menag-resmi-atau-tidak-agama-bukan-otoritas-saya/full&view=ok> accessed 18 May 2019.

48 Jane Monnig Atkinson, 'Religions in Dialogue: The Construction of an Indonesian Minority Religion' (1983) 10 *American Ethnologist* 684, 688.

49 Howard M Federspiel, *Islam and Ideology in the Emerging Indonesian State: The Persatuan Islam (Persis), 1923–1957* (Brill 2001) 4.

50 See Huub de Jonge, 'Discord and Solidarity among the Arabs in the Netherlands East Indies, 1900–1942' (1993) *Indonesia* 73, 75.

51 Syed Farid Alatas, 'The Ṭarīqat Al-'Alawiyyah and the Emergence of the Shi'i School in Indonesia and Malaysia' (1999) 79 *Oriente Moderno* 323, 330.

interpretation of Islam was suited to the background of the Indonesians,[52] formerly influenced by Hinduism, Buddhism and mysticism. Abdullahi Ahmed An-Na'im similarly argues:

> The process of Islamisation in Indonesia happened in peaceful ways, though there were instances of Muslim rulers using force to convert surrounding peoples to Islam. Intensive trade relations with the central regions of the Islamic world and Arab migration, especially from Hadramawt and Yemen, also contributed to the process. However, by its very nature, Islamisation was neither uniform nor comprehensive, as it tended to depend on location, time frame, and circumstances, such as the nature and resilience of pre-existing cultural and religious tradition.[53]

Before declaring independence in 1945, imperial Islam became the state religion in most of Indonesia's coastal kingdoms. The King was identified as supreme defender of the faith, by means of which some of them allowed localised or syncretistic tradition to survive in court rituals, while other Muslim rulers promoted a strict application of Islamic law, threatened apostates and forced religious minorities to convert to Islam.[54] Besides the King, saints and local religious leaders from traditional Islamic schools also became the principal defenders of the Islamic faith, including being able to determine certain punishments for criminal offences. For instance, in the pre-colonial era some members of the nine saints collaborated with the King of Demak Islamic Kingdom to kill Syech Siti Jenar, a renowned *sufi*, accused of spreading heretical Islamic teaching through his ideology, the unity of existence (*wahdat al-wujud*).[55] Until now, some modernist movements have accused Sufism as deviating from the Islamic doctrine, even though that movement was not able to destroy the popularity of Sufism in traditionalist Muslim circles. Thus, Sufism has been prominent throughout the history of Indonesian Islam,[56] but none of the present-day Sufism is affiliated to Syech Siti Jenar because of the dominant influence of the nine saints.

This collaboration also continued in the independence war, by which many sultanates or kings worked together with Islamic fighter groups, mainly religious

52 See ibid 331.

53 Abdullahi Ahmed An Na'im, *Islam and the Secular State* (Harvard University Press 2009) 226.

54 Robert W Hefner, *Civil Islam: Muslims and Democratization in Indonesia* (Princeton University Press 2011) 29.

55 Syech Siti Jenar was a prominent sufi in the history of Islam in Indonesia. His teaching about *wahdat al-wujud* or *Manunggaling Kawulo Gusti*, the teaching of the emergence of God into the soul of human beings, was seen as deviant to the Islamic law practised by nine saints (*wali songo*) who had a significant role in spreading Islam in Indonesia, particularly Java.

56 Martin van Bruinessen, 'Studies of Sufism and the Sufi Orders in Indonesia' (1998) 38 *Die Welt des Islams* 192, 204.

and local leaders from Islamic schools, which succeeded in bringing Islam into the centre of Indonesian society to revolt against the colonialists.[57] The collaborative effectiveness of sultanates or kings, saints and traditional Islamic leaders when utilising Islam as an engine of defence against colonisation confirms that Islam played a critical role in the history of Indonesian society. Islam was not only invoked as a political force but also as the hegemonic idea of national identity, which latterly brought about the occurrence of inextricably overlapping discourses of being religious and being nationalist in the debate of modern Indonesian civil society. The question of relegation or unification of Islam and the state has become an eminent discussion point in the history and current debate of Indonesia. Since the early modern era in Indonesia until now, Muslims have tried to invoke their great tradition of religious scholars or jurists (*ulama*) and Islamic law as symbols of nationhood. On the other hand, some moderate Indonesian Muslims, like the former president Abdurrahman Wahid, believe that Indonesia should not embrace the notion of an "Islamic state". Wahid found Islam to be compatible with Pancasila and its five principles of faith, humanity, unity, democracy and social justice.[58]

In regard to the debate on the relationship of Islam and the state, Nadirsyah Hosen similarly says:

> There are many people who believe that the use of religion for such purposes ultimately results in a violation of the separation of church and state – one basis of a secular state – and thus of other people's religious liberty. Other religious believers, however, argue that it is wrong to exclude religion from public debates, and that such a policy effectively constitutes discrimination against religion and believers.[59]

These contentious discussions reflect the struggle between secular and religious approaches to maintain the relationship between Islam and the state in Indonesia. The discussion shows that most Indonesians have still attempted to formulate how Indonesia as a state must regulate a mode of life for its citizens, either under a theocratic or a secular state. Until now some Indonesian Muslims, however, still prefer to separate Islam and the state and believe that the formal introduction of Islamic law into Indonesian human rights law can effectively constrain rights and freedoms, especially for vulnerable groups.[60] Yet, Islamic revivalism has, in fact,

57 Peacock (n 45) 346.

58 Catroina Croft-Cusworth, 'Islam and Tolerance in Indonesia' (*Lowy Institute* 4 November 2014) <www.lowyinstitute.org/the-interpreter/islam-and-tolerance-indonesia> accessed 18 May 2019.

59 Nadirsyah Hosen, 'Religion and the Indonesian Constitution: A Recent Debate' (2005) 36 *Journal of Southeast Asian Studies* 419, 420.

60 Arskal Salim, *Challenging the Secular State: The Islamization of Law in Modern Indonesia* (University of Hawaii Press 2008) 111.

become stronger recently, even though the legal formal acknowledgement of Islam in Indonesia declined after independence. Since independence Indonesia has become a republic with a presidential system, a system which places the president in the top position in place of the earlier concept of the King.[61] The nation also adopted Pancasila as a state ideology and the 1945 Constitution became the supreme defender of faith and religions, even though there is no single word referring to a particular official religion in the constitution after the deletion of seven words of the Jakarta Charter from the preamble of the constitution.[62] It may be noted that religion in Indonesian law may be defined as "theistic-secular religion" as inferred from the first principle of Pancasila, which affirms that the state believes in One Supreme God.

From an orthodox legal point of view Indonesia is not an Islamic state, since implicit in its constitutional foundations is the doctrine of equality of religions and the absence of any provision conferring preferred status on the Islamic faith.[63] Yet, the discussion of religion, particularly Islam, is without a doubt still significant in the midst of the process of Islamisation in Indonesia.[64] In contemporary Indonesia, Islam is undergoing a renaissance, as evidenced by a growing number of religious schools, mosques, civic groups, media outlets and Islamic political parties or parties associated with Islam.[65] Since 1999, the Islamisation of the country has also been upheld by a policy of decentralisation, as growing numbers of regions have implemented or are willing to implement Islamic law. The world-famous Aceh is the most prominent example of these developments.

Even though it was agreed that Pancasila was the final ideology of Indonesia, the role of religion embedded into society has been very powerful in shaping people's perspective on a particular norm and in engendering the multifaceted human rights discourse in the country. Muslim views on the position of religion are also divergent. Some believe that Islam is only a social and spiritual capital, separated from

61 In the 1950s Indonesia implemented a parliamentary system which placed the prime minister as head of the state, before it was replaced by a presidential system through presidential decree in 1959.

62 The Jakarta Charter included two key clauses; the first asserts that the state is based upon the belief in One Supreme God while the second phrase, which was deleted before the enactment of the 1945 Constitution, constitutes seven words, *dengan kewajiban menjalankan syariah Islam bagi pemeluknya*, which literally means that adherents of Islam are obliged to follow Islamic law. See Sebastiaan Pompe, 'Islamic Law in Indonesia' (1997) 4 *YB Islamic & Middle EL* 180, 184.

63 Justus M van der Kroef, 'The Role of Islam in Indonesian Nationalism and Politics' (1958) 11 *The Western Political Quarterly* 33, 33.

64 The term Islamisation here refers to Mayer's definition, which asserts that Islamisation means official and unofficial programmes of reinstating Islamic norms and values to make societies and the law more Islamic. Some of them, such as the reinstatement of Islamic law as the law of the land and making Islam a more prominent component of political life and social organisations, have already been implemented and some are only at the proposal stage. See Ann Elizabeth Mayer, 'Islam and Justice: Debating the Future of Human Rights in the Middle East and North Africa (Review)' (1997) 19 *Human Rights Quarterly* 875, 129.

65 Edward P Lipton, *Religious Freedom in Asia* (Nova Publishers 2002) 127.

legal and political realms, while others argue that it is a legal universal foundation to determine certain rights and freedoms. Robert W. Hefner argues:

> Although the Muslim world has its share of secular modernists, many practicing Muslims continue to look to their religion for principles of public order as well as personal spirituality. The political ideals they derive from their tradition, however, are not immutable, but vary in a manner that reflect competing views as to how Muslims should respond to the challenges of the late modern world.[66]

Based on this premise, some Muslims say the separation between Islam and the state was necessary if the transcendent truth of Islam was to be subordinated to human rulers.[67] This divergence therefore still brings about much public reasoning and retains its foundation in comprehensive doctrines and in particular foundations of specific understandings of Islam.[68]

It is significant to state that Islamic discourse should not be perceived interchangeably with Islamic law in the Indonesian context. Islamic discourse deals with interrelated concepts of politics, theology, law and human rights. Some individuals and groups of Muslims attempt to apply these concepts in Indonesia as they believe that Islam should not differentiate between public and private domains.[69] On the other hand, Islamic law as asserted by Act No. 3/2006 on Religious Judicature is restricted only to family law, primarily marriage and divorce.[70] All matters related to public law, among other human rights law, fall under the jurisdiction of secular law and public courts.

Indonesian national life is prominently regulated by secular law and the remnants of customary regulation, with religious law having only a small jurisdiction in family law.[71] Yet, the two discourses have overlapped with each other and coexist due to the interchangeable process of Islamisation and secularisation within society. According to John R. Bowen, "what is significant from the discussion of Islam in Indonesia is that the Islamic discursive tradition continues to provide a world-wide universe of past and present interpretations of the Quran and Hadith".[72] However, this hermeneutical authority has frequently overlapped

66 Robert W Hefner, 'Public Islam and the Problem of Democratization' (2001) 62 *Sociology of Religion* 491, 493.

67 ibid 493.

68 Bowen (n 42) 14.

69 Salim (n 60) 17.

70 According to article 49, the Religious Court also has to do with marriage, divorce, inheritance, Islamic economy, gifts (*sadaqah*), wealth tax (*zakat*) and endowment (*infaq*). However, the court mostly deals with marriage and divorce, due to administrative reasons, while the other functions have been practised outside the court (non-litigation).

71 Arskal Salim and Azyumardi Azra, 'Islamic Values, Law and Expectations in Contemporary Indonesia', in Arskal Salim and Azyumardi Azra (eds), *Shari'a and Politics in Modern Indonesia* (Institute of Southeast Asian Studies 2003) 12.

72 Bowen (n 42) 15.

with constitutional interpretation as it is a fact that Islam has continued to expand within Indonesia and has determined the kind of role to play in the modernisation of the country.[73] Those contested authorities also illustrate that human rights discourse in Indonesia cannot merely be examined from the secular state law perspective as it absorbs a collection of religious-cultural concepts of law.

The complex relationship between Islamic discourse and state law in Indonesia engenders the spectrum of human rights in the country. Recognising Islamic discourse in Indonesia as part of legal pluralism on one hand may protect Muslim personal law and Muslim political rights but, on many occasions, it also stimulates the complexity of marginalised groups such as religious minorities within Islam. The main reason for this is that the Indonesian government and a large Indonesian Muslim population prefer to keep the monolithic perspective of Islam rather than admitting various interpretations of Islamic values of human rights. As a consequence, there is no room for the rights of religious minorities within Islam because this kind of religious hermeneutic is considered as a defamation of Islam and a threat to Islamic orthodoxy as part of public order.

The complex relationship between the state and religion seen in the Indonesian case does occur in other parts of the Muslim world too. The expansion of secularism has challenged Islamic orthodoxy as many Muslims still continue to look to their religion for principles of public order. Westernisation and modernism have never succeeded in eliminating Islamic influence in contemporary Indonesia as Muslims commonly perceive Islam as much more than a religion; it is a way of life that encompasses all areas of human activity, private and public; ranging from the theological to the political.[74] In different periods of history, religion including Islam has been used to legitimise political gains and mobilise public opinion in favour of vested interests.[75] Islam has influenced government policies to enact laws suited to the religious, cultural and social conditions of the nation. Sometimes it has apparently influenced judicial institutions to issue verdicts on particular cases and constructed a common understanding of particular ethics and morality within society. Based on this situation, the discussion of human rights, particularly the rights of religious minorities within Islam in Indonesia, should not and cannot ignore religion.

3. Religious minorities within Islam in the religion and state relationship

It has already been noted that religion in Indonesia does not completely retreat from the public stage. The first reason is that Pancasila as the Indonesian state

73 Deliar Noer, *The Modernist Muslim Movement in Indonesia, 1900–1942* (Oxford University Press 1973) 73.

74 Vincent JH Houben, 'Southeast Asia and Islam' (2003) 588 *The Annals of the American Academy of Political and Social Science* 149, 148.

75 Alan Race and Ingrid H Shafer, 'Democracy at the Heart of Islam', in Alan Race and Ingrid H Shafer (eds), *Religions in Dialogue: From Theocracy to Democracy* (Ashgate 2002) 107.

ideology and the supreme source of law, which inspires all regulations including the constitution, clearly acknowledges the role of theistic religion in the country. Secondly, the state has to manage religious diversity as the factual manifestation of the first principle of Pancasila in the public realm. Failing to control religious diversity may threaten religious harmony among religions, especially when particular religious adherents consider their religion as a perfect model of public order and source of ethics. However, this religious authoritarianism generally provokes the practice of inequality and discrimination against marginalised religions. For instance, some cultural and structural Muslims either as intellectuals, bureaucrats or apostles have been very active in the promotion of Islam as the dominant concept in Indonesian socio-cultural life.[76] They have tried to convince Muslims and other Indonesians that Islam is universal and hence should be applied unconditionally.[77] This group of Muslims which particularly represents "puritan-fundamentalist" Muslims insists that Muslims are not allowed to apply other forms of culture such as secularism, pluralism and human rights norms not suited to traditional Islamic teaching.[78]

The discussion of religious minorities within particular religions, especially their rights to embrace and practise their religion in a state-religion relationship, is a complicated issue and becomes more challenging especially when the state tries to administer religious life. The state is required to administer the performance of religious freedom in general to establish public order. But, when the state engages in defining what is true and what is wrong, as the fundamental element of religious freedom, the state then acts as the guardian of religion rather than as the protector of the right to freedom of religion. According to international human rights law standards, the state is allowed to intervene in regard to the right to practise religions or beliefs "*forum externum*" for the purpose of preserving public safety, order, morals, health and the fundamental rights and freedoms of others. Yet, the state must leave enough room for individuals to embrace theistic, non-theistic and atheistic religious beliefs in the *forum internum.*

The state should manage the religious character of the nation by protecting religious freedom but at the same time it should protect religious harmony among religions as a consequence of the pluralistic character of religious life, social integration, public order and national unity. Some Indonesians, especially the proponents of secularism, agree that this can be effectively achieved only when the state refrains from any interference in religious belief. On the other hand, the proponents of the integration of religion and the state suggest that

76 Federspiel (n 49) 77. Cultural Muslims are those who are not in state institutions, compared to chairs of Islamic organisations and private institutions, while structural Muslims are those working for governmental institutions.

77 Rizal Sukma and Clara Joewono, 'Gerakan Salafi di Indonesia: Dari Wahabi Sampai Laskar Jihad', in Rizal Sukma and Clara Joewono (eds), *Gerakan dan pemikiran Islam Indonesia kontemporer* (Centre for Strategic and International Studies 2007) 128.

78 ibid 129.

the state should monitor and regulate religious minority groups which promulgate non-mainstream religious teachings because the spread of their religious teaching is generally accused of bringing about social disintegration.

The government of Indonesia, in fact, established institutions such as the Ministry of Religious Affairs (hereafter MORA) and the Joint-Judiciary Committee of Religious Life (Badan Koordinasi Pengawas Aliran Kepercayaan Masyarakat, hereafter Bakorpakem) as watchdogs of religious life long ago. These institutions have frequently affected the rights of particular religious groups to practise their religion or beliefs. Additionally, the existence of the Indonesian Council of Ulama (hereafter MUI), a state-sanctioned institution, has frequently restricted the rights and influence of religious minorities within Islam because the MUI is authorised to issue religious edicts on religious matters including *fatwas*, which restrict religious minorities within Islam. In many cases, these three institutions have collaborated in restricting the spreading of any forms of non-mainstream Islamic teachings that may, in their view, disturb religious harmony within society.[79] Consequently, many religious minorities within Islam have become victims because the three institutions often label them as deviant or misleading Islam.

Instituting a particular state policy such as the establishment of state official religions or the preservation of religious harmony among religions is not restricted under international human rights law. Yet, when this kind of state policy results in discrimination or any impairment of the rights of particular adherents of religion, such as members of religious minorities within Islam, the international standard of human rights norms must apply. A human rights violation occurs when the government of Indonesia, for the purpose of preserving religious harmony in the country, restricts the rights of religious minorities within Islam to spread their religious teaching. It is because article 18 (3) of the ICCPR only permits restrictions on *forum externum* if limitations are prescribed by law and are necessary to protect public safety, order, health or morals or the fundamental rights and freedoms of others. State policies which restrict the rights of religious minorities within Islam to embrace a particular Islamic teaching as part of unconditional religious freedom are strictly prohibited under international human rights law because this right cannot legitimately be limited in any circumstances.

We will now briefly examine each of the state institutions mentioned above to discuss their human rights perspectives on the issue of religious minorities within Islam in Indonesia.

79 About the collaboration of the MUI, Bakorpakem and MORA which restricts non-mainstream Islamic groups, see generally Bernhard Platzdasch, 'Religious Freedom in Indonesia: The Case of the Ahmadiyah' (2011) 2 ISEAS Working Paper on Politics and Security Series.

3.1. The Ministry of Religious Affairs (MORA)

The MORA is the highest institutional canopy to monitor religious life in Indonesia. It was established in January 1946 to supervise religious life and organise related legal matters.[80] It has been an important institution in accelerating the development of Islam and has largely spearheaded the government-led campaign of Islamisation, nationally directing, regulating and promoting all kinds of religious activities, especially Islamic ones.[81] The MORA has been central to Indonesian Islam until now; not only administering the religious court, supervising curricula for religious education and registering marriage and divorce,[82] but also labelling a particular religion as deviant. Thus, the MORA regularly issues statements on the issue of religious minorities within Islam. Surprisingly, instead of emphasising its argument using legal reasons based on the 1945 Constitution, Pancasila and international human rights instruments, the MORA habitually categorises religious minorities within Islam as deviant and as heretical Islam, based on its preference for Islamic orthodoxy.

In the late 1980s, *Tempo* magazine, for example, disclosed that the hatred against Ahmadiyah in West Java was triggered by brochures circulated by the MORA, wherein Ahmadiyah followers were condemned as infidels.[83] Since then there have been several issues regarding the restriction of religious minorities within Islam to preserve Islamic orthodoxy. One of the closest relationships between the MORA policy on the issue of religious minorities within Islam and Islamic orthodoxy was the banning of Ahmadiyah in the early 1980s, because this policy was enacted by the MORA after the MUI issued a *fatwa* which declared that Ahmadiyah is a misleading Islamic group. It was not surprising because *fatwas* do not only reflect a relationship between MUI as an authoritative Islamic institution to regulate Islamic life and Indonesian Muslim society but also illustrate a complex relationship between MUI and the state, especially the monitoring of religious life.[84] In its development, the MORA also manages to observe all religions including local religions. It occasionally monitors the attendance of followers of minority faiths at their places of worship. Yet, it appears to concentrate more on Islam and tries to closely control religious minorities within Islam whose practices deviate from mainstream Islamic belief.

Limitations on religious manifestation, in strict adherence to the limitations regimes, can be legitimate as long as they are proportionate to the specific need, such as the requirement to protect an individual's fundamental rights.[85] It is due to

80 Lindsey (n 38) 100.
81 See Salim (n 60) 84.
82 Michael Barry Hooker, *Indonesian Syariah: Defining a National School of Islamic Law* (Institute of Southeast Asian Studies 2008) 205.
83 Luthfi Assyaukanie, 'Fatwa and Violence in Indonesia' (2009) 11 *Journal of Religion and Society* 9.
84 Mun'im Sirry, 'Fatwas and their Controversy: The Case of the Council of Indonesian Ulama (MUI)' (2013) 44 *Journal of Southeast Asian Studies* 100, 100–101.
85 'Guidelines on the Legal Personality of Religious or Belief Communities' 2 <https://primarysources.brillonline.com/browse/human-rights-documents-online/guidelines-on-the-legal-personality-of-religious-or-belief-communities;hrdhrd03672015047> accessed 18 May 2019.

the fact that some expressions may promote hatred against individuals or a particular group of people. Thus, if the MORA considers a national law, including a law that has religious nuance, to restrict Ahmadiyah for the purpose of preserving Islamic orthodoxy that is espoused by the government, such a policy is in contravention of the international standard of human rights which protects the right to select a certain Islamic teaching. This policy might bring about a loophole in the law in the Indonesian human rights system because it theoretically does not recognise any religion as a source of law but, in practice, some religious institutions, especially those backed up by the state, are authorised to give privileged treatment to mainstream religions and restrict religions seen as deviant on the grounds of avoiding disruption to public order and peace.

The other problematic matter from the perspective of the MORA is that although it has separate directorates for other religions, these are insignificant. This means that the MORA is in effect a Muslim institution.[86] Additionally, even though the ministry is authorised to monitor religious life, it is not a judicial organization in dealing with issues related to religious freedom. According to article 2 (1) of Act No. 1/PNPS/1965, the MORA, together with the Ministry of the Interior and the Attorney General, are also authorised to issue joint decrees on religious matters such as the building of houses of worship, guidelines of religious propagation and missionary endowment.[87] On some occasions, a joint decree also restricts the rights of religious minorities even though it should be enacted to administer the governing process of the state only. For instance, the MORA, the General Attorney and the Ministry of the Interior enacted Joint Decrees No. 3/2008, No. 33/JA/2008, and No. 199/2008, which restricted the right of Ahmadiyah to spread Islamic teaching due to the disharmonious situation within mainstream Islam. This restriction will be discussed further in Chapter 6.

3.2. The Indonesian Ulama Council (MUI)

The other institution that is significantly influential on human rights discourse, particularly the rights of religious minorities within Islam, is the MUI. This institution was established in 1975 to mobilise Muslim support for government policies.[88] The MUI is generally represented by Sunni Islam, such as those branches called traditionalists, modernists and puritans through whom joint *fatwas* are issued.[89] A *fatwa* is a religious opinion on a particular topic from the point of view of Islamic law, given by an acknowledged expert, and hence it is an excellent source for understanding the social reality of Islam in its various

86 Cornelis van Dijk, 'State-Islam Relations in Contemporary Indonesia: 1915–1990', in Cornelis van Dijk, *State and Islam* (Research School CNWS 1995) 102.
87 See several joint ministerial decrees on these matters in Lipton (n 65) 115–118.
88 Dijk (n 86) 103.
89 Salim and Azra (n 71) 104.

contexts.[90] Therefore, even though *fatwas* are not legally binding in Indonesian national legislation, the majority of Indonesian Muslims see them as the face of Islam and hence rely on such *fatwas* for their understanding of what is and what is not acceptable to the religion.[91]

The MUI is organised at national, provincial and regency level. In theory the regional committees are subordinate but in fact it appears that the regional committees act on their own initiative.[92] Some regional MUI committees are even more conservative, especially in relation to religious minorities within Islam. This can be examined from the *fatwas* of MUI Sampang District and East Java Province, in which both of them declared that Shi'ah is a "misleading" religious minority within Islam even though the central MUI did not do so. Although the MUI is not an institution anchored in law, its *fatwa* becomes a significant document in a court trial because it becomes one of the main considerations for court judges to adopt a verdict.[93]

The position of MUI as an influential and authoritative organisation to determine "true and false Islam" gave the *ulama* a significant role in Indonesian legal and human rights spheres. When the MUI is dominated by conservative groups of Muslims, their *fatwas* will also express a harsh confrontation with religious minorities within Islam. The main problem is not only the authorisation of all levels of MUI at national and regional levels to issue *fatwa*,[94] but also the relationship between MUI and the state organization as well as judicial power. If the MUI enacted a *fatwa* declaring that a certain religious minority within Islam is "misleading", the MORA on behalf of the state would restrict the rights of religious minorities within Islam. In a judicial matter, the court would also consider the *fatwa* when punishing individual members of religious minorities within Islam.

From the orthodox legal perspective, *fatwa* is not defined as law because Indonesian law officially only recognises positive law, primarily adopted from Dutch law, and Indonesian customary law (*adat*) as part of the Indonesian genuine legal framework. According to Moch Nur Ichwan, its production of *fatwa* and non-*fatwa* only contains signs of its changing position as a mediator between state and society, especially on traditional Islamic orthodoxy.[95] He further asserts that the *fatwa* is intended to be an answer to a question and is related to points of Islamic law, ranging from purely legal matters to questions of beliefs, all of which are viewed from an Islamic legal perspective.[96]

90 Nico Kaptein, 'Introduction' (2005) 12 *Islamic Law and Society* 1, 1.
91 Saeed (n 35) 177.
92 Hooker (n 4) 17.
93 See for example the verdict of Sampang court No. 69/PID.B/2012/PN.Spg.
94 For a more detailed analysis of this matter, see Piers Gillespie, 'Current Issues in Indonesian Islam: Analysing the 2005 Council of Indonesian Ulama Fatwa No. 7 Opposing Pluralism, Liberalism and Secularism' (2007) 18 *Journal of Islamic Studies* 202.
95 Moch Nur Ichwan, ''Ulamā', State and Politics: Majelis Ulama Indonesia after Suharto' (2005) 12 *Islamic Law and Society* 45, 46–50.
96 ibid 51.

The MUI has frequently enacted *fatwas* not in accordance with the spirit of Pancasila and the 1945 Constitution as the two main sources of national law. Even though the task of the MUI is to maintain harmonious relations with the other religions, this seems to be in theoretical matters because this institution has shown a conservative Islamic face. It regularly condemns so-called "deviant" sects and requests the government to ban them. The first *fatwa* which restricts non-mainstream Islamic teachings was issued on 1 June 1980 and asserted that Ahmadiyah, especially the Qadiani version, was deviant because this Islamic religious minority did not form a legitimate part of Islam.[97] This *fatwa* was then reasserted in 2005, confirming Ahmadiyah's deviancy and declaring that they should be restricted because their beliefs threatened religious harmony, social integration, public order and national security. In fact, when MUI first declared that Ahmadiyah was deviant, the MORA did not yet do so. It was later in 1984, when the MORA officially issued a circular letter spread across Indonesia saying that Ahmadiyah Qadian was deviant because it believed in Mirza Ghulam Ahmad as a prophet, that the announcement was supported by MUI with the same argument.[98]

In 1994, the MUI also issued a *fatwa* accusing Darul Arqam, a messianic Islamic group and allegedly a deviant Islamic sect. Darul Arqam was declared deviant and the spread of its Islamic teaching was restricted because the messianic issue resulted in dissension and division among Muslims, particularly between traditionalist, modernist and puritan Islam.[99] This research shows that this kind of accusation from the MUI against religious minorities within Islam has still been practised until very recently. As a consequence, some moderate Muslims criticised the MUI as violating human rights and promoting conservative voices on the issue of sectarianism in Islam.

3.3. *The joint-judiciary committee of religious life (Bakorpakem)*

Another institution that has a significant role in monitoring religious life is Bakorpakem. This institution was at first under the MORA. This was sustained until 1961, when the institution was then moved to the Attorney General's office.[100] Based on article 2 (3) of Act No. 15/1961, Bakorpakem on behalf of the Attorney General is authorised to prevent excesses, undesirable deviations and the abuse of power of the charismatic leaders. The authorities regularly crack down on those religious sects or individuals that are considered to lead people astray, that cause divisions in society, that threaten law and order and

97 See the MUI *fatwa* No. 11/2005.
98 Bernard Johan Boland, *The Struggle of Islam in Modern Indonesia* (Springer 2013) 107.
99 Hooker (n 4) 3.
100 Uli Parulian Sihombing, 'MENGGUGAT Bakor Pakem: Kajian hukum terhadap pengawasan agama dan kepercayaan di Indonesia/Uli Parulian Sihombing, Fulthoni, Dadang Trisasongko' (Indonesian Legal Resource Center 2008) 4.

that insult established religion by wrongly interpreting the true nature of God.[101] Since its existence, Bakorpakem has labelled many unofficial religions as deviant and has banned many of them in several regions, especially soon after the 1965 coup, where the Committee restricted some mystical beliefs and syncretistic religions. In its monitoring and supervisory working system, Bakorpakem has jointly collaborated with religious institutions and judicial organs to restrict the religious freedom of unofficial religions.

Together with MUI and MORA, Bakorpakem also jointly collaborates to give recommendations to the judicial institutions on the issue of religious affairs even though none of them can act on behalf of the law by restricting the rights of religious minorities. This affirms that the institutions undertake extra-judicial functions to uphold tolerance, religious harmony and mutual respect among different religious communities.[102] In fact, the existence of these institutions is a major factor in the sustainability of religious minorities within Islam because the institutions act as the hand of mainstream Islam to monitor and discriminate religious minorities within Islam. As a consequence, the court relies much on these three institutions, even though they often monopolise religious hermeneutics to restrict freedom of religion.

It is submitted that these three institutions generally restrict the religious freedom of the other religious groups if, in their view, the manifestation of such a right may threaten "public order" in Indonesian society. The government usually uses "religious orthodoxy, social integration, and national unity" as permissible limitations to restrict the right of religious minorities within Islam to spread their Islamic teaching. Yet, this limitation is in contravention of article 18 of the ICCPR. Their collaboration has significantly influenced government policies in determining a particular right and freedom which can be enjoyed by non-mainstream religious groups, including religious minorities within Islam. Thus, the discussion of religious freedom in Indonesia, particularly the rights of religious minorities within a particular religion in a state-religion relationship, is a complicated issue because state-religious institutions have often discriminated against religious minorities in attempting to "stabilise" religious harmony and social integration within Indonesian society.

4. Perspectives of Islamic organisations on religious minorities within Islam

We will now briefly examine perspectives of other Islamic organisations to see an alternative point of view on the rights of religious minorities within Islam in

101 JA Niels Mulder, 'Aliran Kebatinan as an Expression of the Javanese Worldview' (1970) 1 *Journal of Southeast Asian Studies* 105, 2.

102 Ahmad Suaedy, 'Pengawasan Negara Terhadap Kehidupan Sipil: Kasus Penyesatan Dan Kriminalisasi Yusman Roy', in Ahmad Suaedy (ed.), *Politisasi agama dan konflik komunal: beberapa isu penting di Indonesia* (The Wahid Institute 2007) 114.

Indonesian society. Besides the MORA, MUI and Bakorpakem, there are some other Islamic organisations that regularly issue *fatwa* on religious matters in Indonesia. Those are the awakening *ulama*, known as Nahdlatul Ulama (NU), the followers of Muhammad, known as Muhammadiyah, and the Islamic Unity (Persatuan Islam/Persis). All of these groups have different opinions on human rights, especially human rights for religious minorities within Islam. The divergent Islamic groups also evince that Indonesian Muslim scholars have long advocated for religious pluralism within Islam. This has been noted by Azra:

> Islam basically speaks positively of diversity of tribes, sects, nations, and peoples, as well as races and languages. The verses of the Quran also acknowledge the natural differences in the intellectual and physical capabilities of human beings. They view different ways of living as a natural and even a divine aspect of creation. The Quran nowhere calls for a forcible unification of this diversity.[103]

It may be assumed that the voices of religious human rights among these groups are also divergent and sometimes mixed. Some Islamic organisations are ardent advocates of tolerance, democracy and human rights while others are very reactive and defensive against a broad spectrum of religious human rights. On many occasions, cases of religious freedom in Indonesia have, in fact, been divided between moderate and conservative voices on religious human rights within the different Islamic organisations.

4.1. Nahdlatul Ulama (NU)

Examining Nahdlatul Ulama (NU)'s perspectives on religious minorities within Islam is very significant because NU has become the largest Islamic organisation in Indonesia. NU was founded in 1926 as an attempt to restrict the spread of Islamic puritanism that stemmed from the Wahabi movement in Saudi Arabia.[104] Even though NU follows the Shafi'i school of Islamic law, defending the authority of the four orthodox schools of Islamic law as well as a genuine Javanese style of life were two other main reasons of its establishment.[105] Some prominent NU religious leaders practise Sufism and the majority of its members live in rural areas practising Islamic syncretism. Since the beginning, there has been heated tension between NU and some puritan Islamic organisations. For

103 Azyumardi Azra and Wayne Hudson, 'Religious Pluralism in Indonesia', in Azyumardi Azra and Wayne Hudson (eds), *Islam Beyond Conflict: Indonesian Islam and Western Political Theory* (Ashgate 2008) 12. It must be noted however that some verses of the Qur'an such as Q3:103 and Q21:92 enjoin Muslims to unity and describe them as a "single *ummah*".

104 Rumadi (n 13) 4. This research identifies all theological thoughts affiliated to Wahabi calling for a return to the Qur'an and Hadith as puritanism, even though some researches consider them as representing reformism.

105 See Boland (n 98) 23.

example, the peak tension occurred in the Islamic Congress of 1922, when both NU and puritan groups declared one another to be infidels, idolatrous and heretic because of a trivial difference in beliefs.[106]

Due to its firm adherence to one of the schools of Islamic law, many scholars argue that Nahdlatul Ulama (NU) is a prominent Islamic organisation that represents traditionalist Islam. This proposition has, however, been challenged by some young NU intellectuals. One of the prominent NU scholars who endorses the importance of *ijtihad* is Abdurrahman Wahid. Yet still, the significant identity of the NU majority is, however, that they argue that the gates of *ijtihad* should henceforth be closed because they believe that the human mind is generally incapable of grasping the patterns and intricacies of God's commands without a reliable guide. So, they hold that people should follow (*taqlid*) the founders of the Islamic schools of law who had examined, compiled, explained and interpreted Sharia up to the tenth century.[107] Many confirm that the idea of defending the major Islamic schools of law marks NU as the promoter of traditionalist Islam even though it has been latterly shown that NU can perhaps no longer be exclusively associated with traditionalist Islam, based on the fact that many NU intellectuals have become strident supporters of religious freedom and the rights of religious minorities within Islam as well.

NU is one of the major three Islamic organisations that have for some years regularly issued *fatwa* in response to the problems of Indonesian Muslims.[108] In the case of human rights and the issue of religious minorities within Islam, NU's voice is split into two groups. The first group prefers to follow a conservative Islamic approach in relation to human rights. Some members of this group have even claimed that aspects of international human rights, such as freedom of religion, cannot be fully implemented in Indonesia.[109] Hasyim Muzadi, former chair of NU, for instance, argues:

> The case of Ahmadiyah is not about freedom of religion but it is about defamation of religion as this group actually insults Islamic teachings by claiming Mirza Ghulam as their prophet. Ahmadiyah should establish their own religion outside Islam if they want to be entitled to constitutional rights and freedom as their current religious belief is problematic.[110]

106 For a more detailed explanation about the tension, see generally Rumadi (n 13) 3 and Hooker (n 4) 66.

107 Federspiel (n 49) 4.

108 Greg Fealy and Sally White, 'Online Fatwa in Indonesia: From Fatwa Shopping to Googling a Kyai', in Greg Fealy and Sally White (eds), *Expressing Islam: Religious Life and Politics in Indonesia* (Institute of Southeast Asian Studies 2008) 1.

109 Khanif (n 26).

110 'Hasyim Muzadi: Sebaiknya Ahmadiyah Jadi Agama Sendiri' (*Republika Online* 7 February 2011) <https://republika.co.id/berita/breaking-news/nasional/11/02/07/162871-hasyim-muzadi-sebaiknya-ahmadiyah-jadi-agama-sendiri> accessed 18 May 2019.

In principle, this argument asserts that Indonesia, which upholds theistic religions and advocates religious pluralism, is different from the liberal character of Western countries which promote unlimited religious freedom for individuals, because this right tends to denigrate a theistic concept of religion. Regrettably, Muzadi still has significant numbers of followers in NU as shown in the last NU National Summit (*muktamar*) in August 2015. Some of his followers also persecuted religious minorities within Islam. For example, some local NU leaders in the East Java MUI branch agreed to enact a *fatwa* in 2012 declaring that the Shi'ah are a misleading Islamic group.[111]

The second group generally uses contextual interpretation of Hadith and the Qur'an to respond to human rights problems in Indonesia. Many members of this group claim that Islam should be able to combine Pancasila, the1945 Constitution, international human rights, modernity, democracy and globalisation. Islam should not be understood as a noun, but rather as a verb capable of answering social problems including human rights. With regard to the Shi'ah, Said Aqil Siradj, the successor of Muzadi argues that this Islamic sect is an integral part of Islam and its followers should be considered as Muslims even though many Muslims, including most NU members, in Indonesia believe that Shi'ahs are apostates.[112] Siradj does not officially declare Ahmadiyah as deviant, even though he argued that the emergence of Ahmadiyah was influenced by British colonialism in India. Siradj is also well known as a moderate Islamic thinker. Meanwhile, many of the NU youngsters are advocates of human rights and defenders of religious minorities within Islam. According to this group, judging other religious beliefs as deviating from the truth is absurd because religious heterogeneity is the will of God and hence judging truth and falsehood in religions is only within God's authority. These arguments affirm that NU basically endorses independent juridical reasoning (*ijtihad*) on human rights discourse, pointing out that both encapsulate a spectrum of factions, all working for the causes of the nation and with a genuine desire for reform.[113] As a consequence, the voice of human rights within NU members is divergent and further confirms that the Islamic schools of thought in NU are not monolithic, even though in theological matters the majority members of those two groups within NU generally agree to follow the founder of the Shafi'i School.

NU regularly issues *fatwa* on religious matters. The first *fatwa* was issued by NU in its 16th meeting in 1946, which declared that fighting against the Dutch colonialists was a religious necessity for Muslims.[114] This *fatwa* merely relied on

111 Both two cases will be observed further in Chapter 4.

112 See his argument about the history of Shi'ah during his academic debate against young NU scholars in YouTube *Said Aqil Membela Mati-Matian SYIAH Iran – YouTube* <www.youtube.com/watch?v=oaerCJ-mGFg> accessed 18 May 2019.

113 See Michael Laffan, 'The Fatwā Debated? Shūrā in One Indonesian Context' (2005) 12 *Islamic Law and Society* 93, 1.

114 Muhammad As'ad, 'Seruan Jihad KH Hasyim Asy'ari Selain Resolusi Jihad' (*NU Online* 14 April 2018) <www.nu.or.id/post/read/88764/seruan-jihad-kh-hasyim-asyari-selain-resolusi-jihad> accessed 18 May 2019.

Islamic teaching in calling Muslims to defend Indonesian independence and wage *jihad* against the Dutch army, which was trying to re-establish its power in Indonesia.[115] Related to this, NU also asserted that suicide bombing is forbidden, unless in a time of war. They hold that suicide is illicit if its purpose is political struggle, but it is licit if there is a greater public interest (*maslahah mursalah*) for the Islamic community, such as to destroy unbelievers who attempt to invade the Muslim land.[116]

In 1962, NU issued a *fatwa* stating that inter-religious marriages were not allowed under Islamic law, either. This *fatwa* was further confirmed by another *fatwa* in 1989.[117] Furthermore, in 2004 a group of Islamic leaders in this group issued a controversial *fatwa* declaring it is forbidden (*haram*) for the Islamic community to choose a woman as president of the country. In fact, NU has a Muslim women's association known as *fatayat* and *Muslimat* led by a woman scholar from NU.[118] Thus, this *fatwa* is disagreed with by most of its mass organisations, which see that it is inconsistent with gender equality in Indonesian society.[119] Surprisingly, their disagreement is generally based on gender equality in the West rather than looking at the gender reality in Islamic states such as Pakistan.

The discourse of human rights within NU evinces that the classification of modernists and traditionalists in Indonesia becomes more blurry, because even though the rural traditionalists continued to be culturally conservative, many of their young generations were at the forefront of progressive thought and religious reform.[120] For instance, Abdurrahman Wahid, the late prominent leader of NU and former president of Indonesia, was well known as an ardent spokesperson for religious minorities and pluralist democracy.[121] He also proved that Pancasila represents a kind of civil religion that simultaneously promotes enlightenment values, including protecting democracy and individual freedom of belief.[122] Wahid also examined whether Islam actually has a concept of state and was doubtful whether the Prophet intended to found an Islamic state.[123] Therefore, Wahid maintained that Islam should act as a complementary factor to the

115 Salim and Azra (n 71) 4.

116 Laffan (n 113) 1.

117 Fealy and White (n 108) 171.

118 A former chair of *Muslimat*, Khofifah Indar Parawangsa is appointed as Minister of Social Welfare under President Joko Widodo (2014–2019). Some other prolific NU *Muslimat* members are Professor Musdah Mulia and Professor Zaitunah from the Islamic State University of Jakarta. Yet their thoughts on the issue of religious minorities within Islam are almost invisible from public debate.

119 Daniels (n 44) 3.

120 Greg Barton, *Abdurrahman Wahid: Muslim Democrat, Indonesian President: A View from the Inside* (UNSW Press 2002) 1.

121 Hefner (n 54) v.

122 ibid 3. When he became president, Abdurrahman Wahid, for instance, enacted Presidential Decree No. 6/2000 to regard Confucianism as one of the recognised religions in Indonesia.

123 See Hooker (n 4) 3.

state in developing a socio-economic and political system, besides the fact that Muslims should also accept Pancasila as the Indonesian state philosophy.[124] He further proposed a functional means of integrating the universal perception of Islam with the national perception of a state by "*membumikan Islam*" [indigenising Islam] into the Indonesian context to preserve the national framework of a democratic society and the protection of minorities.[125]

To understand Wahid's position, it might be useful to note that he was essentially a moral philosopher, rather than a strict practitioner of the philosophy of Islamic law. His interest was the moral good of society within the parameters of Islam.[126] Wahid and prominent reformist Indonesian Muslim thinkers assert that Muslims face two choices or paths: to pursue a traditional, static, and legal-formalistic Islam or to fashion a more dynamic cosmopolitan, universal and pluralistic worldview.[127] In this way, it transpires that secularism is the best option for Indonesian society, which is multi-ethnic, multicultural and multi-religious, even though the understanding of secularism in this context is slightly different from the Western perspective, because Indonesian secularism still needs to recognise religious values as a valid tradition within Indonesian society.[128]

4.2. Muhammadiyah

The other mainstream Islamic group that has a significant role in the discourse of human rights in Indonesia is Muhammadiyah. The name of this group literally means the followers of Muhammad. This organisation was established in 1912 and has become the second largest Islamic organisation in Indonesia. Muhammadiyah was founded to spread reformist ideas of Islam among the population and to promote religious life among its members by providing educational institutions, hospitals and other social services.[129] Unlike NU, the purpose of Muhammadiyah was to purify Islam from the corrupting local influences of popular customs and to promote Islamic beliefs based on their *ijtihad* on the Qur'an and Hadith.[130] Muhammadiyah tries to purify Islamic belief based on the Qur'an and Hadith for its legal opinion, by stripping out accretions of non-Islamic elements.[131] Based on its puritan theological approach and commitment to social services, Muhammadiyah is classified as puritan-modernist Islam.

124 See Masdar Hilmy, *Islamism and Democracy in Indonesia: Piety and Pragmatism* (Institute of Southeast Asian Studies 2010) 2.
125 See ibid 3.
126 Hooker (n 4) 3.
127 See Khaled Abou El Fadl, *Islam and the Challenge of Democracy: A Boston Review Book* (Princeton University Press 2015) 1.
128 See and compare with the concept of secularism in India in Race and Shafer (n 75) 3.
129 Noer (n 73) 3.
130 Fauzan Saleh, *Modern Trends in Islamic Theological Discourse in 20th Century Indonesia: A Critical Survey* (Brill 2001) 3.
131 Peacock (n 45) 3.

Soon after Muhammadiyah's establishment, the Islamic voice in Indonesian public spheres increasingly became dominated by advocates of the Egyptian-oriented modernism of Muhammad Abduh and Rashid Rida, who significantly influenced Muhammadiyah's doctrine. Muhammadiyah emphasised a need to move away from what it presented as a derivative understanding of Islamic jurisprudence (*fiqh*) and a fatalistic dependence on the *ulama*; fatalism most attributed to the practitioners of Sufism and traditionalist Islam.[132] They primarily emphasised thoughtful and innovative independent interpretation (*ijtihad*) rather than dull, passive and unimaginative submission to authority (*taqlid*) as the way to modernise Islamic thinking.[133] They assumed that only the fundamental truths had been set down in the Qur'an and Hadith and that in every age these truths had to be newly applied to current conditions. Hence, Muslims should examine the Qur'an and Hadith to discover the legal prescriptions and moral teachings.[134]

This Islamic modernism first came to Indonesia at the beginning of the twentieth century with a progressive and reformist movement.[135] Muhammadiyah sought to establish *tauhid*, pure Islamic monotheism, shorn of all kinds of *shirk*, *bid'ah*, *tahayul* and *khurafat* (polytheism, innovations, superstitions and non-Islamic beliefs).[136] This idea signifies that puritan-modernists seem to prefer to keep Islamic orthodoxy rather than modernising Islamic teachings because they tend to purify Islamic practice in Indonesia from the elements that they believe as superstition. It may be noted that Muhammadiyah is modernist only in its practice and not in terms of ideology, which clings rigidly to *salafi* interpretations eschewing, in the name of *taqlid*, the interpretations of post-*salafi* Islamic scholars.[137] For instance, even though Muhammadiyah has never explicitly declared that Ahmadiyah is deviant, its *fatwa*, issued in 1933, stated that whoever claims prophethood after Muhammad is classified as an infidel. Din Syamsudin, the chairman of Muhammadiyah, who in early 2014 was appointed chair of the MUI, also signed the MUI *fatwa* when he was secretary of the MUI in 1980s. This obliged the government to ban the spread of Ahmadiyah across Indonesia, disband the organisation and outlaw its activities.

Yunayar Ilyas, the chair of Muhammadiyah jurisprudence assembly asserted that it was not necessary for Muhammadiyah to adopt a *fatwa* to accuse Ahmadiyah as a deviant Islamic group because there had been two prominent Islamic organisations (MUI and the World Muslim League) which already declared that

132 Laffan (n 113) 3.
133 Robert Edward Elson, *The Idea of Indonesia: A History* (Cambridge University Press 2008) 1.
134 Federspiel (n 49) 1.
135 Barton (n 120) 1.
136 Daniels (n 44) 1.
137 ibid 103.

Ahmadiyah was deviant.[138] This argument is similar to the argument from some local Muhammadiyah branches which consider that Ahmadiyah was deviant.[139]

In the case of the Shi'ah, Muhammadiyah also did not issue a *fatwa* declaring that this Islamic sect was deviant or apostate. Through its official opinion adopted in 2012, Muhammadiyah only rejects the concept of an infallible *imamiyah* who has divine knowledge and authority and of *al-rafidha*, the rejectionists; that is, those who have rejected community and consensus.[140] Muhammadiyah's voice on the Shi'ah is actually divergent. Yunahar Ilyas, the chair of *fatwa* argues that Shi'ah is not a true faith, while Din Syamsudin notes that Shi'ah is a version of Islam.[141]

The divergent views of Muhammadiyah confirm that this group endorses *ijtihad*. But, its rejection of the beliefs of Ahmadiyah and Shi'ah illustrates that Islamic reformism brought by Muhammadiyah is not intended to develop a modern interpretation of Islamic discourse on human rights. On many occasions this reformism has even provoked legal theological exclusivism which restrains them from responding to contemporary human rights discourse. An-Na'im notes that:

> The fundamental mistake of Islamic modernists is that they sought to achieve their goal through reform within the framework of Sharia. Some of them may have been intimidated by the prospects of challenging what they perceived to be a divine system, while others may have been persuaded to adopt this course of action out of tactical or political reason, thinking that their views would have greater popular appeal if they remained within the confines of Sharia.[142]

Based on An-Na'im's argument, it can be said that classifying religious minorities within Islam as infidels, by using the literal understanding of Islamic sources, demonstrates an out of date Islamic interpretation produced in the early centuries of Islam. This classification also becomes invalid in Indonesia because Islamic law, except in the field of family law, theoretically did not have jurisdiction on human rights after the state adopted Dutch civil law. As a consequence, religious claims against human rights are contradictory to the

138 Ahmad Subakir, 'Menyoal Fatwa MUI Tentang Larangan Aliran (Aqidah) Ahmadiyah' (2009) 6 *Jurnal Kontemplasi* 2.

139 ibid.

140 Peter Clarke, 'Sects in Islam', in Peter Clarke (ed.), *The Oxford Handbook of the Sociology of Religion* (Oxford University Press 2011) 2.

141 Aditya Revianur, 'Din: Muhammadiyah Keberatan Fatwa Sesat Syiah' (*KOMPAS.com*) https://nasional.kompas.com/read/2012/09/07/09330267/Din.Muhammadiyah.Keberatan.Fatwa.Sesat.Syiah accessed 18 May 2019.

142 Abdullahi An-Na'im and edited by Mashood A Baderin, *Islam and Human Rights: Selected Essays of Abdullahi An-Na'im* (Routledge 2017) 34.

concept of a quasi-theistic principle of Pancasila, as this principle protects all religions and beliefs and suggests that the state is not an Islamic state.

Regarding the discourse of a quasi-theistic secularism, Nurcholis Madjid, one of the prominent Muhammadiyah thinkers asserts that Islam does not lend itself to state ideology because it is a true religion and, therefore, the interpretation of the Constitution of Medina is neither relevant nor helpful for contemporary Indonesia.[143] Madjid argues that if Muslims consider that aspects of Islam could be reinterpreted, the noble spirit of humanitarianism should receive greater attention because according to the Qur'an all religions must be protected and followers must be given freedom to carry out their teachings.[144] Madjid further affirms that there should be liberalisation of Islamic thought, which consists of distinguishing between that which is eternal and that which is temporal. Thus, Madjid proposes that Indonesia should not establish an Islamic state, an idea which is seen by many hardline Muslims as blasphemous because they believe in the unity of Islam and the state.[145] Madjid's *ijtihad* on Islamic reform was endorsed by many Indonesian moderate Muslims, including Abdurrahman Wahid from NU. For proponents of Islamic reform, all Muslims must be freed from a monolithic Islamic interpretation because religion is essentially an individual matter.[146]

The late Mohammad Hatta, another Muhammadiyah thinker and the first vice president of Indonesia, also argued that the Qur'an is especially the basis of religion, not a book of law, and so the people of the state themselves must establish orderly law by their mutual deliberations even though the Qur'an establishes a basis for justice.[147] Hatta hence argued that the resulting law will be state law, not religious law, because Indonesia should establish the separation of state affairs and religious affairs.[148] It means that the assurance of a quasi-theistic secular state as stipulated in Pancasila should not be used by the state to intervene in religious affairs but rather to protect freedom of religion. Similarly, Ahmad Dahlan, the founder of Muhammadiyah, considered that the concept of Pancasila is in accordance with the teachings of Islam and that there are always opportunities and openings to uphold and implement the basic principles of Islam within the framework of the Pancasila state.[149]

143 Hooker (n 4) 49.

144 Virginia Matheson Hooker and Amin Saikal, *Islamic Perspectives on the New Millennium* (Institute of Southeast Asian Studies 2004) 33.

145 Assyaukanie (n 83) 33.

146 Virginia Matheson Hooker and Amin Saikal, 'Perspective on Shari'a and the State', in Virginia Matheson Hooker and Amin Saikal (eds), *Islamic Perspectives on the New Millennium* (Institute of Southeast Asian Studies 2004) 34.

147 See Bahtiar Effendy, *Islam and the State in Indonesia* (Institute of Southeast Asian Studies 2003) 45.

148 See ibid 30.

149 See ibid 82.

Like NU, women's voices on religious minorities within Islam in the Muhammadiyah circle are also almost invisible in the public sphere. Even though gender and human rights discourses in Indonesia are a way forward and better than in the Middle East, it happens too often that women's voices are not at the forefront and the centre of human rights debates. Male dominance also occurs in all Islamic organisations, including the hardline Islamic groups below, showing that the history of patriarchy in the discourse of Islamic jurisprudence has not much changed until recently.

4.3. Hardline Islamic groups

The problematical discourse of human rights in Indonesia also refers to puritan-fundamentalists or conservatives. As in many other parts of the Muslim world, the scholars of this group generally argue that Islam has a separate and distinct system of rights and duties and hence they resist the imposition of any foreign human rights system and influences.[150] The hardline Islamic groups in Indonesia generally follow the conservative interpretation of Islamic law and take the position that international human rights law is not applicable or is only partially applicable in their domestic jurisdictions.[151] Since the fall of the New Order in 1998 these groups have occupied public discourses on human rights, especially on the rights of religious minorities within Islam, and have strongly argued that religious minorities within Islam should not be entitled to religious freedom.

These groups have existed in Indonesia since the era of Dutch colonisation, at first as the movement of reformism (*tajdid*) and improvement (*islah*).[152] Puritan-fundamentalism was carried to Indonesia in the 1780s by Indonesians from West Sumatera, who had completed a pilgrimage to Mecca and had imbibed Wahhabiyya doctrines. In the era of colonisation the propagation of Wahhabism produced the Padri Movement, which sought to spread particular beliefs through militant action in the societies of the archipelago.[153] While in the era of modern Indonesia, puritan-fundamentalist Islam is primarily represented by Islamic Unity (Persatuan Islam, Persis), Islamic Defender Front (Front Pembela Islam, FPI), Islamic Community Forum (Forum Umat Islam, FPUI) Jamaah Islamiyah (JI), the Indonesian Party Liberation (Hizbut Tahrir Indonesia, HTI) and the Holy Warriors Council (Majelis Mujahidin Indonesia, MMI). While Persis had already existed in Indonesia since the colonial era, the later groups appeared in Indonesian public discourse after the *Reformasi* in 1998. Persis is

150 Niaz a Shah, *Women, the Koran and International Human Rights Law* (Brill 2006) 45.
151 ibid 2.
152 Nuhrison M Nuh and Achmad Rosidi, 'Kasus Salafi Versus Non-Salafi di Kabupaten Lombok Barat Nusa Tenggara Barat', in Achmad Rosidi, *Kasus-Kasus Aliran/Faham Keagamaan Aktual Di Indonesia* (Departemen Agama, Badan Litbang Agama Dan Diklat Keagamaan, Puslitbang Kehidupan Beragama 2006) 4.
153 Federspiel (n 49) 45.

classified as a puritan-fundamentalist group in the sense that this group calls for "radical *ijtihad*" as already explained earlier in this chapter.

These groups are viewed as puritan-fundamentalists in the sense that they strove to return to the basic tenets of the prophet and his companions by calling for the full application of Islamic law in Indonesia. They strongly believed that the nation was a society shaped around God, that its law should be based on divine law and that the president should be a Muslim.[154] The hardline Islamist groups are highly critical of the secular state, believing that only a state based on Islamic law can be just because they believe that Islam is a total way of life to maintain high standards of Islamic morality.[155] Consequently they promote strict observance of scriptural Islam and reject any meaningful collaboration with non-Muslims.[156] The hardline Islamic groups were convinced that only by referring to Islam could they resist imperialism, including inter alia the concept of religious human rights for religious minorities within Islam. For example, they strongly oppose the far-reaching and profound provision of religious freedom in article 18 of the ICCPR and the UDHR and often translate religious freedom as defamation of religion because this right, according to them, threatens Islamic belief.

This kind of proposition results in repressive ideas against religious minorities in Indonesia, particularly those who practise non-mainstream Islam. Islamic hardline groups such as MMI and FPI believe that Islam is betrayed by moderate reformers such as Nurcholis Madjid, Abdurrahman Wahid, and the Liberal Islamic Network (JIL).[157] They do not refer to Pancasila to understand human rights and the rights of religious minorities as this ideology is seen as not Islamic. The puritan-fundamentalist groups tend to advocate an Islamic state by replacing it with Islamic ideology. Yet their struggle for the establishment of Indonesia as an Islamic state based on Islamic law, by constitutional as well as violent means in the form of armed rebellions, has been unsuccessful since the beginning of Indonesian independence.[158]

The main concern of puritan-fundamentalists is to disseminate ideas by means of public meetings, sermons and study groups and organising schools and publications. They enjoy public debates and challenge other people who do not agree with their ideas and standpoints to debates. For instance, Persis had three significant debates with Ahmadiyah Qadian and with traditionalist Muslims such

154 For further discussion, see Elson (n 133) 168.

155 Julie Chernov Hwang, *Peaceful Islamist Mobilization in the Muslim World: What Went Right* (Springer 2009) 45.

156 Robert Pringle, *Understanding Islam in Indonesia: Politics and Diversity* (Editions Didier Millet 2010) 45.

157 Greg Fealy and Sally White, '"As Long as It's Halal": Islamic Preman in Jakarta', in Greg Fealy and Sally White (eds), *Expressing Islam: Religious Life and Politics in Indonesia* (Institute of Southeast Asian Studies 2008) 45.

158 Zoya Hasan, 'The Indonesian Experience in Implementing Democracy', in Zoya Hasan (ed.), *Democracy in Muslim Societies: The Asian Experience* (SAGE Publications 2007) 56.

as NU in the 1930s.[159] The Persis follower believes that the doctrine of Ahmadiyah is not in accordance with mainstream Islam[160] and hence this religious minority within Islam should be prohibited in Indonesia. The *raison d'être* of puritan-fundamentalists to attack religious minorities within Islam is that they could act with impunity and, in some instances, they have been empowered in their efforts by the MUI, a quasi-judicial institution authorised to issue *fatwas* as earlier discussed above.[161]

Since the beginning, the existence of hardline Islamic groups has not only influenced religious discourse but also legal and human rights discourse in Indonesia. Muhammad Natsir, in his direct discussion with Soekarno in the 1940s, said that Islam did not tolerate nationalism founded on fanaticism, which broke up the bond of brotherhood of all Muslims of various nationalities.[162] Therefore, he voiced a strong rejection of Pancasila as an empty abstraction of colourless neutrality and argued for the establishment of Islam as the ideological foundation of the Indonesian state. Only Islam, he further argued, could serve to ground the constitution in what he believed to be the true feelings and beliefs of the people.[163] He proposed "theistic democracy" – a system in which the sovereignty of the people was to be exercised within certain limits that had been determined by God and then was followed by some contemporary Indonesian Islamists for the formal implementation of Islamic law.[164]

Until recently, some puritan-fundamentalists have also insisted on introducing Islamic values into the Indonesian public sphere without differentiating between the Islamic theological and legal realms. They insist that there are no such things as binary opposites of the private and public spheres because they believe that Islam is both religion and politics.[165] They noted that Islam, from the lifetime of its founder, was the state and that the identity of religion and government is indelibly stamped on the memories and awareness of the faithful from its sacred writings. This makes it not only universal, but indeed much more than an ideology because it is a complete civilisation.[166]

This argument implies that many Muslims still believe that substantive justice and morality in Islamic law will remain ineluctable prisms through which Muslims evaluate international human rights law. Islamic law is perceived by many

159 Noer (n 73) 4.
160 Ahmad Suaedy, 'Diskriminasi Hak Sipil Minoritas: Pelarangan Pencatatan Pernikahan Jemaat Ahmadiyah Kuningan', in Ahmad Suaedy (ed.), *Politisasi Agama dan Konflik Komunal, Beberapa Isu Penting di Indonesia* (The Wahid Institute 2007) 45.
161 Hwang (n 155) 6. It should be noted that many religious persecutions against religious minorities within Islam have been perpetrated by puritan fundamentalist organisations.
162 See Hooker (n 4) 4.
163 See R Michael Feener, *Muslim Legal Thought in Modern Indonesia* (Cambridge University Press 2007) 45.
164 ibid 3.
165 See Hilmy (n 124) 45.
166 Feener (n 163) 4.

Muslims as an expression of God's will for humanity and hence all Muslims should therefore submit themselves specifically to the will of God.[167] This perception can be noted from the view of HTI. HTI's basic proposition is that Islam, especially Islamic law, is a gift from God to the whole of mankind. It will therefore bring good to all, Muslims and non-Muslims alike, and hence it is the duty of Muslims to accept the totality of Islam. Muslims should also convey the message to others as part of being devoted Muslims. Therefore, many other puritan-fundamentalist organisations removed the Western concept of human rights in Indonesian law and highlighted the importance of Islamic law to resolve contemporary human rights problems in Indonesia.

The proponents of Islamism share the same perception – that is, that Islamic law should have been taken more seriously by the state as well as the greater Muslim society. Many Indonesian Muslims perceive Islam as guidance and a solution to all aspects of life. Because 88% of the country's population are Muslims, this fact, they argue, should provide the legitimacy for making Islam the basis of the state – or at least make it possible to recognise Islamic law as a core ingredient or an integral part of the constitution. They also argue that secular-positive law has not brought legal improvements for Muslims in Indonesia.[168] Robert W Hefner has observed that their demand to apply Islamic law is generally due to the lackadaisical attitude of traditionalist and modernist Muslims to strict Islamic devotion and the objection that puritan-fundamentalists should resign themselves to being a marginal minority in a nation dominated by a leadership only nominally committed to the Islamic faith.[169] Additionally, they consider the Indonesian government as un-Islamic and the president an apostate, because the state does not give verbal recognition to Islamic law as the supreme source of law in Indonesia.

According to them, Islam in Indonesia has attracted accretions of non-Islamic elements that must be removed, because purity is to be found in the Qur'an and Hadith. Therefore, the purification of public Islam is the first condition that must be established.[170] One of the ways of doing this is by requesting *fatwa* from the Middle East relating to Islamic issues. For instance, the Forum Komunikasi Ahlus Sunnah wal Jama'ah (FKASWJ), an Indonesian *da'wa* organisation established at the beginning of 1998 under the leadership of Ja'far Umar Thalib, requested *fatwa* to resolve the conflict between Muslims and Christians in Ambon in 2000.[171] Additionally, they requested *fatwa* on *rajam* law (stoning punishment for adultery) in the case of Abdullah, a member of Laskar Jihad

167 Tamara Sonn, *Interpreting Islam: Bandali Jawzi's Islamic Intellectual History* (Oxford University Press 1996) 34.
168 Effendy (n 147) 4.
169 See Azyumardi Azra and Arskal Salim, 'Islamizing Capitalism, On the Founding of Indonesia's First Islamic Bank', in Azyumardi Azra and Arskal Salim (eds), *Shari'a and Politics in Modern Indonesia* (Institute of Southeast Asian Studies 2003) 56.
170 See Hooker (n 4) 4.
171 Kaptein (n 90) 4.

(Jihad Brigade) found guilty of adultery in 2001. Based on Laskar Jihad's own trial, not in a state public court, they sought to apply Islamic law because they believed that the government was un-Islamic and Abdurrahman Wahid, the president, was an apostate.[172]

Due to this mixture of secularisation and communalisation of religion, discussing sensitive human rights questions such as the rights of religious minorities within Islam in Indonesia cannot ignore Islamic organisations as parts of civil society. These organisations constitute an arena of competing values including, among others, human rights discourse because each Islamic organisation tries to influence the public sphere by issuing *fatwas* with its own source of interpretation. Interestingly, the vast majority of *fatwas* hardly refer to the constitution and state ideology even though the essence of some of their arguments is connected to constitutional freedoms and rights. Some Islamic organisations and individuals have tried to introduce Islamic religious prescripts into Indonesian law through their religious interpretation and sometimes such interventions have been accommodated in the formal legal system.

5. Islam within the concept of a quasi-theistic secular state

The recognition of official religions and the establishment of religious or quasi-religious institutions indicates that Indonesia is basically a state that supports religious denominations within the spectrum of Indonesian secularism. Therefore, even though Indonesia is legally not an Islamic state or a state based on particular religious beliefs, it may be called a "quasi-theistic secular state" – a state that upholds secularism in its legislations but at the same time also considers the significant role of theistic religion in the public sphere.[173] This concept signifies that the majority religion (Islam) in Indonesia has peculiar status because it is often placed as a sacred canopy to control the implementation of statutes and strains the application of international human rights instruments in the country.

The concept of a quasi-theistic secularism is designed to stabilise the Indonesian socio-political realm and protect the national unity mandated by the state ideology, Pancasila. The concept is significant because Indonesia was built on the idea of dynamic pluralism, which should accommodate various religions, more specifically orthodox religions, respect different traditions and cultures and keep the nature of Indonesian diversity. This dynamic diversity cannot be preserved if a state is built strictly on the basis of monolithic religious belief. At the same time, religion cannot be relegated from the public sphere as religion is an essential part of national identity. Consequently, a quasi-theistic secularism needs to filter some sorts of rights and freedoms that may or may not be implemented in the country. One example of human rights that is difficult to be

172 Effendy (n 147) 45.
173 Khanif (n 36).

realised is the far-reaching and profound provision of freedom of religion or belief for religious minorities within a particular religion. One of the main reasons is because of the existence of state and non-state religious institutions, which generally determine standards of human rights norms applicable for particular religious groups.

The complexity of religious authority and constitutional interpretation in a quasi-theistic secular Indonesia illustrates that the application of constitutional rights and the norms of international human rights instruments coincide with socio-religious reality within Indonesian society. Some *fatwas* from Islamic organisations have still been permitted by the government even though the essence of *fatwas* is not in accordance with the constitutional human rights provisions. For instance, the MUI *fatwa* which declared Ahmadiyah's deviance has not been challenged by the government even though the right to freedom of religion is clearly guaranteed by Pancasila and the 1945 Constitution.

In some cases, the existence of Islamic mass organisations may also interfere with the independence of judicial institutions by pressuring the institutions on the importance of protecting public order, namely religious harmony and social integration. The existence of "watchdog institutions", such as the MUI, MORA and Bakorpakem, to oversee religious life and the significant influence of civil Islam on legal and theological discourses such as NU, Muhammadiyah and others in Indonesia supports Islam as a public and preferred religion in the country. This means that Indonesia does not embrace French secularist "*laïcité*" but is a religious-secular state, whose public realm is dominated both by religious discourse and human rights discourse. Thus, secularism in Indonesia cannot be defined as "the total disestablishment of religion"[174] from the public sphere as experienced by Christianity in Europe and North America. As argued by An-Na'im, "this kind of secularism should be defined as a set of public policy applied variously in distinct contexts for organising the relationship between religion and state".[175] The relation of state and religion is aimed at protecting the pluralistic religious conditions of the nation in order to safeguard the freedom of religion and the belief of believers and non-believers alike.[176]

The concept of a quasi-theistic secular state in Indonesia is required because the state has to act as a guardian of religious life as a consequence of the separation between the state and religion. This concept is basically required because human rights, particularly the rights of religious minorities within Islam in Indonesia, need some legitimacy from mainstream Islam as the majority religion. Apparently, a purely secular approach to human rights will fail to resolve the problem of

174 The concept of disestablishment results in the privatisation and individualisation of religion because the state is restricted to establishing a particular religion or prohibiting the exercise of religion. See Winnifred Fallers Sullivan, 'Religion, Law and the Construction of Identities. Introduction' (1996) 43 *Numen* 128, 56.

175 Abdullahi Ahmed An-Na'im, 'The Interdependence of Religion, Secularism, and Human Rights: Prospects for Islamic Societies' (2005) 11 *Common Knowledge* 56, 56.

176 See a similar argument at Abdullahi A An-Naim, 'Re-Affirming Secularism for Islamic Societies' (2003) 20 *New Perspectives Quarterly* 36, 37.

religious minorities within Islam in Indonesia, since that will require the majority mainstream Muslims to subordinate their religion to criteria that would be perceived by many as non-Islamic. Thus, a quasi-theistic secular approach in Indonesia provides room for Indonesian people to choose and practise their religion or belief and at the same time it allows the government to occasionally intervene in people's religious lives to protect public order.

The main problem with this concept is how to ensure the neutrality of the state in the case of the rights of individuals who deviate from perceived orthodox religious norms. While many Indonesians could accommodate some religious rights, such as the right to change and adopt a new religion and the right to have inter-religious marriage, many others claim that heretical Islam is strictly prohibited as such a right threatens the Islamic faith. Many Muslims believe that allowing heretical views within Islamic teachings equates with an attack not only on the foundations of the state but also the very essence of religious life within the society.[177] This problem illustrates that Muslims seek an Islamic foundation for human rights. An appropriate solution to overcome human rights problems in Islamic society is therefore to combine religious and secular human rights approaches and not to merely adopt the Western concept of secularism.[178]

Looking at Islam, as the majority religion, to resolve problems of religious minorities within Islam in Indonesia is aimed at getting religious legitimacy because Islam, law and human rights discourse are interdependent. On many occasions, Islam is perceived as a system of belief which contains legal, ethical and moral principles that distinguishes it from other communities. The more Islamic religious perspectives are excluded from human rights discussion, particularly the discussion to resolve problems of religious minorities within Islam, the less likely it is going to be that religious adherents (Muslims) will accept the universality of human rights.[179] Thus the effort to establish a quasi-theistic secularism in Indonesia which does not disregard religious values as one necessary source of law and morality can be seen from the first principle of Pancasila, which provides a basic secular principle of equidistance between all religions in the Indonesian state. Surely, the existence of that principle has an impact on how Islam and the Indonesian state go together.

However, the state should be capable of balancing competing claims among religious adherents because some Islamic religious leaders are becoming, or attempting to become, a new kind of broker for a different sort of culture.[180] This illustrates that the biggest struggle to establish a relationship between the

177 See and compare with Kilian Bälz, 'Submitting Faith to Judicial Scrutiny through the Family Trial: The "Abu Zayd Case"' (1997) 37 *Die Welt des Islams* 135, 150.

178 An-Na'im and Othman propose slightly different methods of reinterpreting Islam on human rights. Othman seeks to liberalise Islam, and is somewhat indifferent to international human rights law, while An-Na'im, by contrast, seeks an Islamic foundation for international human rights law. See Michael Freeman, 'The Problem of Secularism in Human Rights Theory' (2004) 26 *Human Rights Quarterly* 375, 381.

179 An-Na'im (n 175) 61.

180 Geertz (n 30) 4.

state and religion is to protect religious values as one of the sources of law from a corrupt power, which usually allows partial acknowledgement of rights and freedoms or establishes a very strict condition for certain groups and individuals. This reality is very challenging as some Indonesian Muslims still refuse to acknowledge particular human rights norms if the application of such norms threatens Islamic orthodoxy. For example, they do not acknowledge the rights of religious minorities within Islam to claim to be the followers of Islam because this norm may cause disharmony among Islamic religious adherents.

Most Muslim leaders generally determine an authoritative Islamic orthodoxy or allow a certain kind of heterodoxy based on their version of Islamic law. This role in the Indonesian context is frequently played by the MORA, MUI and Islamic mass organisations. These three institutions act as the guardians of Islam and form an exclusive Islamic community. They have determined to exclude groups or individuals from the community who do not share common values, including religious orthodoxy. It is submitted that the claim of religious orthodoxy might endanger the idea of religious pluralism and the recognition of freedom of religion or beliefs for religious minorities within Islam, which habitually constitute the distinctive character of Islamic teaching.

In Indonesia, like in many other Muslim societies, Islam is perceived by its adherents as a complex religious system serving numerous functions including both unifying and conflictive.[181] Thus, keeping religious pluralism in Indonesia as well as helping religious minorities within Islam is very complex because it contains the inextricable relationship between religion, culture, state law and international human rights instruments.[182] It is not simply a matter of accommodating competing claims to religious truth in the private domain of individual faith but it also remains inherently a matter of public policy.[183] Muslim sects and divisions in Indonesia – and apparently in many Muslim societies – have a common belief as the most authoritative Islamic groups and see themselves as the only true Islamic religious sects. From the previous observation, it is submitted that in societies like Indonesia, where religion has a strong influence, such claims are usually owned by the Islamic majorities and become absolute. Thus the recognition of religious freedom or beliefs is a significant cornerstone of the establishment of religious-democratic pluralism, because pluralism not only means the existence of a diversity of interests and competing value systems but also denotes how these different interests and value systems are moderated by means of a democratic mechanism.[184] This idealistic condition can be better achieved when the majority and minority share an egalitarian and liberal concept of human rights in the public sphere as a fair

181 Daniels (n 44) 6.

182 For further discussion on four elements of jurisprudence, see Werner F Menski, 'Flying Kites in a Global Sky: New Models of Jurisprudence' (2011) 7 *Socio-legal Review* 1, 56.

183 Abdulaziz Sachedina, *The Islamic Roots of Democratic Pluralism* (Oxford University Press 2001) 3.

184 Hilmy (n 124) 4.

contestation arena to build universal humanity. If the concepts are widely accepted by a population, basically determined by the majority, then the norms easily become legitimate.

Bibliography

Alatas SF, 'The Ṭarīqat Al-'Alawiyyah and the Emergence of the Shi'i School in Indonesia and Malaysia' (1999) 79 *Oriente Moderno* 323.

Alfitri, 'Religious Liberty in Indonesia and the Rights of "Deviant" Sects' (2008) 3 *Asian Journal of Comparative Law* 1.

An-Na'im AA, 'Re-Affirming Secularism for Islamic Societies' (2003) 20 *New Perspectives Quarterly* 36.

———, 'The Interdependence of Religion, Secularism, and Human Rights: Prospects for Islamic Societies' (2005) 11 *Common Knowledge* 56.

———, *Islam and the Secular State* (Harvard University Press 2009).

An-Na'im A and edited by Baderin MA *Islam and Human Rights: Selected Essays of Abdullahi An-Na'im* (Routledge 2017).

As'ad M, 'Seruan Jihad KH Hasyim Asy'ari Selain Resolusi Jihad' (*NU Online* 14 April 2018) <www.nu.or.id/post/read/88764/seruan-jihad-kh-hasyim-asyari-selain-resolusi-jihad> accessed 18 May 2019.

Assyaukanie L, 'Fatwa and Violence in Indonesia' (2009) 11 *Journal of Religion and Society* 1 <https://dspace.creighton.edu/xmlui/handle/10504/64439> accessed 11 October 2016.

———, *Islam and the Secular State in Indonesia* (Institute of Southeast Asian Studies 2009).

Atkinson JM, 'Religions in Dialogue: The Construction of an Indonesian Minority Religion' (1983) 10 *American Ethnologist* 684.

Atsushi O, Masaaki O and Suaedy A *Islam in Contention: Rethinking Islam and State in Indonesia* (The Wahid Institute 2010).

Azra A and Hudson W, 'Religious Pluralism in Indonesia', in Azyumardi Azra and Wayne Hudson (eds), *Islam beyond Conflict: Indonesian Islam and Western Political Theory* (Ashgate Publishing 2008) 12.

Azra A and Salim A, 'Islamizing Capitalism, On the Founding of Indonesia's First Islamic Bank', in Azyumardi Azra and Arskal Salim, *Shari'a and Politics in Modern Indonesia* (Institute of Southeast Asian Studies 2003) 56.

Bälz K, 'Submitting Faith to Judicial Scrutiny through the Family Trial: The "Abu Zayd Case"' (1997) 37 *Die Welt des Islams* 135.

Barton G, *Abdurrahman Wahid: Muslim Democrat, Indonesian President : A View from the Inside* (UNSW Press 2002).

Boland BJ, *The Struggle of Islam in Modern Indonesia* (Springer 2013).

Bolton R, 'Plato's Distinction between Being and Becoming' (1975) 29 *The Review of Metaphysics* 66.

Bowen JR, *Islam, Law, and Equality in Indonesia: An Anthropology of Public Reasoning* (Cambridge University Press 2003).

Boyle K and Sheen J, *Freedom of Religion and Belief: A World Report* (Routledge 2013).

Bruinessen M van, 'Studies of Sufism and the Sufi Orders in Indonesia' (1998) 38 *Die Welt des Islams* 192.

Burhanudin J, 'Aspiring for Islamic Reform: Southeast Asian Requests for Fatwās in al-Manār' (2005) 12 *Islamic Law and Society* 9.

Clarke P, 'Sects in Islam', in Peter B Clarke (ed.), *The Oxford Handbook of the Sociology of Religion* (Oxford University Press 2011) 2.

Croft-Cusworth C, 'Islam and Tolerance in Indonesia' (*Lowy Institute* 4 November 2014) <www.lowyinstitute.org/the-interpreter/islam-and-tolerance-indonesia> accessed 18 May 2019.

Daniels T, *Islamic Spectrum in Java* (Routledge 2016).

de Jonge H, 'Discord and Solidarity among the Arabs in the Netherlands East Indies, 1900–1942' (1993) 55 *Indonesia* 73.

Dijk C van, 'State-Islam Relations in Contemporary Indonesia: 1915–1990', in Cees van Dijk and Alexander de Groot, *State and Islam* (Research School CNWS 1995) 102.

Effendy B, *Islam and the State in Indonesia* (Institute of Southeast Asian Studies 2003).

——— *Islam in the Contemporary Indonesian Politics* (Ushul Press 2006).

Eliraz G, *Islam in Indonesia: Modernism, Radicalism, and the Middle East Dimension* (Sussex Academic Press 2004).

Elson RE, *The Idea of Indonesia: A History* (Cambridge University Press 2008).

Erlando R, *Said Aqil Membela Mati-Matian #SYIAH Iran* (Forum Kyai Muda 2013).

Fadl KAE, *Islam and the Challenge of Democracy: A Boston Review Book* (Princeton University Press 2015).

Fealy G and White S, '"As Long as It's Halal": Islamic Preman in Jakarta', in Greg Fealy and Sally White (eds), *Expressing Islam: Religious Life and Politics in Indonesia* (Institute of Southeast Asian Studies 2008) 45.

———, 'Online Fatwa in Indonesia: From Fatwa Shopping to Googling a Kyai', in Greg Fealy and Sally White (eds), *Expressing Islam: Religious Life and Politics in Indonesia* (Institute of Southeast Asian Studies 2008) 1.

Federspiel HM, *Islam and Ideology in the Emerging Indonesian State: The Persatuan Islam (Persis), 1923–1957* (Brill 2001).

Feener RM, *Muslim Legal Thought in Modern Indonesia* (Cambridge University Press 2007).

Feener RM and Cammack ME, 'Muslim Legal Thought in Modern Indonesia: Introduction and Overview', in R Michael Feener and Mark E Cammack (eds), *Islamic Law in Contemporary Indonesia: Ideas and Institutions* (Harvard University Press 2007) 14.

Freeman M, 'The Problem of Secularism in Human Rights Theory' (2004) 26 *Human Rights Quarterly* 375.

Geertz C, 'The Javanese Kijaji: The Changing Role of a Cultural Broker' (1960) 2 *Comparative Studies in Society and History* 228.

———, *Islam Observed: Religious Development in Morocco and Indonesia* (University of Chicago Press 1971).

Gillespie P, 'Current Issues in Indonesian Islam: Analysing the 2005 Council of Indonesian Ulama Fatwa No. 7 Opposing Pluralism, Liberalism and Secularism' (2007) 18 *Journal of Islamic Studies* 202.

Hasan Z, 'The Indonesian Experience in Implementing Democracy', in Zoya Hasan, *Democracy in Muslim Societies: The Asian Experience* (SAGE Publications 2007) 56.

Hasugian MR, 'Menag: Resmi Atau Tidak Agama Bukan Otoritas Saya' (*Tempo*, 27 July 2014).

'Hasyim Muzadi: Sebaiknya Ahmadiyah Jadi Agama Sendiri' (*Republika Online* 7 February 2011) <https://republika.co.id/berita/breaking-news/nasional/11/02/07/162871-hasyim-muzadi-sebaiknya-ahmadiyah-jadi-agama-sendiri> accessed 18 May 2019.

Hefner RW, 'Public Islam and the Problem of Democratization' (2001) 62 *Sociology of Religion* 491.

———, *Civil Islam: Muslims and Democratization in Indonesia* (Princeton University Press 2011).
Hilmy M, *Islamism and Democracy in Indonesia: Piety and Pragmatism* (Institute of Southeast Asian Studies 2010).
Hooker MB, *Indonesian Islam: Social Change through Contemporary Fatåawåa* (University of Hawaii Press 2003).
———, *Indonesian Syariah: Defining a National School of Islamic Law* (Institute of Southeast Asian Studies 2008).
Hooker VM and Saikal A, *Islamic Perspectives on the New Millennium* (Institute of Southeast Asian Studies 2004a).
———, 'Perspective on Shari'a and the State', in Virginia Hooker and Amin Saikal (eds), *Islamic Perspectives on the New Millennium* (Institute of Southeast Asian Studies 2004b) 33.
Hosen N, 'Religion and the Indonesian Constitution: A Recent Debate' (2005) 36 *Journal of Southeast Asian Studies* 419.
Houben VJH, 'Southeast Asia and Islam' (2003) 588 *The Annals of the American Academy of Political and Social Science* 149.
Hwang JC, *Peaceful Islamist Mobilization in the Muslim World: What Went Right* (Springer 2009).
Ichwan MN, ''Ulamā', State and Politics: Majelis Ulama Indonesia after Suharto' (2005) 12 *Islamic Law and Society* 45.
Kaptein N, 'Introduction' (2005) 12 *Islamic Law and Society* 1.
Khanif A, 'Questioning a Theistic, Secular Pancasila to Protect Religions' (*The Jakarta Post* 6 January 2015).
———, 'NU Must Deal with Members' Persecution of Minorities' (*The Jakarta Post* 5 August 2015) <www.thejakartapost.com/news/2015/08/05/nu-must-deal-with-members-persecution-minorities.html> accessed 16 October 2017.
Kosel S, 'The History of Islam in Bolaang Mongondow, North Sulawesi' (2010) 38 *Indonesia and the Malay World* 43.
Laffan M, 'The Fatwā Debated? Shūrā in One Indonesian Context' (2005) 12 *Islamic Law and Society* 93.
Lev DS, *Legal Evolution and Political Authority in Indonesia: Selected Essays* (Martinus Nijhoff Publishers 2000).
Lindsey T, *Indonesia: Law and Society* (Federation Press 1999).
———, 'The State and Syariah in Indonesia 1945–1995', in Tim Lindsey (ed.), *Indonesia: Law and Society* (Federation Press 2008) 186.
Lipton EP, *Religious Freedom in Asia* (Nova Publishers 2002).
Mayer AE, 'Islam and Justice: Debating the Future of Human Rights in the Middle East and North Africa (Review)' (1997) 19 *Human Rights Quarterly* 875.
Menski WF, *Comparative Law in a Global Context: The Legal Systems of Asia and Africa* (Cambridge University Press 2006).
———, 'Flying Kites in a Global Sky: New Models of Jurisprudence' (2011) 7 *Socio-Legal Review* 1.
Mulder JN, 'Aliran Kebatinan as an Expression of the Javanese Worldview' (1970) 1 *Journal of Southeast Asian Studies* 105.
Noer D, *The Modernist Muslim Movement in Indonesia, 1900–1942* (Oxford University Press 1973).
Nuh NM and Rosidi A, 'Kasus Salafi Versus Non-Ṣalafi di Kabupaten Lombok Barat Nusa Tenggara Barat', in Ahmad Syafi'i Mufid (ed.), *Kasus-Kasus Aliran/Faham Keagamaan*

Aktual Di Indonesia (Departemen Agama, Badan Litbang Agama Dan Diklat Keagamaan, Puslitbang Kehidupan Beragama 2006) 4.

Office for Democratic Institutions and Human Rights, *Guidelines on the Legal Personality of Religious or Belief Communities* (Office for Democratic Institutions and Human Rights 2014).

Peacock JL, 'The Creativity of Tradition in Indonesian Religion' (1986) 25 *History of Religions* 341.

Pew Forum on Religion and Public Life, 'Muslim Population of Indonesia: Pew Research Center' (4 November 2010) <www.pewforum.org/2010/11/04/muslim-population-of-indonesia/> accessed 15 May 2019.

Platzdasch B, 'Religious Freedom in Indonesia: The Case of the Ahmadiyah' (2011) 2 ISEAS Working Paper on Politics and Security Series.

Pompe S, 'Islamic Law in Indonesia' (1997) 4 *YB Islamic & Middle EL* 180.

Pringle R, *Understanding Islam in Indonesia: Politics and Diversity* (Editions Didier Millet 2010).

Race A and Shafer IH, 'Democracy at the Heart of Islam', in Alan Race and Ingrid H Shafer (eds), *Religions in Dialogue: From Theocracy to Democracy* (Ashgate 2002) 107.

Rais AIM, 'Muhammadiyah's "Progressive Islam": Guideline or Tagline?' (*Jakarta Post*, 3 August 2015) <www.thejakartapost.com/news/2015/08/03/muhammadiyah-s-progressive-islam-guideline-or-tagline.html> accessed 16 May 2019.

Ramage DE, *Politics in Indonesia: Democracy, Islam, and the Ideology of Tolerance* (Routledge 1995) <http://search.ebscohost.com/login.aspx?direct=true&scope=site&db=nlebk&db=nlabk&AN=76332> accessed 14 July 2016.

Revianur A, 'Din: Muhammadiyah Keberatan Fatwa Sesat Syiah' (*KOMPAS.com*) <https://nasional.kompas.com/read/2012/09/07/09330267/Din.Muhammadiyah.Keberatan.Fatwa.Sesat.Syiah> accessed 18 May 2019.

Rumadi, *Islamic Post-Traditionalism in Indonesia* (ISEAS – Yusof Ishak Institute 2015).

Sachedina A *The Islamic Roots of Democratic Pluralism* (Oxford University Press 2001).

Saeed A, 'Towards Religious Tolerance through Reform in Islamic Education: The Case of the State Institute of Islamic Studies of Indonesia' (1999) 27 *Indonesia and the Malay World* 177.

———, 'Interpreting the Quranic Principle of Religious Pluralism', in Abdulla Saeed (ed.), *Approaches to the Qur'an in Contemporary Indonesia* (Oxford University Press 2005) 221.

Saleh F, *Modern Trends in Islamic Theological Discourse in 20th Century Indonesia: A Critical Survey* (Brill 2001).

Salim A, '"Sharia from Below" in ACEH (1930s–1960s): Islamic Identity and the Right to Self-determination with Comparative Reference to the Moro Islamic Liberation Front (MILF)' (2004) 32 *Indonesia and the Malay World* 80.

———, *Challenging the Secular State: The Islamization of Law in Modern Indonesia* (University of Hawaii Press 2008).

Salim A and Azra A, 'Islamic Values, Law and Expectations in Contemporary Indonesia', in Arskal Salim and Azyumardi Azra (eds), *Shari'a and Politics in Modern Indonesia* (Institute of Southeast Asian Studies 2003) 12.

Sihombing UP, 'MENGGUGAT Bakor Pakem: Kajian hukum terhadap pengawasan agama dan kepercayaan di Indonesia/Uli Parulian Sihombing, Fulthoni, Dadang Trisasongko' (2008) (Indonesian Legal Resource Center 2008) 4.

Siregar HB, 'Islamic Law in a National Legal System: A Study on the Implementation of Shari'ah in Aceh, Indonesia' (2008) 3 *Asian Journal of Comparative Law* 1.

Sirry M, 'Fatwas and Their Controversy: The Case of the Council of Indonesian Ulama (MUI)' (2013) 44 *Journal of Southeast Asian Studies* 100.

Shah NA, *Women, the Koran and International Human Rights Law* (Brill 2006).

Sonn T, *Interpreting Islam: Bandali Jawzi's Islamic Intellectual History* (Oxford University Press 1996).

Suaedy A, 'Diskriminasi Hak Sipil Minoritas: Pelarangan Pencatatan Pernikahan Jemaat Ahmadiyah Kuningan', in Ahmad Suaedy, *Politisasi Agama dan Konflik Komunal: Beberapa Isu Penting di Indonesia* (The Wahid Institute 2007a) 45.

———, 'Pengawasan Negara Terhadap Kehidupan Sipil: Kasus Penyesatan Dan Kriminalisasi Yusman Roy', in Ahmad Suaedy, *Politisasi Agama dan Konflik Komunal: Beberapa Isu Penting di Indonesia* (The Wahid Institute 2007b) 44.

Subakir A, 'Menyoal Fatwa MUI Tentang Larangan Aliran (Aqidah) Ahmadiyah' (2009) 6 *Jurnal Kontemplasi* 1.

Sukma R and Joewono C, 'Gerakan Salafi di Indonesia: Dari Wahabi Sampai Laskar Jihad', in Rizal Sukma and Clara Joewono, *Gerakan dan pemikiran Islam Indonesia kontemporer* (Centre for Strategic and International Studies 2007) 128.

Sullivan WF, 'Religion, Law and the Construction of Identities. Introduction' (1996) 43 *Numen* 128.

Tayob A, *Religion in Modern Islamic Discourse* (Hurst Publishers 2009).

van der Kroef JM, 'The Role of Islam in Indonesian Nationalism and Politics' (1958) 11 *The Western Political Quarterly* 33.

4 The complex reality of religious minorities within Islam in Indonesia

1. The discourse of *forum internum* and *forum externum* in international human rights law

As discussed in Chapter 2, the existence of rights for religious minorities, for both intra and inter religious minorities, are basically covered by different international human rights instruments. Based on the factual phenomena of minorities as vulnerable groups of people, religious minorities may receive special rights because this kind of group not only deserves equal rights but also positive measures such as effective protection from the state.[1] Based on Asma Jahangir's report submitted to the HRC in 2003, "one of the main reasons is that minority groups, and particularly religious minorities, are often directly targeted for extra-judicial execution in many countries".[2] Such persecutions are often a consequence of the external manifestation of their religion or beliefs. This means that there should be a synergic relation between international human rights law and domestic law on the regulation of *forum internum* and *forum externum* to protect vulnerable religious groups globally.

International human rights instruments define *forum internum* as freedom of thought or conscience.[3] The HRC similarly points out that *forum internum* encompasses freedom of thought and conscience, or the freedom to have or to adopt a religion or belief of one's choice that is not susceptible to any limitation.[4] The HRC further asserts that freedom to have or to adopt a religion or belief necessarily entails the freedom to choose a religion or belief including, inter alia, the right to replace one's current religion or belief with another, or to adopt atheistic views, as well as the right to retain one's religion or belief.[5] Paul M. Taylor similarly argues that:

1 Nazila Ghanea, 'Are Religious Minorities Really Minorities?' (2012) 1 *Oxford Journal of Law and Religion* 57, 60.
2 E/CN.4/2004/7.2.
3 E/CN.4/2005/61.15.
4 General Comment No. 22, Compilation of General Comments and General Recommendations Adopted by Human Rights Treaty Bodies 2006 22.
5 ibid 345.

> *forum internum* is taken to denote the internal and private realm of the individual against which no state interference is justified in any circumstance. It does not only comprise an individual's "absolute freedom of choice of religion or belief" but also a range of additional freedoms (which shall be referred to as the residual scope of the *forum internum*).[6]

Based on this notion, the concept of religion in international human rights law deals with supernatural phenomena and involves belief, practice and moral prescriptions. It is concerned largely with spiritual matters and for the most part is viewed as a private, personal affair, separate and distinct from the more rational aspects of life.[7] As a consequence, the concept of *forum internum* in international human rights law is built around individual autonomy. Thus, the individual is the centre around which the protection of human rights is construed and legitimised.[8] It may be noted that *forum internum* is the internal source of religious rights and the protection of these rights is a touchstone for the protection of an individual's spiritual integrity, as all individuals are entitled to the right to be different and hold deviating thoughts and beliefs.[9]

Related to this unconditional right, Bart Labuschagne further argues that:

> a final rationale of the *forum internum* is that it guarantees that the believer is taken seriously when he adheres to a not established or known religion and invokes the protection of the freedom of religion. Even when a religion is not widely known, a judge should at least listen carefully to such a believer, in order to find out whether a protectable form of belief is at stake.[10]

This argument proposes that international human rights law regulates equal protection for individuals to profess a religion or belief of their choice. It protects a person from being defined by the terms of a dominant majority and is therefore an indispensable element of the freedom of religion.[11] The concept of *forum internum* asserts that the legal rationale of religious freedom in international human rights law is to manage the difference of religious beliefs and respect the right of others to have religions or beliefs as a matter of inherent rights for human beings.

6 Paul M Taylor, *Freedom of Religion: UN and European Human Rights Law and Practice* (Cambridge University Press 2005) 115.
7 Ahmad Yousif, 'Islam, Minorities and Religious Freedom: A Challenge to Modern Theory of Pluralism' (2000) 20 *Journal of Muslim Minority Affairs* 29, 30.
8 Bart Labuschagne, 'Recognition of Religious Differences under Dutch Law' (2000) 8 *Tilburg Law Review* 159, 65.
9 ibid 166.
10 ibid 165.
11 ibid 166.

Apart from the internal dimension of religious freedom (*forum internum*), the external dimension of religious freedom, known as *forum externum*, is also protected in several international human rights instruments. Those instruments recognise that everyone has the right to display their religion or belief in teaching, practice, worship and observance, either individually or in a community with others.[12] The HRC has additionally pronounced that religious manifestation, or *forum externum*, should be understood as referring to a broad range of acts as stated in the definition of religious freedom, such as inter alia the right to disseminate religious teaching, build places of worship and distribute religious texts or publications.[13] The *forum externum* is invoked both in terms of the positive freedom of persons who wish to wear or display religious symbols and in terms of the negative freedom of persons who do not want to be confronted or coerced. Those religious rights are an integral part of the *forum externum* of all religions and it is the obligation of every state to protect equally the exercise of religious freedom from every religious group.

However, one should bear in mind that *forum externum* can be restricted by law for reasons of public safety, order, health, morals or the fundamental rights of others. With regard to the justified legal limitation of *forum externum*, Jeroen Temperman argues that:

> The manifestation of one's religion is not an absolute right. A number of important interests are recognised as possible grounds for limitation of this second type of freedom. However, restrictions must be prescribed by law and must be necessary to protect other recognised interests. Grounds for limitation include public safety, order, health, morals and the fundamental human rights and freedoms of others.[14]

The limitation of religious manifestation prescribed by law is necessary to uphold the essential characteristic of human rights standards in democratic societies. It means that the restriction by law is important, especially in a state which endorses a particular religion as an integral part of its society, because the law adopted by parliament does not represent authoritarianism but more likely represents the democratic principle and will of the people.

The recognition of the rights and freedoms of others as one requirement to restrict *forum externum* is significant, because every religion has a community of believers which shares collective distinctive religious identity within its own group. Conversely, all individuals who belong to a particular religion should be

12 See *e.g.* article 18 of the UDHR and ICCPR and article 1 of the 1981 Declaration. Article 13 of the UIDHR similarly regulates that everyone has the right to worship in accordance with her or his religious belief.

13 Compilation of General Comments and General Recommendations Adopted by Human Rights Treaty Bodies 333.

14 Jeroen Temperman, *State–Religion Relationships and Human Rights Law: Towards a Right to Religiously Neutral Governance* (Brill 2010) 272.

aware that their religion also belongs to a wider community. It confirms that human beings do not live in a society where all members share a uniform religious belief.[15] Even though the nations of the world are now more interconnected, and the idea of one global village has become commonplace,[16] it seems that the nature of religions demonstrates that diversity and difference remain a key fact of human life. The interdependence of nations, societies and communities may in fact force us to encounter more complex religious issues, because people in any particular place will consequently come from a larger amount of various cultural and religious backgrounds.

Based on this multiplicity of religions, the state, through its legal organs, should regulate proportionately the external manifestation of all religious groups to ensure respect for the fundamental rights of others and to protect public order. This argument is substantiated by the view of the HRC that restrictive measures against the rights and freedoms of people must conform to the principle of proportionality. The Committee then noted that:

> The term proportionality means that such restrictions must be appropriate to achieve their protective function; they must be the least intrusive instrument amongst those which might achieve the desired result; and they must be proportionate to the interest to be protected.[17]

One effort to achieve the proportionality restriction is that the state parties, in principle, should maintain a pluralistic view of public morals.[18] This means that the recognition of official religions and a preferred version of religious teaching by the state parties are theoretically still compatible with article 18 of the ICCPR, as long as they would not be used to discriminate against unrecognised minority religions and unofficial religious teachings from the official religions.

It must be noted that the principle of proportionality to control the practise of religion is meant to protect individuals and communities as adherents of religion, rather than the doctrine of religion itself. The restriction would contain proportionate interference if unease among adherents of certain religions occurred as a consequence of maintaining public order and morals and the fundamental rights of others. For example, the District Court of South Jakarta sentenced Agus Imam Solichin – who claimed he was the Promised Messiah – to two years in prison because he commanded his followers to engage in sexual

15 Jonathan Chaplin, 'Law, Religion and Public Reasoning' (2012) 1 *Oxford Journal of Law and Religion* 319, 319.

16 Arif A Jamal, 'Models of Pluralistic Discourse: A Consideration of the Ismaili Muslim Conciliation and Arbitration Boards in Kenya' (2001) 8 *Yearbook of Islamic and Middle Eastern Law* 86, 87.

17 Compilation of General Comments and General Recommendations Adopted by Human Rights Treaty Bodies 175.

18 Sarah Joseph and Melissa Castan, *The International Covenant on Civil and Political Rights: Cases, Materials, and Commentary* (Oxford University Press Oxford 2013) 577.

intercourse together in one room as a religious ritual.[19] This case suggests that the restriction was applied, not due to Solichin's claim as Messiah, but instead because of the resultant amoral behaviour prohibited under article 289 of the Indonesian Criminal Law. In relation to the *forum externum* right of religious minorities within Islam in Indonesia, discriminatory treatment can be seen from the enactment of Law No. 1/PNPS/1965, or the Blasphemy Law which, among others, restricts non-mainstream versions of Islamic interpretations due to the official recognition of Islam in Indonesia, even though the justification is usually about protecting public order.

2. Freedom to embrace and practise religion in Islamic law

The guarantee of the freedom to embrace religious beliefs in Islamic law can be found in several verses of the Qur'an. For instance, the Qur'an (2:256) clearly regulates that there is no compulsion in religion and emphasises that the non-duress principle to embrace religion is a divine mandate (18:29). The verse says that God addresses his prophet to believe that this truth (Islam) is from your lord, so whoever wills, let him believe, and whoever wills, let him disbelieve. These verses assert that, in principle, Islam provides a religious freedom that is the domain of every individual. Neither the state nor the religious organisations can force Muslims to adopt Islamic belief, because individuals must be willing to comply with Islam in order for their belief to be sincere.

Interpreting the Qur'an (2:256), Niaz Shah opines that the verse in principle asserts that individuals cannot be forced to embrace Islam and that, when she/he becomes a Muslim, nobody can force her/him to follow other Muslims and their beliefs.[20] Thus, all schools of thought in Islam are valid. This argument is also asserted by the Qur'an (4:59), which instructs Muslims to refer any disagreement among Muslims to God and His Prophet. Thus, the verse asserts that in theory Islam acknowledges intra-Islamic pluralism as part of *forum internum* in Islamic law and prevents Muslims from forcing monolithic Islamic teachings on their fellows.

In the history of Islam, there has been a spectrum of struggles over the rights of minority religions and religious minorities within Islam, even though the Qur'an clearly stipulates that there is no compulsion in the religion. The Qur'an supports freedom of belief and affirms that the objectives of Islamic law cannot be fulfilled properly without granting individuals freedom of belief and the freedom to express it.[21] Here, the right to express oneself should be noted inter alia as the right to practise and proselytise one's religious belief as part of the

19 'Monthly Report on Religious Issues' (The Wahid Institute 2011) 38, 3–5.

20 Niaz Shah, 'Freedom of Religion: Koranic and Human Rights Perspectives' (2005) 6 *Asia-Pacific Journal on Human Rights and the Law* 69, 71.

21 Kamali Mohammad Hashim, 'Freedom of Expression in Islam' (2009) 31 *International Journal of Middle East Studies* 450, 103.

recognition of *forum externum*, a principal norm of religious freedom in Islam. This means that in principle Islam not only expects, but also accepts, the reality of difference and diversity within human society. All human diversities are part of divine intent and purpose because God created human beings within diverse nations in order that human beings could know one another.[22]

The Islamic jurisprudence on the rights of religious minorities within Islam can be seen from the case of the Kharijites, which occurred in the very early period of Islam. In this case, the fourth Caliph, Ali b. Abi Thalib, did not declare the Kharijites to be infidels, even though most Muslims at that time regarded them as transgressors. Instead Caliph Ali said that a person who seeks the truth but makes an error is never the same as a person who seeks falsehood and then proceeds to commit it.[23] Also, dissenting opinions about injunctions of the Qur'an were demonstrated by different Muslim leaders in the early days of Islam. For instance, the second Caliph, Umar b. Khattab, on one occasion after a particular war campaign, refrained from taking the booty explicitly prescribed in the Qur'an because he argued that to do so would violate the spirit of the Qur'an in the existing situation of hardship.[24] These findings suggest that Muslims should also realise that Muslim dissenters have existed since the time of the Prophet Muhammad, emerging all throughout Islamic history and up to recent times.

The leading jurists of Islamic jurisprudence agree that it is unlawful to attribute disbelief to anyone merely on the grounds of difference of opinion.[25] The fact that this does not match a lived reality is another matter. Interpreting the Qur'an (4: 94), Hashim Kamali also argues that

> the utterance of the greeting of peace (*salam*) is evidence enough to establish a presumption in favour of a person being a believer, and hence the Quran does not permit inquisitions of any kind to establish the Islamic status of individuals.[26]

This Qur'anic principle is emphasised further in a Prophetic Hadith, which states "whoever prays our prayer, facing the *qiblah* that we face and eats what we have slaughtered, is a Muslim and shall have the same rights and obligations as we have".[27] Based on this discussion, the Qur'an and Hadith, as two supreme

22 See Qur'an 49: 13.
23 Mohammad Hashim (n 21) 186.
24 Amina Wadud, 'Towards a Qur'anic Hermeneutics of Social Justice: Race, Class and Gender' (1995) 12 *Journal of Law and Religion* 37, 44.
25 Mohammad Hashim (n 21) 187.
26 ibid. The translation of the Qur'an (4: 94): "Say not to those who greet you with peace (al-salam): 'you are not a believer'". Kamali: 187 also notes that Ibn Hazm argues that anyone who has uttered the testimonial faith (*kalimat al-shahadah*) and declared faith in the mission and guidance of the Prophet Muhammad is a Muslim.
27 ibid 187–188.

sources of Islamic law, clearly recognise internal plurality of Islamic belief. The Islamic jurisprudence (*fiqh*), which upholds the death sentence for allegedly heretical, blasphemous or any kind of heterodox Islamic teaching, is in conflict with the explicit provision of the religious pluralism of Islamic law. It can also be argued that the belief *forum internum*, as an unconditional right in Islam, can only be confirmed through a person's external manifestation and practise of such a belief (*forum externum*). Individuals cannot properly embrace Islam if they cannot practise their individual religious beliefs.

In relation to non-Muslim minorities, Islamic history also demonstrates the recognition of *forum externum* as a significant element of freedom of religion for all religions. For instance, in the Ummayad period, the governor of Kufa, Hajjaj bin Yusuf, wrote a letter to Muhammad bin Qasim regarding the request from the Hindus and Buddhists of India to restore temples and uphold their religious rights. Hajjaj emphasised that the Muslim ruler had no right whatsoever to interfere in the lives and property of other people, and should permit them to follow their own religion.[28] Similar to that, Umar b. Khattab also showed equal reverence towards the holy site of the Jews when he conquered Jerusalem in 638, while Ali b. Abi Thalib underscored the legal equality between Muslims and the protected minorities (*dhimma*) by saying that the compensation for the killing of a Christian or Jew was the same as that for a Muslim.[29]

Based on this discussion, the Qur'an and the Hadith, as two supreme sources of Islamic law, recognise the plurality of religious beliefs, including differences of opinion (*ikhtilaf*) between Islamic teachings among Muslims. Islam recognises far-reaching *forum internum* because it enjoins Muslims to respect the internal plurality of Islamic belief. Islam also acknowledges that the right to practise a religion or belief or *forum internum*, and the right to embrace a religion or belief or *forum externum*, are two interrelated domains because Muslims cannot properly embrace Islam if they cannot practise their individual religious belief. Islamic jurisprudence, which upholds the death sentence, as stated, is basically in conflict not only with the international conception of religious freedom but also with the explicit provision of religious pluralism in Islamic law.

In several Muslim-majority states, however, there has been repression of religious dissidents – some as apostates or blasphemers, some as heretics or renegades and some simply as infidels. The issue of sects or minority religious movements in Islam is complicated by the fact that international human rights instruments do not provide clear definitions of the concepts of religion, sects or new religious movements. In fact, sects are part and parcel of the phenomenon

28 Reza Shah-Kazemi, *The Spirit of Tolerance in Islam* (IB Tauris 2012) 60.

29 ibid 66–68. Kazemi reported that Umar declined to perform prayer in the Church of the Holy Sepulchre, not for theological reasons but more about his fear that his action may later be taken as a pretext to convert the church into a mosque by Muslims.

of religion. Yet the terms "blasphemers, apostates, heretics and infidels" demonstrate that the term "sects" in Islam, and in some other world religions, now has a pejorative connotation and is frequently regarded as being synonymous with danger, sometimes with a non-religious dimension.[30]

These religious persecutions suggest that Islamic law, as applied by some Muslim-majority states or understood by Muslims in those states, is based on interpretations developed from early Muslim jurists and is fundamentally inconsistent with modern notions of constitutionalism and international human rights law. The persecution of religious minorities within Islam is also perhaps the most controversial and serious human rights violation of religious freedom in many Muslim-majority states today. In relation to this case, Arzt has identified that such religious persecution can generally be grouped into three categories; (1) state-sanctioned enforcement; (2) extra-legal enforcement of apostasy decrees issued by vigilante groups; and (3) mixed cases.[31] These three categories frequently result in multiple negative impacts for religious minorities within Islam, not only for their religious freedom, but also other rights and freedoms.

An example of state-sanctioned enforcement in the Muslim world can be seen in the execution of the Sudanese Muslim reformer, Mahmoud Taha, in 1985. His egalitarian interpretation of Islam, and his call for the establishment of a more just Islamic socialist economic order (in which men and women, Muslims and non-Muslims, had equal rights), was alleged to be heretical and apostate by the Nimeiri regime.[32] Also, in 1996, the Egyptian Court of Cassation ruled that the Egyptian Muslim scholar Nasr Abu Zayd's writings on Islam constituted an act of apostasy.[33] Under traditional Islamic law, apostasy (*ridda*) has far-reaching consequences, ranging from the death penalty to dissolution of marriage and disinheritance.[34] In 2012, the Egyptian government also sentenced a Shi'ah teacher, Mohammed Asfour, to one year in jail for contempt of religion and charged Bassem Youssef, a Sunni comedian and satirist, with insulting Islam in his popular television programme.[35]

30 Donna E Arzt, 'Heroes or Heretics: Religious Dissidents under Islamic Law' (1996) 14 *Wisconsin International Law Journal* 349, 418.

31 ibid 144.

32 See a detailed explanation about this case in Abdullahi Ahmed An-Na'im, 'The Islamic Law of Apostasy and Its Modern Applicability: A Case from the Sudan' (1986) 16 *Religion* 197, 197–224.

33 The court's reasoning was that Nasr Abu Zayd had denied that the Qur'an was the word of God, describing it as "a cultural product" and as being affiliated to a human culture, rendering it an incarnated human text. He described Islam as an Arabic religion, denying its universality and availability to everybody. See detail in Maurits Berger, 'Apostasy and Public Policy in Contemporary Egypt: An Evaluation of Recent Cases from Egypt's Highest Courts' (2003) 25 *Human Rights Quarterly* 720, 720 & 731.

34 Kilian Bälz, 'Submitting Faith to Judicial Scrutiny through the Family Trial: The "Abu Zayd Case"' (1997) 37 *Die Welt des Islams* 135, 137.

35 Katrina Lantos Swett and Mary Ann Glendon, 'Egypt Breaks Faith on Religious Freedom' (*Al-Monitor* 2013).

In the Islamic Republic of Pakistan, where Islamic law is recognised as part of state law, the rights of minorities within Islam have become deeply problematic. Even though its constitution clearly states that every citizen has the right to practise and propagate her/his religion, and every religious denomination and sect thereof shall have the right to establish, maintain and manage its religious institution,[36] the constitutional interpretation of religious rights is generally monopolised by the religious majority to oppress minorities. The Ahmadiyah in Pakistan have been declared non-Muslims since the 1970s. In 1984, Ordinance XX pronounced that the use of certain Islamic epithets by the Ahmadiyah, descriptions and titles, were banned.[37] The Ahmadiyah was charged with blasphemy for actions including wearing an Islamic slogan on a shirt, planning to build an Ahmadiyah mosque and distributing Ahmadiyah literature in a public square.[38] Ahmadiyah members are prohibited from any public expression of their faith because the Pakistani government argues that Ahmadiyah religious practice (in any form) offends the country's Sunni majority.[39]

This kind of restriction is generally adopted by states solely to eliminate non-mainstream religious beliefs. Many states consider that the non-mainstream religions, allegedly deviant religions or foreign religions, are the main source of public unrest and should be eliminated, adjusted or transformed into the majority version. Still to this day, some countries prefer to restrict the rights of minority religions to preserve religious and social harmony, rather than protect them.[40] They perceive minorities as a negation of the majority, undeserving of any rights, and hence states prefer to uphold assimilation by allowing the dominant group to simultaneously universalise itself and particularise the minority as "the other".[41] If the minority resists against the majority perspective of commonality, then the majority defines them as abnormal or deviant. In the context of religious freedom, the word "deviant" derives from the consent of the religious majority to preserve religious orthodoxy. These findings confirm that, in general, there is inequality between religious minorities and the majority, even though all cultures and religions should be equal because there is no superiority of cultures and religions over the others.[42]

36 See Article 20 of Pakistan's Constitution.

37 See article 298-B and C of Ordinance XX.

38 Amjad Mahmood Khan, 'Persecution of the Ahmadiyya Community in Pakistan: An Analysis under International Law and International Relations' 16 *Harvard Human Rights Journal* (2003) 28, 219.

39 Paul Marshall and Nina Shea, *Silenced: How Apostasy and Blasphemy Codes Are Choking Freedom Worldwide* (Oxford University Press USA 2011) 90.

40 For some further information about restriction against minority religions, see Taylor (n 6) 197–198.

41 Adeno Addis, 'Individualism, Communitarianism, and the Rights of Ethnic Minorities' 67 *Notre Dame Law Review* 63, 1224.

42 See Henry J Steiner, Philip Alston and Ryan Goodman, *International Human Rights in Context: Law, Politics, Morals: Text and Materials* (Oxford University Press 2008) 610.

The second type of religious persecution is the extra-legal enforcement of apostasy. The involvement of a religious organisation that sanctions apostasy or blasphemy frequently triggers communal conflict in mixed cases. If not conflict, then it may spur majority groups to persecute individuals or religious minorities within Islam. This can be seen in the case of the murder of Faraq Fouda, one of Egypt's leading secular intellectuals, a vocal critic of militant Islamists as well as of the Egyptian government and an advocate of separation of state and religion. He was murdered by Gama'a al-Islamiya (GI) in June 1992 because his views were considered apostate.[43] Fouda was shot dead by a GI member who discovered a *fatwa* on permitting the killing of a blasphemer, which the extremist certainly considered Fouda to be.[44] The murderers were defended by a senior theologian, Sheik Ahmad Ghazali, who stated in court that Fouda and secularists like him were apostates who should be put to death by the government. The Sheik testified that if the government failed to carry out this duty, then the public should be free to do so instead.[45]

The 1986 blasphemy law in Pakistan that mandates fines, life imprisonment or the death penalty for anyone who insults religion (Islam) has also encouraged mobs to persecute so-called blasphemous individuals or religious minorities within Islam.[46] The Office of the UN High Commissioner for Human Rights (OHCHR), for example, reported that Ahmadiyah in Pakistan faced continuous threats, discrimination and violent attacks. The Ahmadiyah religious community had been declared non-Muslim and was then subjected to a number of undue restrictions and, in many instances, institutionalised discrimination.[47]

The persecution of religious minorities within Islam in the Muslim world suggests that many states actually act contrary to Islam, a religion that has always been subject to various interpretations since the Prophetic era. Their recent policies show that the restriction of religious minorities within Islam is primarily caused by political, social and traditional customs of the country, rather than Islamic law. Many Muslim rulers neglect the fact that one person's interpretation of Qur'anic verses and Hadiths is not identical to another's, even amongst scholars and religious leaders. The principle of *ikhtilaf* (difference of opinion) struggles to find acceptance, much like the Western-dominated principle of pluralism. The Qur'an itself, as a divine revelation, has been a source of different interpretations among Muslim scholars and has made Muslims well-acquainted with differences and diversity in the area of religion.[48] It is a fact that Islam is

43 Arzt (n 30) 145.

44 Luthfi Assyaukanie, 'Fatwa and Violence in Indonesia' (2009) 11 *Journal of Religion and Society* 3.

45 Donna E Arzt, 'The Role of Compulsion in Islamic Conversion: Jihad, Dhimma and Ridda' 8 *Buffalo Human Rights Law Review* 31, 43.

46 Arzt (n 30) 146.

47 OHCHR, *UN Experts Strongly Condemn attacks against Ahmadis in Pakistan* (28 May 2010).

48 Azyumardi Azra and Wayne Hudson, *Islam beyond Conflict: Indonesian Islam and Western Political Theory* (Ashgate 2008) 114.

primarily and essentially defined by the Qur'an and Sunna of the Prophet, but the interpretation and application of the scripts has always been conditioned by the understanding of the Muslim community at any given time and place.[49] As a consequence, while Islamic law will continue to be extremely important in shaping the human rights perspectives of Muslims, all Muslims must still be aware that there is no single interpretation of Islamic law, as Muslim civilisations have applied various conceptions of jurisprudences for over twelve centuries.[50]

3. The complex reality of religious minorities within Islam in Indonesia

It was officially reported by MORA that since the early 1950s the number of religious sects in Indonesia, including within Islam, has grown rapidly. By the middle of 1960, the Deputy Attorney General declared that there were hundreds of such sects throughout Indonesia, which caused the Indonesian government to express official alarm over the proliferation of religious sects.[51] According to official statistics, nearly 400 misleading religious cults are banned, including some Islamic groups that are considered heretical.[52] Until now, the government continues to restrict the religious right to *forum internum* of groups and individuals associated with forms of Islam viewed as outside the mainstream by arresting and charging individuals with heresy, blasphemy and insulting Islam.[53] Based on this policy, the exact number of religious sects is very uncertain, because they often identify themselves as adherents of one of the official religions to avoid persecution.

As the New Order government of Indonesia legally provides religious freedom to five accepted religions, all unrecognised religions are subject to restrictions even though, practically, people are still allowed to embrace them.[54] Adherents of non-recognised religions are free to profess and practise their religions or beliefs as long as they choose to write one of the five recognised religions on their identity cards. This state policy constitutes discrimination against people who embrace non-recognised religious minorities. From the 1970s until the late 1990s, the New Order government, through its watchdog institutions, often stigmatised religious minorities as Communist. Thus, many people who generally participate in Javanese mysticism feel threatened and refuse to register their membership because they have been associated with Communism or an anti-

49 Abdullahi An-Na'im, 'What Do We Mean by Universal?' (1994) 23 *Index on Censorship* 120, 123.

50 Ayla Karmali, 'Sharia and Muslim Legal Thought in the 21st Century: The Paths Ahead' (2006) 13 *Yearbook of Islamic and Middle Eastern Law Online* 3, 3.

51 Justus M van der Kroef, 'New Religious Sects in Java' (1961) 30 *Far Eastern Survey* 18, 18.

52 'Indonesia Annual Human Rights Report Submitted to Congress' (U.S.D.S. 1989) 856.

53 'Indonesia Religious Freedom Report' (United States Commission on International Religious Freedom 2007) 120–126.

54 'Indonesia Annual Human Rights Reports Submitted to Congress' (U.S.D.S. 1997) 772.

Islamic mentality.[55] This was especially so from the period following the *coup d'état* of 1965, which saw the departure of Communism from Indonesia.[56] To rid the country of atheist Communism, people have been put under pressure to acknowledge one of the recognised five religions. Some Islamic groups tried to force the syncretists to show that they had become mainstream obedient Muslims. Yet, most Javanese syncretists agree to be Muslim, as long as they do not have to change their lifestyle or abandon *kebatinan* (mysticism).[57]

After the decline of Communism, religious minorities within Islam were suspected of being puppets of imperialism, secularism, liberalism, Westernisation and anti-Islamic trends and were treated as enemies of Islam, even seen as infidels. Persecution against religious minorities within Islam has become epidemic within the allegedly successful blending of democracy and Islam in the country. Such sects are seen as threats against Islam in different strata, depending on how aggressive the propagation of their belief is. The government and Sunni majorities persecute them in the name of public order and for theological reasons. It is often claimed that the distinctive character of religious minorities within Islam is a threat, rather than representing the nature of Islam as a supposedly uniform – but in reality, immensely diverse – religious grouping. As an overwhelming majority, the Sunnis have the most authoritative religious interpretation and utilise it to accuse religious minorities within Islam as deviant. The Sunni majority habitually collaborates with the government to victimise the religious minorities within Islam to allegedly protect Islamic homogeneity. This suggests that the concept of unity in diversity, as the spirit of the nation, cannot be fully implemented by Indonesian Muslims because some of them still prefer to live in homogeneity or,[58] more precisely, wish to assert Islamic religious orthodoxy in the country.

The religious minorities within Islam in Indonesia accused of being deviant include the Shi'ah, Ahmadiyah, Mahesa Kurung, the bilingual prayer congregation and Inkar Sunnah. Additionally, there are Sunni minorities that have become victims: such as Islam Jamaah, a Messianic Indonesian Islamic group that latterly renamed itself as the Indonesian Islamic Propagation Board (Lembaga Dakwah Islam Indonesia, LDII). The discriminative treatment is not solely due to the difference in theological understanding among the Islamic sects and divisions, but is also related to social, cultural, political and legal reasons. Additionally, the character of persecution varies, ranging from officially state-

55 Jan Anton Niels Mulder, *Aliran Kebatinan as an Expression of the Javanese Worldview* (University of Singapore Department of History 1970) 108–109.

56 According to the decree of the People's Consultative Assembly No. XXV/1966, Communism, Leninism and Marxism were banned throughout the country because the principles of those teachings were not in accordance with the noble religious spirit of the Nation which believes in One Supreme God.

57 Mulder (n 55) 110.

58 Rumadi Ahmad and Ahmad Suaedy, *Politisasi Agama dan Konflik Komunal: Beberapa Isu Penting di Indonesia* (The Wahid Institute 2007) 2.

sanctioned enforcement actions to extra-legal enforcement of blasphemy by religious organisations and mixed cases, which will be further explained in the following section.

3.1. Officially state-sanctioned enforcement actions

The involvement of the state in religious matters, especially in defining the term blasphemy, is not new in the history of Indonesia. Blasphemy has even been used in a wider context, ranging from political and legal to religious reasons. For instance, the Soekarno Old Order (in office from 1945 until 1967) considered its political concept of "*nasakom*" (nationalism, religionalism and Communism) as a sacred policy. Every individual and organisation that refused to acknowledge this policy was seen as heretical. Thus, the *nasakom* concept triggered rebellions from Muslims in some regions, starting from the late 1940s until the early 1950s. Some Muslims in South Sulawesi, South Kalimantan, West Java and Aceh started to rebel against the central government because they argued that Soekarno policies, including the *nasakom* concept, did not mandate Muslims to obey and implement Islamic law.[59] Besides rebelling, these movements also persecuted syncretistic groups due to the allegation of being Communist. During that time there was a high socio-political tension between Communists and the Islamic axis, which led to the victimisation of non-mainstream religions such as syncretism and Javanese mystical belief. These rebellions and the socio-political situation were latterly used by Soekarno, as a leader of guided democracy, to enforce an act on blasphemy in 1965. This is discussed in further detail below.

The New Order Soeharto (in office from 1967 until 1998), in contrast, acknowledged that the prerequisite for being a loyal Indonesian citizen was to believe in God (that is, to not become a Communist) as an essential Pancasila character. Denial of the Pancasila principles (including *asas tunggal* or the sole principle, which will be discussed later) was not merely seditious, but heretical as well.[60] Some Islamic and revolutionary Marxist organisations that refused to use Pancasila as their sole foundation or ideology were labelled as deviants. It can be noted that at that time the blasphemy law, enacted in 1965, was exploited by the government to silence political opposition, government critics and other dissidents.

Apart from the conception of political blasphemy, there are other state policies that can be categorised as officially state-sanctioned enforcement actions aimed at restricting religious freedoms. The first category of official state actions

59 Siti Hanna, 'Pencegahan Penodaan Agama (Kajian atas UU NO.1 TAHUN 1965)' (2010) 13 *RELIGIA* 4.

60 Arief Budiman, 'The New Order State: Language, Ideology, Hegemony', in Arief Budiman (ed.), *State and Civil Society in Indonesia* (Centre of Southeast Asian Studies, Monash University 1990) 132.

is the enactment of laws that implicitly restrict the religious right to *forum internum*. Such laws provide authority for the government to intervene in religious matters. Secondly, official state action can also be seen from state policies that advocate extra-legal enforcement of apostasy declarations by religious organisations. These two categories of state actions generally provoke the imprisonment of members of religious minorities within Islam in order to restrict them from allegedly insulting the officially recognised and mainstream Islam.

Religious persecutions of religious minorities within Islam and individuals occur as the government is legally authorised to restrict religious minorities seen as deviants. These state actions are basically based on the Presidential Decree, also known as Act No. 1/PNPS/1965 on the Prevention of Blasphemy and Abuse of Religions, hereinafter 1965 Blasphemy Law, and article 156a of the Indonesian Criminal Code (Kitab Undang-Undang Hukum Pidana, KUHP), hereinafter KUHP Blasphemy Law. Article 1 of the 1965 Blasphemy Law says that:

> everyone is prohibited in public from intentionally conveying, endorsing or attempting to gain public support for any interpretation of a certain religion embraced by people in Indonesia or undertaking religious activities that resemble religious activities of the religion, where the interpretation and activities are in deviant from the basic teachings of the aforesaid religion.

Article 2 (1) of this law then says that whoever violates article 1 is warned and ordered to stop her/his conduct based on the joint ministerial decree from the MORA, Attorney General and Interior Ministry. Article 2 (2) further provides that if the violation mentioned in paragraph 1 of this article is performed by an organisation or a mystical belief, the President of the Republic of Indonesia can disband such organisation and, after receiving considerations from the MORA, the Attorney General and Interior Ministry can declare it an illegal organisation.

Article 3 of the 1965 Blasphemy Law further states that if individuals violate article 1 of the Act and the three ministerial offices or the president have already carried out policies to stop blasphemous actions, then individuals who remain within the "blasphemous organisations" are liable for penalties of up to five years in prison. While this article theoretically applies to both individuals and organisations, practically most blasphemy cases in Indonesia deal with individuals. These articles are further emphasised by article 156a of the KUHP Blasphemy Law, which says that whoever conveys, endorses or attempts to spread misleading religious teachings is liable on conviction to up to five years in prison.

The two blasphemy laws, in fact, have frequently been enforced by district courts in several regions to sentence individuals who are considered as heretical or blasphemous. Besides using the blasphemy laws to target religious minorities within Islam, the court has also used the laws to victimise some religious sects in other religions. These actions show that the KUHP Blasphemy Law is not applied to protect the very foundation of religious plurality and public order from the negative effect of abusive actions and expressions but more to facilitate discriminatory treatment of minority religious sects. In 2004, for example, the

Priest Mangapin Sibuea, leader of the Judgment Day Christian Sect, was arrested and sentenced to three years in prison by the District Court of Bandung West Java.[61] This sect was seen by Protestant and Catholic Christian groups such as the Forum for Christian Communication in Indonesia (FKKI) as "deviant" due to its non-mainstream Christian belief.[62]

Within Islam, the District Court of Malang, East Java sentenced Muhammad Yusman Roy in 2005 to two years in jail for reciting Muslim prayers in the Indonesian language, which MUI said tarnished the purity of Arabic-based Islam. In the same year, the District Court of Probolinggo East Java also sentenced Ardi Husain, a leader of the Narcotic and Cancer Rehabilitation Centre, because he performed misleading interpretations of the Qur'an and published it as a book.[63] He was sentenced to four and a half years of imprisonment.[64] The court also sentenced five editors of the book to five-year terms, while an employee who sold a copy to a neighbour received three years.[65] A similar case happened in West Sulawesi Province in 2006, when Sumardin Tappaya was sentenced to six months in jail. Sumardin, a Muslim teacher, was accused of heresy, a crime punishable with up to five years in prison, because he whistled during prayers, an action deemed as a deviant religious act.[66]

In 2011, one Ahmadiyah member was convicted to seven months in prison by the District Court of Serang Banten because he was accused of perpetrating a communal conflict. The other perpetrators were also convicted by the district court to imprisonment ranging from three to six months. In fact, this communal conflict, which involved Sunni and Ahmadiyah followers in Cikeusik Banten, resulted in the killing of three members of the Ahmadiyah group and damage to Ahmadiyah properties.[67] This might be the most interesting recent case concerning the Ahmadiyah in Indonesia because the government has never banned Ahmadiyah's *forum internum*, but only restricts its religious propagation.[68]

61 Wiyana D, 'Mangapin Dituntut Hukuman Tiga Tahun Penjara' (2004) *Tempo*. Mangapin claimed himself to be the last Prophet, said he had met the Holy Spirit and predicted that the Day of Judgement would come on 10 November 2002.

62 'Kiamat Sekte Sibuea Diundur Hingga 2007' (2003) *Tempo*.

63 Some of Ardi's writing that was alleged to be deviant to mainstream Islamic teaching includes that he believes the prophet is still alive, the devil (*shaitan*) is more faithful than humans and the holy book is still being revealed to him. He also claims that he meets God, Islam is only for Arabs, going to heaven should not be limited to being a Muslim and being a true Muslim should not be limited to embracing Islam.

64 Siti Aminah and Muhammad Khoirul Roziqin, 'Pemantauan Kasus Kasus Penodaan Agama Di Indonesia Periode 2012–2014' (2015) 5 *Jurnal Keadilan Sosial* 36–37.

65 Richard C Paddock, 'Separation of Mosque, State Wanes in Indonesia' (*Los Angeles Times* Los Angeles 20 March 2006).

66 Melissa Crouch, *Law and Religion in Indonesia: Conflict and the Courts in West Java* (Routledge 2013) 144–145.

67 *Cikeusik Case* (2011) Public Court of Serang District 314/Pid.B/2011/PN.SRG.

68 The imprisonment of the Ahmadiyah members and perpetrators of the communal conflict was solely based on criminal acts. Apart from this case, none of the Ahmadiyah members were convicted by any court even though this Islamic group has been severely persecuted in Indonesia.

Even though the government, through its joint ministerial decree in 2008, did not ban Ahmadiyah's *forum internum*, it did express support of MUI's *fatwa* adopted in 2005, which stated that Ahmadiyah is a misleading religious form outside Islam and that Muslims who follow Ahmadiyah are apostates.[69] Some local governments also enacted laws that limited or banned Ahmadiyah as an Islamic religious sect, while some government officials, particularly at the local level, were involved in atrocities against Ahmadiyah.

In the Cikeusik case, the restriction of Ahmadiyah's right to *forum internum* was caused by the fact that the Muslim majorities consider all Ahmadiyah activities a threat to Sunni-Islamic orthodoxy and religious harmony. This is why the Muslim majorities in Cikeusik tried to disband the Ahmadiyah congregation by attacking them.[70] The court did not use the 1965 and KUHP Blasphemy Laws as a legal consideration to make a verdict because those laws specifically regulate religious realms while the conflict had already resulted in criminal offences *i.e.* killing three members of Ahmadiyah and the destruction of Ahmadiyah property. Thus, it should be noted that this case was motivated by a refusal of the Muslim majorities to accept the Ahmadiyah belief. The attack against Ahmadiyah was followed by local government restrictions and a refusal from Muslim majorities to allow Ahmadiyah members to return to their villages.[71] When they were attacked by the Muslim majority and restricted by state organs, Ahmadiyah's right to *forum internum* was partly affected because the internal dimension of belief in Islam must be manifested freely, without fear.

A similar case also occurred against the Shi'ah sect in some parts of Indonesia. For instance, the persecution against the Shi'ah in Sampang East Java in 2012, which resulted in the killing of one Shi'ah member and the burning of Shi'ah properties, also ended up with the imprisonment of Tajul Muluk, a local Shi'ah leader. He was convicted and sentenced to two years in prison by the District Court of Sampang. This was doubled to four years in prison by the Appeal Court of East Java. The PT argued that the increase of punishment was based on Tajul Muluk's frequent efforts to spread hostility and for attempting to disgrace Islamic religious belief from around 2003 to 2011, which was seen to result in religious communal conflicts between the Shi'ah and the Sunni in the locality. In its verdict, the court relied on MUI's *fatwa* and article 156a of the KUHP Blasphemy Law.[72] After this case, Shi'ah followers could not return to their village because the Muslim majorities in Karang Gayam village still refused to accept them and considered them as transgressors of Islam. Meanwhile, the

69 The government adopted a joint ministerial decree (Surat Keputusan Bersama, SKB) of the MORA No. 3/2008; The General Attorney No. Kep-033/A/JA/6/2008; and the Interior Ministry No. 199/2008. About the *fatwa*, see MUI *fatwa* No. 11/MUNAS VII/MUI/15/2005.

70 *Cikeusik Case* (n 67).

71 Elaine Pearson, *In Religion's Name: Abuses against Religious Minorities in Indonesia* (Human Rights Watch 2013) 65–66.

72 *Tajul Muluk Case* (2012) Appeal Court of East Java 481/PID/2012/PT.SBY.

local government in Sampang advised them not to return to their village to avoid a similar conflict.

Besides sentencing individuals, the government has also banned or disbanded religious minorities within Islam, such as Islam Jamaah, a messianic Islamic group. This group started to exist in Indonesia in the 1950s. Islam Jamaah was declared deviant by MUI and banned by the government in 1971.[73] Such cases disclose that the implementation of the blasphemy laws gives preferential treatment to certain mainstream religious denominations and attempts to curb dissenters' freedom of religion and choice.[74] Moreover, the blasphemy laws help to foster a climate of intolerance and are used to justify extra-legal discrimination against religious minorities. The government and Muslim majority groups use these laws as justification to take things into their own hands.[75] Consequently, many communal conflicts directed at persecuting religious minorities within Islam were triggered by reference to blasphemy laws and state policies, even though others have also been triggered by MUI's *fatwa*.

In the context of international religious freedom, state parties are restricted to protecting a particular religious teaching that can hinder individuals from embracing different kinds of religious teachings. Enacting regulations inspired by religious norms is a common feature in the Indonesian legal system due to the close relationship between religion and the state, as well as the concept of a quasi-theistic secular state. In addition to that, adopting the blasphemy law, which restricts non-mainstream religious teachings, is another matter. This law does not provide an equal environment for all religions to flourish in reality, and hence the principle of equality for dissident religious groups is almost impossible when it provides and uses a definition of religion favoured by a singular version of religious belief backed by the state. The majority groups frequently employ religious justification to criminalise non-mainstream religious teachings, while the government regards this criminalisation to control religious activities of the religious minorities within Islam as a means of preserving religious harmony and social stability. If this religious justification is legalised by the state through legislation, such as by enacting a blasphemy law, all rights to *forum internum* and *forum externum* of the religious minorities within Islam will be criminalised. Thus, this blasphemy law has no place in a democratic Indonesia which, based on Pancasila as the supreme source of law, basically provides freedom for all – regardless of anyone's religious conviction.

73 *Fatwa* of MUI on Islam Jamaah.

74 Karl-Heinz Ladeur and Ino Augsberg, 'The Myth of the Neutral State: The Relationship between State and Religion in the Face of New Challenges' (2007) 8 *German Law Journal* 143, 148.

75 Freedom House, 'Policing Belief: The Impact of Blasphemy Laws on Human Rights' (Freedom House 2010) 47.

3.2. Extra-legal enforcement of blasphemy decrees

As analysed earlier in Chapter 3, the influence of Islamic authority on state law in Indonesia is very obvious, even though Islam is not declared the religion of the state. This influence can be seen in Howard Federspiel's argument. Federspiel noted that since the early twentieth century, Indonesia has used the MUI to interpret Islamic law and to resolve contentious matters.[76] Until the latter half of 2013, religious institutions with official or unofficial government backing, such as the MUI and MORA, frequently used reference to the blasphemy law to impose state-sanctioned interpretations of religious doctrine on members of religious minorities within Islam that are deemed deviant or heretical.[77] The MUI, through its *fatwas*, frequently challenges the secular framework of human rights in Indonesian law and international human rights instruments because the *fatwas* are based on so-called conservative Islamic teachings. Since the fall of the Soeharto regime in 1998, the MUI has been more conservative in its approach towards religious pluralism, especially regarding the rights of religious minorities within Islam.

During the early phase of Islamisation in Indonesia Islam was spread widely by traders, as well as "the nine saints", through accommodative approaches. Islam, at that time, had been made to sanction a number of mystical beliefs common to the traditional religious outlook.[78] In the era of colonialism, most Indonesian Muslims even rejected the coming of Wahhabism brought by some Indonesian Muslims in the early eighteenth century.[79] The tension among traditionalist-syncretist, puritan-modernist and puritan-fundamentalist Muslims in Indonesia started to occur in the early nineteenth century. The Muhammadiyah movement, which introduced independent legal reasoning and the idea of an evangelical return to the Qur'an and Hadith as the supreme sources of the Muslim faith, was challenged by traditional Muslim organisations like NU, who believed that the door of *ijtihad* was already closed and subscribed to religious and cultural accretions. Since then, the moderate and conservative Muslims in those organisations have attempted to dominate the public sphere through official and unofficial government backing, like the MORA and MUI, because such institutions have a significant role in defining true Islam in Indonesia. For example, some NU and Muhammadiyah members, who became members of MUI in East Java, supported a *fatwa* on the banning of the Ahmadiyah even

76 Howard Federspiel, 'Islamic Values, Law and Expectations in Contemporary Indonesia' (1998) 5 *Islamic Law and Society* 90, 93.

77 Freedom House (n 75) 2. See also Peter Henne, 'Latest Trends in Religious Restrictions and Hostilities' (Pew Research Center 2015).

78 Justus M Van Der Kroef, 'The Role of Islam in Indonesian Nationalism and Politics' (1958) 11 *The Western Political Quarterly* 33, 37.

79 This is especially clear in the case of the Padri Movement in Sumatera in the 1820s. See Jeffrey Hadler, 'A Historiography of Violence and the Secular State in Indonesia: Tuanku Imam Bondjol and the Uses of History' (2008) 67 *The Journal of Asian Studies* 971, 971–1010.

though those Muslim organisations opposed the joint ministerial decree, which restricted the right to *forum externum* of the Ahmadiyah in 2008.[80]

In relation to its *fatwas* on the rights of religious minorities within Islam, the MUI has, through another *fatwa*, established ten main criteria of apostasy, namely: (1) repudiating one element of the six basic foundations of Islamic faith (*rukn iman*), (2) believing in or following a belief contrary to the Qur'an and Hadith (as interpreted by the MUI), (3) believing in revelation after the Prophet Muhammad, (4) denying the divine validity of the Qur'an, (5) performing misleading Qur'anic interpretation, (6) repudiating Hadith as one of the sources of Islam, (7) insulting the Prophet Muhammad, (8) denying the Prophet Muhammad as the seal of the prophets, (9) changing, adding or decreasing the basic principles of Islamic ritual, and (10) calling other Muslims infidels.[81] These elements of the MUI *fatwa* on apostasy are drawn from the multi-faceted MUI extra-legal cases against different religious minorities within Islam in Indonesia between 1980 and 2007. It should be noted that the central MUI and its different branches, in collaboration with the MORA and Bakorpakem, actively issued *fatwas* long ago, not only to accuse religious minorities within Islam as deviant Muslims but also to persecute non-Islamic religious minorities.

The first extra-legal enforcement of apostasy on religious minorities within Islam was the MUI's *fatwa* on the Ahmadiyah in 1980. This *fatwa* was a response to social unrest among Sunni Muslims since the arrival of the Ahmadiyah in Indonesia in the 1920s.[82] Before this *fatwa*, discrimination against the Ahmadiyah had actually occurred all over Indonesia since its arrival in the country. For example, some mainstream Islamic religious leaders and Muslim organisations, such as NU, Muhammadiyah and the Masyumi Islamic political party, had earlier denounced the Ahmadiyah sect and its teachings as deviant from mainstream Islam.[83] Thus, the subsequent enactment of MUI's *fatwa* in 1980 significantly pushed the Ahmadiyah case into becoming a national issue.

The MUI's *fatwa*, which many Indonesians see as a non-binding but influential opinion, asserts that the Ahmadiyah, especially the Qadiani version, is deviant and that this Islamic religious minority does not form a legitimate part of mainstream Islam.[84] This *fatwa* was then reasserted in 2005 with the new *fatwa* No. 11/Munas VII/MUI/15/2005, which reconfirmed that the Ahmadiyah was deviant and should be restricted because its beliefs threatened religious harmony, social integration, public order and national security.[85] The essence of

80 Pearson (n 71) 18–19.

81 'Fenomena Aliran Sesat Di Indonesia' (2010) 61 *Ikhlas Beramal Magazine* 3.

82 Aris Mustafa, *Ahmadiyah: Keyakinan yang Digugat* (Pusat Data & Analisa Tempo 2005) 3.

83 Melissa Crouch, 'Judicial Review and Religious Freedom: The Case of Indonesian Ahmadis' (2012) 34 *Sydney Law Review* 3.

84 The *fatwa* of MUI dated 1 June 1980.

85 Khoiruddin Nasution, 'Fatwa Majelis Ulama Indonesia (MUI): On Ahmadiyah' (2008) 7 *Millah: Jurnal Studi Agama* 4.

the *fatwa* was based on the Qur'an and Hadith, as well as the decision of the Mujamma al-Fiqh al-Islami of the Organisation of Islamic Conference (OIC), dating back to 1976.[86] It appears that the issuance of MUI's *fatwa* was essentially influenced by global Muslim responses to the Ahmadiyah sect in the Muslim world around that time.[87] Although the broad tone and timing of the issuance of the *fatwa* coincided with the vigorous hard-line policy of the Pakistani government against Ahmadiyahs in Pakistan during the same period, the connection of the Indonesian case with that of Pakistan could only be speculated.[88]

In 1984, the MUI also issued a non-*fatwa*, known as *tadzkirah* or admonition, on the Shi'ah. However, this admonition did not explicitly declare the Sh'iah as deviant.[89] This non-*fatwa* only admonished the Sunni to be aware of Shi'ah proliferation in Indonesia because its theological teaching exclusively relies on the doctrines of *Ahlul Bait* or *Imamiyyah*, which believe in the sanctity of the Shi'ah *imams* and the establishment of *Imamiyyah* as part of Islamic teachings.[90] The MUI also noted that Shi'ah theological understanding was exclusive because of its claim that Sunni Muslims had manipulated some Prophetic Hadiths to promote their political interest.[91] This MUI *tadzkirah* was primarily purposed to advise Muslims about this theological distinction, but was eventually interpreted differently by the Sunnis to persecute and discriminate against the Shi'ahs. This *fatwa* was then disagreed with by the MUI of East Java province because, in 2012, the East Java MUI declared that the *Imamiyyah*

86 For more detail about the *fatwa*, see ibid, 8–10.

87 The first MUI *fatwa* in 1980 was basically influenced by Saudi Arabia and a recommendation of the OIC dating back to 1976. See Yew-Foong Hui, 'Religious Freedom in Contemporary Indonesia: The Case of the Ahmadiyah', in Hui Yew-Foong (ed.), *Encountering Islam: The Politics of Religious Identities in Southeast Asia* (Institute of Southeast Asian Studies 2013) 44.

88 M Atho Mudzhar, 'Fatwas of the Council of Indonesian Ulama: A Study of Islamic Legal Thought in Indonesia, 1975–1988' (UCLA 1990) 4.

89 The admonition has five arguments which emphasise theological distinctions between the Sunni and the Sh'iah: (1) the Sh'iah rejects Hadiths narrated by other than the *Ahlul Bait* (members of the Prophet's family) while the Sunni do not discriminate against any Hadiths as long as the transmitters are reliable, (2) the Sh'iah regards *imams* as *ma'sum* (free from making mistakes) while Sunnis believe that *imama* are ordinary humans, (3) the Shi'ah do not recognise *ijma* without the approval of an *imam* while Sunnis argue that *ijma* is an independent agreement among Muslim scholars, (4) the Shi'ah consider the establishment of an Islamic leadership or government is one of the principles of Islam while Sunnis assert there is no preference for any system of political leadership as long as it serves and protects public interests, and (5) the Shi'ah considers the four caliphs before Ali as usurpers. See the recommendation of the MUI on the Shi'ah, dated 7 March 1984.

90 MUI Recommendation dated 7 March 1984.

91 Nuhrison M Nuh and Achmad Rosidi, 'Ikatan Jama'ah Ahlul Bait Indonesia (IJABI) Kota Bandung – Jawa Barat', in Ahmad Syafi'i Mufid (ed.), *Kasus-Kasus Aliran/Faham Keagamaan Aktual Di Indonesia* (Departemen Agama, Badan Litbang Agama Dan Diklat Keagamaan, Puslitbang Kehidupan Beragama 2006) 33.

Shi'ah, also known as *Ahlul Bait*, was misleading. This *fatwa* applied the central MUI's *fatwa* to ten criteria of apostasy. It was also based on the Shi'ah's principal religious interpretations. The *fatwa* recommended the central and local governments around Indonesia to take the necessary actions, such as banning the spread of Shi'ah teaching.[92]

Besides issuing *fatwas* on the Shi'ah and Ahmadiyah, the MUI also issued some *fatwas* on other religious minorities within Islam. The *fatwas* were enacted to respond to the spread of religious teaching accused of endangering religious harmony within society. For example, in the 1980s, the MUI issued a *fatwa* on Islam Jamaah, a Sunni-Messianic Islamic group, which latterly renamed itself as LDII, the Indonesian Islamic Propagation Board.[93] In this *fatwa*, the MUI explained that Islam Jamaah was deviant because the group declared that other Muslims outside of their membership were infidels.[94] In May 2005, the MUI issued another *fatwa* on bilingual Islamic prescribed prayers performed by Yusman Roy. The MUI again declared that this kind of prayer was deviant and invalid because Roy used Bahasa Indonesian and Arabic in his prayers.[95]

The blasphemy law is also enforced extra-judicially by Islamic organisations through extra-judicial monitoring and restricting and persecuting of alleged misleading religious activities. For example, a verdict of Tajul Muluk in Sampang Court considered information from NU Sampang branch, rejecting the Shi'ah. The rejection of the Shi'ah Sampang was also endorsed by the Sampang MUI branch. The information from these two Islamic organisations was then used by the court to apply the blasphemy law to sentence Tajul Muluk because of the supporting opinions from the majorities during the trial.[96] Declaring religious minorities within Islam as deviant or misleading is also performed by local MUI in some regions. These examples show that the MUI does not share inclusive interpretation of Islamic teaching. Declaring other Muslims as misleading is not in accordance with the spirit of religious pluralism and is in contravention of international human rights instruments on religious freedom. If the position of religion is as a pillar of collective identity within a society, this *fatwa* can then trigger religious persecution against minorities because the majority claims to have a justification to do so.

The extra-legal enforcement of blasphemy or apostasy by government-backed Islamic organisations has occurred with respect to protecting the basic historical sources of Islam, contrary to the views of some religious minorities within Islam (seen as deviants or infidels). Principally, the MUI *fatwa* is not a legally binding instrument in the Indonesian legal system but in many instances the *fatwas*

92 *Fatwa* of East Java MUI No. Kep. 01/SKF-MUI/JTM/I/2012.

93 Islam Jamaah was founded by Nurhasan in 1951. See Sutiyono, *Benturan Budaya Islam: Puritan & Sinkretis* (Penerbit Buku Kompas 2010) 124.

94 *Fatwa* of MUI on Islam Jamaah. Because of this *fatwa* and unrest among the Sunni majority, this group changed its name into LDII.

95 *Fatwa* of MUI on Bilingual Prayer, dated 7 May 2005.

96 *Tajul Muluk Case* (n 72).

influence Indonesian Muslims. If the *fatwa* is intolerant, such as declaring religious minorities within Islam as deviants or infidels, it is then very likely to be followed by communal conflict between the majorities and the minorities because the majorities claim to have religious justification to persecute religious minorities within Islam. The government has never repealed any MUI *fatwas*, including the *fatwa* on Ahmadiyah, even though this *fatwa* is clearly inconsistent with the international standard of religious freedom and the protection of religious minorities. Some local governments have even endorsed the *fatwas* to restrict the rights of religious minorities within Islam. For example, the regional representative office of the MORA in West Nusa Tenggara issued a ban on thirteen religious sects in October 2005, including the Ahmadiyah and nine other forms of traditional beliefs (*aliran kepercayaan*), for being deviations of an official religion.[97]

The question is why did the government keep silent about intolerant *fatwas* that are inconsistent with the international protection standard of religious minorities? The government must realise that any attempt to manipulate a version of religious teaching may disrupt people's religious freedom. Inter and intra religious pluralisms are the nature of religion. On the other hand, labelling other religious groups as apostate or misleading is also the nature of religion, not only in Islam but also in other religions. Yet, this must be circulated to all internal members of a religion instead of being declared publicly, because the latter may trigger communal conflict among religious followers. The government must control the issuance of *fatwas* on doctrinal matters because all the *fatwas* are very likely to be followed by Muslims. If the *fatwa* contains hatred and incitement, such as labelling religious minorities within Islam as apostate or infidel, the government may interfere with it because the *fatwa* may be used by the majorities to persecute them. Thus, interference against the *fatwa* is justified under international human rights law because this policy is proportionate to protect minorities and to preserve public order.

There have been disagreements among members of the MUI since its establishment in 1975, especially regarding some *fatwas* on social and moral matters. In some cases, a school of Islamic law was chosen to deal with one matter and then another school was chosen for other matters.[98] This method was chosen by the MUI to avoid rigidity or exclusiveness in order to reform *fiqh* approaches, because most Indonesian Muslims strictly follow the Syafi'i school of law.[99] Yet the MUI displayed a very rigid and conservative approach to the issue of religious minorities within Islam, particularly on the Ahmadiyah. Thus, it can be

97 Asian Indigenous & Tribal People Network, *Indonesia, Piecemeal Approaches to Systemic and Institutionalised Discrimination: A Shadow Report to the Initial to Third Periodic Reports (CERD/C/IDN/3) to the CERD Committee* (Asian Indigenous & Tribal Peoples Network 2007) 3.

98 About different *fatwas* of MUI, see Nadirsyah Hosen, 'Behind the Scenes: Fatwas of Majelis Ulama Indonesia (1975–1998)' (2004) 15 *Journal of Islamic Studies* 147, 147–179.

99 ibid 160.

noted that the MUI *fatwa*, issued in 2005 declaring the Ahmadiyah as deviant, was in fact the MUI attempting to emulate the spirit of the 1998 *Reformasi*, which acknowledged far-reaching religious freedom in the 1945 Constitution and Human Rights Act. In this case, the MUI attempted to justify dominant Muslim voices, not only on the national level but also in the Muslim world, which restricted the rights of religious minorities within Islam. This meant that the MUI was more inclined to work with the Muslim majorities to put into practice the restrictions on religious minorities in Islam.

3.3. Mixed cases

All the aforesaid examples and discussion points confirm that *fatwas* have had two significant effects in relation to the protection of the rights of religious minorities within Islam in Indonesia. The first is that *fatwas* have frequently influenced official state-sanctioned actions, such as government policies and court decisions against religious minorities within Islam. The *fatwa* has been used by the courts as evidence to sentence individuals belonging to different religious minorities within Islam for blasphemous actions. Secondly, besides endorsing state-sanctioned actions on the implementation of the 1965 and KUHP Blasphemy Law, the MUI *fatwa* on religious minorities within Islam has also triggered communal conflicts between religious minorities within Islam and the mainstream Sunni majority in Indonesia. Thus, Muslim majority groups believe that their action in suppressing religious minorities within Islam is encouraged by MUI's *fatwas* and the government's policies, resulting in a critical situation for religious freedom. For example, in 2006, due to the urging of local clerics, 500 angry villagers in Bondowoso East Java attacked 150 Shi'ah members who were conducting routine prayers. This was because local Sunni residents were objecting to the presence of the Shi'ah in their community and accusing them of "deviant" Islamic beliefs and heresy.[100] In 2011, a mob of youths from a Sunni school attacked a Shi'ah-affiliated Yapi Islamic traditional school *(pesantren)* in Pasuruan, East Java. A year later, the Shi'ah in Sampang East Java were attacked by Sunni residents, who burnt some Sh'iah properties and displaced hundreds of Shi'ah followers because some of the local *ulama* and the local MUI had issued a *fatwa* asserting that the Shi'ah were deviants.[101]

In 2007, dozens of Sunni Muslims in Pasuruan East Java raided two houses belonging to M. Thoyib and Rochamim, because the men were accused of practising heretical Islamic rituals by conducting animistic prayer ceremonies at cemeteries.[102] Additionally, Sunni Muslims in local Bogor West Java beat Alih

100 Bureau of Democracy, Human Rights and Labor, 'Indonesia: International Religious Freedom Report' (United States Department of State 2010).
101 *Fatwa* of the MUI Sampang East Java No. 0-35/MUI/SPG/1/2012 and a statement from the NU Islamic organisation which supported the MUI's *fatwa*.
102 Bureau of Democracy, Human Rights and Labor, 'Indonesia: Report on International Religious Freedom' (United States Department of State 2007).

bin Hadi to death because his teaching allegedly endorsed Muslim travel to a nearby mosque, rather than to Mecca, for pilgrimage and paying alms (*zakat*) after *Eid Fitri*.[103] In 2012, Tarekat At-Tijaniyah's property at Cimahi West Java was burnt by Sunni Muslims because the leader of the sect believed that there would be a tsunami in the capital city of Indonesia (Jakarta) and that the Day of Judgement would occur on 17 August 2012. Even if these groups were considered to be included in the seventy-two sects that are deviant and misleading based on Islamic doctrine,[104] the persecution of these groups is still unlawful under Islamic and Indonesian law. Muslims must understand that diversity of belief, including the different interpretation of Islamic teachings, is divinely initiated.[105] Their right to *forum internum* is also guaranteed by international human rights law, as long as their belief does not breach public order, morality and the fundamental rights of others.

The collaborative efficacy of state-religious institutions and Islamic organisations has also frequently incited the majority of mainstream Sunni communities to socially alienate and publicly restrict the Ahmadiyah in different localities around Indonesia. Some members of the Ahmadiyah were forced either to leave their village, to convert to mainstream Islam, to establish a new religion other than Islam or not to claim being Muslim. However, it must be understood that there are still many unreported cases of persecutions of the Ahmadiyah and other religious minorities within Islam, especially in local areas. The main reason for this is because of the decentralisation policy, applied in 1999. This triggered the spread of religious persecutions of religious minorities within Islam, some of which are pursued through legislation, policies and decisions issued by the local executive or the legislature.[106] As of 2012, there have been thirty local government policies that prohibit the teaching of Ahmadiyah doctrines in Indonesia.[107]

The previous examples assert that religious minorities within Islam in Indonesia face a very complex situation. The legislation that discriminates against the minority right to disseminate non-mainstream religious beliefs is exploited by the Muslim majorities. They use exclusive interpretation of Islamic teachings to back up the legislation through the state-backed organisations, while the Muslim majorities argue that the persecution is justifiable, not only under state

103 ibid.

104 The Hadith which explains that Islam is divided into seventy-three sects, see Hadith narrated by Abu Dawood 4067. This Hadith exists in the Sunnis as well as in the Twelver Shi'ah, including the Zaydis with their different versions. See Zulfikar Hirji, 'Pluralism and Islamic Traditions of Sectarian Division', in Zulfikar Hirji, *Diversity and Pluralism in Islam: Historical and Contemporary Discourses amongst Muslims* (IB Tauris 2010) 33.

105 ibid 42.

106 According to article 1 of the Decentralisation Law No. 32/2004, all regional governments are authorised to maintain their governing process and the interest of their society.

107 See HRWG, 'Alternative Report of Indonesia's ICCPR State Report, Article 18: Freedom of Religion and Belief' (Human Rights Working Group 2012) 3.

legislation but also under Islamic law. This is because authoritative Islamic organisations, such as the MUI, also endorse the legislation. Thus, both the 1965 and KUHP Blasphemy Laws and the MUI's *fatwas* do not only criminalise religious minorities within Islam but also trigger the Muslim majorities to persecute them. These complex realities spread across several regions because the local governments justified their discriminatory treatments against religious minorities within Islam based on the 1965 and KUHP Blasphemy Laws. Moreover, the local Muslim majorities generally relied on the MUI's *fatwas* or simply urged the local MUI to adopt similar *fatwas* to justify the persecution of religious minorities within Islam.

The above cases also demonstrate that the conflict among Muslims is mainly about those who represent religious authority to determine who is right and who is wrong, and ultimately who is most faithful to the religious precepts and values.[108] All believers in Islam argue that their religious interpretation is the most authoritative, but when supported by the political realm the authoritative interpretation generally rests with the majority groups. The religious persecution of religious minorities within Islam seeks to imply that the minorities are on the wrong side because the majority has the power to affirm that non-mainstream Islam is deviant or even a group of apostates. For instance, the Shi'ah's belief that the Companions of the Prophet, including the first three caliphs, were usurpers of political power that should have legitimately fallen to Ali is highlighted by the Sunni majority's propensity to associate many of the Shi'ah with heresy and even apostasy.[109] In contrast, in situations where the Shi'ah is a majority, the Sunni are also often discriminated against as a non-mainstream Islamic group and are treated as second-class citizens.

4. The complex reality of religious minorities within a theocratic society

The previous examples suggest that many Indonesian Muslims still perceive Islam as the primary source for validating the rights of religious minorities within Islam, even though Indonesia is not a theocratic state. In Indonesia, the state provides formal secular norms of human rights, while Muslim society is still regimented by adherence to Islamic law.[110] This concept leads to the close relationship between a religious-democratic state and the religiosity of society. The religious majority in Indonesia is represented by religious organisations and their followers promote a common religious norm, which does not permit the total separation of religious doctrine and state policy. They opine that the implementation of human rights does not solely depend on legal written documents but also depends on the acceptance of the religious majority. Thus, any freedom or right not in line with the consensus among the majority should be rejected.

108 Abdullah Saeed, *Freedom of Religion, Apostasy and Islam* (Routledge 2017) 23.
109 ibid 25.
110 See Sita Ram Goel, *Freedom of Expression: Secular Theocracy versus Liberal Democracy* (Voice of India 1998). New Delhi: Voice of India.

The Indonesian context also illustrates the unavoidable contention between various religious groups in Muslim-majority states and the difficulty of the state to stay completely neutral without any intervention. The religious majority would usually practise religious communalism through the establishment of different religious organisations and institutions within the state, playing a significant role in the affairs of the state. In Indonesia, it is impossible for religious institutions, such as MUI, to be set up by the state. The reason for this is because leaders of religious majorities usually restrict religious freedom for religious minorities, even though others may seek to enable the minorities to follow their own religions or beliefs.[111] This divergent view signifies how religious minorities are seen as aliens by the majority, creating a disadvantaged situation. This is contrary to the international perception that human rights norms should be conceived as incontestable standards of human behaviour, applicable to individuals in all countries.

The refusal of some Muslims to accept the rights of religious minorities within Islam, and their swift reaction against Muslims who criticise Islam or perform non-mainstream religious activities, shows that the doctrine of human rights, which specifically stresses the equality of all people and the need to respect the equal dignity of all, may encounter problems when it explicitly supports the rights of minorities against the majorities.[112] This is because, in Indonesia, there is lack of unanimity amongst the majority of Muslims on the scope of the rights of religious minorities within Islam, even though some Muslim scholars like Abdurrahman Wahid and Nurcholis Madjid have proposed the compatibility of the Islamic doctrine with international human rights. Additionally, there remains a wide variety of Muslim voices on the issue of human rights generally,[113] which affects the Islamic discourse on the universality of human rights amongst the Muslim populace. It signifies the fact that the contention about the rights of religious minorities within Islam, in Indonesia and in any other Muslim-majority state, is not strictly based on Islam as a religion but is a matter relating to the political realm and Muslim hermeneutical perspectives.

The existence of extra-legal enforcement on the blasphemy law by the MUI confirms that Islam in Indonesia is perceived by Muslims as more than just a system of thought or belief. It is seen as a way of life, consisting of a divine element and a core identity of the Muslim existence. Islam, like other religions, encompasses beliefs and a world-view that illuminates the very ground of being, investing life with divine-ultimate meaning and direction.[114] Therefore, it is difficult for Muslims and religious adherents to solely follow secular norms of human rights and to give

111 Asghar Ali Engineer and Uday Mehta, 'Religion and Secularism', in Asghar Ali Engineer and Uday Mehta (eds), *State Secularism and Religion: Western and Indian Experience* (Ajanta Publications 1998) 3.

112 Roger Trigg, *Equality, Freedom, and Religion* (Oxford University Press Oxford 2012) 65.

113 Heiner Bielefeldt, 'Muslim Voices in the Human Rights Debate' (1995) 17 *Human Rights Quarterly* 587, 587.

114 Donald A Giannella, 'Religious Liberty, Nonestablishment, and Doctrinal Development. Part I. The Religious Liberty Guarantee' (1967) 80 *Harvard Law Review* 1381, 1425.

up Islamic norms that they perceive as God-given rights.[115] Many Muslims perceive that the Islamic tradition is fully formed and take very seriously the aspiration of their religion to inform their ordinary lives in its own mould. Islam is perceived as universal because it encompasses previous Abrahamic religions and then supersedes them. Therefore, Muslims perceive Islam as final-universal guidance, not only in socio-legal matters but also in their personal daily lives.[116] Apart from being a religion, Islam also theoretically provides a sense of Islamic culture among Muslims, by which religious attachment to the Islamic culture creates stronger control within Muslim societies.[117] They argue that whoever threatens Islam is not only seen as threatening Islamic religious beliefs but also Islamic society.

The earlier discussion shows that most Indonesian Muslims still perceive Islam as an integral part of their religious and social lives, including legal and human rights matters. This shows that Islam in Indonesia plays a very significant role in shaping Muslims' perspectives on many human rights issues. Ignoring Islam as a substantial component of Muslims' daily culture would underestimate its power and significance because Islam is not just an individual matter but it flourishes in society.[118] Islam constructs an Indonesian Muslim's common understanding about particular ethical and moral values. It tells of the doctrine of cultural relativism and asserts rules about morality that vary from place to place because the understanding of certain values depends on the cultural context.[119] Additionally, it asserts that moral claims derive from, and are enmeshed in, a cultural context which is itself the source of validity because there is no universal morality.[120]

It signifies that the main difficulty with working to establish a universal standard of human rights across cultural, and particularly religious, boundaries (like in Indonesia's case) is that each tradition has its own internal frame of reference because each tradition derives the validity of its precepts and norms from its own sources.[121] Thus, dismissing a strong influence of religion in any society, particularly in Indonesia where religion has a significant role in the public sphere, is problematic even though it is true that the behaviour of believers is not always motivated by total fidelity to their

115 Geoff Gilbert, 'Religious Minorities and Their Rights: A Problem of Approach' (1997) 5 *International Journal on Minority and Group Rights* 97, 107.

116 Marshall GS Hodgson, *The Venture of Islam: The Classical Age of Islam* (University of Chicago Press 1974) 217.

117 Mashood Baderin, 'Islam and the Realization of Human Rights in the Muslim World: A Reflection on Two Essential Approaches and Two Divergent Perspectives' (2007) 4 *Muslim World Journal of Human Rights* 15.

118 The original concept is taken from Trigg (n 112) 155–156.

119 Raymond John Vincent, *Human Rights and International Relations* (Cambridge University Press 1986) 37.

120 ibid.

121 Abdullahi Ahmed An Na'im, *Toward an Islamic Reformation: Civil Liberties, Human Rights, and International Law* (Syracuse University Press 1996) 146.

faith.[122] This problem indicates that there is an intricate and complex relationship between religion, human rights, state and socio-legal political context in Indonesian society. Therefore, Muslims should consider establishing a universal religious rationale society, which embraces all human beings by granting them equal distribution of rights and equality before the law.[123] This can be done by disfavouring a jurisprudence that upholds religious intolerance against vulnerable groups, like religious minorities within Islam. Thus, all Indonesian Muslims must use egalitarian principles from the Qur'an to support their human conduct to preserve the universalism of human rights and establish religious humanism in Islam.

In view of the above analyses, Islam in Indonesia can play a positive and important normative role in endorsing international and national human rights provisions. Even though the history of relationships between Islam, the law and the state in Indonesia is full of areas of tension, Indonesian Muslims need to strongly understand that Islam does not only provide spiritual capital but can also be used as social capital to generate humanitarian principles for all human beings. As Islam plays a significant role, Muslim scholars and leaders of Islamic organisations must endorse egalitarian morality and human rights because the government and society will consider their *ijithad* as a significant consideration in applying a particular human rights norm.

Bibliography

Addis A, 'Individualism, Communitarianism, and the Rights of Ethnic Minorities' (1993) 67 *Notre Dame Law Review* 63.

Ahmad R and Suaedy A, *Politisasi Agama dan Konflik Komunal: Beberapa Isu Penting di Indonesia* (The Wahid Institute 2007).

Aminah S and Roziqin MK, 'Pemantauan Kasus Kasus Penodaan Agama Di Indonesia Periode 2012–2014' (2015) 5 *Jurnal Keadilan Sosial* 25.

An-Na'im AA, 'The Islamic Law of Apostasy and Its Modern Applicability: A Case from the Sudan' (1986) 16 *Religion* 197.

———, 'What Do We Mean by Universal?' (1994) 23 *Index on Censorship* 120.

———, *Toward an Islamic Reformation: Civil Liberties, Human Rights, and International Law* (Syracuse University Press 1996).

An-Na'im AA and Henkin L, 'Islam and Human Rights: Beyond the Universality Debate' (2000) 94 *Proceedings of the Annual Meeting (American Society of International Law)* 95.

Arzt DE, 'Heroes or Heretics: Religious Dissidents under Islamic Law' (1996) 14 *Wisconsin International Law Journal* 349.

———, 'The Role of Compulsion in Islamic Conversion: Jihad, Dhimma and Ridda' (2002) 8 *Buffalo Human Rights Law Review* 31.

122 Abdullahi A An-Na'im and Louis Henkin, 'Islam and Human Rights: Beyond the Universality Debate' (2000) 94 *Proceedings of the Annual Meeting (American Society of International Law)* 95, 95.

123 ibid 368–370.

Asian Indigenous & Tribal People Network, *Indonesia, Piecemeal Approaches to Systemic and Institutionalised Discrimination: A Shadow Report to the Initial to Third Periodic Reports (CERD/C/IDN/3) to the CERD Committee* (Asian Indigenous & Tribal Peoples Network 2007).

Assyaukanie L, 'Fatwa and Violence in Indonesia' (2009) 11 *Journal of Religion and Society* 1.

Azra A and Hudson W, *Islam beyond Conflict: Indonesian Islam and Western Political Theory* (Ashgate Publishing 2008).

Baderin M, 'Islam and the Realization of Human Rights in the Muslim World: A Reflection on Two Essential Approaches and Two Divergent Perspectives' (2007) 4 *Muslim World Journal of Human Rights* 1.

Bälz K, 'Submitting Faith to Judicial Scrutiny through the Family Trial: The "Abu Zayd Case"' (1997) 37 *Die Welt des Islams* 135.

Berger M, 'Apostasy and Public Policy in Contemporary Egypt: An Evaluation of Recent Cases from Egypt's Highest Courts' (2003) 25 *Human Rights Quarterly* 720.

Bielefeldt H, 'Muslim Voices in the Human Rights Debate' (1995) 17 *Human Rights Quarterly* 587.

Budiman A, 'The New Order State: Language, Ideology, Hegemony', in Arief Budiman (ed.), *State and Civil Society in Indonesia* (Centre of Southeast Asian Studies, Monash University 1990) 132.

Bureau of Democracy, Human Rights and Labor, 'Indonesia: Report on International Religious Freedom' (United States Department of State 2007).

———,'Indonesia: International Religious Freedom Report' (United States Department of State 2010).

Chaplin J, 'Law, Religion and Public Reasoning' (2012) 1 *Oxford Journal of Law and Religion* 319.

Compilation of General Comments and General Recommendations Adopted by Human Rights Treaty Bodies (2006) HRI/GEN/1/Rev.8.

Crouch M, 'Judicial Review and Religious Freedom: The Case of Indonesian Ahmadis' (2012) 34 *Sydney Law Review* 545.

———, *Law and Religion in Indonesia: Conflict and the Courts in West Java* (Routledge 2013).

Engineer AA and Mehta U, 'Religion and Secularism', in Asghar Ali Engineer and Uday Singh Mehta (eds), *State Secularism and Religion: Western and Indian Experience* (Ajanta Publications 1998) 3.

Federspiel H, 'Islamic Values, Law and Expectations in Contemporary Indonesia' (1998) 5 *Islamic Law and Society* 90.

Freedom House, 'Policing Belief: The Impact of Blasphemy Laws on Human Rights' (Freedom House 2010).

Ghanea N, 'Are Religious Minorities Really Minorities?' (2012) 1 *Oxford Journal of Law and Religion* 57.

Giannella DA, 'Religious Liberty, Nonestablishment, and Doctrinal Development. Part I. The Religious Liberty Guarantee' (1967) 80 *Harvard Law Review* 1381.

Gilbert G, 'Religious Minorities and Their Rights: A Problem of Approach' (1997) 5 *International Journal on Minority and Group Rights* 97.

Goel SR, *Freedom of Expression: Secular Theocracy versus Liberal Democracy* (Voice of India 1998).

Hadler J, 'A Historiography of Violence and the Secular State in Indonesia: Tuanku Imam Bondjol and the Uses of History' (2008) 67 *The Journal of Asian Studies* 971.

Hanna S, 'Pencegahan Penodaan Agama (Kajian atas UU NO.1 TAHUN 1965)' (2010) 13 *RELIGIA* 2.

Henne P, 'Latest Trends in Religious Restrictions and Hostilities' (Pew Research Center 2015).

Hirji Z, 'Pluralism and Islamic Traditions of Sectarian Division', in Zulfikar Hirji (ed.), *Diversity and Pluralism in Islam: Historical and Contemporary Discourses Amongst Muslims* (IB Tauris 2010) 33.

Hodgson MGS, *The Venture of Islam: The Classical Age of Islam* (University of Chicago Press 1974).

Hosen N, 'Behind the Scenes: Fatwas of Majelis Ulama Indonesia (1975–1998)' (2004) 15 *Journal of Islamic Studies* 147.

HRWG, 'Alternative Report of Indonesia's ICCPR State Report, Article 18: Freedom of Religion and Belief' (Human Rights Working Group 2012).

Hui Y-F, 'Religious Freedom in Contemporary Indonesia: The Case of the Ahmadiyah', in Hui Yew-Foong (ed.), *Encountering Islam: The Politics of Religious Identities in Southeast Asia* (Institute of Southeast Asian Studies 2013) 44.

'Indonesia Religious Freedom Report' (United States Commission on International Religious Freedom 2007).

Jamal AA, 'Models of Pluralistic Discourse: A Consideration of the Ismaili Muslim Conciliation and Arbitration Boards in Kenya' (2001) 8 *Yearbook of Islamic and Middle Eastern Law* 86.

Joseph S and Castan M, *The International Covenant on Civil and Political Rights: Cases, Materials, and Commentary* (Oxford University Press Oxford 2013).

Karmali A, 'Sharia and Muslim Legal Thought in the 21st Century: The Paths Ahead' (2006) 13 *Yearbook of Islamic and Middle Eastern Law Online* 3.

Khan AM, 'Persecution of the Ahmadiyya Community in Pakistan: An Analysis under International Law and International Relations' (2003) 16 *Harvard Human Rights Journal* 28.

Labuschagne B, 'Recognition of Religious Differences under Dutch Law' (2000) 8 *Tilburg Law Review* 159.

Ladeur K-H and Augsberg I, 'The Myth of the Neutral State: The Relationship between State and Religion in the Face of New Challenges' (2007) 8 *German Law Journal* 143.

Marshall P and Shea N, *Silenced: How Apostasy and Blasphemy Codes are Choking Freedom Worldwide* (Oxford University Press USA 2011).

Mohammad Hashim K, 'Freedom of Expression in Islam' (2009) 31 *International Journal of Middle East Studies* 450.

'Monthly Report on Religious Issues' (The Wahid Institute 2011) 38.

Mudzhar MA, 'Fatwas of the Council of Indonesian Ulama: A Study of Islamic Legal Thought in Indonesia, 1975–1988' (UCLA 1990).

Mulder JAN, *Aliran Kebatinan as an Expression of the Javanese Worldview* (University of Singapore Department of History 1970).

Mustafa A, *Ahmadiyah: Keyakinan yang Digugat* (Pusat Data & Analisa Tempo 2005).

Nasution K, 'Fatwa Majelis Ulama Indonesia (MUI): On Ahmadiyah' (2008) 7 *Millah: Jurnal Studi Agama* 2.

Nuh NM and Rosidi A, 'Ikatan Jama'ah Ahlul Bait Indonesia (IJABI) Kota Bandung – Jawa Barat', in Ahmad Syafi'i Mufid (ed.), *Kasus-Kasus Aliran/Faham Keagamaan Aktual Di Indonesia* (Departemen Agama, Badan Litbang Agama Dan Diklat Keagamaan, Puslitbang Kehidupan Beragama 2006) 33.

Paddock RC, 'Separation of Mosque, State Wanes in Indonesia' (*Los Angeles Times* 20 March 2006).
Pearson E, *In Religion's Name: Abuses against Religious Minorities in Indonesia* (Human Rights Watch 2013).
Rosyidin M, 'Fenomena Aliran Sesat Di Indonesia' (2010) 61 *Ikhlas Beramal* magazine.
Saeed A, *Freedom of Religion, Apostasy and Islam* (Routledge 2017).
Shah N, 'Freedom of Religion: Koranic and Human Rights Perspectives' (2005) 6 *Asia-Pacific Journal on Human Rights and the Law* 69.
Shah-Kazemi R, *The Spirit of Tolerance in Islam* (IB Tauris 2012).
Steiner HJ, Alston P and Goodman R, *International Human Rights in Context: Law, Politics, Morals: Text and Materials* (Oxford University Press 2008).
Sutiyono, *Benturan Budaya Islam: Puritan & Sinkretis* (Penerbit Buku Kompas 2010).
Swett KL and Glendon MA, 'Egypt Breaks Faith on Religious Freedom' (*Al-Monitor* 2013).
Taylor PM, *Freedom of Religion: UN and European Human Rights Law and Practice* (Cambridge University Press 2005).
Temperman J, *State–Religion Relationships and Human Rights Law: Towards a Right to Religiously Neutral Governance* (Brill 2010).
Tempo, 'Kiamat Sekte Sibuea Diundur Hingga 2007' (2003) (*Tempo* magazine).
Trigg R, *Equality, Freedom, and Religion* (Oxford University Press Oxford 2012).
Van Der Kroef JM, 'The Role of Islam in Indonesian Nationalism and Politics' (1958) 11 *The Western Political Quarterly* 33.
———, 'New Religious Sects in Java' (1961) 30 *Far Eastern Survey* 18.
Verdict of Cikeusik Case (2011) Public Court of Serang District 314/Pid.B/2011/PN.SRG.
Verdict of Tajul Muluk Case (2012) Appeal Court of East Java 481/PID/2012/PT.SBY.
Vincent RJ, *Human Rights and International Relations* (Cambridge University Press 1986).
Wadud A, 'Towards a Qur'anic Hermeneutics of Social Justice: Race, Class and Gender' (1995) 12 *Journal of Law and Religion* 37.
Wiyana D, 'Mangapin Dituntut Hukuman Tiga Tahun Penjara' (2004) (*Tempo* magazine).
Yousif A, 'Islam, Minorities and Religious Freedom: A Challenge to Modern Theory of Pluralism' (2000) 20 *Journal of Muslim Minority Affairs* 29.

5 Protecting *forum internum* for religious minorities within Islam in Indonesia

1. Legal framework of *forum internum* in Indonesia

Discussing the *forum internum* of religious minorities within Islam in the Indonesian context is unequivocally complex. The concept of *forum internum* as asserted in the 1945 Constitution and international human rights instruments ratified by Indonesia is understood differently by the government and the general Muslim populace. The state frequently challenges the rights of religious minorities within Islam due to the influence of traditional Islamic orthodoxy and the practices of Indonesian customary law. The mixture of traditional Islamic orthodoxy and customary norms with Indonesian legal positivism has created serious complexity for human rights enforcement in the country, including the freedom to hold a certain version of the Islamic creed that is not in line with the majority. Based on this interwoven legal system, it is necessary to examine the legal spectrum of *forum internum* in relation to the concept of Pancasila. Pancasila is fundamental to understanding Indonesian human rights because as a national ideology and the supreme source of law, Pancasila is subject to interpretation. It can be interpreted in a relatively open and liberal way or in a monolithic and restrictive way, depending mostly on the regime and society in a particular era.

Pancasila consists of five, unamendable principles and has also become the highest source of law in the Indonesian legal system.[1] This means that Pancasila becomes the supreme source of law in the Indonesian hierarchical order of legislative rules.[2] The five principles of Pancasila are also mentioned in the preamble of the 1945 Constitution, which emphasises that these principles are established as the supreme source of the constitution. Even though there have been progressive legal and many human rights developments in Indonesia, particularly after the *Reformasi* era in 1998, such as the amendment of constitutional

1 See article 1 (3) of the Peoples' Consultative Assembly (Majelis Permusyawaratan Rakyat, MPR) Decree No. III/MPR/2000.

2 According to article 2 of the MPR Decree, the hierarchy of Indonesian law is as follows: The 1945 Constitution, MPR's Decree (TAP MPR), Act (UU), Substitute Act (Perpu), Government Regulation (PP), Presidential Decree (Kepres) and Bylaw (Perda).

human rights provisions and the enactment of the Human Rights Act, these Pancasila principles have not been amended. Broadly speaking, Pancasila should inspire legal and human rights development in Indonesia and hence the accurate understanding of Pancasila's religious principle is required to understand the scope of protection of all religions, including sects within a particular religion.

Indonesians should therefore invoke the spirit of Pancasila, particularly its religious, humanitarian and just principles to overcome human rights problems and to protect religious minorities within Islam. The National Alliance for Freedom of Religion and Belief (*Aliansi Kebangsaan untuk Kebebasan Beragama dan Berkeyakinan*, AKKBB) has been a leader in this and their advocacy of the freedom of religion for religious minorities within Islam proclaimed that Pancasila was the ideological basis for religious freedom and tolerance. AKKBB believes that the actions of particular religious groups such as the Islamic conservatives actually violate and endanger religious freedom.[3] This group highlighted the fact that Indonesia guarantees religious freedom for all of its citizens and noted further that this religious freedom is the essence of the unity in diversity slogan that serves as a foundation of Indonesia.[4]

According to Pancasila, the concept of monotheistic religion and God is basically sociological, so that God and religion here is purely a matter of interpretation.[5] The flexible interpretation of God and religion in Pancasila might be influenced by Soekarno's argument that "God is infinite and inclusive".[6] The word "inclusive" refers to a multi-faith God. Thus, all Indonesians have an equal right to interpret religion and God in Pancasila if their interpretation is in accordance with the spirit of pluralism. This would allow Christians, followers of local religions and Muslims to interpret God and religion based on their own unique, religious teachings. In Islam, some Muslim scholars have argued that the Indonesian Muslim majority believes that Pancasila is only in accord with Islamic belief. This is because the first principle of Pancasila, in their opinion, is simply another reformulation of the Islamic belief in the One Supreme God (*Tauhid*).[7] Others argue that the humanitarian principle can be interpreted by Muslims as the Islamic noble spirit of humanitarianism (*habl min al-nas*), which constitutes the second aspect of Islamic teachings after the spirit of godliness (*habl min-Allah*).[8]

3 Bernhard Platzdasch, *Religious Freedom in Indonesia: The Case of the Ahmadiyah* (Institute of Southeast Asian Studies 2011) 12.
4 ibid.
5 Ahmad Syafii Maarif, *Islam dan Pancasila Sebagai Dasar Negara: Studi Tentang Perdebatan Dalam Konstituante* (LP3ES 2006) 146.
6 Soekarno, Iman Toto K Rahardjo and Suko Sudarso, *Bung Karno, Islam, Pancasila, NKRI* (Komunitas Nasionalis Religius Indonesia 2006) 333.
7 Virginia Matheson Hooker and Amin Saikal, 'Political Islam in Post-Soeharto Indonesia', in Virginia Matheson Hooker and Amin Saikal (eds), *Islamic Perspectives on the New Millennium* (Institute of Southeast Asian Studies 2004) 137.
8 Virginia Matheson Hooker and Amin Saikal, 'Indonesian Muslims Enter a New Age', in Virginia Matheson Hooker and Amin Saikal (eds), *Islamic Perspectives on the New Millennium* (Institute of Southeast Asian Studies 2004) 2.

The late Muhammad Hatta, the first vice president of Indonesia, argued that "the monotheistic principle of Pancasila is a principle that should guide all other principles".[9] Hatta elevates the first principle of Pancasila to a supreme, religious level because, according to him, it inspires every legal and social development of the nation. This supreme religious principle of Pancasila remains flexible and applicable to all monotheistic religions as there is not an explicit assignment to Islam. The flexible interpretation of Pancasila's religious principle does not have a particular designation and hence any constructive interpretation of this principle is generally accepted by society. If we combine monotheism and humanitarianism, they are both quite compatible with the religious aspect of Pancasila because these principles stress that all religions, whether mainstream or not, practised by Indonesians must be protected.

Despite a clash of opinions among Indonesian Muslims, even as early as 1945 when Pancasila was first established, some leading Muslim thinkers such as the late Abdurrahman Wahid and the late Nurcholish Madjid strongly emphasised that Pancasila is the philosophy of the state and must be accepted by all Indonesians.[10] Thus, Indonesian Muslims do not need to interpret Islam as being in conflict with Pancasila because Pancasila reflects, relatively, the concept of *Tauhid* in Islam. In contrast, Pancasila's religious concept was intended to facilitate religious pluralism in Indonesia and encompasses all aspects of positive religious developments in the country. Accordingly, all religious sects including religious minorities within Islam must have an equal opportunity to develop, if they accept Pancasila as the ideology of the state.

However, the ongoing religious persecution of religious minorities within Islam indicates that some Indonesian Muslims see this broad interpretation of the concept of monotheistic religion as unsatisfying. In fact, this dissatisfaction manifested itself in entire attempts to establish a separate, Islamic state. These attempts have existed as early as the state's founding in 1940. Two notable leaders were Kahar Muzakkar, the leader of the Islamic movement in South Sulawesi, and S. M. Kartosuwirdjo, leader of Darul Islam in West Java. These men led a nationalist movement against Soekarno and Hatta, intending to establish separate Islamic states.[11] They served as the inspiration for Daud Beureuh, who declared an Islamic state in Aceh and Ibnu Hadjar in South Kalimantan.[12] Since then, Pancasila has been seen by some Muslims as an insufficient tool or "a failed ideology" that is incapable of covering all problems in the country. In response, these disgruntled individuals proposed Islam as an alternative doctrine to respond to social problems, including human rights. Some Muslims stated that the Republic of Indonesia, as the largest Muslim country, should adopt

9 Maarif (n 5) 157.
10 Yoyon Sukron Amin, 'Gus Dur Dan Riwayat Islam-Pancasila' (*The Wahid Institute* 2013).
11 Abdullahi An-Na'im, *Islam and the Secular State* (Harvard University Press 2009) 229.
12 Siti Hanna, 'Pencegahan Penodaan Agama (Kajian atas UU NO.1 TAHUN 1965)' (2010) 13 *RELIGIA* 4.

a constitution and laws which are in accordance with Islam or not in conflict with the teachings of this religion.[13] Therefore, some Muslims like Saifuddin Zuhri, a minister of the MORA in the Soekarno era, urged the government to enact a new law to theistically interpret the secular Pancasila because they argued that the Pancasila's principle is too broad.[14] They argued that there should be a more specific law to interpret the broad range of "belief in One Supreme God", noting that if every person can interpret this principle based on his or her belief, it endangers public order, national stability and religious pluralism itself.[15] Consequently, Soekarno agreed to enact Law No. 1/PNPS/1965, or the Blasphemy Law, to protect the rights of religious believers of established religions.[16]

Thus, since independence, although many Muslims agreed to the adoption of a theistic secular ideology and constitution, they nevertheless held that the state should promulgate laws in accordance with the Islamic creed. This means that the dispute over the relationship between Islam and the state ideology, especially over the rights of Muslims, first occurred in the first decade of modern Indonesia. This suggests that some Muslims, especially the orthodox, have experienced a long-lived dissatisfaction with Pancasila, including the theistic secular principle. They regard this interpretation as an attempt to undermine the dominant status of Islam, because by awarding all religions equal status it replaces religion with a secular ideology.[17] Thus, most Muslims argue that the 1965 Blasphemy Law was designed in principle as a tool to help implement the religious aspect of Pancasila and to protect all majority religions including Islam.

2. Protecting theistic religious freedom: problems and challenges

This book has defined Indonesia as a quasi-theistic secular state because it recognises One Supreme God, and leaves room for the interpretation of which God is meant. The book also argues that Indonesia has developed a reputation for pluralism and a moderate form of Islam and does more to protect freedom of expression than many of its neighbours. Additionally, the quasi-theistic concept can also be defined as a state which upholds secularism in its legislation but

13 See Bernard Johan Boland, *The Struggle of Islam in Modern Indonesia* (Springer Science & Business Media 2013) 44. The contention is especially about the constitutional clause which regulates the obligation of Muslims to carry out *Sharia*. See also Arskal Salim, *Challenging the Secular State: The Islamization of Law in Modern Indonesia* (University of Hawaii Press 2008) 1.

14 Salim (n 13) 160. See also Al Khanif, 'Questioning a Theistic, Secular Pancasila to Protect Religions' (*The Jakarta Post* 6 January 2015).

15 Khanif (n 14).

16 This law in principle restricts the spread of so-called "misleading interpretations" of religious teaching.

17 Sidney R Jones, '"It Can't Happen Here": A Post-Khomeini Look at Indonesia Islam' (1980) 20 *Asian Survey* 311, 320.

at the same time also takes into consideration the significant role of theistic religion in the public sphere.[18] However, because a fundamental aspect of the first principle of Pancasila is belief in One Supreme God, spreading atheism (which relates to *forum externum*) is legally forbidden,[19] although atheism is still allowed in practice in the private realm in conformity with *forum internum*. For example, the Padang Public Court (Pengadilan Negeri, PN) did not explicitly forbid individuals to embrace atheism. The court instead applied Act No. 11/2008 on Electronic Transactions and Information to restrict the spreading of atheism. According to this Act, individuals are prevented from spreading information that may incite hatred and hostility among individuals or groups based on, inter alia, religion.[20]

On the one hand, it has been observed that Indonesia has, with its unique legal and ideological state, become a model for the complex integration of democracy and Islam,[21] has succeeded in strengthening gender equality and has protected the right to change religion and belief even though these two rights remain controversial in other Muslim-majority countries.[22] Apart from the ongoing process of improving economic, cultural and educational rights, political rights have also been developed since the resignation of Soeharto in 1998. Most notable was a December 2007 Constitutional Court decision that found Articles 154 and 155 of the Indonesian Criminal Code (KUHP), which criminalised insults and similar offences against the government, to be in violation of constitutional guarantees of freedom of expression.[23]

On the other hand, however, the issue of so-called deviant religious beliefs has remained untouchable until recently and, in fact, has been considered as the most serious criminal offence against the recognised official religions. With regard to Islam, perhaps the Muslim minority sect most persecuted in the *Reformasi* era is Ahmadiyah. This sect's treatment has inflicted a sort of interpretive calamity on the right to freedom of religion in the country. The reason for this is that the government maintains a right to define what constitutes "a true religion" in Indonesia and has ensured through its policies that its citizens can only follow what it has deemed as an accepted religious faith.[24] In 1959, parliament

18 Khanif (n 14) 24.

19 In June 2012, the West Sumatra Court sentenced Alexander Aan to thirty months in prison and a fine of 100 million rupiah (US$11,000) for "inciting public unrest" via Facebook postings espousing atheism. See Human Rights Watch (HRW), 'World Report 2013' (*Human Rights Watch* 2013).

20 See the verdict of Muaro Court No. 45/PID.B/PN.MR/2012.

21 Freedom House, 'Policing Belief: The Impact of Blasphemy Laws on Human Rights' (Freedom House New York 2010) 43.

22 Until recently, the right to change religion was still prohibited in some Muslim countries. In Saudi Arabia, for instance, apostasy is forbidden and is considered as a serious crime for all Muslims. See further in Nicholas Garces, 'Islam, Till Death Do You Part: Rethinking Apostasy Laws under Islamic Law and International Legal Obligations' (2010) 16 *Southwestern Journal of International Law* 229.

23 See verdict of the Constitutional Court No. 6/PUU-V/2007.

24 Alfitri, 'Religious Liberty in Indonesia and the Rights of "Deviant" Sects' (2008) 3 *Asian Journal of Comparative Law* 1, 2.

asked the MORA to propose God, a Holy Book, prophets and principles of life to be followed by adherents of religion as fundamental criteria in defining a religion.[25] This definition was aimed at differentiating religion from mystical belief but until the present day this definition is not officially acknowledged by the MORA. That proposal by parliament in 1959 suggests that even though Pancasila should inspire the secular character of Indonesian human rights law and the broad understanding of religion, the massive movement and impact of Islamisation in the country has affected the government's definition of religion and consequently the *forum internum* of unrecognised religious minorities.

The main reason for the complexity of the right to religious freedom in Indonesia is that Pancasila as the highest legal canopy comprises short, simply constructed sentences that allow for a wide range of interpretation. With regard to the first principle, which is related to the belief in "One Supreme God", all monotheistic religions should theoretically be protected by this principle but, at the same time, non-theistic religions including minorities within a theistic religion cannot be discriminated against because Indonesia is also bound by international standards of human rights. Yet, the ongoing cases of religious persecutions, especially of religious minorities within Islam, show that this principle only applies to six recognised religions, which were established in a 2006 decision by the Ministry of Religious Affairs. It should also be noted that there are multiple interpretations of this principle among the official religions. Many Indonesians assume that it consists of abstract law that should further be elucidated in Indonesian derivative law, like the blasphemy law already mentioned in the previous section. Even though Pancasila was made the basis of the integration of different values, some intellectuals have come to perceive Pancasila as "a bowl without substance".[26] In this conception, Pancasila is viewed as a flexible ideology that can be interpreted differently by Indonesians.

Some believe that Pancasila as a national ideology contains all the noble ideals of Indonesia and sources of law thereafter established should not deviate from the values implicit in Pancasila.[27] Drijarkara, a great Indonesian philosopher for example, argued that "Pancasila is the best possible formulation of the relationship between religion and the Indonesian state because Indonesian culture, in general, is religious and sees life as a journey towards God".[28] The first Indonesian president, Soekarno, similarly argued that Pancasila becomes the guardian of the identity of the nation where the Muslims remain Muslim, the Christians remain Christian, the Buddhists remain Buddhist, the Hindus remain Hindu and so on.[29] He further

25 Rahmat Subagya, *Kepercayaan, Kebatinan, Kerohanian, Kejiwaan, dan Agama* (Kanisius 2002) 118.

26 Shigeo Nishimura, 'The Development of Pancasila Moral Education in Indonesia' (1995) 33 *Southeast Asian Studies* 303, 27.

27 Hesti Setyowati and M Harris S Toengkagie, 'Introduction to the Indonesian Legal System: Major Developments in the Past Decade' (2006) 13 *Yearbook of Islamic and Middle Eastern Law Online* 57, 58.

28 Alfitri (n 24) 5.

29 Sjafruddin Prawiranegara, 'Pancasila as the Sole Foundation' (1984) 38 *Indonesia* 74, 78.

noted that "Pancasila as the basis of Indonesian nationalism is not for just one person, not for just one group, such as the group of nationalists, or the group of the rich, but for all".[30] With his community outlook, Soekarno tried to use Pancasila to unite the Indonesian people into one single nation, a Pancasila Nation that does not privilege any one group over another but protects citizens equally.

Soekarno also asserted that Indonesia should have its own concept of political rights which was not absolute and confrontational in nature, but more inclined to deliberation, consensus and harmony.[31] His argument was based on his view of the state as an embodiment of the whole people, which was therefore bound to protect the people.[32] However, even though Soekarno was well known as a "Pancasilaist" and a strident supporter of secularism for the country, his policies on the protection of religious freedom remain controversial. For instance, Pancasila was Soekarno's alternative to a Muslim state, and any group that campaigns too vocally for Muslim interests such as upholding the establishment of an Islamic state was accused of undermining Pancasila.[33] In relation to the right of religious minorities, the Presidential Decree No. 1/1965, the Blasphemy Law, which is still being implemented, became his most controversial legacy on the history of religious minorities in modern Indonesia.

The Indonesian legal scholar Supomo, in early independent Indonesia, also asserted that the inner spirit and spiritual nature of the Indonesian people are characterised by the ideal of the unity of life of the people and their leaders in a totalitarian-integralistic concept of the Indonesian people.[34] In this system, the state is always obliged to maintain the unity and harmony of society because its leaders are at one with the people.[35] However, the state should not identify itself with the most powerful groups of society but should rather transcend all groups and individuals, identifying itself with the whole people in every level in the spirit of justice, peace and harmony.[36] Unfortunately, the spirit of harmony often influenced the state apparatus, including polices and judges, to discriminate against vulnerable groups or individuals in the name of the public interest.

The spirit of harmony had been bolstered by the second president, Soeharto, during his 32 years in power. He understood Pancasila as the principle of harmony and balance that should prioritise the community.[37] Soeharto further

30 Robert Edward Elson, 'Another Look at the Jakarta Charter Controversy of 1945' (2009) 88 *Indonesia* 105, 1112.

31 T Mulya Lubis, *In Search of Human Rights: Legal-Political Dilemmas of Indonesia's New Order, 1966–1990* (PT Gramedia Pustaka Utama 1993) 57.

32 ibid 58.

33 Jones (n 17) 320.

34 Herbert Feith, *Indonesian Political Thinking 1945–1965* (Equinox Publishing 2007) 198–190.

35 ibid 190.

36 ibid 191.

37 Eka Darmaputera, *Pancasila and the Search for Identity and Modernity in Indonesian Society: A Cultural and Ethical Analysis* (Brill 1988) 181.

proposed that "the unconditional acceptance of Pancasila was essential for continued national stability and unity".[38] The government frequently used Pancasila to safeguard the national interest, positioning individuals as bound by and subordinated to the public interest. Through his policies, Soeharto made Pancasila sacrosanct by repressing any attempts to challenge it. It was sacred because Pancasila was seen as an articulation of the historical experience of the Indonesian people and was also defined as an aspiration for the future. It may be argued that all of these propositions interpret Pancasila as a tool to preserve public interest rather than individual rights. When individuals demand and practise freedoms and rights, they should also conform to the particular ethics and morality that apply within their community, otherwise the government will curb individual rights to preserve the order and stability of the state.

During the Soeharto era, the religious principle of Pancasila was forcibly applied to all recognised and non-recognised religions, enhancing the theistic religious concept in society. This concept remained absolute because Soeharto's policy stipulated that all people should adopt a monotheistic religion as mandated by the state philosophy of belief in One Supreme God.[39] He asserted that:

> The position of the state was as a guardian of religion and an upholder of religious freedom and the spread of a religion may not be accompanied by intimidation because religion is based on one's personal conviction and because freedom of religion is fundamental human rights.[40]

However, his encouragement of greater religiosity in the nation and his advocacy of more than one religion are merely a reflection of efforts to eliminate the influence of Communism in Indonesia, rather than implementing equal religious freedom for all religions.[41] This can be seen from his policies which gave privileges to recognised official religions while individuals or groups that practised so-called deviant religious teaching were banned and arrested. Nearly 400 unrecognised religious cults labelled as misleading were banned in 1989, including some religious minorities within Islam.[42] His government also simultaneously monitored religious minorities within Islam considered to be in danger of deviating from orthodox Islamic tenets and some of them, such as the messianic Islamic sect Darul Arqam (LDII), were dissolved.[43] During this era, the government

38 Douglas E Ramage, *Politics in Indonesia: Democracy, Islam and the Ideology of Tolerance* (Routledge 2002) 35.

39 Robert Pringle, *Understanding Islam in Indonesia: Politics and Diversity* (Editions Didier Millet 2010) 91.

40 Boland (n 13) 41.

41 For further discussion about Soeharto's policy on religious piety, see Arskal Salim, 'The Influential Legacy of Dutch Islamic Policy on the Formation of Zakat (Alms) Law in Modern Indonesia' (2006) 15 *Pacific Rim Law & Journal Policy* 19, 684.

42 Indonesia: Annual Human Rights Report Submitted to Congress (U.S.D.S. 1989) 855–866.

43 Indonesia: Annual Human Rights Report Submitted to Congress (U.S.D.S. 1995) 783.

did not protect religious minorities within Islam that were seen as deviant and even advocated on behalf of MUI's *fatwa* on Ahmadiyah. Some of Soeharto's policies had also encouraged communal conflict between the majorities and minorities. An example was the fact that the hatred of Ahmadiyah was triggered by brochures circulated by the MORA and speeches in mosques, whereby Ahmadiyah was condemned as "infidel".[44]

This case shows that Soeharto used Pancasila as an authoritarian framework for legal unification. He ignored the diversity of Indonesia by enforcing a monolithic interpretation of Pancasila and hence it became entrenched in Indonesian legal, social, religious and political life. Like his predecessor, Soeharto used Pancasila as a tool of highly partisan social and ideological management.[45] Soeharto's authoritarian interpretation of Pancasila brought about the discourse of national unity described as a means of maintaining control over an extremely disparate and varied society. His emphasis on national unity imposed an artificial harmony and a "forced pluralism" in Indonesia that has begun to break down since the "*Reformasi* era" in 1998.[46]

In the *Reformasi* era, Pancasila underwent a new phase of "desacralisation", lacking a vision of the future of Indonesia. It is beleaguered by religious fundamentalism, extra-legal authoritarianism, internationalism and reformative euphoria in a messy, complex and fragile institutionalised process of democratisation. In this era, the Pancasila foundation of the republic is challenged by Islamist calls for "Shariatisation" across the nation.[47] Some Indonesian Muslim leaders such as Habib Rizieq Shihab, Abu Bakar Baasyir and members of the MUI have subordinated Pancasila by referring to their traditional Islamic orthodoxy to interpret religious freedom for the rights of religious minorities within Islam. Some people argue that the decline of Pancasila is caused by the long abuse of Pancasila in both the Old and New Order eras. Thus, in the *Reformasi*, Pancasila lost its central position even though it still regained some of its earlier potency as a symbol of an energetic, if sometimes beleaguered, Indonesian desire for unity, freedom and tolerance.[48] For example, Susilo Bambang Yudhoyono (SBY), the Indonesian president from 2004 to 2014, observed that "Pancasila is the principle, the foundation of the state and an open ideology, a living ideology that should become the source of enlightenment, the source of inspiration and at the same time the source of solutions for Indonesia's problems".[49]

44 Luthfi Assyaukanie, 'Fatwa and Violence in Indonesia' (2009) 11 *Journal of Religion and Society* 4.

45 Robert Elson, 'Pancasila's Contemporary Appeal: Relegitimizing Indonesia's Founding Ethos' (2012) 168 *Journal of the Humanities and Social Sciences of Southeast Asia and Oceania* 132.

46 Freedom House (n 21) 45.

47 Ann Black, 'Finding the Role for Shari'a Law in Post-Reformasi Indonesia' (2008) 2008 *Lawasia Journal* 165, 166.

48 Elson (n 45) 132.

49 Susilo Bambang Yudhoyono, *Indonesia on the Move: Selected Speeches and Articles by the President of the Republic of Indonesia* (Bhuana Ilmu Populer 2006) 49.

SBY's definition of Pancasila as a source of enlightenment in responding to contemporary human rights problems seems paradoxical. One important piece of evidence is that religious persecution of the so-called "deviant" religious minorities within Islam still occurred and has become even more serious. Even though SBY's government made progress by ratifying the ICCPR in 2005, which committed Indonesia to protecting and promoting human rights[50] and providing equal opportunity for religious believers to establish religious places,[51] the rights of religious minorities within Islam remain ignored. He frequently supported religious tolerance and pluralism and promised to protect religious minorities and hold perpetrators of sectarian violence to account, yet he also expressed support for a 2008 decree banning Ahmadiyah activities.[52] It may also be argued that during a decade in power, SBY has been criticised for his hands-off policy towards the persecution of religious minorities within Islam and for his slow response toward religiously motivated violence.[53]

3. Examining theistic *forum internum* within Pancasila principles

In examining religious freedom, particularly *forum internum* in Pancasila, one must consider its first principle, belief in One Supreme God. As previously mentioned, this theistic religious principle does not refer to any particular God and religion and hence many Indonesians argue that the secular-religious principle of Pancasila is compatible with all religions and beliefs practised by Indonesians, and that none of these religions or beliefs has a higher status in the country. Thus, it does seem clear that all traditional beliefs as well as mainstream religions are compatible with and protected by state ideology and hence official Islam and other official religions can claim no special place under the law.[54]

The first principle of Pancasila also means that Indonesia is a religious state, though not a theocratic one by which all religions have a recognised place. Thus, as analysed in Chapter 3, Indonesia is a theistic secular state where religion and the state must be clearly distinguished. Such a compromised distinction is important in order to avoid both the politicisation of religion and the religionisation of politics.[55] Yet the two are and remain connected. In terms of religious freedom, the cooperation of the state is necessary in avoiding the discriminatory manipulation of religious principles in legal instruments. Through

50 ibid 193.
51 U.S.D.S., 'Indonesia; Annual Human Rights Report 2005,' 30, 833.
52 U.S. Commission on International Religious Freedom, 'Annual Report 2012' (US Commission on International Religious Freedom 2012) 33.
53 Dian AH Shah, *Constitutions, Religion and Politics in Asia: Indonesia, Malaysia and Sri Lanka* (Cambridge University Press 2017) 224.
54 Michael Morfit, 'Pancasila: The Indonesian State Ideology According to the New Order Government' (1981) 21 *Asian Survey* 838, 849–850.
55 Benyamin Fleming Intan, *'Public Religion' and the Pancasila-Based State of Indonesia: An Ethical and Sociological Analysis* (Peter Lang 2006) 4.

this principle, the government is committed to not adopting any religion as a state religion but considers religion as an important aspect of life, not only for the sense of religion itself but also for ensuring basic human rights.[56] In this neutral stance, the quasi-theistic secular state is principally neither allowed to favour nor to discriminate against certain professions of faith. Additionally, it should generally withdraw from religious issues, especially the political act of defining what can legitimately be classified as religion and religious behaviour.[57]

The theistic religious principle underlying Pancasila guarantees equal protection for all religions and beliefs and all forms of religious difference. Pancasila was created to preserve Indonesian religious and cultural diversity. Through it, Soekarno's vision of a secular state was safeguarded, and Indonesia's Pancasila nationalist ideology became the strong protector of not only Islam but also Christianity and other minority faiths.[58] It is important to note here that the theistic character of Pancasila differs from religious freedom as understood in international human rights law. Here, Pancasila theoretically does not recognise non-theistic religions as well as the right not to profess any religion or belief as guaranteed under international human rights instruments.[59] However, while theoretically non-mainstream religions such as mystical beliefs and some unofficial religions are not protected, they should be permitted because the government's responsibility is to promote mutual tolerance. This state responsibility is based on the first principle of Pancasila. This mentions belief in One Supreme God, which is conceived as a general statement, broad enough to encompass a wide variety of religions and beliefs.[60] The broad definition of "Supreme God" in Pancasila is a result of a national compromise between Islamic and nationalist groups to establish a non-denominational state that is capable of maintaining religious diversity throughout the vast country. Hence, in its vagueness and broad definition of "Supreme God", Pancasila should become the constitutional basis for unity in a society characterised by plural ethnic and religious groups.[61]

Based on this argument, the religious principle of Pancasila should be understood as an attempt from the founders of Indonesia to advocate religious diversity rather than to preserve religious orthodoxy. It should not be used as

56 Lubis (n 31) 75.

57 Karl-Heinz Ladeur and Ino Augsberg, 'The Myth of the Neutral State: The Relationship Between State and Religion in the Face of New Challenges' (2007) 8 *German Law Journal* 143–144.

58 Nathan Jones, 'Rediscovering Pancasila: Religion in Indonesia's Public Square' (2005) 3 *The Brandywine Review of Faith & International Affairs* 23, 25.

59 The question of non-theistic religions will not be examined as this thesis is focused specifically on the question of protecting minorities within Islam. For the question of non-theistic religions in Indonesia see *e.g.* Subagya (n 25) 36.

60 Morfit (n 54) 840.

61 Donald E Weatherbee, 'Indonesia: The Pancasila State' (1985) *Southeast Asian Affairs* 133, 134.

religious justification to discriminate against those who have different interpretations of God and His divine revelation as part of *forum internum* protected by international human rights law. As asserted by Soekarno, Pancasila as the supreme source of Indonesian law promotes the interests of all religions and beliefs including unrecognised sects within official religions.[62] In this religiously accommodating state, religious communities not only maintain their autonomy but also are encouraged to make a vital contribution to the nation's public life through their particular beliefs, because their beliefs are protected equally.[63] The principle of a religiously accommodating state explicitly thrusts religion into the public sphere, not only as an inspiration for national development but also more particularly as an ethical and moral basis on which to implement humanitarian and religious principles; for instance, by guaranteeing religious freedom for all Indonesians.

Since the early days of independence, many Muslims have held the belief that the five principles of Pancasila, particularly the belief in One Supreme God, were in accordance with Islamic teachings and therefore many of them became prominent defenders of Pancasila.[64] The mixture of religious and humanitarian principles of Pancasila is also in accordance with the concept of *adamiyyah* (personhood or humanity) established by Imam Abu Hanifah, previously mentioned in Chapter 2. Thus, Indonesian Muslims must understand that individuals who believe in a Supreme God should be entitled to basic rights and be equally protected from any kind of discriminatory treatment. The focus of human rights in Pancasila should be understood as moral and legal principles to outlaw discrimination, because humanitarianism is created by God and hence individuals will be granted rights and freedom as long as they have theistic faith. It implicitly confirms that under the religious principle of Pancasila, discrimination is prohibited because it will infringe upon God's creations.

The secular defenders of Pancasila in contrast assume that the religious principle of Pancasila is a compromise between international human rights law and Islamic law. They view Pancasila as a secular ideology that combines secular principles of international human rights law with the religious principle of Islamic law and argue that this principle should not be defined as relating to a monotheistic God because it does not refer to any particular religion. Their argument then leads to the proposition that secularisation is very much compatible with the character of Pancasila and vice versa.[65] This can also be seen from the joining of the religious principle and the humanitarianism principle to promote the non-discrimination principle in the multicultural and religious society

62 Intan (n 55) 4. The plural word of religions was interpreted by Soekarno to define religion in a broad sense, including mystical beliefs, unrecognised religious sects and official religions.

63 ibid 5.

64 For further exploration of the relationship between Muslims and Pancasila, see generally R Michael Feener, *Muslim Legal Thought in Modern Indonesia* (Cambridge University Press 2007) 118.

65 Intan (n 55) 18.

of Indonesia. It is the manifestation of the unity in diversity principle (*Bhinneka Tunggal Ika*), as religious diversity is and will always be a fact in Indonesia. Today, it seems even to be more diverse and plural, evidence that Indonesian society has never been a monolithic society, especially religiously.[66] Thus, trying to impose a monolithic, religious interpretation would mean not only breaching the principle of belief in a multi-faith God but also undermining the humanitarian principle of Pancasila. Hence, Indonesian unity as asserted in the third principle means non-discriminate integration and respect for diversity of ethnicity, culture and religion.

Regardless of the reason, Pancasila is neither a religion nor a substitute for religion and people who believe in theistic religion should enjoy rights and a respected place in the Pancasila-based state.[67] The theistic secular character of Pancasila is intended to make it a neutral ideology and a source of law that protects religious and ethnic diversity. It shows that the character of unity in diversity inspired Indonesia's founding fathers to create an open and inclusive state ideology of Pancasila as part of the 1945 Constitution, the primary foundation of the nation-state, which transcends ethno-religious boundaries.[68]

It can be concluded that Pancasila, especially the first principle, which is belief in One Supreme God, theoretically recognises and protects all religions and beliefs. Under this principle, there should be no priority in religion because the state equally recognises all religions and no religious labelling such as mainstream religion, heretic or blasphemer, even though heterodoxy is a common feature of religion.[69] Even though the character of a theistic religious freedom in Pancasila differs from religious freedom in international human rights law, the recognition of a multi-faith God and the absence of a specifically named religion suggest that this protection should also include intra-religious sects within a particular religion. This means that religion should not be used to justify discrimination against those who have different religious interpretations because religion is conceptualised as a multi-faith belief which is open to human interpretation. Thus, all religious groups including religious minorities within Islam are protected equally under Pancasila. All six official religions have no right to restrict religious sects within their religions because this would be contrary not only to the secular-religious principle of Pancasila but also the second principle of a Just and Civilised Humanity. Additionally, discrimination against non-mainstream religions including religious minorities within Islam is in conflict with international standards of religious freedom and minority protection.

Any forms of discriminatory treatment against religious minorities are solely influenced by religious and socio-political reasons of the state and majority groups

66 Darmaputera (n 37) 167.
67 Prawiranegara (n 29) 4.
68 Sumanto Al Qurtubi, 'In the Spirit of Tolerance, a Merry Christmas to My Christian Friends' (*Jakarta Globe* Jakarta 24 December 2010).
69 Khanif (n 14).

to preserve social harmony and religious orthodoxy. The persecution of religious minorities within Islam occurs because the secular-religious principle of Pancasila is mingled with the so-called Islamic orthodoxy demanded by the MORA, MUI and Sunni Islamic organisations. This intermingling of law and religion in Pancasila brings together secular and religious principles which attempt to establish a civilised religious state and advocate universal human rights, thus making it very complex. One reason for this complexity is that in this context, balancing religious rights for the religious majority and religious minorities in Indonesia depends partly on the role of majority Islamic organisations. The majorities often define Pancasila to preserve their interests and discriminate against any religious groups that subscribe to different religious beliefs. Consequently, Pancasila as a state ideology and a supreme source of law works with diversity and the freedom of the people, operating like "a bowl without substance" to protect religious minorities.

4. The legal framework of *forum internum* in the 1945 Constitution

After examining the protection of *forum internum* in Pancasila, this section then examines the characteristic of religious freedom in the 1945 Constitution to understand the constitutional regulation of *forum internum*. This section will aid in understanding the hierarchical relationship of the religious principle of Pancasila and the freedom of religion in the constitution. Additionally, it is important to scrutinise the constitutional limitation of human rights in relation to the complexity of *forum internum* among religious minorities within Islam in Indonesia. The first part of the section examines the discourse of individualism in the constitution, its problems and how human rights were previously regulated in the constitution before the amendment. The second part discusses the characteristic of *forum internum* in the second amendment of the constitution. The section concludes with a discussion on the limitations of the constitution's treatment of human rights.

4.1. Between individual religious freedom and socio-religious harmony

The five principles of Pancasila are incorporated in the preamble of the 1945 Constitution. This preamble is understood normatively as a supreme source of the constitution, which also signifies that Pancasila serves as the basis of the 1945 Constitution that establishes the foundation of law for the Republic of Indonesia.[70] The immersion of the five principles in the 1945 Constitution confirms that the Pancasila values are intended to be the formulaic representation of the idea of the Indonesian state.[71] The ideological monopoly of Pancasila, which was created during the Soeharto era, has theoretically

70 Prawiranegara (n 29) 4.
71 Ramage (n 38) 185.

diminished.[72] Yet, since the *Reformasi* era, the moral and legal substances of Pancasila remain integral to the 1945 Constitution.[73]

Before the *Reformasi* era, the 1945 Constitution left constitutional human rights ambiguous because it only comprised thirty-seven articles, most of them on the most basic aspects of governance.[74] Limited provisions on civil and political rights were guaranteed, such as equality before the law (article 27), freedom of association and expression (article 28) and freedom of religion (article 29 (2)), which provided that "the State guarantees all persons the freedom of worship according to his/her own religion or belief". This signifies that the founders of Indonesia advocated for religious freedom even though the constitution was made during the chaotic period of the independence war and the long debate regarding the integralistic state. The problem, however, is that the right to religious freedom was neither practically nor comprehensively protected and implemented. Instead, the state could deal with such rights as it saw fit, including restricting or suspending them.[75] For instance, even though Pancasila and the 1945 Constitution guaranteed the freedom of religious belief, this was interpreted in practice by the New Order regime as requiring every citizen to have a religion, while at the same time it sought to restrict the activities of religious minorities within Islam and mystical traditions.[76] The experience of the New and Old Order regimes confirms that constitutional provisions of human rights did not work well because the government had frequently subordinated the rights of people to safeguard its political interest.

In the Indonesian legal system, it is common for privileged laws and documents like the 1945 Constitution to provide general principles, while the detailed elaboration of the principles is generally provided by special enactment at the lower level.[77] In principle, both Pancasila and the 1945 Constitution provide the protection of inter-religious minorities; specifically between Islam as the majority religion and Christianity, Hinduism, Buddhism and Confucianism as minorities. The main reason is that both types of religion had participated in the

72 What I mean by the abolition of the monopoly of Pancasila refers to Soeharto's policies which used Pancasila as a partisan tool to safeguard his power. See Decree of the People Consultative Assembly (MPR) No. XVIII/MPR/1998 which repealed Decree of the MPR No. II/MPR/1978 on Guidelines for Understanding and Practices of Pancasila (*Pedoman Penghayatan dan Pengamalan Pancasila*, abbreviated as P4).

73 Philip Eldridge, 'Human Rights in Post-Suharto Indonesia' (2002) 9 *The Brown Journal of World Affairs* 127, 130.

74 Ted L McDorman and Margot Young, 'Constitutional Structures and Human Rights in Southeast Asia: Cambodia, Indonesia, Thailand and Vietnam' (1998) 47 *University of New Brunswick Law Journal* 85, 98.

75 Timothy Lindsey, 'Constitutional Reform in Indonesia: Muddling toward Democracy', in Timothy Lindsey (ed.), *Indonesia, Law and Society* (2nd edn, The Federation Press 2008) 4.

76 Andrew Ellis, 'The Indonesian Constitutional Transition: Conservatism or Fundamental Change?' (2002) 6 *Singapore Journal of International & Comparative Law* 38, 132.

77 J Leyser, 'Legal Developments in Indonesia' (1954) 3 *The American Journal of Comparative Law* 399, 401.

formation of the nation. They made major contributions to the formation of nationalism during the colonial era by generating religious inspiration to support the Indonesian nationalist movement, thereby promoting national unity against Dutch colonialism.[78] However, none of them explicitly spoke about the right to religious minorities within religions during the formulation of the constitution.

The concept of the integralistic state proposed by Indonesia's founders may have also influenced the absence of human rights protection. In this concept, the state is the embodiment of the people and hence the adoption of human rights provisions in the constitution was considered unnecessary because the state automatically provides equal protection for all people. However, the absence of an unequivocal provision on the protection of minority rights in the 1945 Constitution left room for the religious minority problem. In practice, the government privileges the religious majority and has recently upheld the concept of religious uniformity in favour of Islam. As holders of public power in their religious roles, the major religious organisations also potentially "religionise" human rights law and government policies, which generally results in the suppression of the rights of religious minorities within the recognised religions. In relation to this, the nature of Indonesian society is like an Islamic society, which emphasises the protection of public or communal interest (*maslaha umma*).

It has been commonly understood that international human rights law prioritises individual autonomy while the Islamic (and local Indonesian) traditions present a communal view in which the concept of the self is realised collectively and defined through traditions and concepts of honour.[79] Muslims claim their identity is formed in terms of their religious community and this connection is essential. Thus, because the religious community is necessary for social identity, the state and the law have an obligation to protect it.[80]

In relation to the individualism of human rights in Indonesia, Huub Lems rightly argues that:

> The rights of individuals must be balanced by those of the community, by the obligation to display respect for the rights of others, the rights of society and the rights of the nation, Indonesian culture, as well as Indonesian customary laws; and a high priority is placed on the rights and interests of society or the nation without however, in any way ignoring or minimalising the rights of individuals and groups. Indeed, the interests of the latter are fully taken into account in the traditional practice of deliberations firmly embedded in Indonesia's national socio-legal and political institutions.[81]

78 Intan (n 55) 4.
79 Marty M Slaughter, 'The Salman Rushdie Affair: Apostasy, Honor, and Freedom of Speech' (1993) 79 *Virginia Law Review* 153, 155.
80 ibid 185.
81 Huub Lems, *'Freedom of Religion' in Indonesia: Some Thoughts from an International Perspective* (Brill 2010) 96–97.

The balance between individual rights and duties demonstrates that the Indonesian human rights concept emphasises that demanding individual rights without considering the obligation to respect the interests of society is generally seen as a taboo. Most people believe that freedom, especially individual freedom, needs to be controlled; if not, this could result in a potentially violent transition to a new form of rule.[82]

In examining the complexity of individualism in Indonesia, Knut Asplund says that:

> Individualism is perceived as a characteristically Western trait; a life stance able to find foothold only within a society where the link between the person and the community has been cut. The individual is thus someone who is not complying with prevailing norms in a given place, someone who is not bound by the village's unwritten rules, and someone who has escaped his obligation to support fellow villagers. Such an individual opposes and threatens the social order.[83]

Asplund's argument is relevant for examining the Indonesian attitude to preserve socio-religious harmony while also ensuring the rights of individuals or groups that adopt distinctive religious beliefs. Most Indonesians believe that Indonesian culture is different from the West and that the imposition of absolute individualism will disturb social harmony.

Because of this emphasis on community in Indonesia, the government usually argues that the imprisonment of individuals who embrace heterodox religious belief is not solely an enforcement of the blasphemy law but more about restoring social-religious harmony within a particular community that has been broken by an unlawful act which threatens socio-religious harmony.[84] In this sense, community is woven into most aspects of Indonesian traditional society and thus the demands of strict individualism as asserted by international human rights law may lead to the collapse of social norms. Human rights, especially rights related to religious and moral values in Indonesia, do not solely depend on written laws but are also influenced by unwritten rules within the society. These unwritten rules in many ways limit the independence of judicial institutions and the application of the constitutional provision of human rights, leading to the incompetency of the state to protect vulnerable groups, including religious minorities, within Islam.

Thus, both legal process and justice have become major issues in Indonesia as a politically complex, socially and religiously diverse and economically changing country.[85] Resolving cases in this legal trajectory does not only mean bringing a case to court and winning the case, but it is more about showing goodwill

82 Knut Asplund, 'Resistance to Human Rights in Indonesia: Asian Values and Beyond' (2009) 10 *Asia-Pacific Journal on Human Rights and the Law* 27, 33.

83 ibid.

84 ibid 30.

85 Daniel Lev, *Legal Evolution and Political Authority in Indonesia: Selected Essays* (Brill Nijhoff 2000) 11.

and proposing compromise to neutralise the intense conflict.[86] This argument is drawn from the fact that the imprisonment of individuals who embrace distinctive Islamic religious belief demonstrates that personal rights are subordinated to the greater value of socio-religious harmony among Muslims. This means the concept of neutralising conflict in the courtroom has been reinforced by the state to curb rights and freedoms seen as threatening social order within society.

4.2. The legal guarantee and scope of forum internum

The 1998 *Reformasi* era brought fundamental constitutional human rights provisions, challenging the concept of rights balance within Indonesia. At the beginning of that era, the 1945 Constitution was no longer viewed as sacrosanct for all Indonesian law, but rather as a document that could be reassessed and updated to reflect the needs and realities of contemporary Indonesia; except the preamble, which should be retained.[87] Thus, parliament offered a massive constitutional review of human rights provisions to transform Indonesia from authoritarianism into a democratic state. Many Indonesians know that in the thirty years of Soeharto's New Order, authoritarian rule was wrapped in the self-styled ideology of Pancasila, ostensibly based on ethnic harmony, national unity and decision-making by consensus.[88] Diversity and identity were highly state-managed affairs during the New Order regime and hence members of ethnic and religious minority groups saw the beginning of *Reformasi* as a new era in which their identity and way of life would be protected and valued within Indonesia's new democracy.[89]

The process of reform began in 1998 and stands on three pillars: democratisation and good governance, respect for and protection of human rights and the rule of law.[90] In terms of the protection of human rights, besides preserving the original version of religious freedom in article 29 (1), article 28 in the Human Rights Section also regulates *forum internum*. Article 28E of this section provides that:

1. Every person shall be free to choose and to practise the religion of his/her choice, to choose one's education, to choose one's employment, to choose

86 About peace or compromise in legal disputes, Lev correctly reported his own experience during his short stay in Yogyakarta, Indonesia. See ibid 189–190.

87 Timothy Lindsey, 'The Trajectory of Law Reform in Indonesia: A Short Overview of Legal Systems and Change in Indonesia', in Timothy Lindsey, *Indonesia, Law and Society* (2nd edn, The Federation Press 2008) 3.

88 Catharin E Dalpino, 'Indonesia's Democratic Difficulty: The Center Will Not Hold' (*Brookings* 30 November 1AD) 86.

89 Dominic Berger, 'Communal Violence in Indonesia : Implications for Democracy and the Role of the State' (Friedrich Ebert Stiftung 2011) 1.

90 N Hassan Wirajuda, 'The Democratic Response' (2002) 9 *The Brown Journal of World Affairs* 15, 18.

one's citizenship, and to choose one's place of residence within the state territory, to leave it and to subsequently return to it.
2. Every person shall have the right to the freedom to believe his/her faith, and to express his/her views and thoughts, in accordance with his/her conscience.

Additionally, article 28I (1) also regulates that, among others, freedom of thought, conscience and religion cannot be limited under any circumstances. Besides recognising religious freedom, article 28I (2) of the constitution guarantees that every person shall have the right to be free from discriminatory treatment based upon any grounds whatsoever and shall have the right to protection from such discriminative treatment.

All of these constitutional regulations on religious freedom are repeated by the Act No. 39/1999 on Human Rights (Human Rights Act). All words of article 28I (1) of the amended constitution are transplanted to article 4, and article 29 (2) of the previous constitution is transplanted to article 20 (2) of the Human Rights Act. Thus, the guarantee and the incorporation of religious freedom in Pancasila, the 1945 Constitution (as amended) and the Human Rights Act together confirm that Indonesian religious freedom is now in accordance with the spirit of international human rights instruments. The only difference under the Indonesian *forum internum* and international human rights instruments is that neither article 29 nor 28 of the constitution on religious freedom explicitly provides the right to change religion or belief. The absence of this right is due to the influence of Islam as the majority religion in the making of the 1945 Constitution, even though there is no explicit Islamic reference in Indonesian legislation.[91]

The influence of Islam can also be seen from the acknowledgement of a multi-faith God as one of the legal considerations to promote and protect human rights. For instance, besides being recognised in the preamble of the constitution, the Indonesian Human Rights Act also asserts that:

> Human rights are a set of rights bestowed by One Supreme God in the essence and being of humans as creations of God which must be respected, held in the highest esteem and protected by the state, law, Government, and all people in order to protect human dignity and worth.[92]

The significant influence of religious references to God in Indonesian legal development can also be seen from regulations of the state and verdicts of the courts. These sources often assert that the regulations and verdicts are

91 The influence of Islam can also be seen from the preamble of the 1945 Constitution, which says that the independence of Indonesia could be achieved due to the grace of "Allah" the Almighty and motivated by the noble desire to live a free national life.

92 Article 1 (1) of the Human Rights Act.

successfully adopted due to the mercy of the One Supreme God.[93] Based on this, since the beginning of modern Indonesia it is difficult to separate the character of legal and human rights development from religion in Indonesia. Most Indonesians will consider that the influence of religion is closely associated with Islam as the majority religion in Indonesia. Based on this argument, the right to change religion or belief and to hold heterodox religious teaching are considered as sensitive rights, regardless of if, in reality, religious conversion and heterodoxy occur in society if kept privately without public declaration.

The absence of significant regulation of the protection of minority rights in Indonesian law is often based on article 1(1) of the 1945 Constitution, which upholds the concept of the unitary state in the form of the Republic to manage ethnic, religious and cultural differences. This argument is reflected in the state's declaration in respect of article 1 of the ICCPR, to the effect that article 1 on the right of self-determination of the ICCPR does not apply to a section of people within the country. It is understandable that the declaration is aimed at protecting the unity of Indonesia because it comprises many different peoples, cultures and religions and beliefs.[94] The state does not make reservation on article 27, which specifically regulates minority rights, because the substance of article 27 is in accordance with Pancasila, the 1945 Constitution and the character of the nation which in principle have advocated tolerance of "ethnic, religious and cultural minorities".

This second amendment illustrates that the constitution establishes an expansive construction of freedom of religion and the protection of *forum internum* for religious minorities, including religious minorities within Islam. In relation to this, Samantha Knights argues that:

> The protection afforded by freedom of religion is important for society as a whole and minorities in particular. Minorities are especially vulnerable to biased perceptions and negative stereotyping and may not easily be able to secure their rights through the normal democratic process. At the same time there is a need to place limits on the freedom so that it does not become a means of infringing the freedom and rights of others. Throughout history, religious orthodoxies that began as the views of a persecuted minority, once associated with power have become the basis for persecution of others.[95]

93 See for example the verdict of Serang Court No. 308/Pid.B/2011/PN.Srg on Ahmadiyah, which says "on behalf of Justice based on One Supreme God". This sentence is always written in every court verdict, including verdicts of the constitutional court.

94 Kevin Boyle and Juliet Sheen (eds), *Freedom of Religion and Belief: A World Report* (1 edn, Routledge 1997) 200.

95 Samantha Knights, *Freedom of Religion, Minorities, and the Law* (Oxford University Press 2007) 1–2.

Based on Knights' argument, the constitutional protection of equal religious freedom for all religious adherents in a plural society is essential to the workings of constitutional democracy. The denial of religious freedom as one of the constitutional human rights will lead to undemocratic and authoritarian rule that potentially discriminates against and persecutes vulnerable groups.[96]

Yet, while religious freedom should be defined as a constitutional guarantee, it should operate as an equal protection for all religions without giving licence to the destruction of other religions, beliefs and cultures.[97] The equal protection means that in principle Indonesia implements positive neutrality towards religion. This would result in an absence of inferiority and superiority among religions and beliefs due to the absence of a specifically named religion in the constitution. In this regard, the state is free to support religions so long as it is not done in a way that favours one religion over another.[98] If there is a conflict between and within religious groups, the obligation of the state is not to remove the cause of tension by eliminating pluralism, such as imprisoning individuals, but to ensure that the competing groups tolerate each other.[99]

In this context, Indonesia theoretically accepts and recognises the universal validity of religious freedom, but the role of traditional religious orthodoxy is frequently mingled with the secular conception of human rights in the constitution. The existence of the MUI and the MORA and demands from the Sunni majority Islamic organisations suggest that the constitutional interpretation of religious matters should consider only orthodox Islamic law. Under this concept, constitutional human rights protections are accepted as long as these elements of constitutionalism are in line with their formal interpretation of Islamic law. Consequently, balancing *forum internum* for the Islamic religious majority and religious minorities within Islam in Indonesia depends partly on the role of Islamic organisations and the state religious institution, which usually use the exclusive interpretation of religious values.

The exclusive interpretation of religious values by religious institutions would lead to the emergence of theocratic constitutionalism, which engenders constitutional alienation of the rights of vulnerable religious groups such as religious minorities within Islam. This concept in principle allows particular groups to use their religious understanding to subordinate religious communities and individuals who have different religious teachings. Such theocratic constitutionalism generally prioritises an official interpretation of religious teachings from a particular institution.[100] This means that the essence of belief does not truly

96 Li-ann Thio, 'Constitutional Accommodation of the Rights of Ethnic and Religious Minorities in Plural Democracies: Lessons and Cautionary Tales from South-East Asia' 22 *Pace International Law Review* 60, 50.
97 Makau Mutua, *Human Rights: A Political and Cultural Critique* (University of Pennsylvania Press 2013) 97.
98 Knights (n 95) 15.
99 ibid 87.
100 Larry Backer, 'Theocratic Constitutionalism: An Introduction to a New Global Legal Ordering' (2006) 16 *Indiana Journal of Global Legal Studies* 85 (2009) 108.

rest on the individual's choice, because the state interferes in it through policies, laws and religious institutions backed by the state. For instance, the MUI issued a *fatwa* limiting the application of international human rights by comparing it with the Cairo Declaration on Human Rights in Islam to preserve equilibrium rights, balancing the equivalence of individual rights and individual duties, individual and social rights and freedom and duties.[101] This *fatwa* is one evidence that all constitutional clauses of human rights in Indonesia, in particular religious rights for minorities within Islam, are interpreted by Muslims based on Islamic values. If a particular constitutional clause does not fit with the official interpretation, then its substance will be lost. Thus, religious minorities within Islam who normally have insufficient representatives in formal and public spheres become disadvantaged because they cannot challenge this interpretation.

It may be concluded that the *forum internum* of religious minorities within Islam in Indonesia depends highly on the reception of Islamic majority groups rather than constitutional clauses. As a consequence, there have been continued persecutions of religious minorities within Islam, even though the second amendment of the 1945 Constitution adopted a progressive formula of civil liberties. One significant reason is that the government tends to adopt religious purism to interpret religious values and curb intra-religious pluralism. This kind of interpretation frequently establishes theocratic constitutionalism, which inhibits any possibility of interpreting Islamic law and allowing for the diversity of Islamic jurisprudence.

Bibliography

Al Qurtubi S, 'In the Spirit of Tolerance, a Merry Christmas to My Christian Friends' (*Jakarta Globe* Jakarta 24 December 2010).

Alfitri, 'Religious Liberty in Indonesia and the Rights of "Deviant" Sects' (2008) 3 *Asian Journal of Comparative Law* 1.

Amin YS, 'Gus Dur Dan Riwayat Islam-Pancasila' (The Wahid Institute 2013).

An-Na'im A, *Islam and the Secular State* (Harvard University Press 2009).

Asplund K, 'Resistance to Human Rights in Indonesia: Asian Values and Beyond' (2009) 10 *Asia-Pacific Journal on Human Rights and the Law* 27.

Assyaukanie L, 'Fatwa and Violence in Indonesia' (2009) 11 *Journal of Religion and Society* 1.

Backer L, 'Theocratic Constitutionalism: An Introduction to a New Global Legal Ordering' (2006) 16 *Indiana Journal of Global Legal Studies* 85 (2009).

Berger D, 'Communal Violence in Indonesia: Implications for Democracy and the Role of the State' (Friedrich Ebert Stiftung 2011) 1.

Black A, 'Finding the Role for Shari'a Law in Post-Reformasi Indonesia' (2008) 2008 *Law-asia Journal* 165.

101 Moch Nur Ichwan, ''Ulamā', State and Politics: Majelis Ulama Indonesia after Suharto' (2005) 12 *Islamic Law and Society* 45, 68.

Boland BJ, *The Struggle of Islam in Modern Indonesia* (Springer Science & Business Media 2013).

Boyle K and Sheen J (eds), *Freedom of Religion and Belief: A World Report* (1st edn, Routledge 1997).

Dalpino CE, 'Indonesia's Democratic Difficulty: The Center Will Not Hold' (*Brookings*, 30 November 1AD).

Darmaputera E, *Pancasila and the Search for Identity and Modernity in Indonesian Society: A Cultural and Ethical Analysis* (Brill 1988).

Dhont F, 'Pancasila's Contemporary Appeal: Relegitimizing Indonesia's Founding Ethos' (Sanata Dharma University 2012).

Eldridge P, 'Human Rights in Post-Suharto Indonesia' (2002) 9 *The Brown Journal of World Affairs* 127.

Ellis A, 'The Indonesian Constitutional Transition: Conservatism or Fundamental Change?' (2002) 6 *Singapore Journal of International & Comparative Law* 38, 132.

Elson RE, 'Another Look at the Jakarta Charter Controversy of 1945' (2009) 88 *Indonesia* 105.

Feener RM, *Muslim Legal Thought in Modern Indonesia* (Cambridge University Press 2007).

Feith H, *Indonesian Political Thinking 1945–1965* (Equinox Publishing 2007).

Freedom House, 'Policing Belief: The Impact of Blasphemy Laws on Human Rights' (Freedom House New York, 2010).

Garces N, 'Islam, Till Death Do You Part: Rethinking Apostasy Laws under Islamic Law and International Legal Obligations' (2010) 16 *Southwestern Journal of International Law* 229.

Hanna S, 'Pencegahan Penodaan Agama (Kajian atas UU NO.1 TAHUN 1965)' (2010) 13 *RELIGIA* 4.

Hooker VM and Saikal A, 'Indonesian Muslims Enter a New Age', in Virginia Hooker and Amin Saikal (eds), *Islamic Perspectives on the New Millennium* (Institute of Southeast Asian Studies 2004a) 2.

———, 'Political Islam in Post-Soeharto Indonesia', in Virginia Hooker and Amin Saikal (eds), *Islamic Perspectives on the New Millennium* (Institute of Southeast Asian Studies 2004b) 137.

Human Rights Watch (HRW), 'World Report 2013' (*Human Rights Watch* 2013).

Ichwan MN, ''Ulamā', State and Politics: Majelis Ulama Indonesia after Suharto' (2005) 12 *Islamic Law and Society* 45.

Intan BF, *Public Religion and the Pancasila-Based State of Indonesia: An Ethical and Sociological Analysis* (Peter Lang 2006).

Jones N, 'Rediscovering Pancasila: Religion in Indonesia's Public Square' (2005) 3 *The Brandywine Review of Faith & International Affairs* 23.

Jones SR, '"It Can't Happen Here": A Post-Khomeini Look at Indonesia Islam' (1980) 20 *Asian Survey* 311.

Khanif A, 'Questioning a Theistic, Secular Pancasila to Protect Religions' (*The Jakarta Post* 6 January 2015).

Knights S, *Freedom of Religion, Minorities, and the Law* (Oxford University Press 2007).

Ladeur K-H and Augsberg I, 'The Myth of the Neutral State: The Relationship between State and Religion in the Face of New Challenges' (2007) 8 *German Law Journal* 143.

Lems H, *'Freedom of Religion' in Indonesia: Some Thoughts from an International Perspective* (Brill 2010).

Lev D, *Legal Evolution and Political Authority in Indonesia: Selected Essays* (Brill Nijhoff 2000).

Leyser J, 'Legal Developments in Indonesia' (1954) 3 *The American Journal of Comparative Law* 399.

Lindsey T, 'Constitutional Reform in Indonesia: Muddling toward Democracy', in Timothy Lindsey (ed.), *Indonesia, Law and Society* (2nd edn, The Federation Press 2008a) 4.

———, 'The Trajectory of Law Reform in Indonesia: A Short Overview of Legal Systems and Change in Indonesia', in Timothy Lindsey (ed.), *Indonesia, Law and Society* (2nd edn, The Federation Press 2008b) 3.

Lubis TM, *In Search of Human Rights: Legal-Political Dilemmas of Indonesia's New Order, 1966–1990* (PT Gramedia Pustaka Utama 1993).

Maarif AS, *Islam dan Pancasila Sebagai Dasar Negara: Studi Tentang Perdebatan Dalam Konstituante* (LP3ES 2006).

McDorman TL and Young M, 'Constitutional Structures and Human Rights in Southeast Asia: Cambodia, Indonesia, Thailand and Vietnam' (1998) 47 *University of New Brunswick Law Journal* 85.

Morfit M, 'Pancasila: The Indonesian State Ideology According to the New Order Government' (1981) 21 *Asian Survey* 838.

Mutua M, *Human Rights: A Political and Cultural Critique* (University of Pennsylvania Press 2013).

Nishimura S, 'The Development of Pancasila Moral Education in Indonesia' (1995) 33 *Southeast Asian Studies* 303.

Platzdasch B, *Religious Freedom in Indonesia: The Case of the Ahmadiyah* (Institute of Southeast Asian Studies 2011).

Prawiranegara S, 'Pancasila as the Sole Foundation' (1984) 38 *Indonesia* 74.

Pringle R, *Understanding Islam in Indonesia: Politics and Diversity* (Editions Didier Millet 2010).

Ramage DE, *Politics in Indonesia: Democracy, Islam and the Ideology of Tolerance* (Routledge 2002).

Salim A, 'The Influential Legacy of Dutch Islamic Policy on the Formation of Zakat (Alms) Law in Modern Indonesia' (2006) 15 *Pacific Rim Law & Journal Policy* 19.

———, *Challenging the Secular State: The Islamization of Law in Modern Indonesia* (University of Hawaii Press 2008).

Setyowati H and Toengkagie MHS, 'Introduction to the Indonesian Legal System: Major Developments in the Past Decade' (2006) 13 *Yearbook of Islamic and Middle Eastern Law Online* 57.

Shah DAH, *Constitutions, Religion and Politics in Asia: Indonesia, Malaysia and Sri Lanka* (Cambridge University Press 2017).

Slaughter MM, 'The Salman Rushdie Affair: Apostasy, Honor, and Freedom of Speech' (1993) 79 *Virginia Law Review* 153.

Soekarno, Rahardjo ITK and Sudarso S, *Bung Karno, Islam, Pancasila, NKRI* (Komunitas Nasionalis Religius Indonesia 2006).

Subagya R, *Kepercayaan, Kebatinan, Kerohanian, Kejiwaan, dan Agama* (Kanisius 2002).

Thio L, 'Constitutional Accommodation of the Rights of Ethnic and Religious Minorities in Plural Democracies: Lessons and Cautionary Tales from South-East Asia' (2010) 22 *Pace International Law Review* 60.

US Commission on International Religious Freedom, 'Annual Report 2012' (US Commission on International Religious Freedom 2012).

Weatherbee DE, 'Indonesia: The Pancasila State' (1985) 133 *Southeast Asian Affairs* 1.
Wirajuda NH, 'The Democratic Response' (2002) 9 *The Brown Journal of World Affairs* 15.
Yudhoyono SB, *Indonesia on the Move: Selected Speeches and Articles by the President of the Republic of Indonesia* (Bhuana Ilmu Populer 2006).

6 Regulating *forum externum* to protect religious minorities within Islam

1. Restricting hate speech to protect religious minorities

Similar to international human rights instruments, the 1945 Constitution also recognises certain limitations of human rights. The distinctive character of human rights limitation is regulated by article 28J (2) of the 1945 Constitution. It says:

> In exercising his/her rights and freedoms, every person shall have the duty to accept the restrictions established by law for the sole purposes of guaranteeing the recognition and respect of the rights and freedoms of others and of satisfying just demands based upon considerations of morality, religious values, security and public order in a democratic society.

The recognition of religious values without referring to any particular religions in the second amendment asserts that the constitution advocates the "religionisation" of Indonesian society rather than the Islamisation of the country. It can be argued that the religious clause may not be used by a certain religious doctrine to restrict a particular manifestation of religious right. The constitutional clause of limitation should be interpreted as saying that all limitations on the manifestation must be applied necessarily to protect public safety, order, health or morals and the fundamental rights and freedoms of others.

As previously mentioned, religious minority rights are generally concerned with protecting collective aspects of individual rights and therefore require positive measures from the government to preserve group identity.[1] One such positive measure is the restriction of religion-inspired hate speech which may breach public order and the fundamental rights of others. This restriction is justified under Article 19(3) of the ICCPR, which requires state parties to fulfil their respective obligations against certain expressions which reach the threshold of incitement to hatred.[2] Additionally, the restriction itself must fulfil the fundamental requirements of human rights restrictions.

1 Nazila Ghanea, 'Minorities and Hatred: Protections and Implications' (2010) 17 *International Journal on Minority and Group Rights* 423, 423.

2 See article 19 of the ICCPR.

For example, the intervention must be necessary to protect the democratic environment or address a pressing social need and must not have an adverse discriminatory effect on certain sectors of the population within a particular society.[3] Taking action against hate speech is classified as an obligation of the state to engage actively in the protection of vulnerable groups such as religious minorities within Islam.

The state, under Article 28 G (1 & 2) of the 1945 Constitution, is mandated to restrict freedom of expression if it consists of incitement that may trigger violence and direct discrimination against a particular group.[4] The provisions of Article 28 are in accordance with international anti-hate speech provisions. For example, CERD states that Indonesia, as a state party, should take appropriate measures such as condemning hate speech and propaganda for the sole purpose of securing individuals the right to enjoy or exercise human rights and fundamental freedoms.[5] The restriction of hate speech is further regulated in Article 156 of the Indonesian Criminal Code. This article states:

> Anyone who expresses feelings of hostility, hate or humiliation towards one or several Indonesian social groups, is threatened with up to four years in prison. The term group in this article and the following article refers to any part of Indonesian society that is different from other groups due to race, country of origin, religion, place, origin, ancestry, nationality, or status according to state administrative law.

This limitation also coincides with article 20 (2) of the ICCPR, which obliges states to prohibit inter alia religious hatred that constitutes incitement to discrimination, hostility or violence. The HRC has similarly stated that the manifestation of religion or belief may be restricted if it uses, inter alia, physical force or hateful propaganda to compel others to adhere to its religious beliefs and congregation or propaganda that constitutes incitement to discrimination, hostility or violence.[6] This proposition suggests that states may prohibit religious manifestations such as hateful religious speech or publications which promote racial or religious discrimination, hostility or violence because they threaten the rights of others and may incite violence that will disturb public order. Some states also decree that the practise of religion and other rights can be restricted to protect the fundamental character of a democratic society.[7]

3 Susannah C Vance, 'The Permissibility of Incitement to Religious Hatred Offenses under European Convention Principles' (2004) 14 *Transnational Law & Contemporary Problems* 201, 209.

4 This article basically regulates that everyone has freedom from fear and is free from any action that might violate her or his dignity.

5 See CERD with particular reference to article 2 and 4. Indonesia ratified the convention on 25 June 1999.

6 General Comment No. 22, Compilation of General Comments and General Recommendations Adopted by Human Rights Treaty Bodies 2006 3.

7 For further discussions in Canada and Italy, see Sarah Joseph, 'Human Rights Committee: Recent Cases' (2001) 1 *Human Rights Law Review* 305, 83–94.

Additionally, states may interfere with people's freedom of expression in order to deal with possible conflicts between the rights of a group to preserve some aspects of substantive minorities' identity.[8]

Unfortunately, these articles are hardly applied to the restriction of hate speech. Hate speech against religious minorities within Islam has become a topic of sermons in some mosques, which has consequently increased the persecution of religious minorities within Islam.[9] For example, a Muslim cleric in West Nusa Tenggara, Izzi Muslim, called for the expulsion of and fought against the Ahmadiyah, declaring them deviant Muslims. Izzi confirmed that his harsh speeches against Ahmadiyah were based on the MUI *fatwa*, which opined that the Ahmadiyah were heretical.[10] Even though his hate speech inspired a local attack against Ahmadiyah, Izzi remains free.

In cases such as that of Izzi Muslim and the Ahmadiyah, the government should take appropriate measures to restrict religion-inspired hate speech because protecting religious minorities within Islam is an uneasy matter, particularly in Indonesia. It is a fact of religious phenomena that all religious groups denounce one another and claim to be the most truthful group. Most Muslims in Indonesia, and in other parts of the Muslim world, commonly denounce and threaten religious minorities within Islam because they are accused by the majority of insulting orthodox Islamic beliefs. Consequently, places of worship and villages of religious minorities within Islam have been the target of religiously motivated attacks by several mainstream Islamic groups.[11] In the last ten years, violence against Ahmadiyah mosques around Indonesia has increased, many incidents being triggered by hate speech.[12] Increased violence suggests that the religious freedom of Muslims and freedom of expression are distorted because all groups and individuals claim their rights and freedoms in a scenario of intense competition and contestation.

Regarding the freedom to express hostility against other groups, the state may allow individuals to speak about religious hatred to their own congregation in private spheres, which could then instigate non-violent acts of racial or religious discrimination.[13] However, the state must restrict the freedom of individuals who publicly disseminate their expressions of hostility, such as in mass media or

8 Nazila Ghanea, 'Are Religious Minorities Really Minorities?' (2012) 1 *Oxford Journal of Law and Religion* 57, 76.

9 From the period of January to July 2013, Setara Institute reported 122 cases of religious persecutions. In 2012, the number of cases slightly increased to 264 from 244 cases in 2011. See further detail in www.setara-institute.org/en/content/report-freedom-religion-and-belief-mid-2013

10 Arghea Desafti Hapsari and Panca Nugrah, 'MUI Fatwa Feeds Flames of Clerics' Hate Speech' (Jakarta 17 January 2011).

11 Melissa Crouch, 'Regulating Places of Worship in Indonesia: Upholding Freedom of Religion for Religious Minorities?' (2007) 96 *Singapore Journal of Legal Studies* 116.

12 Jeremy Menchik, 'Why Is a New York Rabbi Giving a Tolerance Award to Indonesia's Intolerant President?' (*Tablet Magazine* 21 May 2013).

13 Ghanea (n 1) 430.

through direct verbal attack, which could jeopardise public order.[14] Legitimate interference in response to public hate speech is based on the HRC's argument that:

> The state party can take strict measures against any dissemination of ideas that constitute discrimination of superiority and inferiority groups or which attempt to justify violence, hatred or discrimination against descent-based communities, including through the internet.[15]

The restriction against religious hatred to protect vulnerable religious groups may be classified as the state's obligation to treat its citizens with equal concern and respect. Additionally, it should ensure that all citizens are entitled to equal concern and respect from other citizens.[16]

Verbal offences against religious minorities within Islam are a very serious matter in Indonesia, threatening the ability to live in peace and security. In some public media, such as on the internet or in print-based media, mainstream Islamic groups have claimed that religious minorities within Islam do not have the right to claim to be Muslims and can, therefore, be justifiably killed.[17] They usually cite state practices in other parts of the Muslim world, the MUI *fatwa* and the Indonesian blasphemy law to justify their hatred. This kind of stereotyping speech is an act of aggression generally directed against vulnerable groups and should therefore be controlled by the state. They should not be allowed to publicly express their hatred towards religious minorities within Islam. If this right is not restricted it may provoke discriminatory or even violent action against members of the targeted group.[18]

It is noted that in such situations the state can justifiably interfere in freedom of speech constituting incitement or hateful expression against individuals or a particular group of people in order to protect the rights and reputations of others. In the context of the general protection of religious minorities, the rights and reputation of religious minorities within Islam should also be protected. Additionally, the management of hate speech is required to anticipate the causal link between the expression and the poisoned environment that may

14 Jeroen Temperman, 'Freedom of Expression and Religious Sensitivities in Pluralist Societies: Facing the Challenge of Extreme Speech' (2011) 2011 *BYU Law Review* 729, 732.

15 General Recommendation XXIX, HRI/GEN/1/Rev.7 at 229.

16 Rhoda E Howard-Hassmann, 'Canadians Discuss Freedom of Speech: Individual Rights versus Group Protection' (2000) 7 *International Journal on Minority and Group Rights* 109, 133.

17 See, for instance, Sobri Lubis's statement (Secretary General of the Islamic Defender's Front (FPI)), which incites hatred against the Ahmadiyah and urges Muslims to kill Ahmadiyah members. *Ceramah Penghasutan Untuk Membunuh Anggota Ahmadiyah Dan Mengacaukan NKRI.*

18 Henry J Steiner, Philip Alston and Ryan Goodman, *International Human Rights in Context: Law, Politics, Morals: Text and Materials* (Oxford University Press 2008) 640.

harm minority groups.[19] The freedom to express religious differences must be balanced with the rights of minority religious groups. In other words, the majority, in fact, may express their religious orthodoxy as their religious human right, yet they must also consider that the minority has the right to be different. It is the duty of the majority to respect this difference. The state may be more sensitive towards the majority, but it also has obligations to protect the rights of the minority. Such restriction is required not only to protect public order and the rights of others, but also to educate people about the importance of religious pluralism as a fundamental characteristic of Indonesia.

Although there is no universally accepted definition of hate speech, for the purposes of this chapter it can be defined as including speeches that promote or lead to religious hatred against a particular group of persons, defined by reference to their religious beliefs or a lack thereof.[20] Such religion-inspired hate speech would also involve incitement to hostility against other persons, triggered by one's interpretations of his or her own beliefs.[21] In other words, the fundamental idea of hate speech covers abusive, denigrating, harassing speech based on, inter alia, a group or individual's religious identity.[22] However, it should be emphasised that the focus of hate speech is not to protect religious doctrine, but rather to insult individuals or groups and strategically arouse hatred against them. It is different from the concept of blasphemy, which focuses on the protection of religious doctrine. In the restrictive concept of hate speech, everyone is acknowledged as having the freedom to express their opinions,[23] but this right can be restricted or censored if it consists of the incitement of violence or discrimination against a particular group or individual for religious reasons.[24]

The main issues regarding the restriction of religion-inspired hate speech are that the persecution of religious minorities is very often triggered by the overlapping of the freedom of expression and religious freedom of two religious groups. Tension between competing freedoms occurs because religious freedom is the business of faith communities, which are generally understood by religious communities as being interested only in their own rights and not the equivalent rights of others.[25] Even though religious freedom and freedom of expression are considered individual rights, many cases of persecution of minorities within Islam are related to group rights, and in particular the rights of those minorities. Minorities such as religious minorities within Islam therefore require stronger

19 HRC, CCPR/C/70/D/736/1997. para. 11.5–6.

20 Vance (n 3) 1.

21 Temperman (n 14) 748.

22 Steiner, Alston and Goodman (n 18) 639.

23 See *e.g.* article 19 of the UDHR and ICCPR and article 28 (E) paragraph 3 of the 1945 Constitution of Indonesia.

24 See, *e.g.* article 20 (2) of the ICCPR and article 28J (2) of the 1945 Constitution of Indonesia.

25 Malcolm Evans, 'Advancing Freedom of Religion or Belief: Agendas for Change' (2012) 1 *Oxford Journal of Law and Religion* 5, 8.

protection from the state because of their legal and political vulnerability. That is why the UN has recognised minority rights as special rights which require effective protection from the state.[26] Hence, the state is not only mandated to respect the rights of minorities but is also obliged to take the necessary steps to protect them, such as restricting religion-inspired hate speech. This allows members of minorities to start off from a platform of equality on a par with majorities.[27]

2. Restricting hate speech: the Rizieq Shihab case

As is the case in many parts of the Muslim world, religious minorities within Islam in Indonesia face discrimination both from government and non-government actors. Unlike in other parts of the Muslim world, however, the main reason for the repression of religious minorities within Islam is not the concept of an Islamic theocratic state, in which the state is the manifestation of the social group that adheres to the Islamic religion.[28] Repression of those who deviate from mainstream Islam occurs as a consequence of the uneasy relationship between religion and state, as well as the position of religion as a pillar of collective identity. The de facto boundaries of religion and state in the country are blurred, at best, and continually contested in both political and judicial spheres.[29] In the realm of religious rights, religious dimensions – especially theology and morality – have long combined and competed with state law, putting the individual religious rights of vulnerable groups at stake. One best example is the case of freedom of expression that incites hate speech against religious minorities within Islam.

One religious hate speech case in Indonesia brought before the court was the case of Habib Rizieq Shihab (hereafter Shihab), leader of the FPI, and Munarman, leader of the Commando of Islamic Army (KLI), in 2008. The District Court of Central Jakarta convicted Shihab and Munarman, sentencing them to 18 months in prison for inciting an attack on the Ahmadiyah during a mass demonstration at the National Monument in Jakarta in 2008 and thereby disturbing public order.[30] Munarman was imprisoned due to his direct involvement in attacking the victims, which breached article 170 (1) of the Indonesian Criminal Code, while Shihab was accused of triggering violence through hate speech against the Ahmadiyah, even though he was not directly involved in the incident. The court found that Shihab's speeches, either exclusively addressed to his followers or expressed in mass media and constituting hatred against the

26 Ghanea (n 8) 60.

27 Ghanea (n 1) 424.

28 Azyumardi Azra and Wayne Hudson, *Islam beyond Conflict: Indonesian Islam and Western Political Theory* (Ashgate 2008) 19.

29 Ran Hirschl, 'Juristocracy vs. Theocracy: Constitutional Courts and the Containment of Sacred Law' (2009) 1 *Middle East Law and Governance* 129, 131.

30 Verdict of the District Court of Central Jakarta No. 1616/PID/B/2008/PN.JKT.PST.

Ahmadiyah, were the main factor instigating his followers to attack the rally, bringing injury to many people.[31]

In his defence during the trial, Shihab opined that Islam tolerates religious freedom and restricts forced religious conversion but does not tolerate those who denigrate Islam as a religion.[32] In the case of the Ahmadiyah, he opined that the Islamic group is not Muslim but a group of apostates or hypocrites. He claimed that the Ahmadiyah, therefore, do not have a right to claim Muslim status and urged all Muslims to fight against them.[33] Shihab did not quote a single provision from written state laws or any applicable laws in the Indonesian criminal legal system. Rather, he further defended his argument that hostility against the Ahmadiyah, and those who deviated from mainstream Islam, was protected by Islamic law.[34] Even though he quoted some Qur'anic verses, such as 16:125 and 3:159, which urge Muslims to invite others to Islam with wisdom and virtuous propagation, deal gently with people and surrender all matters to Almighty God, he also quoted, albeit out of context, the history of the Prophet's revenge against those who insulted Islam.[35]

Shihab repudiated other Hadiths that regulate the question of apostasy requiring particular circumstances, such as the intention of the apostating person to split themselves from the community and actively engage in fighting against the Muslim community.[36] The Islamic law on the death penalty for apostasy is related to law in a time of war. The Qur'an does not suggest that those engaged in hostilities should be forced to convert to Islam.[37] This argument is supported by the fact that there is no single verse in the Qur'an which explicitly commands Muslims to persecute anyone who deviates from mainstream Islam or does not believe in it at all. One Hadith, usually cited as legal justification for persecuting apostates or any form of Islamic deviant, was classified as belonging to the solitary or *ahad* category, because Ibn Abbas, who transmitted it, was only thirteen years old at the time of the

31 ibid 71. See also Human Rights Watch, 'In Religion's Name | Abuses against Religious Minorities in Indonesia' (*Human Rights Watch* 28 February 2013) 37.

32 Shihab used several Qur'anic verses to support his defence, such as 9: 73, 66: 9, 48: 29, and 3: 159, and several Hadiths as well as Islamic jurisprudence from Ali b. Thalib. See further in Habib Rizieq Shihab, 'Mengadili Perjuangan Pembubaran Ahmadiyah' (District Court of Central Jakarta 20 October 2008) 37.

33 ibid 10–13.

34 Besides citing Qur'anic verses, he also quoted several *Sunna* and the tradition of the companions. For instance, he quoted Ali b. Abi Thalib's message to his companions, saying that Muslims may convince themselves to use force if they think that it is the best way to resolve a dispute. See ibid 36.

35 Rizieq Shihab quoted Qur'anic verses (9: 107–8) which describe the *munafiqun* group who established the opposition mosque to divide Muslims. See ibid 33–39.

36 Abdullah Saeed notes several Hadiths which clarify the death penalty for apostasy in Islam, such as Hadiths transmitted by Abu Dawud, Imam Bukhari and Imam Muslim. See further discussion in Abdullah Saeed, 'The Islamic Case for Religious Liberty' (*ABC Religion & Ethics* 24 February 2012).

37 ibid.

Prophet's death.[38] This is contrasted by the actual conduct of the Prophet Muhammad, who allowed a man wanting to convert to his former religion, after embracing Islam, to go free without imposing any penalty on him.[39]

The Shihab case suggests that most conservative Muslim clerics still understand religious freedom as freedom to enter into Islam but not freedom to leave it.[40] Clerics in some Muslim-states also extend restricted freedom to Muslims practising different interpretations of Islam. In Indonesia, for example, it is believed by most conservative Muslim majorities that such restrictions are applicable to religious minorities within Islam as well as to individuals who advocate the urgency and need to rejuvenate Islamic hermeneutics and therefore deviate from mainstream Islam. This conservative view unfortunately persists today, even though the Qur'an states that Muslims are family and issues a divine mandate for all Muslims to settle disputes among themselves peacefully.[41] It is regrettable that when Islamic law offers a choice between two or more solutions, some Muslims opt for the most severe, which generally disapproves of rights and freedoms.[42] Consequently, they do not recognise Muslims' freedom to have different interpretations of Islamic law, as this right is mostly considered by the ruling Islamic groups as an affront to Islam by so-called deviant Islamic beliefs.

The Shihab case also shows that some Muslims still prefer to quote Qur'anic verses and Hadiths out of context in order to support an oppositional view of human rights, even though others apparently support various modern human rights principles such as religious freedom.[43] Shihab's continuous hate campaign against religious minorities within Islam not only denies the divine mandate of the Qur'an and Hadith to promote Islam in a peaceful way, but also repudiates Islamic jurisprudence on personal religious freedom and expression, as in the case of the Kharijites in the era of the Caliph Ali b. Abi Thalib. The freedom to express opinions is guaranteed so long as opposition is not accompanied by acts of violence or supported by force.[44] This argument should also apply to the rights of Muslim dissidents to practise their different Islamic interpretations. In general, it seems that when Shihab insisted that religious minorities within Islam, such as the Ahmadiyah, should be restricted or even killed, his authority basically surpassed the Prophet Muhammad; the Prophet was only mandated by God to deliver Islam, not to compel individuals to embrace Islam.[45] It is regrettable

38 Mohamed Charfi, *Islam and Liberty: The Historical Misunderstanding* (Zed Books 2005) 49.
39 Saeed (n 36).
40 Charfi (n 38) 48.
41 See Qur'an 49:10.
42 For further discussion about the controversy of the death punishment and the politicisation of Islamic law in the Islamic world, see Charfi (n 38) 48–59.
43 Abdullahi Ahmed An-Na'im, 'Islam and Human Rights: Beyond the Zero-Sum Game' (*ABC Religion & Ethics* 9 April 2018).
44 Ahmed Zaki Yamani, 'Humanitarian International Law in Islam: A General Outlook' 7 *Michigan Journal of International Law* 28, 193.
45 See Qur'an 64: 12.

that this kind of conservative voice appears to be dominating the discourse of Islam and human rights in many parts of the Muslim world.

In Indonesia, religious hatred has frequently been utilised in campaigns by Shihab and hardline Islamic groups to demonise religious minorities within Islam and individuals who advocate independent juridical reasoning (*ijtihad*) to rejuvenate the right to religious freedom in Islam. These hardliners persuade other Sunni moderate Islamic groups, as well as judicial institutions, to restrict the Ahmadiyah and the Shi'ah because they believe that these groups threaten their orthodox Islamic beliefs.[46] They claim that religious minorities within Islam like Ahmadiyah and the Shi'a in fact violate their religious rights, namely their version of orthodox Islamic rights, and as a result they adopt extra-legal enforcement by issuing *fatwas* to defend their rights. For instance, in 2002 a *fatwa* was issued by the Unity of Islam (Persis), the Prosperous Justice Party (PKS) and the mainstream Muhammadiyah movement accusing Ulil Absar Abdalla of blasphemy because he said that the Prophet Muhammad was primarily a historical figure and questioned the basis of Islamic law.[47] These orthodox Islamic groups opined that Abdalla's critical interpretation of the Qur'an and the Prophet may be classified as blasphemous belief. They threatened Abdalla with jail under Indonesian law and further argued that anyone who slanders Islam can be punished with death in accordance with Islamic law.[48] However, Abdalla has still not been tried and remains free, even though his critiques of Islam caught the attention of radical orthodox Islamic groups.

The Abdalla and Shihab cases suggest that Indonesia basically promotes freedom of expression irrespective of criticising religious beliefs. At the same time, it also restricts hate propaganda to preserve religious pluralism and vibrant democracy as substantive characters of the nation. Even though it is the obligation of the state to guarantee freedom of expression, the Shihab case confirms that everyone is restricted from engaging in activities that violate the rights of others.[49] Freedom of speech is not a value which requires absolute protection, but it is a value that must be balanced against non-discrimination, multiculturalism and social harmony equally.[50] Crowley has correctly observed in that regard that:

> We may believe whatever we want; our minds are private and not the province of legislators or police. But we are not entitled to act on beliefs or

46 Ismail Hasani and Bonar Tigor Naipospos, *Wajah Para Pembela Islam* (Pustaka Masyarakat Setara Jakarta 2010) 124.

47 Citra Nur Noviansi and M Fakhruddin Budiarti, 'Jaringan Islam Liberal: Gerakan Liberalis Islam Serta Pergerakan Dan Perkembangannya Di Indonesia (2001–2010)' (2013) 10 *Jurnal Sejarah Lontar* 24.

48 Paul Marshall and Nina Shea, *Silenced: How Apostasy and Blasphemy Codes Are Choking Freedom Worldwide* (Oxford University Press USA 2011) 163.

49 Ghanea (n 1) 431.

50 Howard-Hassmann (n 16) 137.

> ideas that impinge on the protected sphere of rights and personal security that we promise to all other members of society.[51]

His argument suggests that hate speech should be restricted not solely to prevent interference in individuals' freedoms, but more to establish constructive social conditions for minorities which are commonly targeted by such speech. Intervention is also required to decrease the particularistic religious identities of the majority, which frequently brings about increasing ferocity against vulnerable individuals and minority groups.

The case of Shihab generally suggests that the court demands people to balance their thoughts and acts in particular situations even though they may find a standard behaviour uncomfortable. It is very reasonable that publicly expressed religious hatred should be restricted because it generally constitutes hatred against a group of persons defined by reference to religious belief.[52] Also, hate speech generally consists of verbal coercion, promotes discrimination, intimidates members of society and potentially triggers riots and violence among religious adherents, thereby disturbing public peace and order.

Based on these destructive impacts, the restriction of religious hatred may be classified as a reasonable or proportionate interference from the state, not only to avoid the breach of public order and vulnerable groups' fundamental rights but also to advance the goal of equality between minority and majority groups. Restrictions on religion-inspired hatred suggest that the state is committed to proclaiming the importance of minority protection and defending the rights and freedoms of all. In ensuring the protection of religious minorities within Islam in Indonesia, interference is required from the state because minority religious rights are generally understood by mainstream orthodox Islamic groups as dubious rights which should not be respected. As a consequence, religious minorities within Islam are easily isolated and discriminated against by the Islamic majority because of their different religious (Islamic) interpretations.[53]

3. Protecting the inclusive character of *forum externum*

After the fall of the Soeharto regime in 1998, the normative framework of religious freedom in Indonesia has been relatively stronger, as this right is stipulated in various national legislations. In terms of freedom of expression and other forms of political and civil rights, Indonesia is still considered more democratic

51 Brian Lee Crowley, 'Religion No Excuse for Illegal, Hateful Acts' (*Vancouver Sun* 27 May 2013).

52 Ben Clarke, 'Freedom of Speech and Criticism of Religion: What Are the Limits?' (2007) 14 *eLaw Journal* 28, 108.

53 Gulazat Tursun, 'Integrating Minorities Through Legislation: A Chinese Point of View' (2011) 12 *Asia-Pacific Journal on Human Rights and the Law* 27, 27.

than other countries in Southeast Asia.[54] The transitional democracy in Indonesia that began in 1998 was seen by many scholars as a phenomenon that enabled significant democratic advances because the country put forward human rights as an agenda of constitutional reforms to advance democratic norms and practices in the country.[55] Since then, Indonesians by comparison enjoy much greater rights and freedoms, especially political rights.[56] However, Indonesia continues to struggle with challenges including discrimination and violence against religious minorities within Islam. The report by Freedom House shows that apart from the impressive democratic gains since the fall of Soeharto in 1998, the government of Indonesia continued to tolerate the persecution of religious minorities within Islam.[57]

The contrasted achievements demonstrate that the human rights advancement is, however, not fully enjoyed by minorities, including religious minorities within Islam. Even though relationships between different religious and ethnic groups in Indonesia are largely harmonious today, there remains acute sectarian discontent between Muslim majorities and religious minorities within Islam. Theoretically, the constitution declares that religious freedom is a legal and constitutional right. It also stipulates that the state is not theocratic, but the recent evidence of religious persecution shows that the preferential treatment of a particular Islamic orthodoxy frequently interferes with the rights of religious minorities within Islam. As a consequence, the persecution of numerous so-called deviants or breakaway sects, or of individual heretics in Indonesia, is striking.[58] Since the *Reformasi* era in 1998, there has been a dramatic increase in the persecution of religious minorities within Islam, suggesting inconsistency in human rights protection. Inconsistency claims are reinforced by the fact that the state has been accused of failing to protect its citizens and, in some cases, of being actively involved in violating the rights of minority, non-orthodox, "deviant" Muslim groups.[59] Factors regarding this are analysed below.

3.1. Exclusive religious rights as the root of deviant accusation

Most of the persecution of religious minorities within Islam in Indonesia has been triggered by religious sentiments between mainstream orthodox Islamic

54 For further discussion about the civil and political rights index in Southeast Asia, see Donald K Emmerson, 'Southeast Asia: Minding the Gap between Democracy and Governance' 23 *Journal of Democracy* 62–73.

55 Dian AH Shah, *Constitutions, Religion and Politics in Asia: Indonesia, Malaysia and Sri Lanka* (Cambridge University Press 2017) 1.

56 Marcus Mietzner, 'Indonesia's Democratic Stagnation: Anti-Reformist Elites and Resilient Civil Society' (2012) 19 *Democratization* 209, 210.

57 Freedom House, 'Indonesia' (Freedom House 2019).

58 Temperman (n 14) 730.

59 Nicola Colbran, 'Realities and Challenges in Realising Freedom of Religion or Belief in Indonesia' (2010) 14 *The International Journal of Human Rights* 678, 678–680.

groups and religious minorities themselves. Hateful sentiments are exacerbated not only by state systems, which legally and politically denounce religious minorities within Islam by displaying negative stereotyping and antipathy or downright hostility towards heterodox minorities,[60] but also by cultural conditions. Segregation of the religious public sphere, such as a mosque, often causes social and religious disharmony for Muslims. One of the seeds of discontent from which hate blooms is the mainstream orthodox Muslim claim that the character of religious minorities within Islam is exclusive.

The exclusive character of *forum externum* – freedom to practise one's faith in the way one chooses – is, however, protected under international human rights law. Indeed, there seems to be a global consensus on the necessity to interpret human rights instruments as the guardian of individual rights.[61] In other words, international human rights law asserts that every individual has the freedom to practise their religious belief the way they choose without being obstructed by others. However, this is generally perceived by most Indonesians as a legal concept that tends to promote and protect exclusive individual rights. Exclusivity can also be interpreted as being individualistic, which is considered an alien characteristic in Indonesian legal norms and culture.

The exclusivity argument suggests that the majority generally accuses the minority of being deviant or misleading because they break or challenge established community norms and the communal character of religious practices. As articulated by Djojodigoeno:

> Individualistic and liberalistic views do not live in the minds of Indonesians. We are socio- and traditio-bound people: every one of us has to act and to behave as all others do; one has to be common, *biasa* (Javanese *lumrah*). Being different from others is being strange, astonishing, wicked, condemnable. In this course of ideas an individualistic state of mind and an individualistic pattern of behaviour and action will arouse opposition, disapproval and condemnation.[62]

Djojodigoeno's argument was further emphasised by former Indonesian foreign minister Ali Alatas, who opined that "the rights of individuals in Indonesia are balanced by the rights of the community because Indonesian customary laws have traditionally put high priority on the rights and interests of the society or nation".[63] This argument suggests that Indonesian legal norms and culture are

60 Evans (n 25) 11.

61 Jill Marshall, *Personal Freedom Through Human Rights Law?: Autonomy, Identity and Integrity under the European Convention on Human Rights* (Martinus Nijhoff Publishers Boston 2009).

62 MA Jaspan, 'In Quest of New Law: The Perplexity of Legal Syncretism in Indonesia' (1965) 7 *Comparative Studies in Society and History* 252, 256.

63 Anthony J Langlois, *The Politics of Justice and Human Rights: Southeast Asia and Universalist Theory* (Cambridge University Press 2001) 19.

similar to some Asian countries whose legal traditions generally endorse "soft authoritarianism". Soft authoritarianism refers to a political system in which laws generally force individuals into subservience for the good of the community, and the good of the community is generally determined through various mechanisms of consensus by elders who act as informal judicial practitioners.[64]

For many Indonesian societies, solidarity on the common ground of religion and ethnic identity as an ideology has become more important than economic structures, not only in defining political movements as asserted by Kahn but also in interpreting international human rights norms.[65] Many people also resist several religious teachings, instead adapting religious norms to local culture in order to create a common religious identity in a particular Indonesian society.[66] If religious exclusivity is considered a "strange" or "deviant" religious characteristic, it becomes a form of social confrontation, or more specifically a human rights confrontation; a clash between individualism and communitarianism. Additionally, such a human rights confrontation may encounter strong resistance from Muslim individuals and organisations, which then challenges official or unofficial capacities to protect these vulnerable groups. This proposition is rooted in the fact that many Islamic organisations in Indonesia still strongly consider Islamic or Indonesian criteria in acknowledging human rights. For example, the MUI argues that the Western concept of human rights is narrowly focused on individual rights, whereas human rights in Islamic and in Indonesian contexts emphasise equally individuals and their responsibilities within society.[67]

In rural communities, this argument is related to customary laws which generally give precedence to community over individuals.[68] This legal perspective has existed prominently in many Indonesian communities for centuries and has been used by different judges in their verdicts. For instance, the light sentences against the defendants in the case of Cikeusik[69] demonstrate that the verdict was adopted by the court not only to punish the defendants who breached the law but more to reconstruct and ensure local social harmony among the people.[70] These findings

64 ibid 24.

65 Joel S Kahn, 'Ideology and Social Structure in Indonesia' (1978) 20 *Comparative Studies in Society and History* 103, 120.

66 A very popular case is about Islamic law on inheritance, by which many Muslims around Indonesia do not apply Islamic law to share inheritance but choose to apply local traditions because the traditions were practised by people for centuries before the coming of Islam to the area.

67 Melissa Crouch, 'Indonesia's Blasphemy Law: Bleak Outlook for Minority Religions' (2012) *Asia Pacific Bulletin*, No. 146 26.

68 For further discussion about the communalist character of Indonesian law, see for instance Timothy C Lindsey, 'Square Pegs & Round Holes: Fitting Modern Title into Traditional Societies in Indonesia' 7 *Pacific Rim Law and Policy Journal* (1998) 699–719.

69 Verdict of Serang Court No. 314/Pid.B/2011/PN.Srg.

70 Based on article 5 of the Judicial Power No. 48/2009, judges are obliged to search justice and understand laws existing within society. There will be further analysis of this in Chapter 7.

may suggest that the concept of individualistic religious human rights, which tends to force individuals to be free from religious communal association, may be confronted by social values as living law within a particular Indonesian society. One of the reasons for this is that most Indonesians are embedded in the social practices of the community. This makes it difficult for them to question the fairness of their experiences even though the socio-legal construction works disadvantageously against them.[71]

Responding to the communitarian cultural argument, Andrew Rosser similarly argues:

> Cultures in developing countries, it is argued, tend to stratify individuals in ways that enhance dignity for some categories of people but leave other categories dishonoured, without dignity or respect, rather than see them as equals with a common set of rights.[72]

Indonesia, based on Rosser's perspective, then, has experienced problems with human rights violations, particularly involving minority groups. Rights violations on the minority-majority line are not simply because of weaknesses in the country's legal framework for human rights and rights implementation; rather, they are the result of extremely diverse ethnic, religious, legal and cultural contexts.[73] As a consequence, forms of individualistic human rights are often understood to be arrogant, alien to Indonesian culture and prohibited by religious belief. This argument suggests that much of the discrimination against and persecution of religious minorities within Islam is not only triggered by discriminatory state policies, but also by exclusive religious characteristics found in ordinary people, and by a lack of knowledge about human rights and, in particular, respecting differences in others.

The Islamic religious majorities usually argue that Ahmadiyah is an exclusive group. Even though prophethood is considered the main trigger of discrimination, the exclusivity of Ahmadiyah is similarly significant. Ahmadiyah's approach is criticised due to its exclusive doctrines; among others, the refusal to perform prayer behind a non-Ahmadiyah imam is one such criticised doctrine.[74] If a group of Ahmadiyah are particularly sizeable, they generally build their own mosque for their own congregation, even though many mosques already exist proximately within the community.[75] The exclusive characteristics of

71 Marshall (n 61) 19.

72 Andrew Rosser, 'Towards a Political Economy of Human Rights Violations in Post-New Order Indonesia' (2013) *Journal of Contemporary Asia* 248.

73 A/HRC/8/23/Add.1 at 2.

74 Herman L Beck, 'The Rupture between the Muhammadiyah and the Ahmadiyya' (2005) 161 *Journal of the Humanities and Social Sciences of Southeast Asia* 210, 219.

75 Rumadi Ahmad, 'Diskriminasi Hak Sipil Minoritas: Pelarangan Pencatatan Pernikahan Jemaat Ahmadiyah Kuningan', in Ahmad Suaedy, *Politisasi Agama dan Konflik Komunal: Beberapa Isu Penting di Indonesia* (Wahid Institute 2007) 2.

Ahmadiyah's *forum externum* are criticised for being unsociable, provoking non-Ahmadiyah people and groups as well as the government to seek their disbandment in order to protect religious harmony. For instance, the legal reasoning of the decree – jointly signed by the Head of Regency, the Head of the Judiciary and the Head of Religious Affairs – to resolve the Ahmadiyah case in Kuningan Regency West Java in 2004, asserted that the Ahmadiyah were accused of giving rise to religious disharmony and anarchism within society and of disturbing public order and social stability.[76]

Similarly, Islamic religious majorities also observe that the group known as Messianic Islam (LDII) performs "exclusive" religious activities. So LDII also faces persecution in Indonesia. The exclusion of outsiders, including other Muslims, from LDII's prayers is based on a strict internal religious hierarchy and boundary-maintaining personal purity norms.[77] LDII also refers to other Muslims outside of its congregation as infidels (*kafir*).[78] It believes that there can be no proper prayers outside of a congregation, which is only legitimate if it is based on an oath of allegiance to a leader (*amir*). The *amir* himself is sacred because his authority derives from God through the Prophet.[79] The exclusiveness of LDII is viewed as the most dangerous form of Islam: "exclusive and un-Indonesian in spirit, rigid and potentially subversive in doctrine".[80] The exclusivity of LDII is seen by mainstream, orthodox Indonesian Muslims as indicative of an exclusivist social orientation not in accordance with the spirit of being with the people (*bermasyarakat*), which is culturally significant in Indonesia and its state ideology of Pancasila.[81] In short, its worship is perceived as socially and politically damaging to the solidarity of "the people".[82]

The conflict between traditionalist Islam, the majority, and *Salafi* or puritan Islam, a minority group, in Lombok West-Southeast Nusa (NTB) in 2005 was also triggered by exclusivity and harsh propagation, because *Salafi* Islam often called other Islamic groups deviant. The *Salafi* openly criticise cultures and religious rituals practised by the majority because they do not conform to what they see as authentic Islamic teaching. This religious minority simply denies that Islam in Indonesia, or anywhere, can be culturally, politically and theologically divergent. They repudiate wide variance in individual expressions of Islamic faith.[83] There are Sharia-oriented reformers, Sufi reformers, adherents of the mystic synthesis, rural *kyai* (Islamic preachers), the followers of messianic movements and many more who are not attracted to reformed versions of

76 ibid 56.
77 John R Bowen, 'Salat in Indonesia: The Social Meanings of an Islamic Ritual' (1989) 24 *Man* 600, 607.
78 Sutiyono, *Benturan Budaya Islam: Puritan & Sinkretis* (Penerbit Buku Kompas 2010) 124.
79 ibid.
80 Bowen (n 77) 608.
81 ibid.
82 ibid 609.
83 Toby Evans, 'Separation of Mosque and State in Indonesia' (2011) *Policy* 6, 37.

Islam.[84] The character of harsh propagation pushes traditionalists to accuse the *Salafi* of seeking to Arabise Indonesian Islam and insult their Islamic belief, therefore habitually engendering religious disharmony and social distrust between the two.

As a consequence of this disharmony in relations, the *Salafi* decided to establish a mosque of their own because they were disappointed with the local people and their refusal to accept the *Salafi* in the community.[85] Such exclusive congregation and houses of worship, however, did worsen tensions with more mainstream Islamic groups because they exacerbated perceptions of religious exclusivity. The traditionalist majority argues that establishing new mosques and congregations threatens "public order", namely religious communality in Islam. They also say that the Islamic community (*umma*) will be segregated. This can be seen to reveal that the *Salafi* are truly exclusive because they do not want to socialise with the majority of Muslims in one mosque.[86] The majority argue that practising prayer exclusively is not in accordance with religious harmony or the spirit of the nation. Therefore, the *Salafi* is considered a group misleading Islam, because it does not perform or follow mainstream Indonesian Islam but rather interprets textual Islam without local wisdom.[87] For instance, the *Salafi* argues that doing *tahlilan* – reciting Qur'anic verses and other forms of Islamic rituals for the deceased – is *bid'ah*, or an innovation, as rituals were not done by the Prophet. For the *Salafi*, *bid'ah is* more sinful than committing adultery with one's mother.[88]

The problem of religious exclusivity and a lack of human rights knowledge among religious adherents can be seen in NU vs. Muhammadiyah. This case suggests that victims of religious persecution are not always those groups labelled "deviant", but may also be mainstream Islamic groups that become a minority in a particular area. In 2011, the Muhammadiyah's mosque in a largely populated NU area in Jember, East Java was destroyed because the *imam*, or leader, of the mosque had said that *tahlilan* was heretic. The *imam* also established Friday prayer for his congregation in his own mosque even though there was already a mosque for Friday prayer nearby. No one was arrested in this case and no further legal action was taken by the *imam* or by the police even though multiple properties, including a house, mosque and classrooms, were severely damaged.[89]

84 Greg Fealy and Sally White, 'Religion, Politics and Social Dynamics in Java: Historical and Contemporary Rhymes', in Greg Fealy and Sally White (eds), *Expressing Islam: Religious Life and Politics in Indonesia* (Institute of Southeast Asian Studies 2008) 3.

85 Nuhrison M Nuh and Achmad Rosidi, 'Kasus Salafi Versus Non-Salafi di Kabupaten Lombok Barat Nusa Tenggara Barat', in Nuhrison M Nuh and Achmad Rosidi, *Kasus-Kasus Aliran/ Faham Keagamaan Aktual Di Indonesia* (Departemen Agama, Badan Litbang Agama Dan Diklat Keagamaan, Puslitbang Kehidupan Beragama 2006) 3.

86 ibid 26–27.

87 ibid 27–30.

88 ibid 30.

89 Data collected during research observation.

The above cases of persecution indicate that the role of the mosque in relation to the rights of religious minorities within Islam in Indonesia is significant, as the mosque is the public realm that should in principle be inclusive for all Muslims regardless of their background. Demanding and establishing a separate and exclusive mosque is often seen as deviating from social-religious solidarity, a characteristic and tradition that is highly treasured by most Indonesian Muslims, especially the mainstream majority. Hence it is not surprising to note that the use of an exclusive mosque or a religious place for particular congregations has exaggerated religious disharmony in Indonesia.[90] For most Indonesian Muslims, mosques are central, not solely as a place of worship but also as a visible manifestation of particular Islamic sects' religious and cultural identities. In many places, the establishment of new mosques, or places allocated for Islamic congregations and certain Islamic groups, has encountered community resistance, created social unrest and caused fragmentation to Islamic religious unity. The results of these cases support the assertion that religious conflicts among different Indonesian Islamic groups frequently emerge as a consequence of religious discord and a particular group's desire to control society through the mosque and religious rituals.

Related to religious rituals, a report on religious life in Indonesia by the Center for Religious and Cross Cultural Studies (CRCS) at the Gadjah Mada University argues:

> The exclusive practice of religion is legally not a crime. Everyone has the right to choose their congregation but the potential of social disharmony due to the exclusive religious behaviours needs to be controlled so that it will not bring about negative stereotypes and abhorrence among religious adherents.[91]

Based on this argument, religious conflict is generally about who represents religious authority to determine who is right and who is wrong, and who is most faithful to religious precepts and values.[92] In most parts of the Muslim world, those who are in power and have authority to define matters generally also control the interpretation of religious beliefs and the legal definition of rights and duties because, as asserted by Anthony Chase, "Islam is often seen as controlling the content of politics and law".[93] In that regard, most state policies and the behaviour of the majority Muslims towards religious minorities within Islam are

90 In Indonesia, Muslims generally have many kinds of Islamic religious places such as mosques, small mosques (*mussalla*) or places that are established to run continuous Islamic rituals and unite congregations such as houses, offices and/or school classes.

91 Zainal Abidin Bagir, 'Laporan Tahunan Kehidupan Beragama Di Indonesia 2012' (*Center for Religion and Cross Culture Studies* 2012) 21.

92 Abdullah Saeed and Hassan Saeed, *Freedom of Religion, Apostasy and Islam* (Routledge 2017) 23.

93 Chase Anthony, 'Liberal Islam and "Islam and Human Rights": A Sceptic's View' in (2006) 1 *Religion and Human Rights* 2, 151.

legally questionable under international human rights law and the Indonesian human rights scheme, yet are politically validated by the government in order to gain social stability.

In this context, the Indonesian government ignores that many exclusivists perceive any kind of religious difference as a threat rather than the nature of religion. They tend to ignore the fact that the history of Islam has never been strictly monolithic and should not be monopolised by a single Islamic group. The discourse of *ikhtilaf* (differences of opinion) suggests that all believers confirm that their respective religious interpretation is authoritative, but when it is confronted with the political realm the authoritative interpretation generally rests with the majority groups. When the majority claim to represent the will of the people and the source of morality, they usually wish to oppress a part of their number: their minority fellows. Consequently, minority groups are threatened not only by the state but also by the social majority, which then renders minorities vulnerable to significant injustice at the hands of the majority.[94]

3.2. The regulation of place of worship: a critique

It is evident from current policies that the Indonesian government considers the distinctive characteristic of exclusivity among Islamic religious minorities in establishing mosques and congregations as a potential cause of religious disharmony and disturbance of public order which needs to be controlled. In response to potential religious disharmony, the government introduced the Joint Ministerial Decree on the Administrative Procedure of the Construction of Places of Worship (hereafter the Decree on Places of Worship). The decree was first enacted in 1969 and superseded by a new decree signed by the Ministry of the Interior and the MORA in 2006. This decree regulates two main matters: (1) protecting religious harmony and (2) controlling the establishment of places of worship. Even though the Decree on Places of Worship was enacted by the government to prevent conflict and preserve religious harmony, in practice it has caused more religious violence than it has prevented.[95]

The key problems with this decree are that on the one hand it acknowledges religious freedom as an unconditional right and it is duly the obligation of the state to protect this right; however, on the other hand, the decree also acknowledges that everyone may practise their religious freedom as far as it does not disturb inter alia peace and public order.[96] The decree acknowledges the enhancement of national development of religious sectors, too, including religious harmony as a part of national harmony.[97] Considerations found in the

94 Neera Chandhoke, *Beyond Secularism: The Rights of Religious Minorities* (Oxford University Press 1999) 6.

95 Crouch (n 11) 106.

96 See consideration of the decree.

97 ibid.

decree illustrate that the government desires to establish norms of religious freedom, but it also tends to preserve particular aspects of Indonesian culture, which generally privilege community over individuals. This perspective suggests that Indonesian legal culture is antithetical to the protection of religious minorities within Islam. Thus, the decree remains ambiguous and controversial because it does not provide a better opportunity for religious minorities within Islam to develop equally with the country's religious majority.

The main controversy relating to the decree on *forum externum*, however, is that the government frequently uses the need for public order to restrict the rights of religious minorities within Islam. Apparently, this policy is pursued to preserve religious harmony as asserted by Article 1 (1) of the Decree on Places of Worship. Article 1 (1) states:

> Harmony among religions is a certain relationship condition among religious adherents based on tolerance, mutual understanding, and respect for equality of all religions to practice religious beliefs and live in cooperation with people in society within the framework of Pancasila and the 1945 Constitution.

To support the idea of harmony among religions, the Decree on Places of Worship establishes the Forum of Religious Harmony among Religions (FKUB) to oversee the establishment of places of worship in particular areas. The aim to preserve harmony can also be seen within the FKUB's main tasks, such as conducting dialogue with religious leaders and followers, accommodating the aspirations of the religious community organisation and the community, formulating policy recommendations and making efforts to educate the community.[98]

The FKUB is established at provincial and regency levels and consists of representatives from all recognised religions and government officials such as governor, regent, chair of the local MORA and chair of the Politics and the Indonesian Unity Body (Badan Kesatuan Bangsa dan Politik, Bakesbangpol).[99] The composition of the local FKUB should mirror the composition of believers in the area, meaning that a Muslim-majority area may have significantly more Muslim members than Christian ones, and vice versa, always placing religious minorities at a distinct disadvantage in obtaining a permit. Muslim representatives are usually chosen from mainstream Islamic organisations such as the NU and Muhammadiyah. In general, there is no representative from religious minorities within Islam, such as Shi'ah and Ahmadiyah, nor from non-official religions. The composition of these official harmony-establishing groups suggests that the right of religious minorities to build a place of worship depends on a consensus dominated by mainstream religions, which generally favours the voices of the community.

98 Crouch (n 11) 109.
99 Article 10 of the decree.

The second problem is that Article 14 of the Decree on Places of Worship requires each religious organisation to obtain sixty signatures from local people as neighbours who agree to support the establishment of the place of worship, and agreement from ninety people who will use the place as their religious congregation. Even though this regulation is meant to ensure that the establishment of a place of worship is solely to provide religious needs for people in a locality, the required number of people's signatures for agreement is highly contentious and arguably suggests that this regulation is effectively intolerant of religious minorities. The main reason is that as a group of people numerically inferior in a given society, religious minorities will have difficulty fulfilling the requirements due to their limited members. Assenting to such a declaration also identifies certain people as members of a minority, and thus carries potential risks. Additionally, their distinctive religious characteristics may still be seen as a threat to the existing beliefs embraced by most people. In other words, the restriction in this decree does not fulfil the required standards prescribed by law to fulfil a pressing social need, but rather reflects a government attempt to restrict equal opportunity for minorities to have places of worship.

Related to the signature requirement, Crouch argues that:

> The 90/60 requirement discriminates against groups with less than 90 members. One has to wonder how a religious group without a place of worship could boast of anywhere near 90 members, unless they were presently worshipping in a building without a permit, given that religious groups are not even allowed to meet in homes. Granting of a permit should not be based on the mere size of the group, but rather on the right of religious groups to have a place of worship – as guaranteed by law.[100]

If we look at the cases of persecution of the aforementioned religious minorities within Islam, this decree may be considered an intolerant restriction of equal opportunity. It may, on the other hand, be argued that obtaining 90 and 60 community supporters as a threshold requirement applied to all religions is not necessarily discriminatory treatment for all religions, as religious minorities may get support from non-members. Thus, the administrative procedures to build places of worship regulated by the decree can inadvertently portray that places of worship in Indonesia are not sites of religious freedom but are rather contested places of tension and violence.[101]

4. The case of the Ahmadiyah in Indonesia

As the most persecuted religious minority, the case of Indonesia's Ahmadiyah has become a national and international issue. Unlike their Ahmadiyah counterparts in other Muslim-majority countries such as Pakistan, where they are not

100 Crouch (n 11) 111.
101 ibid 116.

recognised as Muslims, verdicts from some religious courts in Indonesia have confirmed the legal status of the Ahmadiyah in Indonesia as Muslims. Ahmadiyah members are required to register their marriages under the jurisdiction of religious courts. Still, their right to practise *forum externum*, especially the right to build mosques for their congregation and disseminate their interpretation of Islamic teachings, is still discriminated against by the state and mainstream majority Muslims. Due to this problematic situation, the last part of this chapter examines two contrasting aspects: the legal recognition of the Ahmadiyah as Muslims and their prohibition from disseminating religious doctrines and exercising their religious *forum externum*.

4.1. Judicial recognition of the Ahmadiyah as Muslims

According to Article 1 (1) of Law No. 50/2009 on Religious Courts (hereafter the Law on Religious Courts), the religious court is an exclusively Muslim justice-administration office with the authority to administer Muslim marriages. Based on Article 63 of Law No. 1/1974 on Marriage, the religious court has authority inter alia to administer Muslim marriages. This means that all individuals who bring their case before this court must be recognised as Muslim by the court. Even though this law clearly specifies the criteria of parties before the court, religious courts in some regions have a different understanding of the law, which has created some kind of discrimination for Islamic religious minorities, including Ahmadiyah members.

Some reports suggest that several Muslim minorities have experienced discrimination regarding the right to exercise their civil rights under this law. For instance, the Coordinating Board for Monitoring Mystical Belief (Bakorpakem) of the Kuningan Regency West Java issued a decision, addressed to the local MORA, not to issue identity cards and marriage documents for Ahmadiyah members.[102] Due to this discriminatory treatment, until 2012 some Ahmadiyah members had to travel to other regions to register their marriages.[103]

Interestingly, this current study finds that some Ahmadiyah members have succeeded in bringing their cases before the religious court in several other regions. The success of these cases confirms, legally, that the Ahmadiyah are still considered Muslim by the court. According to article 49 and 50 of the Law No. 3/2006 on Religious Courts, all Muslims should register cases regarding their marriage in a religious court. As a consequence, disputes in relation to marriage – such as divorce, inheritance or married people's right to take care of their children or others – need to be brought before the religious court. Thus, according to these findings, the Ahmadiyah in Indonesia are legally Muslim.

102 Nuh and Rosidi (n 85) 1.

103 ibid 49. Nuh and Rosidi also reported that some regencies were pleased to register their marriages, such as Jakarta, Cirebon, Bekasi, Tangerang and Semarang.

Several cases brought by the Ahmadiyah can be examined in the following description. The first case is a verdict of the Religious Court of Cimahi District, West Java which decided one case of divorce (*talaq*) brought before the court by an Ahmadiyah member in 2013. The complainant brought this case before the court because he wanted to divorce his wife, who did not agree that they should live together under the marriage contract after the complainant converted to Ahmadiyah. The court granted his application by allowing him to divorce his wife. The court also cited Qur'anic verse (2: 227) which regulates the right of a man to divorce his wife.[104] There is no further clarification and consideration of the complainant's Islamic belief. This verdict differs from a similar case which was brought before the Religious Court of Padang District, West Sumatra in 2012. In this case, the wife as complainant asked the court to dissolve her marriage because her husband had converted to Ahmadiyah. She reported that her husband had asked her to follow his new religious belief.[105] In granting the complainant's application to dissolve the marriage, the court observed in its consideration that the defendant's husband was a person who had converted to another religion (without mentioning a specific religion).[106]

Rika Zulkarini, a female Ahmadiyah, likewise brought a similar case to the Religious Court of East Jakarta District in December 2011.[107] The court cited a Qur'anic verse (30: 21) as one of their considerations and the Judge ruled that the wife could divorce her husband if her hatred for her husband increased.[108] The court also granted the complainant's application to take care of their two children, even though the court knew that she was Ahmadiyah.[109] None of these cases were brought before the Appeal or Supreme Court and until now there has been no single verdict from the Supreme Court overruling any of these religious courts' decisions.

The significant discussion from these cases is that the religious courts knew that the parties before the courts were Ahmadiyah, but the court still used Qur'anic verses and did not discriminate against the Ahmadiyahs' civil rights as Muslim litigants before the court. Apparently, this confirms that the Ahmadiyah are legally considered Muslims, as the courts accepted them as such and resolved the respective cases based on the Qur'an as a supreme source of Islamic law. Thus, if we look at discrimination against Ahmadiyah by several other state organs, such as Bakorpakem, the MORA, MUI and non-judicial institutions, we can legitimately argue that the various kinds of discriminations against Ahmadiyah are a political matter and not reflected in the case law as analysed below.

104 Verdict of Cimahi Religious Court No. 1199/Pdt.G/2013/PA.Cmi.
105 Verdict of Padang Religious Court No. 1040/Pdt.G/2012/PA.Pdg.
106 ibid.
107 Her identity as Ahmadiyah was declared by her husband during the trial, who said that his wife's big family were Ahmadiyah members and she did not deny this claim. See Verdict of East Jakarta Religious Court No. 2731/Pdt.G/2011/PAJT at 10.
108 ibid 22–23.
109 ibid 25.

4.2. The joint ministerial decree on the Ahmadiyah

In contrast to the practice of the religious courts and the recognition of Ahmadiyah members as Muslims in divorce cases, as discussed above, Ahmadiyah are discriminated against in other areas and prohibited by legislation from disseminating their Islamic teachings around Indonesia. In 2007, for example, the Supreme Court held that the joint decision enacted by some state officials in Bogor District, restricting the Ahmadiyah's rights to perform religious practices, was legally justifiable.[110] The joint decision was collectively signed by chairs of local government sectors and religious leaders in Bogor West Java.[111] An edict was endorsed by the joint decision signatory to freeze the Mubarak Ahmadiyah Campus in Parung Bogor District as a result of pressure from some Islamic hardliner groups such as the Muslim People Movement (Gerakan Umat Islam, GUI).

In this case, several lawyers, including well-known Muslim human rights advocate Adnan Buyung Nasution, who supported the Ahmadiyah's rights, appealed the joint decision made by several institutions in Bogor District West Java before the Supreme Court. Regrettably, the Supreme Court upheld the verdict made by the Appeal Court of West Java, which rejected the appeal and upheld the joint decision, collectively agreeing to close down the Ahmadiyah campus and restrict Ahmadiyah's rights for the sake of public order.[112] This appeal was brought before the court by the Ahmadiyah and their advocates because they claimed that the decision was administratively illegal. Additionally, it negatively affected the Ahmadiyah's right to exercise religious and social activities after the joint decision was put into force in 2005.[113] The Bogor case is only one example of discrimination faced by the Ahmadiyah in many regions.

Yet after the 1980s – when discriminatory policies first started to target them – no other similar cases were brought before the court by the Ahmadiyah until early 2016. Mahmud Mubarik Ahmad, an Ahmadiyah spokesperson, claimed that the Ahmadiyah had already submitted many cases to the courts. The writer tried to search these cases in all online sources,[114] but still could not find any other relevant cases.[115] Other similar cases related to the rights of religious minorities within Islam were usually brought forth by human rights

110 It should be noted that a joint decree is not a type of legislation in the Indonesian legal system. The decree is enacted to regulate administrative matters.

111 The decision was made by the local branch of the Indonesian Ulema Council, Bogor, the Mayor of Bogor, the chair of the Police Office of Bogor, the head of the Army Office of Bogor, the Local Attorney-General of Bogor, the Local Office of the Ministry of Religious Affairs of Bogor, the District Court of Bogor, the Air-Base Command of Bogor and the Local Parliament of Bogor.

112 Verdict of Supreme Court No. 182 K/TUN/2007 at 3.

113 ibid 6.

114 Since 2008, all court verdicts in Indonesia can be accessed publicly without subscription.

115 Interview with Mahmud Mubarik Ahmad, a spokesman of Ahmadiyah Qadiani Indonesia around January 2014.

advocates, as in the 2009 and 2012 judicial review of blasphemy law, which will be examined further in Chapter 7. All other published materials related to the Ahmadiyah and other Islamic religious minorities are mostly written by Indonesian scholars as well as human rights organisations. The Ahmadiyahs usually speak in seminars or conferences held overseas due to safety concerns, despite similar and relevant seminars being successfully held in Indonesia.

It must be noted that the various kinds of persecution and discrimination described thus far are generally triggered by a *fatwa* of the MUI (1980 and 2005), which label Ahmadiyah as heretical. This is made worse by the Joint Ministerial Decree on Ahmadiyah (hereafter as the Decree on Ahmadiyah) adopted by the government in 2008, which restricted religious dissemination by Ahmadiyah. The decree principally consisted of two main regulations. The first provision of the decree was adopted to restrict Ahmadiyah proselytism, and the second part also ordered the public not to conduct any unlawful act that may harm Ahmadiyahs. The regulation that restricts Ahmadiyah rights says:

> Ahmadiyah are warned and ordered, as long as they consider themselves to hold to Islam, to discontinue the promulgation of interpretations and activities that are deviant from the principal teachings of Islam. Any Ahmadiyya member who does not comply with this warning and order as specified in the first and second articles shall be liable to penalties as prescribed in regulatory laws and such penalties shall extent to the organisation and legal body.[116]

In its 2008 annual report to the HRC, the Indonesian government argued that the Decree on Ahmadiyah was not meant to restrict Ahmadiyah's *forum internum*, but rather was adopted to protect Ahmadiyah members.[117] The state's non-interference in Ahmadiyah religious belief was asserted by the Indonesian government as follows:

> The issuance of the Decree does not outlaw the belief, but orders its followers to halt their proselytization activities and to fully respect the existing laws and regulations; it appeals to the Ahmadiyah followers to return to the Islamic mainstream and at the same time appeals to the others to refrain from violent acts against them. The issuance of such a decree is never meant to be an intervention of the State in people's freedom of religion. It is merely an effort by the Government to uphold law and public order and the protection of the followers of Ahmadiyah from criminal attack. In other words, the Government limits its role to the levels of maintaining law and

116 The Joint Ministerial Decree on Ahmadiyah was signed by the MORA through its decision No. 03/2008, the Attorney General through its decision No. KEP-033/A/JA/6/2008 and the Interior Ministry through its decision No. 1993/2008.

117 HRC, '8th Session of the Human Rights Council' (June 2008) 134.

> order and the protection of citizens. It does not interfere with religious doctrines or limit religious freedom.[118]

The phrase "to return to the Islamic mainstream" indicates that the government basically applies non-proportionate interference when it uses the religious criteria of the mainstream majority as a requirement to restrict the rights of Ahmadiyah. Additionally, the government's statement suggests that it monopolises religious interpretation to transform Ahmadiyah into a version of Indonesian mainstream Islam. This means the government repudiates the freedom of Ahmadiyah to perform different religious teachings as an aspect of their freedom of religion, which encompasses freedom from conformity and freedom from the practices of a mainstream religion.[119]

Responding to the criticism of the HRC on the way the government has handled the issue of the Ahmadiyah, Indonesia reiterated that it has never interfered in interpreting religious doctrine or limiting religious freedom in the country, further suggesting that the Ahmadiyah issue is not simply a question of religious freedom. Extra caution is needed since this issue is highly sensitive and involves multiple aspects; government responsibility for promoting a harmonious life amongst religions and their believers, the duty to uphold law and order and the commitment to eradicate extremism and radicalism.[120] The government further assumes that the decree was considered proportionate interference because its purpose was to prevent the communal conflict triggered by the polemic of the Ahmadiyah. On the one hand, it consists of proportionate interference by compelling the Ahmadiyahs' opponents to refrain from committing acts of religious intolerance, while also mandating the Ahmadiyah not to disseminate their religious teaching to anyone else.

This aforesaid argument was based on the second regulation of the Decree on Ahmadiyah, which states:

> All members of the public are ordered to protect and maintain harmonious religious life as well as peaceful and orderly community life by not conducting unlawful activities and or actions against Ahmadiyya. Any member of the public who does not comply with this warning and order as specified in the first and fourth articles shall be liable to penalties and prescribed in regulatory laws.[121]

From this regulation, it can be noted that the Indonesian government, in fact, does not restrict Ahmadiyah's *forum internum* but only restricts their religious

118 ibid.

119 Jerold Waltman, 'Communities in Conflict: The School Prayer in West Germany, the United States and Canada' (1991) 6 *Canadian Journal of Law & Society* 27, 40.

120 '8th Session of the Human Rights Council' (n 117) 137.

121 Decree on Ahmadiyah.

proselytisation (*forum externum*). It means that the problem of the Ahmadiyah lies between the state obligation to promote and protect the Ahmadiyah as a religious minority and the state obligation to maintain public order and religious harmony as a fundamental aspect of the religious-national development plan.

In the 2012 Universal Periodic Review, Indonesia reaffirmed its commitment to ensuring religious freedom for all individuals.[122] With regard to the Ahmadiyah, Indonesia held dialogue to promote mutual understanding and respect between Muslim majorities and religious minorities within Islam.[123] Yet, the reality of religious minorities within Islam in the country, especially the Shi'a and Ahmadiyah, seems to be different. Discrimination and persecution against them still occurs in some places. The state legal apparatus did not conduct adequate investigations and legal steps to stop persecution, resulting in the displacement of members of religious minorities within Islam from their villages.[124] This persecution is not only motivated by religious sentiment among Muslim majorities, but is also triggered by government policies, including the adoption of the Decree on the Ahmadiyah.

The Decree on the Ahmadiyah is designed to meet a pressing social need but is only relevant and sufficient to temporarily end the conflict. This type of settlement is well known in Indonesia as one that promotes harmony and Indonesian unity, although in reality it disrupts the values of written human rights laws. Harmony in Indonesian society has been a tradition for years and it is hence important in the settlement of disputes because it maintains the prevailing social values. The Decree on the Ahmadiyah reinforces that harmony as a prerequisite of establishing Indonesian unity is an imperative guideline in dealing with human rights fulfilment.

The form of dispute settlement involving the restriction of *forum externum* for particular religious groups may not permissibly be imposed for discriminatory purposes or applied in a discriminatory manner.[125] The limitation on a particular *forum externum* should address the concept of proportionality as required by international human rights law. The Decree on the Ahmadiyah and other forms of *forum externum* restrictions for religious minorities within Islam would be legally understandable if they prohibited proselytisation for all religions because this is deemed to threaten peace and harmony among religions in Indonesia. Additionally, if a certain religious group is allowed to disseminate its religious teaching, or demonstrate and speak publicly with the conviction that another religious group is apostate and heretical and further ask the government

122 Human Rights Watch, 'UN Human Rights Council: Statement for the 2012 Universal Periodic Review of Indonesia' (*Human Rights Watch* 2012).

123 '8th Session of the Human Rights Council' (n 117) 134.

124 'UN Human Rights Council' (n 122).

125 Compilation of General Comments and General Recommendations Adopted by Human Rights Treaty Bodies 34.

to ban them, it would be justifiable if the state also allowed such a group to spread its religious beliefs and to express the opinion that its rights are being threatened.

Apparently, the Decree on the Ahmadiyah, together with other restrictions against heterodox religious practices inspired by the 1965 Blasphemy Law, was meant to limit religious opposition to the government.[126] In their recent application, however, the blasphemy-inspired regulations are generally adopted by the government to control non-mainstream religious teachings, which then threatens the rights of citizens and is defendable not only by the words of the constitution but by the institutions involved in the due process of law.[127] In the case of the Ahmadiyah, the government opined that the protection of religious minorities and the general implementation of human rights should consider religious harmony and the existing and prevailing culture. It suggests that the government has tried to reconcile the big gap between international human rights standards for religious minority rights and the majorities' primordial attachment to religious faith because Indonesia's diverse religious society brings about a divergent concept of religious freedom minorities. On the one hand, international human rights law proposes far-reaching individual freedoms for persons to embrace religions or beliefs of their choice, while most Muslims in Indonesia are still attached to the Islamic primordial religious faith which rejects any ideas not compatible with their beliefs.

The Decree on the Ahmadiyah does not outlaw the beliefs of the Ahmadiyah, but the failure of the government to protect the right to practise religion consists of discriminatory treatment. This can be said because the decree does not restrict other religious groups from doing so. This means that the disruption of Ahmadiyah's *forum externum* in order to achieve other goals, such as gaining harmony and thereby Indonesian unity, cannot be justified because Ahmadiyah religious preaching does not practically harm and violate the rights of other Muslims per se. The government should acknowledge that the violation of human rights is not limited to physical threats, but also includes the failure or neglect of the government itself to ensure rights for its people. To violate people's rights does not merely mean to commit an offence against the right-holders, but also to fail to give them the rights and protections to which they are entitled.[128]

In Indonesia, the recognition of freedom of thought, conscience and religion and its practice are the most vital elements of believers' identities and their conception of life. Therefore, the recognition of religious freedom for all individuals

126 John Olle, 'The Campaign against Heresy – State and Society in Negotiation in Indonesia', *Paper presented in Biennal Conference*, Wollongong Australia (26–29 June 2006) at 1.

127 Timothy Lindsey, 'The Rechtsstaat and Human Rights', in Timothy Lindsey (ed.), *Indonesia, Law and Society* (Federation Press 2008) 183.

128 Jack Donnelly, 'Human Rights and Human Dignity: An Analytic Critique of Non-Western Conceptions of Human Rights' (1982) 76 *The American Political Science Review* 303, 304.

does not only require non-interference from the government but also its compliance to ensure "proportionate measures", such as the legal guarantee to be free from discriminatory national regulations. Based on this proposition, the Decree on the Ahmadiyah and any other restriction against non-mainstream religions must be interpreted with caution, because it is adopted by the government to transform minorities into a version of the majority with the aim of preserving religious harmony.

These restrictive policies also suggest that community discourse, which is closely related to social and religious harmony, is one of the major pillars of Indonesian law, democracy and human rights. Community discourse is endemic to Indonesian legal life and hence confirms that the enforcement of the rights of minorities not only requires the enforcement of written laws on human rights but also considers the existence of social values as an unwritten legal consensus among people. On behalf of the community, the majority wishes to silence a religious deviant or heretic through restricting minority proselytisations. On this basis, Ahmadiyah members and supporters generally argue that even though these kinds of regulations were purportedly aimed at protecting the Ahmadiyah and keeping the peace, the government was punishing them rather than their attackers. This argument was based on many cases which demonstrate that the Indonesian authorities often did little to prevent the attacks or prosecute those responsible, instead blaming Ahmadiyahs for provoking the violence.[129]

In summary, the Decree on the Ahmadiyah may suggest that in the Indonesian legal system a judgment is generally made not to apply written law in strict ways but to seek equity and fairness.[130] It means that the application of international human rights instruments, which relies heavily on written regulations, would tend to impose socio-legal norms that are alien to many communities and ethnic groups, which generally gives rise to social dislocation in a particular Indonesian society.[131] This type of juristic preference can be noted from within President Yudhoyono's argument in his speech at the Appeal of Conscience Foundation in 2013, when he was awarded the World Statesman Award. He argued that the government would not tolerate any unlawful and violent acts committed by a certain group that will violate the rights of others, yet at the same time he stated that maintaining peace and public order can never be taken for granted.[132] Based on these propositions, the effort to protect Ahmadiyah cannot be separated from communitarian discourses, as the government and most Indonesian people opine that Ahmadiyahs' rights cannot be separated from Ahmadiyah responsibility to preserve religious harmony in Indonesia.

129 Marshall and Shea (n 48) 41.
130 Jaspan (n 62) 257.
131 ibid.
132 Mong Palatino, 'Does Indonesia's SBY Deserve the World Statesman Award?' (13 June 2013).

Bibliography

Ahmad R, 'Diskriminasi Hak Sipil Minoritas: Pelarangan Pencatatan Pernikahan Jemaat Ahmadiyah Kuningan', in Ahmad Suaedy (ed.), *Politisasi Agama dan Konflik Komunal: Beberapa Isu Penting di Indonesia* (Wahid Institute 2007) 2.

An-Na'im AA, 'Islam and Human Rights: Beyond the Zero-Sum Game' (*ABC Religion & Ethics* 9 April 2018).

Anthony C, 'Liberal Islam and "Islam and Human Rights": A Sceptic's View' (2006) 1 *Religion and Human Rights* 2, 151.

Azra A and Hudson W, *Islam beyond Conflict: Indonesian Islam and Western Political Theory* (Ashgate Publishing 2008).

Bagir ZA, 'Laporan Tahunan Kehidupan Beragama Di Indonesia 2012' (*Center for Religion and Cross Culture Studies* 2012).

Beck HL, 'The Rupture between the Muhammadiyah and the Ahmadiyya' (2005) 161 *Journal of the Humanities and Social Sciences of Southeast Asia* 210.

Bowen JR, 'Salat in Indonesia: The Social Meanings of an Islamic Ritual' (1989) 24 *Man* 600.

Chandhoke N, *Beyond Secularism: The Rights of Religious Minorities* (Oxford University Press 1999).

Charfi M, *Islam and Liberty: The Historical Misunderstanding* (Zed Books 2005).

Clarke B, 'Freedom of Speech and Criticism of Religion: What are the Limits?' (2007) 14 *eLaw Journal* 28.

Colbran N, 'Realities and Challenges in Realising Freedom of Religion or Belief in Indonesia' (2010) 14 *The International Journal of Human Rights* 678.

Compilation of General Comments and General Recommendations Adopted by Human Rights Treaty Bodies 2006 HRI/GEN/1/Rev.8.

Crouch M, 'Regulating Places of Worship in Indonesia: Upholding Freedom of Religion for Religious Minorities?' (2007) 96 *Singapore Journal of Legal Studies* 116.

———, 'Indonesia's Blasphemy Law: Bleak Outlook for Minority Religions' (2012) *Asia Pacific Bulletin*, No. 146.

Crowley BL, 'Religion No Excuse for Illegal, Hateful Acts' (*Vancouver Sun* 27 May 2013).

Donnelly J, 'Human Rights and Human Dignity: An Analytic Critique of Non-Western Conceptions of Human Rights' (1982) 76 *The American Political Science Review* 303.

Emmerson DK, 'Southeast Asia: Minding the Gap between Democracy and Governance' (2012) 23 *Journal of Democracy* 2.

Evans M, 'Advancing Freedom of Religion or Belief: Agendas for Change' (2012) 1 *Oxford Journal of Law and Religion* 5.

Evans T, 'Separation of Mosque and State in Indonesia' (2011) 27 *Policy* 4.

Fealy G and White S, 'Religion, Politics and Social Dynamics in Java: Historical and Contemporary Rhymes', in Greg Fealy and Sally White, *Expressing Islam: Religious Life and Politics in Indonesia* (Institute of Southeast Asian Studies 2008) 3.

Freedom House, 'Indonesia' (Freedom House 2019).

Ghanea N, 'Minorities and Hatred: Protections and Implications' (2010) 17 *International Journal on Minority and Group Rights* 423.

———, 'Are Religious Minorities Really Minorities?' (2012) 1 *Oxford Journal of Law and Religion* 57.

Hapsari AD and Nugrah P, 'MUI Fatwa Feeds Flames of Clerics' Hate Speech' (Jakarta 17 January 2011).

Hasani I and Naipospos BT, *Wajah Para Pembela Islam* (Pustaka Masyarakat Setara Jakarta 2010).

Hirschl R, 'Juristocracy vs. Theocracy: Constitutional Courts and the Containment of Sacred Law' (2009) 1 *Middle East Law and Governance* 129.

Howard-Hassmann RE, 'Canadians Discuss Freedom of Speech: Individual Rights versus Group Protection' (2000) 7 *International Journal on Minority and Group Rights* 109.

HRC, '8th Session of the Human Rights Council' (June 2008).

Human Rights Watch, 'UN Human Rights Council: Statement for the 2012 Universal Periodic Review of Indonesia' (*Human Rights Watch* 2012).

———, 'In Religion's Name | Abuses against Religious Minorities in Indonesia' (*Human Rights Watch* 28 February 2013).

Indofakta, *Ceramah Penghasutan Untuk Membunuh Anggota Ahmadiyah Dan Mengacaukan NKRI.* (YouTube 2008).

Jaspan MA, 'In Quest of New Law: The Perplexity of Legal Syncretism in Indonesia' (1965) 7 *Comparative Studies in Society and History* 252.

Joseph S, 'Human Rights Committee : Recent Cases' (2001) 1 *Human Rights Law Review* 305.

Kahn JS, ''Ideology and Social Structure in Indonesia' (1978) 20 *Comparative Studies in Society and History* 103.

Langlois AJ, *The Politics of Justice and Human Rights: Southeast Asia and Universalist Theory* (Cambridge University Press 2001).

Lindsey T, 'Square Pegs & Round Holes: Fitting Modern Title into Traditional Societies in Indonesia' (1998) 7 *Pacific Rim Law and Policy Journal* 699–719.

———, 'The Rechtsstaat and Human Rights', in Tim Lindsey (ed.), *Indonesia, Law and Society* (Federation Press 2008) 183.

Marshall J, *Personal Freedom through Human Rights Law?: Autonomy, Identity and Integrity under the European Convention on Human Rights* (Martinus Nijhoff Publishers Boston 2009).

Marshall P and Shea N, *Silenced: How Apostasy and Blasphemy Codes Are Choking Freedom Worldwide* (Oxford University Press USA 2011).

Menchik J, 'Why Is a New York Rabbi Giving a Tolerance Award to Indonesia's Intolerant President?' (*Tablet Magazine* 21 May 2013).

Mietzner M, 'Indonesia's Democratic Stagnation: Anti-Reformist Elites and Resilient Civil Society' (2012) 19 *Democratization* 209.

Noviansi CN and Budiarti MF, 'Jaringan Islam Liberal: Gerakan Liberalis Islam Serta Pergerakan Dan Perkembangannya Di Indonesia (2001–2010)' (2013) 10 *Jurnal Sejarah Lontar* 1.

Nuh NM and Rosidi A, 'Kasus Salafi Versus Non-Salafi di Kabupaten Lombok Barat Nusa Tenggara Barat', in Nuhrison Nuh and Achmad Rosidi, *Kasus-Kasus Aliran/Faham Keagamaan Aktual Di Indonesia* (Departemen Agama, Badan Litbang Agama Dan Diklat Keagamaan, Puslitbang Kehidupan Beragama 2006) 3.

Palatino M, 'Does Indonesia's SBY Deserve the World Statesman Award?' (13 June 2013).

Rosser A, 'Towards a Political Economy of Human Rights Violations in Post-New Order Indonesia' (2013) 43 *Journal of Contemporary Asia* 2.

Saeed A, 'The Islamic Case for Religious Liberty' (*ABC Religion & Ethics* 24 February 2012).

Saeed A and Saeed H, *Freedom of Religion, Apostasy and Islam* (Routledge 2017).

Shah DAH, *Constitutions, Religion and Politics in Asia: Indonesia, Malaysia and Sri Lanka* (Cambridge University Press 2017).

Shihab HR, 'Mengadili Perjuangan Pembubaran Ahmadiyah' (District Court of Central Jakarta 20 October 2008).
Steiner HJ, Alston P and Goodman R, *International Human Rights in Context: Law, Politics, Morals: Text and Materials* (Oxford University Press 2008).
Sutiyono, *Benturan Budaya Islam: Puritan & Sinkretis* (Penerbit Buku Kompas 2010).
Temperman J, 'Freedom of Expression and Religious Sensitivities in Pluralist Societies: Facing the Challenge of Extreme Speech' (2011) 2011 *BYU Law Review* 729.
Tursun G, 'Integrating Minorities through Legislation: A Chinese Point of View' (2011) 12 *Asia-Pacific Journal on Human Rights and the Law* 27.
Vance SC, 'The Permissibility of Incitement to Religious Hatred Offenses under European Convention Principles' (2004) 14 *Transnational Law & Contemporary Problems* 201.
Waltman J, 'Communities in Conflict: The School Prayer in West Germany, the United States and Canada' (1991) 6 *Canadian Journal of Law & Society* 27.
Yamani AZ, 'Humanitarian International Law in Islam: A General Outlook' (1985) 7 *Michigan Journal of International Law* 28.

7 Repealing blasphemy law to protect religious minorities within Islam in Indonesia

1. Religion, defamation and religious freedom under international human rights law

In the context of religious freedom and minority rights, international human rights law has attempted to strike a balance, not only between religious beliefs and freedom of expression as asserted in articles 18, 19 and 20 of the ICCPR[1] but also to establish equal relations between the respective majority and minority groups, as asserted by article 27 of the ICCPR. Against the historical background of persecutions of vulnerable minority groups, the international human rights movement has basically succeeded in establishing international human rights standards for minorities in general as well as religious minorities in particular.[2] State parties responsible for the implementation of relevant human rights instruments are required not only to guarantee freedom of religion as an individual human right but also to protect communal dimensions of religions, because most religions are practised communally.[3] If the states only protect the individual as a believer of religion and not communal religious rites, the individual may consider this policy as a kind of insult against his/her religion. Based on this argument, the state parties are legally and morally also obliged to undertake proactive actions to protect the right of every person to embrace a religion of their choice and to respect the communal observance of religious rites as part of religious freedom.

To regulate the communal character of religion, the state parties must acknowledge that the recognition and protection of the rights of believers in a world characterised by inter and intra diversities and rivalry of beliefs becomes very significant because religious belief and religious identity are both significant personally and communally.[4] Additionally, religion is like a double-edged

1 M Bassiouni, 'Speech, Religious Discrimination, and Blasphemy: Remarks' (1989) 83 *American Society of International Law Proceedings* 427, 3.

2 Geoff Gilbert, 'Religious Minorities and Their Rights: A Problem of Approach' (1997) 5 *International Journal on Minority and Group Rights* 97, 18.

3 Nazila Ghanea-Hercock, 'Introduction', in Nazila Ghanea-Hercock, *The Challenge of Religious Discrimination at the Dawn of the New Millennium* (Springer 2013) 1.

4 ibid 2–3.

sword,[5] either serving as a source of prejudice and discrimination or becoming a source of reconciliation and healing.[6] Religion is able to construct public consciousness with its transcendental and supernatural values because it is perceived by many people as the most influential element in the creation of peace and this can be achieved when people respect the differences that exist within or between religions. Related to this, Hans Küng confidently argues that "there is no world peace without peace among religions and no peace among religions without accurate knowledge of one religion to another".[7] This signifies that attempting to create peace holistically will be difficult to accomplish without introducing and accepting inter and intra religious pluralism for all religious groups.

To respond to these complex realities of religion, international human rights law gives preference to protecting human beings as believers rather than protecting religions. There are no instruments that explicitly define religion because those instruments tend to demarcate religion into the private domain and assign priority to human rights in the public sphere.[8] This assumes that religion is a private matter and hence it solely involves man and his God. Because of this, the state must be separated from the Church.[9] This perspective apparently upholds the human being as the sacred element in human rights while religion on the other hand is considered as a complementary element of the human being.

Since 9/11, however, the human rights movement has shifted into a new area of demarcation of religion and human rights because religious defamation became an increasingly prominent matter of debate in the UNHRC.[10] Starting from 1999, until 2010, there had been approximately 20 UN resolutions relating to the defamation of religion.[11] One of these was Resolution 7/19, adopted in 2008 in response to the dramatic rise of Islamophobia in the world and global protests stemming from the controversy about the cartoon published by the Danish newspaper *Jyllands-Posten* in 2005.[12] In principle, the resolution was

5 About double-edged sword theory, see Carolyn Evans, 'The Double-Edged Sword: Religious Influences on International Humanitarian Law' (2005) *Melbourne Journal of International Law* 1.
6 J Paul Martin, 'The Three Monotheistic World Religions and International Human Rights' (2005) 61 *Journal of Social Issues* 4, 828.
7 Hans Küng, *Global Responsibility: In Search of a New World Ethic* (Wipf and Stock Publishers 2004) 105.
8 Ghanea-Hercock (n 3) 115.
9 See the separationist theory which advocates the separation between law and religion in Mashood A Baderin, 'Religion and International Law: Friends or Foes?' (Social Science Research Network 2009) 643.
10 The Human Rights Commission was disbanded in 2006 and was replaced by the Human Rights Council. See Brett G Scharffs, 'International Law and the Defamation of Religion Conundrum' (2013) 11 *The Review of Faith & International Affairs* 66, 67–68.
11 ibid 68.
12 Michael Kimmelman, 'Outrage at Cartoons Still Tests the Danes' (*The New York Times* 20 March 2008).

a result of a debate between Muslim-majority countries which supported the resolution and Western countries, which ended with the passing of a non-binding resolution condemning the defamation of religion, particularly Islam.[13] This resolution in principle emphasises the duties and responsibilities of every person in exercising his/her freedom of speech and expression, which means that this right does not include the right to insult religions or beliefs.[14]

However, after long contentious debates the UNHRC has, since 2011, departed from adopting resolutions protecting religions and turned its attention to the protection of believers. In 2011, the UNHRC adopted Resolution 16/18 which focuses more narrowly on combating religious intolerance, which usually targets individuals on the basis of their religion or belief.[15] This shift is important because human rights bodies affirm their neutral position toward religions and further emphasise their focus on human beings as the subject of human rights legislation.

2. The complex application of blasphemy law

The prohibition of blasphemy and its negative impact on the rights of religious minority groups and other rights and freedoms is still a worldwide phenomenon, despite the great advancement in international human rights law. In general, blasphemy laws may interfere with the rights of religious minority groups. Additionally, the allocation of an official religion as in Indonesia could potentially incline the state to protect the official religion and to possibly use a religious doctrine favoured by the majority to persecute religious minorities. In this context, the principle of universal religious freedom and the protection of religious minorities becomes very vulnerable.

In the Muslim world, blasphemy laws are applied widely, not only to prosecute acts that are considered insulting to Islam but also to oppress religious minorities within Islam. Many cases show that the offence of blasphemy has a low threshold, is very broad and can be used to persecute Islamic dissidents. These cases carry different kinds of punishments, ranging from life imprisonment to the death sentence.[16] Consequently, blasphemy, heresy and even apostasy have been applied interchangeably despite different definitions within Islamic law.[17] Blasphemy is basically defined as any kind of action which insults the Islamic sacred symbols.[18] In Islamic Sunni jurisprudence for instance,

13 Human Rights Council Res. No. 7/19 on Combating Defamation of Religions.

14 Abdullahi An-Naim, 'Best of 2010: Religious Freedom and Defamation' (*ABC* 10 November 2010).

15 A/HRC/RES/16/18.

16 Mark Gretason, 'A Law on Religious Hatred Entrenching Pluralism' (2003) 150 *Law & Justice – The Christian Law Review* 37, 3.

17 About multi-faceted descriptions and case studies of blasphemy and apostasy, see David Forte, 'Apostasy and Blasphemy in Pakistan' (1994) 10 *Connecticut Journal of International Law* 27, 68.

18 Hashemi, *Religious Legal Traditions, International Human Rights Law and Muslim States* (Brill Nijhoff 2008) 31.

blasphemy is known as *sabb*, which means the offence of insulting Islamic sacred symbols such as God, the Angels and the Prophet.[19] Some Shi'ah jurists argue that the offence of blasphemy should include insults against the twelve Shi'ah imams and the daughter of the Prophet, Fatimah.[20] Some Sunni Muslims in Indonesia also hold that insulting prominent Islamic religious leaders is considered blasphemous.[21] Evidently, the term "insulting" is relative, being heavily dependent on the context.

There is *ikhtilaf*, or differences of opinion among Muslim scholars about the punishment of blasphemy in Islam. Some argue that if a Muslim blasphemes, she/he remains a Muslim but may be punished for committing the offence of blasphemy. Other interpretations deem that a Muslim who commits blasphemy becomes an apostate.[22] This argument seems to overlap with the concept of apostasy because apostasy is considered by many Muslim scholars as a crime exclusively applied to Muslims who reject Islam either by word or deed.[23] It means that the very ambiguity of the definition of blasphemy serves as a possible device for the state and Islamic majority groups "to punish apostates, heretics, non-Muslims who criticise Islam and political dissenters as well".[24]

Heresy or religious dissidence (*zandaqah*) in Islam is generally related to the idea of Muslims considered by the majority to be inconsistent with mainstream or orthodox Islam.[25] In other words, heresy can be defined as non-mainstream Islamic teaching or a reform within Islam seen as dangerous to the social order.[26] Heresy is often considered dangerous by the majority groups because its non-mainstream views indicate attempts to subvert the community of believers.[27] As a consequence, since the first century of Islam after the death of the Prophet, the Islamic majorities utilised blasphemy and heresy as a means of silencing political and theological opponents.[28] Some Muslims define heresy as

19 ibid.
20 ibid 32.
21 The case of Saleh, a young Muslim in Situbondo District, East Java Indonesia, who was sentenced to five years in prison in 1996, illustrates that insulting a *kyai*, an Islamic religious leader, is considered blasphemous under article 156a of the Indonesian Criminal Code. See the case in Uli Parulian Sihombing, Pultoni, Siti Aminah and Muhammad Khoirul Roziqin, *Ketidakadilan Dalam Beriman: Hasil Monitoring Kasus-Kasus Penodaan Agama Dan Ujaran Kebencian Atas Dasar Agama Di Indonesia* (The Indonesian Legal Resource Center 2012) 20–22.
22 Abdullah Saeed, *Freedom of Religion, Apostasy and Islam* (Routledge 2017) 38.
23 Nicholas Garces, 'Islam, Till Death Do You Part: Rethinking Apostasy Laws under Islamic Law and International Legal Obligations' (2010) 16 *Southwestern Journal of International Law* 229, 230.
24 Forte (n 17) 49.
25 Garces (n 23) 236.
26 Bernard Lewis, 'Some Observations on the Significance of Heresy in the History of Islam' (1953) 1 *Studia Islamica* 43, 55.
27 Anthony Chase, 'Legal Guardians: Islamic Law, International Law, Human Rights Law, and the Salman Rushdie Affair' 11 American University International Law Review 3, 399.
28 Abdullah Saeed, 'The Islamic Case for Religious Liberty' (*First Things* 2011).

an intellectual rebellion insulting to the Prophet's honour.[29] Others consider heresy to include a false belief or the denial of orthodox belief by a rival school of thought. This results in a situation where any attempt to reform or revise orthodox Islamic beliefs could be considered heresy.[30] These jurisprudential differences then deeply influence the broad practices of blasphemy law in the Muslim world. Saeed, for instance, reports that "many well-known and highly respected Islamic scholars were accused of apostasy, unbelief or heresy because of the school they belonged to or because of their intellectual orientation",[31] as well as their political affiliation.

Neither the Qur'an nor the Prophet clearly regulated the existence of an offence of blasphemy and heresy or a specific punishment for it in the world.[32] The penalisation of blasphemy and heresy started in the post-prophetic Islamic jurisprudence to restrain and persecute freedom of expression as well as to marginalise dissenting opinions within Islam. A number of political leaders and Islamic majority groups interpret the Qur'an and the *Sunnah* as a means of silencing dissenting voices among Muslims, such as Kharijis, Shi'ah,[33] Ahmadiyah and any other Muslim minorities. The majority considers them not only blasphemers but also heretic (*zindiq*), because their profession of Islam seems to them not to be sufficiently sincere.[34] Some others also accused them as non-Islamic groups which threaten Islamic belief. Thus, even though the early Islamic jurists did not have unanimous opinions on heresy, some Muslim states and Islamic majority groups usually viewed it more ruthlessly than they did apostasy.[35] In many Muslim-majority states, some Muslims and religious minorities within Islam seen as heretical have experienced dramatic forms of persecution, have been excommunicated from the mainstream Islamic community and have experienced severe legal and social sanctions.[36]

In other countries, the debate on whether the offence of blasphemy should be retained, reformed or abolished has also been raised by many human rights advocates. In some Western countries, blasphemy laws, even though rarely used, frequently deal with freedom of speech and expression.[37] Blasphemy is also defined differently based on the religious context in particular states. It is

29 Abdullah Saeed and Hassan Saeed, *Freedom of Religion, Apostasy and Islam* (Routledge 2017) 39.

30 Donna E Arzt, 'Heroes or Heretics: Religious Dissidents Under Islamic Law' (1996) 14 *Wisconsin International Law Journal* 349.

31 For detailed information and lists of Islamic scholars persecuted in the early stage of Islam since the death of the Prophet, see Saeed and Saeed (n 29) 30–31.

32 ibid 3.

33 ibid 39.

34 ibid.

35 ibid 41.

36 Heiner Bielefeldt, 'Muslim Voices in the Human Rights Debate' (1995) 17 *Human Rights Quarterly* 587, 599.

37 Jeroen Temperman, 'Blasphemy, Defamation of Religions & Human Rights Law' (Social Science Research Network 2012) 518.

common policy among a majority of states, not only Muslim but also some Western states, to pass legislation which restricts religious insult.[38] Some countries enact such laws to protect the feelings of religious believers from offensive materials being used against the sacred elements of their religions.[39] Other countries use such laws to back state-sponsored religious orthodoxy, which brings about potential discrimination against non-mainstream religious interpretation. Thus, under such laws, non-mainstream interpretations are seen by the orthodox religious majority as threatening their claims of superiority, exclusivity and monopoly of interpreting religious texts, thereby making religious minority groups vulnerable.[40]

It can be concluded that blasphemy does not need the intention to commit a crime, but merely the perceived negative impacts of the blasphemous act.[41] In many cases, the application of blasphemy law not only affects freedom of expression but also discriminates against minority religions considered as un-established religions in a given country. The law is applied in states that recognise official religions to uphold religious orthodoxy and by democratic states, generally with the aim of preserving public order. In the Muslim world, the orthodox religious majority usually rejects non-mainstream religious interpretations because those interpretations are seen as advocating internal reform or non-mainstream interpretations of Islam contrary to the orthodox Islamic doctrine.[42] Thus, blasphemy law or state-favoured interpretations of religion are often applied to legitimise rules based on an exclusivist religious identity that cannot tolerate affirmations of equality of minority Muslim groups.

3. Blasphemy law within religious plurality: an Indonesian case

Indonesia has experienced a complex and long history with human rights development, involving both Indonesian human rights scholars and Islamic figures.[43] The country has long dealt with the mixture of Indonesian legal traditions and secular Dutch civil law, as well as attempting to absorb religious values into the legal arena. Indonesia has also attempted to incorporate social actions and

38 Hashemi (n 18) 44–51.

39 Temperman (n 37) 666. See *e.g.* the Irish Defamation Act No. 31/2009.

40 Mohamed SM Eltayeb, *A Human Rights Approach to Combating Religious Persecution: Cases from Pakistan, Saudi Arabia, and Sudan* (Intersentia 2001) 95–96.

41 JW Montgomery, 'Can Blasphemy Law Be Justified?' (2000) 145 *Law & Justice – The Christian Law Review* 6, 9.

42 Hashemi (n 18) 33.

43 A good example was the deletion of the seven words which explicitly referred to the application of Sharia in the preamble of the 1945 Constitution during the preparation of Indonesian Independence in 1945 because most Muslims believed that this clause may have divided Indonesia into many groups. See for example Arskal Salim and Azyumardi Azra, 'The State and Sharia in the Perspective of Indonesian Legal Politics', in Arskal Salim and Azyumardi Azra (eds), *Shari'a and Politics in Modern Indonesia* (Institute of Southeast Asian Studies 2003) 4.

religious aspirations into its legislation. As a consequence, Indonesian law is characteristically secular. Yet it also cooperates with religious values without mentioning a particular religion, to provide an environment in which minority religions may also flourish. This, then, indicates that the concept of "secularism" is also a plural phenomenon in Indonesia.

Practically, however, several legislations enacted to protect public order and religious harmony among people have been frequently used to silence dissident religious groups. A good example is the Indonesian 1965 Blasphemy Law.[44] Many Indonesians speculate that the 1965 Blasphemy Law was inspired by article 147 of the Dutch criminal law on blasphemy even though the distinctive relationship is dubious.[45] Unlike the Dutch blasphemy law which only restricts the incitement of hate speech against persons on the grounds of their religion or belief,[46] Article 1 of the 1965 Blasphemy Law does not only restrict freedom of expression that may be harmful against the six recognised religions (Islam, Christianity, Protestantism, Buddhism, Confucianism and Hinduism) but also restricts religious teachings that deviate from the official religions.[47] This article authorises leaders of the official religions to set boundaries on what is official doctrine and to determine the most authoritative understanding of religion as well as restrict the so-called "deviant" interpretation of the respective religions.[48]

The 1965 Blasphemy Law was first proposed by the Ministry of Religious Affairs, under Saifudin Zuhri, in response to socio-political situations in the country at the time. During this time, Indonesia endured multiple Islamic rebellions and ideological conflicts between the Communist Party and Islamic organisations.[49] This law has now, nevertheless, been politically interpreted by the government and by many people as discriminating against members of religious minorities.[50]

44 Basically, this law was first enacted as a presidential decree, the law below an Act in the Indonesian legal hierarchy. After the enactment of Law No. 5/1969 which provides that every presidential decree or presidential regulation enacted before this law should be considered as an Act, presidential decrees were elevated to the same level as Acts.

45 Article 147 of the Dutch Criminal Code restricts persons who publicly offend religious sensibilities by malign blasphemies as a serious offence against public order.

46 Jeroen Temperman, 'Freedom of Expression and Religious Sensitivities in Pluralist Societies: Facing the Challenge of Extreme Speech' (2011) 2011 *BYU Law Review* 729, 748.

47 This article asserts that everyone is prohibited in public from intentionally conveying, endorsing or attempting to gain public support for any interpretation of a certain religion embraced by people in Indonesia or undertaking religious activities that resemble religious activities of the religion, where the interpretation and activities deviate from the basic teachings of the aforesaid religion.

48 Temperman (n 37) 4.

49 Siti Hanna, 'Pencegahan Penodaan Agama (Kajian Atas UU No.1 tahun 1965)' (2017) *RELIGIA* 159–160.

50 Binawan for instance reported that the Ministry of Defense circulated a Decree in 1981, stating that people that belong to "unrecognised religions" were restricted from serving in the Indonesian army. See Alexius Andang L Binawan, 'Declarations and the Indonesian Constitution on Religious Freedom' (2011) 49 *Al-Jami'ah: Journal of Islamic Studies* 361, 381.

This regulation is further emphasised by article 156a of the Indonesian Criminal Code (hereinafter KUHP Blasphemy Law), which threatens to jail people for up to five years for blasphemous actions. The KUHP Blasphemy Law was originally inspired by the 1965 Blasphemy Law, but unlike the 1965 Blasphemy Law the KUHP Blasphemy Law does not explicitly restrict so-called "deviant" religious beliefs. Some Indonesians argue that the two laws prevent hate speech and abusive actions and expressions against certain religions to protect public order and religious harmony. Others argue that these laws protect the official religious doctrine, not the believers of religions.[51] It is apparent from the different cases of blasphemy in Indonesia that there is a close relationship between the 1965 Blasphemy Law and the KUHP Blasphemy Law, with many judges frequently interpreting the laws to protect religious orthodoxy to the detriment of religious minorities within the official religions.

Even though Indonesia has experienced many blasphemy cases in the court room, the Ahmadiyah, as the most persecuted religious minority within Islam, has never had the opportunity to be represented.[52] Neither the Supreme Court nor the district courts have applied blasphemy laws to the Ahmadiyah, even though verdicts have been in favour of restricting Ahmadiyah activities. In one case, for example, the Supreme Court found that the restriction of Ahmadiyah activities by the collective decision of heads of the local military, police, district prosecution office, religious affairs ministry, air force, parliament and district court of Bogor was legal.[53] However, the verdict did not cite the blasphemy law as this was an administrative case. In the case of the Ahmadiyah, blasphemy law is generally applied by executive state organs such as the central government[54] and local governments in the political realm[55] to restrict Ahmadiyah rights based on pressure from the orthodox Islamic religious majority groups. The central and local governments argue that the blasphemy law inspired them to restrict religious minorities within Islam solely to preserve religious harmony and respond to pressing social needs in a democratic society.[56] In this context, the government has the power to determine the rights of a particular religion. In these cases, the majority religion is able to decide on whim if

51 See Sihombing and others (n 21) 10–11.

52 To read detailed information regarding individuals and groups charged with blasphemy law, see ibid 11–16.

53 Verdict of Supreme Court No. 182K/TUN/2007.

54 One example is the Joint Decree on Ahmadiyah in 2008 which restricted the spread of Ahmadiyah, collectively signed by the MORA, the Interior Ministry and the Attorney General.

55 In 2011, several local governments enacted regulations which principally restricted Ahmadiyah activities. See more detailed information in Azhari, M. S., (coord.) 2011. 'Lampu Merah Kebebasan Beragama, Laporan Kebebasan Beragama Dan Intolerensi Di Indonesia 2011' (Wahid Institute) 8.

56 See *e.g.* Decree of the East Java Governor No. 188/94/KPTS/013/2012, which restricted Ahmadiyah activities, and Decree No. 55/2012, which restricted the spread of so-called "deviant" religious teaching.

a minority religion can freely exist.[57] With the majority religion behind them, the government is then authorised to restrict a minority even though such religious activity does not actually incite or produce lawless action.[58]

These facts indicate that the blasphemy law has become an issue of public morality, commonly determined by the religious majorities to exclude religious groups which share non-mainstream religious teachings with them. This is similar to restrictions against organisations as these are often a prelude to an official ban.[59] This demonstrates that the blasphemy law is in fact inconsistent with the nature of religious plurality in Indonesia. The Indonesian blasphemy law does not make specific reference to Islamic law or sources, so the country also generally considers the practices of other Muslim-majority countries against religious minorities within Islam and argues that Indonesia should act accordingly. This means that this law perceives "Islamic" differently and on a case by case basis. One reason for this is that Indonesia has not officially incorporated the OIC Cairo Declaration on Human Rights in Islam into its national legislation, including human rights and criminal law, yet it still may consider the moral content of the Declaration and Islamic criteria as justification to enact a particular policy.[60]

4. Judicial review of the Indonesian blasphemy law

The establishment of the Constitutional Court of the Republic of Indonesia (Mahkamah Konstitusi, MK) in 2003 was meant to oversee the parliament, which has broad powers in enacting regulations and controlling executive power through the amendment of the 1945 Constitution. Since its establishment, the MK has become the highest guardian of constitutional human rights because all citizens can submit a judicial review of the Acts that discriminate against their rights and are in contradiction with the 1945 Constitution. Thus, the establishment of the MK enhances "democratic norms and the rule of law principles and to strengthen the principle of legal certainty in the country".[61] The state

57 Susannah C Vance, 'The Permissibility of Incitement to Religious Hatred Offenses under European Convention Principles' (2004) 14 *Transnational Law & Contemporary Problems* 201, 210.

58 See AD Hapsari, 'Failure to Revise Blasphemy Law Would "Limit Role of Religion"' (*The Jakarta Post* 20 March 2010).

59 Adiaan Bedner, *Administrative Courts in Indonesia: A Socio-Legal Study* (Brill Nijhoff 2001) 172.

60 See Judge Natabaya's opinion and his support of the death penalty for drug traffickers, Verdict of Mahmakah Konstitusi (hereafter verdict of MK) No. 2 & 3/PUU-V/2007 on Judicial Review of Act No. 22/1997 on Narcotic at 43. Indonesia signed the OIC Cairo Declaration without officially adopting it into its national legislation and hence in normative legal matters Islamic law does not have binding rules in its human rights and criminal law, as none of the human rights and criminal codes in Indonesian legislation specifically refer to Islamic law.

61 Petra Stockmann, *The New Indonesian Constitutional Court: A Study Into Its Beginnings and First Years of Work* (Hanns Seidel Foundation 2007) 100.

considers the 1945 Constitution was created based on the contract between government and citizens, and thus this judicial review exists to prevent politicians from reneging on the founding contract with citizens.[62] Thus, the establishment of the MK should set up an accountability system which plays an important role in furthering democratic reform, the rule of law and human rights enforcement.[63] An important case brought before the MK was for the judicial review of the 1965 Blasphemy Law in October 2009. The applicants included Islamic leaders, Muslim scholars and human rights activists, while the government was represented by the MORA, the Minister of Justice and the parliament.[64] Both sides also invited religious and human rights organisations and some individuals as *amici curiae* or friends of the court during the court hearing.

4.1. Examining law in the MK hearings

One of the most significant elements in the Indonesian legal system is the principle of judicial independence. This principle requires that all judges and judicial institutions be independent in their decisions. This is to protect the law from external interference and to allow judges to reach independent verdicts.[65] However, this principle cannot be translated into judge-made law as practised in the common law tradition.[66] It is more properly interpreted to mean that all judges must creatively search for the living law in society. In many sensitive cases brought before the courts, the judges consider popular values within society to interpret the constitution. This implies that judges generally perceive societal values as an important factor in ensuring justice and the effective realisation of the constitution as well.

The judges are required to independently search for law and justice using their own legal perspective as protected by article 5 of Law No. 48/2009 on Judicial Powers. This article provides that:

> All judges including the Constitutional Court judges are required to search, keep abreast of and understand legal values and justice living within Indonesian society.[67]

62 Tom Ginsburg, *Judicial Review in New Democracies: Constitutional Courts in Asian Cases* (Cambridge University Press 2003) 23.

63 Matthew Draper, 'Justice as a Building Block of Democracy in Transitional Societies: The Case of Indonesia' (2001) 40 *Columbia Journal of Transnational Law* 391, 392.

64 See the list of advocates and applicants in *Judicial Review of 1965 Blasphemy Law* (2009) Constitutional Court of Indonesia 140/PUU-VII/2009 1–4.

65 See *e.g.* articles 4 and 28 of Law No. 4/2004 on Judicial Power, article 5 of Law No. 48/ 2009 on Judicial Power and article 24 of the 1945 Constitution.

66 Leslie Scarman, 'Codification and Judge-Made Law: A Problem of Coexistence' (1967) 42 *Indiana Law Journal* 355, 358.

67 Translation by the writer.

This article demonstrates that understanding the Indonesian legal tradition should not be restricted to written documents. There also needs to be consideration for all sources of law which derive from unwritten documents, both from religions and from traditions practised by people. This factual legal pluralism becomes more complex as there are different kinds of communities within Indonesian society. These communities can be categorised as: the religious community, which generally perceives tenets of its religion as a source of law; the secular community, which considers the constitution as its supreme law; and the traditional community, which still practises its own traditional norms. These three kinds of communities often do not share the same legal values and hence judges are expected to consider legal perspectives from all communities to do justice in the cases before them.[68] This clearly reflects a deep recognition of legal pluralism in the official Indonesian legal framework.

The court searches for living law within the society by inviting *amici curiae* or friends of the court, whether Indonesians or foreigners. The *amici* do not need to be legal practitioners or bodies who have particular legal skills related to the case. They could be religious leaders, philosophers, social activists or any relevant body possessing education or experience relevant to the case before the court. These *amici* are generally proposed by the parties or invited by the MK during the court hearing to give their independent "expert" opinions related to the case brought before the MK.[69] In the case of judicial review of blasphemy law for instance, Cole Durham was proposed by the complainants to emphasise the reasons for revoking the blasphemy law. Other kinds of foreign legal and human rights scholars have been proposed by parties in different cases since the establishment of the MK.[70] The main objective of inviting *amici* to a hearing is to enable the judge, pursuant to article 5 of Law No. 48/2009 on Judicial Powers, to appreciate and weigh the diversity of legal perspectives regarding a case before reaching a decision either in favour of or against it.

Additionally, the MK judges are free to consider their previous jurisprudence in similar cases. Some other judges refer to similar cases from other countries which have different concepts of laws, such as common law countries. For instance, Judge Maruarar Siahaan quoted the 1945 constitution and referred to several cases from the USA to support his dissenting opinion when advocating the abolition of the death penalty.[71] Judges also considered verdicts from the constitutional courts of South Korea and South Africa to support their

68 See Roger Cotterrell, *Law, Culture and Society: Legal Ideas in the Mirror of Social Theory* (Ashgate 2006) 35.

69 See article 1 (13) of MK Regulation No. 06/PMK/2005 on Litigation Procedure in the MK.

70 Some legal and human rights scholars invited by the MK to give their expert opinions during court hearings are Professor William A. Schabbas, Professor Jeffrey Fagan and Professor Philip Alston, who were asked to give their opinion regarding the judicial case against the death penalty for drug traffickers. See Verdict of MK No. 2 and 3/PUU-V/2007.

71 ibid 70. para. 5.4.

arguments.[72] In other cases, arguments and considerations from the MK judges may consider various kinds of legal perspectives depending on the case and arguments from the parties.[73]

The MK may also refer to various kinds of binding and non-binding legal instruments and other sources of law. Some judges consider international instruments, not only ratified by the country, such as the ICCPR, but also relevant instruments that do not have legally binding effect. Reference to non-binding international instruments is not limited to the UDHR but also the European Convention of Human Rights (ECHR), the American Convention of Human Rights (ACHR), the protocol of the ICCPR and protocols of the Geneva Convention.[74] Another non-binding instrument that is referred to is the OIC Cairo Declaration on Human Rights in Islam. For instance, Judge Natabaya argued that Indonesia as the largest Muslim country and a member of the OIC should, in examining the matter of the death penalty, morally consider the Cairo Declaration, especially article 2A of the Declaration.[75]

An important characteristic of court hearings in the MK is that all parties may present their own legal perspectives. Then, the judges will counter those arguments with the same sources. This means that judges generally use legal consideration on a case by case basis. Consequently, in some cases they may use the constitution and Islamic law, while in other cases they only consider the constitution and international human rights instruments. For instance, the MK considered Qur'an, Hadith and Islamic jurisprudences to reject an application for the judicial review of Act No. 1/1974 on Monogamous Marriage because the majority of the parties involved in the court hearing, including the complainants, quoted the constitution and Islamic law to defend their arguments.[76] From all these facts, examining law and human rights in the MK can be very broad and a matter may not be examined from one single source, including the constitution itself.

Normally, presented arguments and considerations are written in the verdict summary. In this way, people will know that the MK judges decided the case not solely based on their authoritative legal view but also considered empirical legal perspectives from the parties and witnesses during the court hearing. The MK often attempts to harmonise all legal perspectives and guarantee that the law is part of Indonesian social life, based not only on written legislation but also acknowledged social norms within Indonesian society and international perspectives. This is to guarantee that all MK verdicts are sensitive to Indonesian socio-cultural diversity by

72 ibid 76–77.

73 This practice is similar to the practice of the South Africa Constitutional Court. See David D Caron, Joan Fitzpatrick and Ron C Slye, 'Republic of South Africa v. Grootboom. Case No. CCT 11/00. 2000 (11) BCLR 1169 and Minister of Health v. Treatment Action Campaign. Case No. CCT 8/02' (2003) 97 *American Journal of International Law* 669, 675.

74 ibid 44. para. 3.24. Until now Indonesia has never ratified any additional protocols of the convention.

75 ibid 43. para. 3.24.

76 See Verdict of MK No. 12/PUU-V/2007.

negotiating the positivistic view of the constitution and legal empirical perspectives from society. This distinctive judicial approach is chosen by the MK to ensure that the verdicts can bridge the interests of all parties because all MK decisions are binding and final. It indicates that the judges ensure that written legislation is not in confrontation with social norms because they believe that social norms constitute another source of law that should also be considered by the court in reaching its final decisions.[77]

One significant consequence of considering "Indonesian social norms" to adopt a verdict is the complexity of state obligations to obey international human rights law standards. In the context of judicial review on blasphemy law, the judges on behalf of the state will consider arguments from *amici curiae* which mainly represent Sunni-mainstream Islam. Additionally, Indonesian Muslims' own interpretation of "deviant Islam", which represents religious minorities within Islam, would very likely be considered by the judges.

4.2. Legal rationales of the judicial review

The plaintiffs in the 1965 Blasphemy Law judicial review application believed that the blasphemy law needed to be revoked because the state must not intervene in religious matters as religious interpretation is in fact non-monolithic. The plaintiffs argued that in the Islamic tradition the differences of thought in religious interpretation are relevant in branches of the law (*furu'iyya*) and more fundamental matters (*usuli*).[78] This argument is true because the history of Islam in Indonesia reveals that religious difference is not only related to religious minorities within Islam but is also encountered within the mainstream orthodox Sunnis. The Muhammadiyah, which advocates purifying Islam from heretical practices, even experienced a harsh welcome by local Muslims in its early period, while until recently the NU has also been accused of introducing innovation (*bid'ah*) by the Muhammadiyah and other puritan Sunnis. More complications arise when the blasphemy law deals with mystical beliefs (*aliran kepercayaan*) because these beliefs generally do not define religion. Such examples confirm that the definition of religion is relative and so, too, are blasphemous actions. The state cannot adopt a particular definition of blasphemy from a specific religion.[79] The plaintiffs concluded that the government cannot interfere in religious freedom and cannot declare one particular religion as deviant and apostate because belief is a divine and individual matter. However, the plaintiffs claimed that religious organisations could theologically declare that another religious group is

77 To read about the confrontation between social norms and legal instruments, see Bedner (n 59) 266.
78 *Judicial Review of 1965 Blasphemy Law* (n 64) 34.
79 ibid 3.

deviant because declaring one particular religion apostate has enlivened the history of religion and in fact lies within the nature of religions.[80]

The plaintiffs contended that article 1 of the 1965 Blasphemy Law, which prescribes a term of up to five years in jail for those who deliberately spread so-called "deviant religious teaching", is unconstitutional and against international human rights provisions on religious freedom. Article 2 (1&2) of the 1965 Blasphemy Law also discriminates against individuals' freedom of assembly and association because the government is authorised to ban and disband so-called deviant organisations.[81] Frans Magnis Suseno, a philosopher *amicus* proposed by the plaintiffs, emphasised that the interpretation of the terms deviant or apostate is relative and has been frequently used by a strong group to declare a vulnerable apostate.[82] JE Sahetapy, a criminal law professor *amicus* from the plaintiffs, also argued that the blasphemy law is diametrically in contradiction with the preamble of the 1945 Constitution, both as a foundation and as a philosophical view of Indonesia. Another *amicus* from the plaintiffs, Cole Durham, also proposed that the blasphemy law is against the spirit of international dimensions of religious freedom in the ICCPR.[83]

The government on the other side argued that the 1965 Blasphemy Law still plays a significant role in preserving religious harmony and Indonesian unity. Chaeruman Harahap, member and representative of the parliament, who gave his opinion during the hearing, argued that the 1956 Blasphemy Law is still relevant to sociologically prevent communal violence; to judicially protect legal certainty of religious freedom based on Pancasila and the 1945 Constitution; and to limit human rights based on article 18 (3) of the ICCPR.[84] This argument was endorsed by the Minister of MORA, Suryadharma Ali, who argued that the state does not restrict individuals to interpreting any kind of religious belief and only limits their *forum externum* right to "publicly convey or spread" their so-called misleading religious interpretation to avoid conflict among religious adherents.[85] Additionally, the Minister of Justice, Patrialis Akbar, asserted that if the 1965 Blasphemy Law

80 This argument was proposed by Frans Magnis Suseno and Lutfhie Assaukanie, the *amici* from the plaintiffs. See ibid.
81 The plaintiffs argued that this article is against article 28E (3) of the 1945 Constitution, which guarantees individuals the right to have freedom of association, assembly and expression, ibid 233.
82 ibid 345.
83 ibid 3. During the court hearing, this argument was partly or entirely supported by the Indonesian Church Association (PGI), the Indonesian Bishops Conference (KWI), the National Commission of Women's Human Rights (Komnas Perempuan), the Board of Mystical Belief Cooperation (BKOK), the Association of Mystical Followers (HPK) and the National Human Rights Commission (Komnas HAM). The Church Union further clarified that the blasphemy law was required to preserve the divinity of the holy book, but the substantive element of blasphemy law should be amended because it is still multi-interpretive.
84 ibid 240.
85 ibid 241.

was repealed, there would be uncontrollable slander among religious followers that may disturb the well-established religious harmony in the country.[86]

The government also proposed sixteen *amici curiae* ranging from Muslim leaders to scholars to support their arguments. One *amicus*, Hasyim Muzadi, former chair of NU argued that:

> The concept of unity in diversity in Indonesia allows pluralism but it is for sociological pluralism which requires the state to protect religions, not theological pluralism because the latter substantially engenders liberalism of religion. The liberalism of religion is when individuals perform misleading religious interpretation on behalf of democracy, a kind of interpretation which then leads to secularism and discriminates against religions.[87]

Nur Syam, another *amicus* from the NU, who advocated Muzadi's argument, stated that religious freedom is closely correlated with social duties because the relation of the state and religion in Indonesia is interdependent.[88] Theologically, Islam does not restrict an individual from embracing another religion, nor even from becoming an atheist, but when they become Muslims they must follow the authentic principles of Islamic belief. This argument was supported by Hafidz Usman, another *amicus*, who believed that Islam recognises consensus *(mujmaalaih)* and tolerates religious difference *(mukthalafalaih)* and asserted that the 1965 Blasphemy Law was not in contradiction with the spirit of justice and the 1945 Constitution.[89] Rony Nitibaskara, a legal scholar *amicus*, concluded that *forum internum* is absolute, but said that it is practically related to the role of the state to restrict public *ijtihad*, which may bring about social disintegration.[90]

The government's arguments represented that *forum internum* as the essential part of religious freedom in Indonesia is the corollary of duties owed to God, but this is more social than individual. Muslims should also uphold good behaviour towards their neighbours because Pancasila, the 1945 Constitution, the Indonesian Human Rights Act and ratified international human rights instruments protect individual religious freedom comprehensively and the principles of brotherhood, national unity and harmony cannot simply be ignored. In this

86 ibid 241.
87 ibid 242.
88 ibid 243.
89 ibid 246.
90 ibid 249. This argument was supported by the MUI, NU, Muhammadiyah, Islamic Association (Persis), Islamic Irena Center, Al Irsyad, Confucius Union (Matakin), Parisada Hindu Dharma, Islamic Society Union (FUI), Indonesian Mosque Council (DMI), HTI, FPI, Ittihadul Mubalighin, Association of Islamic Schools in Madura (Bassra), Development and Unity Party (PPP), Indonesian Buddhist Society (WALUBI) and Indonesian Islamic Propagation Board (DDII). The Matakin argued that the blasphemy law was required to protect religious minorities and rejects the application to repeal the Law before the government enacts a new just law. See ibid 251. para. 3.27.

context, individuals can get their rights as long as they obey certain morals and ethics prescribed by particular religions as public order instruments.

Regarding the relationship between demanding particular rights and good behaviour, Abdul Aziz Said argues that such behaviour is:

> prescribed by Muslim social order based upon sincerity and good deeds and organised around a community of believers. The integration of personality is realised through the disintegration of self, when human beings act for the good of the community rather than to achieve their own selfish desires.[91]

This proposition suggests that the concept of human rights in Islam is not only about rights but also about truth, justice and duty emanating from the divine word and the best way for human beings to achieve this is by considering their obligations,[92] not only to their religion but also to the community of believers.

Said's argument may be used to examine the interwoven relationship of religiosity and human rights in Indonesia. Even though Islam does not have a formal influence on human rights, Islamic values as part of the unwritten rules developed in a given society should not be ignored. The government, during the hearing, opposed the international human rights concept of religious freedom because it solely relies on individualism and confirmed that individual freedom is supreme. Individual freedom ends where the freedom of the community begins.[93] Thus, the government argued that the state recognises religious freedom and confirms that Islam protects the right to profess religion. However, the right for intra-Islamic difference is exceptional. This argument apparently ignores the fact that since the death of Prophet Muhammad, Islam has been and continues to be plural.

In contrast, the plaintiffs believed that the 1965 Blasphemy Law confirmed the state's interest in upholding a monolithic interpretation of religion to protect the officially recognised religions. Thus, it challenges both the individual concept of religious freedom in international human rights law as well as the pluralism in Islam. Additionally, the immense plurality of customary and religious practices leads some scholars to speak of "Islams" rather than of Islam.[94] There is in fact a rich diversity of belief, practice and emphasis among those who accept the divinity of Islam in the Muslim world and the variety of interpretations of what it means to be a Muslim is more diverse in Indonesia.[95]

91 Abdul Aziz Said, 'Precept and Practice of Human Rights in Islam' (1979) 1 *Universal Human Rights* 63, 64.
92 ibid 63.
93 ibid 73.
94 Werner F Menski, *Comparative Law in a Global Context: The Legal Systems of Asia and Africa* (Cambridge University Press 2006) 281.
95 Mark Cammack, Lawrence A Young and Tim Heaton, 'Legislating Social Change in an Islamic Society – Indonesia's Marriage Law' (1996) 44 *The American Journal of Comparative Law* 45, 47.

Islamic diversity can be preserved well if a state is neutral. On the one hand a state should recognise the important role of religion, but it must also limit its intervention on religious matters such as avoiding definitions of "good Muslims" and "deviant Muslims". The state cannot apply or adopt a monolithic interpretation of Islam and thereby punish other practices allegedly deviant to one particular Islam because this will affect individual rights. Related to this, An-Na'im argues:

> Muslims everywhere, whether minorities or majorities, are bound to observe Sharia as a matter of religious obligation, and that this can best be achieved when the state is neutral regarding all religious doctrines and does not claim to enforce Sharia principles as state policy legislation.[96]

An-Na'im's argument points out that Islam and states which have a majority Muslim population have some basic divergences from the international human rights law concept of individual rights. The concept of rights and the individual is, in Islam, distinguishable from the international human rights law versions because the conception of rights and freedom is linked with duties. Individuals possess certain obligations towards God, fellow humans and nature, all of which are defined in Islamic law. Here, the individual is placed in the context of the community of believers, because some Muslims believe Islam maintains that humans are not created for impervious individuality. Although it is different for liberal democratic states based on an individualistic philosophy, groups with a more collectivist orientation find it difficult to conform to international human rights law.[97] A Muslim is not the autonomous individual of Western philosophy but somebody who submits him/herself as a servant of God.[98] Thus, some Muslims argue that the duties of Muslims towards God are given more emphasis than the rights of individuals.[99] The history of Islamic jurisprudence, including the arguments of the government and its advocates in the 1965 Blasphemy Law case, shows a different line of argumentation and development. Some Muslim jurists have agreed that the larger interest of Muslim society takes precedence over the interest of the individual because individual freedom is only sacred as long as he/she does not deliberately violate religious law or transgress the rights of others.[100] The problem is still that the interpretations of what constitutes a transgression are a human assessment. Therefore, this puts one interpretation against the other and becomes political.

96 'Abd Allāh Aḥmad Na'īm, *Islam and the Secular State* (Harvard University Press 2009) 3.

97 Ahmad Yousif, 'Islam, Minorities and Religious Freedom: A Challenge to Modern Theory of Pluralism' (2000) 20 *Journal of Muslim Minority Affairs* 29, 31.

98 Donna E Arzt, 'The Application of International Human Rights Law in Islamic States' (1990) 12 *Human Rights Quarterly* 202, 206.

99 Arskal Salim, *Challenging the Secular State: The Islamization of Law in Modern Indonesia* (University of Hawaii Press 2008) 81.

100 Yousif (n 97) 35.

The 1965 Blasphemy Law demonstrates that *forum internum*, as the essential element of religious freedom of Pancasila and the 1945 Constitution, is challenged by one kind of exclusive interpretation of Islam when the MUI, MORA and majority Islamic organisations force religious minorities within Islam to follow one favoured Sunni orthodox religious interpretation. They project Islam as a monolithic religion which implicitly controls the country's rulers, especially in relation to the government's policies on religious freedom. The community at large is also arranged according to the principles and criteria of that specific religion. Other religions are accordingly either declared illegal or are, at most, tolerated as long as they do not interfere or clash with the ruling religion.[101] This does not only violate the basic principle of religious freedom protected by domestic legislations but also contradicts international religious human rights norms.

The 1965 Blasphemy Law also shows that the diversity of Islamic hermeneutics gives preferential treatment to Sunni majorities over religious minorities within Islam in Indonesia. This kind of alleged majoritarian religious interpretation considers other Islamic groups which do not share their religious interpretations as un-Islamic even though they still practise the basic tenets of Islam. Thus, it was submitted that legally the 1965 Blasphemy Law should be repealed because it is inconsistent with the spirit of religious pluralism of the Indonesian constitution and Pancasila. The authorisation of the blasphemy law also demonstrates that forcing a particular religious interpretation on everyone is inconsistent with Islamic law and international human rights law.

4.3. Arguments of the Constitutional Court

The MK rejected the case even though the court confirmed that the right to embrace a religion, including having a different interpretation of religious teaching, is an essential part of religious freedom regulated in Pancasila and the 1945 Constitution. The MK emphasised that Indonesia is a religious secular state in which every citizen, either individually or collectively, must accept Pancasila's indivisible principles including the supreme religious principle. The MK further confirmed that the religious character of the nation is confirmed in the court decisions, concluding that the performance of the judicial organ is based on belief in the One Supreme God.[102] Another religious character is provided by the preamble and in the essence of the 1945 Constitution: that is, the spirit of education to increase an individual's faith and piety advanced in article 31(3) of the constitution.[103] It can be noted that the theistic character of the nation establishes a distinctive Indonesian religious freedom.[104]

101 Juan Vorster, *Constitutional Implementation of Religious Freedom* (Brill 2010) 167.
102 Every court verdict starts with the saying "justice on behalf of the One Supreme God". This means the judges believe that the decision they make is not solely based on their own efforts but is also influenced by their belief in a theistic Supreme God.
103 *Judicial Review of 1965 Blasphemy Law* (n 64) 222.
104 ibid 273.

The MK also explained that the concept of "religious values", which limits the application of human rights in article 28J (2) of the 1945 Constitution, is in accordance with the Indonesian constitutional character of human rights. Hence, the ratification of international human rights instruments should be in accordance with state philosophy (Pancasila) and the 1945 constitution.[105] This is interesting because even though the state enacted Law No. 12/2005 to domesticate the ICCPR into Indonesian law, the court suggested that human rights provisions should still be in accord with Indonesian domestic law.

The reality, as previously discussed, is that law in the Indonesian context, especially in the courtroom, is very complex and not limited to written legislation but may also derive from societal norms, which the MK has to acknowledge. Thus, international human rights instruments are implemented by the courts taking into account Pancasila, the 1945 Constitution and empirical legal perspectives as well. The history of Pancasila and the 1945 Constitution earlier analysed in Chapter 5 vividly demonstrates this approach. This distinctive legal approach is also reflected in the conceptualisation of the principle of rule of law by the MK as follows:

> The principle of rule of law or *negara hukum* in Indonesia should not be the same as the principle of rule of law in other countries. The principle of *negara hukum* should be seen from the perspective of the 1945 Constitution; belief in One Supreme God as the main principle and religious values which construct the development of the state and the nation, not a state which separates religion and the state and Indonesia does not uphold individualism and communalism principles.[106]

This observation by the MK explicitly indicates that the significance of rule of law can only be understood in a specific Indonesian context because this term is in fact an imported concept. The court claimed that by analogy, similar pluralist-sensitive understanding should be given to the concept of religious freedom, whereby the religious character of a particular nation may restrict the freedom to be an atheist and forbid individuals to abuse religious teachings. This argument is, then, different from the secular legal character of the West because belief in One Supreme God and constitutional religious values in Indonesia become the measurement of bad law or good law and of constitutional law or unconstitutional law.[107]

The MK also observed that religion is not only associated with the private sphere but also consists of sociological, cultural and historical aspects within a given society. In other words, religion is not solely a private matter. Individuals are unable to exclusively or individually interpret pluralism, liberalism or fundamentals of religion in a unilateral manner, because any interpretation of these concepts should consider the 1945 Constitution as a general agreement of

105 ibid 274–275.
106 ibid 275.
107 ibid 275.

the nation.[108] Based on this argument, it is obvious that the MK did not only consider religious freedom in the context of the written legislation per se to resolve the case of blasphemy law, but also considered other perspectives such as the Indonesian rule of law, democracy, human rights, public order and the "religious values" embraced by people in the country.[109] This signifies that the MK acts as an interpreter of the constitution by using its authoritative constitutional interpretation, as well as becoming the master of living laws by relying on its legal wisdom.

These considerations led the MK to decide that the Indonesian blasphemy law does not place a restriction on *forum internum* for non-mainstream religious teachings because it only controls the spread of thoughts or actions that consist of hatred or abuse of a particular religion. It was therefore constitutional to limit the spread of the so-called "deviant" religious interpretations based on the essence of the recognised religions practised in Indonesia. The law does not restrict individuals from interpretations of a particular religious teaching as long as this is done in the private sphere without the fear of disturbing public order.[110] The MK emphasised that believing in a particular religious teaching (*forum internum*) cannot be restricted and the perpetrator cannot be convicted, but this right can be limited when it deals with other parties within a given society (*forum externum*).[111] In many other states, this kind of limitation is generally justified due to the need to protect public order which can be disturbed by communal conflicts in society. The next question would then be whether the restriction against the rights of religious minority groups to propagate their belief is necessary to preserve public order and the rights of others in a democratic society.

The MK further asserts that the blasphemy law protects individual, social and state interests. If there is a social conflict caused by religious expressions from different religious groups, the state does not need to manage the substance of religion but should manage citizens' behaviour,[112] which means that the law is required to uphold general protection and prevent social conflict within society. The MK also noted that the blasphemy law might be amended but cannot be repealed as long as there is no new law which regulates the same matter. However, enacting a new law is beyond the MK's authority as this is restricted to parliament. Even though the Law No. 23/2003 on the Constitutional Court does not explicitly empower the MK to require or recommend that the parliament should amend a law, it could be interpreted that the MK "implicitly ruled" that parliament should enact a new law to regulate religious freedom and religious claims among religious adherents.[113]

108 ibid 278–279.
109 ibid 279–280.
110 ibid 287.
111 ibid 288.
112 ibid 300.
113 ibid 283.

These arguments were articulated by the MK to achieve legal harmony or "*jalan tengah*", an attempt to adopt some sort of margin of appreciation[114] between the interests of the plaintiffs and the state.[115] The court tends to emphasise that the promotion and protection of the rights of religious minorities within Islam should be inspired by Indonesian values, cultures and traditions even though Indonesia has ratified international human rights instruments. The court argues that there must be balance and harmony in order to interpret human rights norms in the country. First, the balance between the rights of individuals within religious minority groups and their responsibility to the community. Second, the court attempts to negotiate the demands from both parties. On the one hand, the court recognises the unconditional right of religious minorities within Islam to have different Islamic teachings. On the other hand, the court does not repeal the blasphemy law as the main hindrance of the protection of religious minorities within Islam. Finally, the court attempts to establish a balance between the international standard of human rights and Indonesian legal and human rights characteristics.

The phrase *jalan tengah* is very common in Indonesia within legal, political and social matters. In this context, Indonesia should be able to achieve the right balance between Secularism and Islamism and Individualism and Communitarianism. This compromise can be seen from the MK's verdict, which acknowledges the unconditional character of theistic religious freedom to protect the rights of religious minorities within Islam in Indonesia, rejects the application of a judicial review of the blasphemy law and implicitly emphasises that the law needs to be revised by legislative organs. This type of legal harmony generally occurs in post-colonised countries that have a complex, constantly contested amalgam of state laws, religious values, philosophical and moral ethics and socio-cultural norms that require careful negotiation of law and justice over time.

The MK's argument confirms that religious freedom and the protection of religious minorities within a particular religion within the spectrum of rule of law in Indonesia is solely guaranteed in written legislation and embraces many kinds of socio-legal and theological aspects. All types of monolithic approaches that seek to wipe out other socio-legal perspectives appear unrealistic because they fail to account for the inherent plurality of law.[116] In the Indonesian

114 For a discussion on margin of appreciation in relation to human rights and Islamic law, see Mashood A Baderin, *International Human Rights and Islamic Law* (Oxford University Press Oxford 2003) 231–235.

115 *Judicial Review of 1965 Blasphemy Law* (n 64) 222. It should be noted here that there was one dissenting opinion from Judge Maria Farida Indrati, who argued that even though the blasphemy law does not explicitly mention official religions in practical terms it only protects recognised official religions, while unrecognised religions should follow certain regulations from the recognised religions. She concluded that substantially this law is against religious freedom and human rights provisions in the 1945 Constitution.

116 Werner F Menski, *Comparative Law in a Global Context: The Legal Systems of Asia and Africa* (Cambridge University Press 2006) 596.

context, the legal system reflects an ongoing balancing act between multiple pluralities, such as state laws, religious laws and customary law.[117] Also considered are international dimensions; international law and Islamic law in the Muslim world.[118] It confirms that the substantive source of law in Indonesia may derive from customary law (tradition); the living law of actual practice, a national or local sense of justice; state law and jurisprudence; and international legal rules,[119] as well as the diversity of Islamic law. Consequently, examining the protection scheme for religious minorities within Islam in Indonesia is not sufficient if one only looks at written legislation such as the constitution and international human rights instruments. Much attention should also be given to unwritten rules within a Muslim society such as Islamic values and customary law, which uphold communitarianism.

The case of a judicial review of the blasphemy law simply exposes the complexity of Indonesian Islam and its relationship with deeply rooted competing normative systems, as was recognised even by late colonial state policies.[120] One significant reason is that Islam has a strong institutional basis within Indonesian state structures, with a variety of institutions specifically established to administer religion like the MORA and MUI.[121] The MK's argument, which acknowledges the necessity of the blasphemy law to protect society and the state's interests, confirms that the concept of rule of law is understood and interpreted as the preservation of harmony among the various competing legal systems. In the context of the judiciary, this concept is frequently interpreted by jurists to accommodate the interests of the parties. For instance, the Cikeusik case in which the perpetrators of communal conflict between the Ahmadiyah and Sunni Islam received a light sentence (six months in prison), even though three Ahmadiyah members were killed, simply illustrates the preservation of harmony between the parties.[122]

117 Franz von Benda-Beckmann, Keebet von Benda-Beckmann and Anne Griffiths, 'Balancing Islam, Adat and the State, Comparing Islamic and Civil Courts in Indonesia', in Franz von Benda-Beckmann, Keebet von Benda-Beckmann and Anne Griffiths (eds), *The Power of Law in a Transnational World: Anthropological Enquiries* (Berghahn Books 2012) 217.

118 If we look at Menski's kite model, the corner of international law or, in my own words, the international dimension of law generally does not have as much power as the other laws. This argument can be seen from the MK's verdict, which confirms that the international standard of religious freedom can be side-tracked if it transgresses the domestic standard of religious freedom. See Werner F Menski, 'Flying Kites in a Global Sky: New Models of Jurisprudence' (2011) 7 *Socio-Legal Review* 1.

119 See Timothy C Lindsey, 'Between State and Society: Professional Lawyers and Reform in Indonesia', in Timothy C Lindsey (ed), *Indonesia: Law and Society* (The Federation Press 2008).

120 Sebastiaan Pompe, 'Islamic Law in Indonesia' (1997) 4 *Yearbook of Islamic and Middle Eastern Law Online* 180, 183. The colonial policies recognised that Indonesians as indigenous people could use unwritten rules or Indonesian legal tradition to settle disputes among them, while the Dutch and other European people had to apply Dutch law.

121 ibid 199–200.

122 Verdict No. 314/Pid.B/2011/PN.SRG.

The MK consideration of "religious values" embraced by Indonesians also confirms that the MK does not ignore religion as a source of legal justification in Indonesia.[123] The MK's argument about the philosophical, sociological, theological and constitutional aspects of religious freedom also endorses that Indonesia does not follow legal positivism.[124] The MK searched for law in a wider legal-cum-sociological context by considering legal texts and sociological arguments from different organisations and individuals during the hearing. This consideration simply establishes that the MK's perception of human rights not only relies on scriptural edicts but also depends on societal and people's perceptions.

The MK argument, which upholds religious values in the constitution as a unique character of the nation, also confirms that the MK tries to understand the processes of interaction associated with the idea of law.[125] The MK attempted to convince us that the constitutional clause of religious values, as one of the elements restricting human rights, is a unique character of Indonesia asserted by Pancasila and the preamble of the 1945 Constitution. In this context, however, the public sphere is regulated through religious norms that define a pious society, an upright rule and a just order.[126] This precept therefore results in the interdependence of religious freedom, religious orthodoxy and state law within Indonesian quasi-theistic secularism. The interdependence can be seen from the MK's verdict emphasising the absolute protection of the *forum internum* as an unconditional right. But it also acknowledged that religious interpretation is not immune and absolute with regard to the *forum externum*. It says that public religious interpretation should follow the essence of the generally established religious methodology based on established religious teachings.[127] This interpretation becomes the highest source of legal interpretation of the religious values in article 28J (2) of the Constitution, as all MK's verdicts are final and binding. Additionally, no other laws provide a contrary standard of interpretation of constitutional religious values. The MK thereby advocates a strict, religious interpretation of a particular religious group as generally embraced by the group's mainstream majority over the others and which protects the religion from abuse on grounds of public order. Consequently, the MK believes that if there is a communal conflict caused by the abuse of religion

123 See Marc Hertogh, 'A "European" Conception of Legal Consciousness: Rediscovering Eugen Ehrlich' (2004) 31 *Journal of Law and Society* 457, 459.

124 Positivism here is used to describe the tradition of legal philosophy that sees law as emanating from state authority rather than from God or some other sources. Once laws are made by the legitimate authority, they must be obeyed by all, including those who made them. See David Bourchier, 'Positivism and Romanticism in Indonesian Legal Thought' (1999) *Law and Society in Indonesia* 186, in Timothy Lindsey, *Indonesia: Law and Society* (Federation Press 1999) 95.

125 Hertogh (n 123) 461.

126 Reza Afshari, 'An Essay on Islamic Cultural Relativism in the Discourse of Human Rights' (1994) 16 *Human Rights Quarterly* 235, 267.

127 Verdict of MK No. 140, *supra* note 83, at 289. para. 3.52.

protected by the 1965 Blasphemy Law, the protection of the religion is held supreme over the right of religious followers.

This case asserts that the protection of religion is considered as the maintenance of social order and becomes the source of law.[128] The uniformity of religious values as social ordering in written legal documents in Indonesia seems to be the most complicated legal protection for religious minorities within Islam. Any laws meant to protect public order and harmony are monopolised by Muslim majorities to persecute religious minorities within Islam. Regulating the uniformity of religious values would result in the internal confusion of the complex legal system.[129] This legal complexity attempts to accommodate customary norms within the overarching system and clearly is the dominant, legal development of protecting religious minorities. In this context, written law is theoretically given privilege over the unwritten norms.[130] This blasphemy case shows that unwritten norms subsume written law because the MK gives consideration to the standard interpretation of practised religious teaching. No single word in the 1945 Constitution and other legal instruments explicitly explains that laws should be written, because the 1945 Constitution emphasises that the state still recognises unwritten norms.[131] The MK searches for "laws" either in law as *ius scriptum* or *ius non scriptum*, because the latter is administratively prehistory within Indonesian law but is substantially still practised by people and applied by judicial organs.

The problem with this so-called legal consensus in Indonesia is that Indonesian legal culture generally refers to majoritarianism. Hence the matters discussed here are issues of power. This concept is predicated on the assumption that the will of the majority is absolute and is the final authority when defining the limits of individual rights and freedoms.[132] Consequently, the collective interest seems to be predominant over individual rights and the fact that public officials as decision-makers have a key role to protect the credibility of the law. Thus, the blasphemy case sanctions arrived at by means of international human rights and Indonesian human rights law, with their emphasis on individual rights and impersonal rules, were considered inappropriate.[133] This disagreement is exacerbated when the role of state-religious institutions and religious organisations gives effect to the application of domestic and international legal dimensions of human rights. As a consequence, the right to embrace a particular religion or belief as well as the right to hold a different interpretation of religious teachings

128 Dolores A Donovan, 'Codification in Developing Nations: Ritual and Symbol in Cambodia and Indonesia' (Social Science Research Network 2008) 704.
129 Michael G Peletz, 'Islamic Justice, State Law, and Cultural Politics in Indonesia: A Review Essay' (2005) *Indonesia* 161, 164.
130 Donovan (n 128) 721.
131 See article 18B of the 1945 Constitution.
132 Derek O'Brien and Vaughan Carter, 'Chant down Babylon: Freedom of Religion and the Rastafarian Challenge to Majoritarianism' (2002) 18 *Journal of Law and Religion* 219, 219.
133 Bourchier (n 124) 97.

as the integral part of an individual's religious freedom is frequently subsumed by the collective rights of the Muslim majorities.

5. Questioning blasphemy law in a quasi-theistic secular state

The blasphemy law case demonstrates that Indonesia's religious freedom protections qualify as secular. However, a more accurate categorisation is quasi-theistic because Pancasila does not mention any particular religion as dominant. This enables individuals and communities to reach their own conclusions about Pancasila's implementation. By doing this, it has the secular objective of preventing communal conflict caused by the abuse of religion and protecting public order.

The secular nature of the 1965 Blasphemy Law may become influenced by Islamic jurisprudence if the MK invites Islamic religious leaders as *amici*. These *amici* will generally not speak as legal scholars, but as the guardians of Islam.[134] The MK's argument asserts that the blasphemy law does not only contain legal matters but also has social and moral values. This means the court needs to consider Islamic religious leaders' arguments as the guardians of the Islamic conscience.[135] This consideration becomes problematic when considering religious freedom as Islamic scholars tend to simply follow traditional orthodox Islamic principles in the context of the blasphemy law, which potentially leads to human rights violations of religious minorities within Islam. The law does not specify the kinds of acts that constitute religious abuse and consequently targets religious minorities who adhere to non-mainstream interpretations of Islam[136]

The 1965 Blasphemy Law in many ways gives particular religions the right to enjoy social authority in Indonesia, allowing them to ignore or reject the human rights paradigm. The principle of quasi-theistic secularism is generally misinterpreted by the majority as referring to an effort to preserve the religious orthodoxy of the six official religions. Whoever does not share this orthodoxy is seen as a threat against the community of believers, the state and the essence of religious belief as well. For instance, even though most Muslims believe that depictions of Muhammad are blasphemous,[137] the depictions of the Prophet in fact have many interpretations ranging from physical, behavioural and authoritarian. In many Indonesian cases, the term depiction is more related to the authority of the Prophet, such as the authority to introduce new law or even a new Holy Book. Additionally, the term "depiction" in the 1965 Blasphemy Law also

134 According to article 22 of the MK Decree No. 06/PMK/2005 on Litigation Procedure in the MK, an *amicus* is anybody who does not have a conflict of interest with the case.

135 On the discussion of religious leaders as the guardians of Islam, see Noel Coulson, *History of Islamic Law* (Edinburgh University Press 2014) 83.

136 Freedom House, 'Policing Belief: The Impact of Blasphemy Law on Human Rights' (Freedom House 2010) 48.

137 Joshua Foster, 'Prophets, Cartoons, and Legal Norms: Rethinking the United Nations Defamation of Religious Provisions' (2017) 48 *Journal of Catholic Legal Studies* 28.

includes the depiction of Archangel Gabriel, the Qur'an, God and other Islamic symbols.

The enactment of the 1965 Blasphemy Law indicates that religious institutions and the state are considered as contemporary expressions of divine rule, not only in terms of moral protectionism but also as part of the definition of offences against common values.[138] As a consequence, believing in a religion as the most fundamental individual religious right is frequently subsumed by communitarian aspects of religion. All religions have communal aspects and a public life, such as forming a religious congregation.[139] However, the close cooperation between Islamic religious institutions and the state potentially results in the narrow, Islamic communitarian ideology that influences blasphemy cases in Indonesia. This ideology considers that the supremacy of the Islamic community should be honoured above the individualistic nature of human rights.[140] This argument principally confirms that the 1965 Blasphemy Law transgresses its legal boundaries by entering into social and political spheres, which are the two main spheres considered by judges when they adopt a verdict in cases before them.

Even though religion is perceived as the foundation of the state, there is still no constitutional reason to treat a particular religious group as deserving special benefits or being subject to persecution.[141] It can be noted that applying the 1965 Blasphemy Law to restrict so-called heretical religions simply demonstrates that the state not only upholds the institutionalised definition of religions, but also institutionalises the legitimacy to divide religious adherents within religions. Regarding the case of religious minorities within Islam, this law is meant to be the legitimacy of the majority to act as God's collective representative in order to implement the Islamic conscience politically and legally. This means that the law also risks ignoring plurality as part of religion's nature. It suggests that this law is in contradiction with Indonesian religious pluralism and international human rights, because more conflicts will arise between the practices of religious minorities and laws crafted by members of the majority.[142]

It also implies that the role of religious non-governmental organisations like the NU, Muhammadiyah and others in defining restrictive and tolerable religious freedom remains influential in judicial processes. Even though the state is

138 Justin Kirk Houser, 'Is Hate Speech Becoming the New Blasphemy? Lessons from an American Constitutional Dialectic' (2009) 114 *Penn State Law Review* 572.

139 David M Kirkham, Tore Lindholm and W Cole Durham, 'Liberal Secularism and European Islam: A Challenge to Muslims and Non-Muslims', in W Cole Durham, David M Kirkham and Tore Lindholm (eds), *Islam and Political-Cultural Europe* (Ashgate Publishing 2013) 9.

140 Martin (n 6) 836.

141 Bret Boyce, 'Equality and the Free Exercise of Religion' (Social Science Research Network 2009) 497.

142 Paul Horwitz, 'The Sources and Limits of Freedom of Religion in a Liberal Democracy: Section 2(a) and Beyond' (1996) 54 *University of Toronto Faculty of Law Review* 1, 3.

constitutionally neutral with regards to particular conceptions of the good life,[143] the socio-religious realities are interpreted by judges as social will which establishes the condition of religious freedom. The question then arises about who owns the right to define true and false belief in an Indonesian quasi-theistic secular state which constitutionally upholds open interpretation of what religion and religious freedom are meant to be. In the Indonesian case, an offence against religious harmony is seen as an offence against the state because religious harmony is the most substantial part of national security and religion is perceived as the foundation of the state. This concept is an antithesis of liberalism, due to its focus on the maximisation of community over individual, obligation over will, tradition over freedom and communitarianism over the autonomous individual.[144]

In this context, individual religious freedom, especially the right to embrace religion in Islam, is perhaps the most difficult right to be examined. This right does not only have a divine element of rights and freedoms but, as shown in this research, this divine element also has been frequently interpreted in the hands of the majority to curb non-mainstream religious interpretation, reflecting power struggles. The distinctions are mainly between "us", which refers to the majority, and "them", which generally refers to allegedly heretical, apostate and blasphemous groups and individuals. This kind of division is an unnecessary effect of the 1965 Blasphemy Law and threatens the integration principle of democratic society and religious plurality in the country.

Bibliography

Afshari R, 'An Essay on Islamic Cultural Relativism in the Discourse of Human Rights' (1994) 16 *Human Rights Quarterly* 235.

An-Na'im A, 'Best of 2010: Religious Freedom and Defamation' (*ABC* 10 November 2010).

Arzt DE, 'The Application of International Human Rights Law in Islamic States' (1990) 12 *Human Rights Quarterly* 202.

———, 'Heroes or Heretics: Religious Dissidents under Islamic Law' (1996) 14 *Wisconsin International Law Journal* 349.

Baderin MA, *International Human Rights and Islamic Law* (Oxford University Press Oxford 2003).

———, 'Religion and International Law: Friends or Foes?' (Social Science Research Network 2009).

Bassiouni M, 'Speech, Religious Discrimination, and Blasphemy: Remarks' (1989) 83 *American Society of International Law Proceedings* 427.

Bedner A, *Administrative Courts in Indonesia: A Socio-Legal Study* (Brill Nijhoff 2001).

Benda-Beckmann F von, Benda-Beckmann K von and Griffiths A, 'Balancing Islam, Adat and the State, Comparing Islamic and Civil Courts in Indonesia', in Franz von Benda-

143 ibid 13.

144 To read about the character of liberalism, see ibid 14.

Beckmann, Keebet von Benda-Beckmann and Anne Griffiths (eds), *The Power of Law in a Transnational World: Anthropological Enquiries* (Berghahn Books 2012) 217.
Bielefeldt H, 'Muslim Voices in the Human Rights Debate' (1995) 17 *Human Rights Quarterly* 587.
Binawan AAL, 'Declarations and the Indonesian Constitution on Religious Freedom' (2011) 49 *Al-Jami'ah: Journal of Islamic Studies* 361.
Bourchier D, 'Positivism and Romanticism in Indonesian Legal Thought', in Tim Lindsey (ed), *Law and Society in Indonesia* (The Federation Press 1999) 186.
Boyce B, 'Equality and the Free Exercise of Religion' (Social Science Research Network 2009).
Cammack M, Young LA and Heaton T, 'Legislating Social Change in an Islamic Society – Indonesia's Marriage Law' (1996) 44 *The American Journal of Comparative Law* 45.
Caron DD, Fitzpatrick J and Slye RC, 'Republic of South Africa v. Grootboom. Case No. CCT 11/00. 2000 (11) BCLR 1169 and Minister of Health v. Treatment Action Campaign. Case No. CCT 8/02' (2003) 97 *American Journal of International Law* 669.
Chase A, 'Legal Guardians: Islamic Law, International Law, Human Rights Law, and the Salman Rushdie Affair' 11 *American University International Law Review* 3.
Cotterrell R, *Law, Culture and Society: Legal Ideas in the Mirror of Social Theory* (Ashgate Publishing 2006).
Coulson N, *History of Islamic Law* (Edinburgh University Press 2014).
Donovan DA, 'Codification in Developing Nations: Ritual and Symbol in Cambodia and Indonesia' (Social Science Research Network 2008).
Draper M, 'Justice as a Building Block of Democracy in Transitional Societies: The Case of Indonesia' (2001) 40 *Columbia Journal of Transnational Law* 391.
Eltayeb MSM, *A Human Rights Approach to Combating Religious Persecution: Cases from Pakistan, Saudi Arabia, and Sudan* (Intersentia 2001).
Evans C, 'The Double-Edged Sword: Religious Influences on International Humanitarian Law' (2005) *Melbourne Journal of International Law* 1.
Forte D, 'Apostasy and Blasphemy in Pakistan' (1994) 10 *Connecticut Journal of International Law* 27.
Foster J, 'Prophets, Cartoons, and Legal Norms: Rethinking the United Nations Defamation of Religious Provisions' (2017) 48 *Journal of Catholic Legal Studies* 28.
Freedom House, 'Policing Belief: The Impact of Blasphemy Law on Human Rights' (Freedom House 2010).
Garces N, 'Islam, Till Death Do You Part: Rethinking Apostasy Laws under Islamic Law and International Legal Obligations' (2010) 16 *Southwestern Journal of International Law* 229.
Ghanea-Hercock N, 'Introduction', in Nazila Ghanea-Hercock, *The Challenge of Religious Discrimination at the Dawn of the New Millennium* (Springer 2013).
Gilbert G, 'Religious Minorities and Their Rights: A Problem of Approach' (1997) 5 *International Journal on Minority and Group Rights* 97.
Ginsburg T, *Judicial Review in New Democracies: Constitutional Courts in Asian Cases* (Cambridge University Press 2003).
Gretason M, 'A Law on Religious Hatred Entrenching Pluralism' (2003) 150 *Law & Justice – The Christian Law Review* 37.
Hanna S, 'Pencegahan Penodaan Agama (Kajian Atas UU No.1 tahun 1965)' (2017) *RELIGIA* 159–160.
Hapsari AD, 'Failure to Revise Blasphemy Law Would "Limit Role of Religion"' (*The Jakarta Post* 20 March 2010).

Hashemi, *Religious Legal Traditions, International Human Rights Law and Muslim States* (Brill Nijhoff 2008).
Hertogh M, 'A "European" Conception of Legal Consciousness: Rediscovering Eugen Ehrlich' (2004) 31 *Journal of Law and Society* 457.
Horwitz P, 'The Sources and Limits of Freedom of Religion in a Liberal Democracy: Section 2(a) and Beyond' (1996) 54 *University of Toronto Faculty of Law Review* 1.
Houser JK, 'Is Hate Speech Becoming the New Blasphemy? Lessons from an American Constitutional Dialectic' (2009) 114 *Penn State Law Review* 572.
Judicial Review of 1965 Blasphemy Law (2009) Constitutional Court of Indonesia 140/PUU-VII/2009.
Kimmelman M, 'Outrage at Cartoons Still Tests the Danes' (*The New York Times* 20 March 2008).
Kirkham DM, Lindholm T and Durham WC, 'Liberal Secularism and European Islam: A Challenge to Muslims and Non-Muslims', in W Cole Durham, David M Kirkham and Tore Lindholm (eds), *Islam and Political-Cultural Europe* (Ashgate Publishing 2013) 9.
Küng H, *Global Responsibility: In Search of a New World Ethic* (Wipf and Stock Publishers 2004).
Lev DS, 'Between State and Society: Professional Lawyers and Reform in Indonesia', in Timothy Lindsey (ed), *Indonesia: Law and Society* (Federation Press 2008) 48.
Lewis B, 'Some Observations on the Significance of Heresy in the History of Islam' (1953) 1 *Studia Islamica* 43.
Lindsey T (ed), *Indonesia: Law and Society* (Federation Press 1999).
Martin JP, 'The Three Monotheistic World Religions and International Human Rights' (2005) 61 *Journal of Social Issues* 827.
Menski WF, *Comparative Law in a Global Context: The Legal Systems of Asia and Africa* (Cambridge University Press 2006).
———, 'Flying Kites in a Global Sky: New Models of Jurisprudence' (2011) 7 *Socio-legal Review* 1.
Montgomery JW, 'Can Blasphemy Law Be Justified' (2000) 145 *Law & Justice – The Christian Law Review* 6.
Na'īm 'Abd AA, *Islam and the Secular State* (Harvard University Press 2009).
O'Brien D and Carter V, 'Chant down Babylon: Freedom of Religion and the Rastafarian Challenge to Majoritarianism' (2002) 18 *Journal of Law and Religion* 219.
Peletz MG, 'Islamic Justice, State Law, and Cultural Politics in Indonesia: A Review Essay' (2005) 80 *Indonesia* 161.
Pompe S, 'Islamic Law in Indonesia' (1997) 4 *Yearbook of Islamic and Middle Eastern Law Online* 180.
Saeed A, 'The Islamic Case for Religious Liberty' (2011) *First Things*.
———, *Freedom of Religion, Apostasy and Islam* (Routledge 2017).
Saeed A and Saeed H, *Freedom of Religion, Apostasy and Islam* (Routledge 2017).
Said AA, 'Precept and Practice of Human Rights in Islam' (1979) 1 *Universal Human Rights* 63.
Salim A, *Challenging the Secular State: The Islamization of Law in Modern Indonesia* (University of Hawaii Press 2008).
Salim A and Azra A, 'The State and Sharia in the Perspective of Indonesian Legal Politics', in Arskal Salim and Azyumardi Azra (eds), *Shari'a and Politics in Modern Indonesia* (Institute of Southeast Asian Studies 2003) 4.
Scarman L, 'Codification and Judge-Made Law: A Problem of Coexistence' (1967) 42 *Indiana Law Journal* 355.

Scharffs BG, 'International Law and the Defamation of Religion Conundrum' (2013) 11 *The Review of Faith & International Affairs* 66.

Sihombing UP, Pultoni, Siti Aminah and Muhammad Khoirul Roziqin, *Ketidakadilan Dalam Beriman: Hasil Monitoring Kasus-Kasus Penodaan Agama Dan Ujaran Kebencian Atas Dasar Agama Di Indonesia* (The Indonesian Legal Resource Center 2012).

Stockmann P, *The New Indonesian Constitutional Court: A Study into Its Beginnings and First Years of Work* (Hanns Seidel Foundation 2007).

Temperman J, 'Freedom of Expression and Religious Sensitivities in Pluralist Societies: Facing the Challenge of Extreme Speech' (2011) 2011 *BYU Law Review* 729.

———, 'Blasphemy, Defamation of Religions & Human Rights Law' (Social Science Research Network 2012).

Vance SC, 'The Permissibility of Incitement to Religious Hatred Offenses under European Convention Principles' (2004) 14 *Transnational Law & Contemporary Problems* 201.

Vorster J, *Constitutional Implementation of Religious Freedom* (Brill 2010).

Wahid Institute, 'Lampu Merah Kebebasan Beragama, Laporan Kebebasan Beragama Dan Intolerensi Di Indonesia 2011' (Wahid Institute 2011).

Yousif A, 'Islam, Minorities and Religious Freedom: A Challenge to Modern Theory of Pluralism' (2000) 20 *Journal of Muslim Minority Affairs* 29.

8 Conclusion

This book has critically examined the complex issue of protecting religious minorities within Islam in Indonesia within the context of international human rights law and Islamic law. This concluding chapter provides a summary of the research findings and, on the basis of those findings, recommends at the end an integrated legal spectrum as a means of effectively protecting the religious rights of minorities within Islam in Indonesia. Firstly, the chapter summarises the general insights of the book on the problematic position of religious minorities within Islam generally and the role and responsibility of Muslim-majority states in that regard. This is followed by a summary of the specific challenges to the protection of religious minorities within Islam in Indonesia.

The preceding chapters of this book show that in relation to the protection of religious minorities within Islam, the position of Indonesia as a quasi-theistic state becomes crucial because the state has a duty to regulate the freedom of religion of all religious groups and individuals. This is achieved generally by, on the one hand, ensuring the protection of their religious rights and, on the other hand, preventing groups from violating the religious rights and freedoms of others. Such a crucial role of the state is necessitated by the fact that all religious groups and individuals often claim that freedom of religious expression and manifestation is part of their religious belief, while at the same time they also often argue that their religious belief cannot be interfered with. These two claims engender the overlapping of the private and public spheres of religious rights especially when the state provides regulations that can be used by the religious majorities to persecute religious minorities within Islam. In this situation, the state is often caught between the need to protect the right of religious minorities within Islam to embrace their own understanding of the religion, and the pressure of the Muslim majorities on the state to protect the religious orthodoxy of the majority from what they consider to be a violation by the minority. Striking a proper balance between these two positions continues to be problematic for most Muslim-majority states, including Indonesia.

Even though international human rights law dictates that the state cannot interfere in any way with the private sphere of individual religious freedom,[1] this book identified that many countries, including Indonesia, cannot clearly differentiate between the private and public spheres of freedom of religion and, in fact, often interfere with the personal beliefs of individuals, particularly minorities. Usually, in allowing the enjoyment of religious freedom by religious majorities, states inadvertently restrict the fundamental rights of religious minorities. As a consequence, the exercise of religious freedom by religious minorities within Islam to disseminate their religious beliefs is often seen to clash with fundamental doctrines of Islam as professed by the majorities. This is very prevalent in respect of Indonesia, because for most Indonesians religious identity, either politically or legally, is considered as a part of the essential identity of the state. This kind of state system generally considers that threatening the religious identity adopted by the state also amounts to endangering public order or national security. Thus, the state often applies restrictive rules against the rights of religious minority groups or individuals who dissent from the prevailing religious orthodoxy adopted by the majority on grounds of protecting public order. In that regard, Indonesia often applies discriminatory policies against minorities within Islam, defining disfavoured minorities within Islam as heretics, ineligible for the international human rights protection awarded to religious minorities.

In relation to this complexity in finding a balance between the protection of the right to religious belief and practice and the right to spread so-called "deviant" religious teaching, Paul Taylor correctly observes that:

> Distaste of proselytism is rooted in issues of culture or national identity, which is in principle separate from matters of doctrine, especially in states that recognise official religions and consider that a certain religion is part of the national identity.[2]

Taylor's argument signifies that to be entitled to equal religious rights, minority religions and religious minorities within a particular religion are often forced to adjust their religious beliefs and rituals to conform to those of the majorities or orthodox religions recognised by the state. If the minorities do not do so, the state can restrict the activities of dissimilar religions or faiths on grounds of protecting social harmony and the national identity of the state.

In the case of the protection of religious minorities within Islam, this kind of restriction is generally employed by states to eliminate non-mainstream religious beliefs, alleged to be deviant religions and the main source of public unrest that should be eliminated, attuned or transformed into the majority version. In the

1 Jill Marshall, 'Conditions for Freedom? European Human Rights Law and the Islamic Headscarf Debate' (2008) 30 *Human Rights Quarterly* 631, 634.

2 Paul M Taylor, *Freedom of Religion: UN and European Human Rights Law and Practice* (Cambridge University Press 2005) 65.

context of religious freedom, the term "deviant" derives from the intention of the religious majority to preserve religious orthodoxy backed by the state, which certainly leads to discrimination and inequality between religious minorities and the majority. When a particular religion is formally endorsed by the state as the state religion, a political force and the main source of legislation and the judicial interpretation of laws,[3] the state may also easily manipulate sacred texts to oppress those who deviate from mainstream politics and religious beliefs. With regard to this, An-Na'im has argued that "when principles of religious law are enacted as positive law of a state, they generally cease to be the religious law and become the political will of that state".[4] He then contends that if Muslim majorities are in power, "they usually deny the rights of religious minorities because the outcome of policy and legislation that they make will be political rather than religious".[5] In this context, Islam may then be turned into Islamism, a tyranny which is generally intolerant of others because in such a system the state frequently privileges the majority religious groups and disfavours proselytism for minorities or those who deviate from the mainstream religion.

The continued persecution of religious minorities within Islam in Indonesia shows that religious domination and repression could still continue in Muslim-majority states, despite these states having ratified international human rights treaties and modified their constitutions to respect religious freedom. The persecution of religious minorities within Islam also suggests that Indonesia is actually not living up to the spirit of Islam, a religion that has always been subject to various interpretations since the Prophetic era. A major finding of this book, however, is that similar to the case in other Muslim-majority countries, the persecution of religious minorities within Islam in Indonesia is primarily influenced by political factors, social custom and traditions of the country rather than Islamic law per se. This also means that the significant role of religion in the Indonesian public sphere as a consequence of the concept of a quasi-theistic secular state cannot override the constitution. The position of the state, then, is to ensure that any kind of abuse of religion is prohibited; whoever does not comply with this basic principle should be liable to penalties prescribed by law.

The complex reality of religious minorities within Islam in Indonesia demands that the Muslim majority should realise that in a state like Indonesia, where Islam is not legalised as a religion of the state, the possible divergent interpretation of Islamic teachings in principle is not protected by religious law but defended by a constitution. Yet, this book shows that religious orthodoxy becomes one of the significant sources to determine a particular right for religious minorities. One of the reasons is the validity of blasphemy law, which

3 Ran Hirschl, 'Juristocracy vs. Theocracy: Constitutional Courts and the Containment of Sacred Law' (2009) 1 *Middle East Law and Governance* 129, 130.

4 Abdullahi Ahmed An-Na'im, 'Why Muslims Need the Secular State' (*ABC Religion & Ethics* 15 November 2011).

5 ibid.

protects religious orthodoxy. Thus, public awareness of the need to respect divergent interpretations of religious teaching is required to protect religious minorities within Islam. The need for such awareness is significant because if searching for the law is not restricted to written documents, understanding human rights, religious freedom and social harmony should also consider common sense within society. This common sense can be achieved when the majority Muslims appreciate that differences of interpretation of Islamic teachings among Muslims are a bounty of God to promote peace and harmony in society.

Based on this interwoven legal system, the challenge to protect religious minorities within Islam is caused by disintegration of the legal system in Indonesia and one best possible method to protect religious minorities within Islam is through promoting and ensuring an integrated legal spectrum within the Indonesian legal system. In this context, there is often a mix-up between international standards and national law on the protection of religious minorities within Islam, the protection of theological differences in Islamic law and the practice of the courts. The Indonesian case as examined in this book shows that state officials, including judges and others, generally endeavour to stand in-between to seek harmony among parties, while explaining their willingness to reinforce human rights. This mechanism frequently involves the rights of religious minorities within Islam, because on the one hand the government faces major challenges in enforcing international standards of human rights protection while on the other hand it also wants to accommodate the interests of Islamic majority groups who insist on establishing orthodox versions of official mainstream Islamic teachings.

The government argues that this need for balancing is meant to preserve political stability and national unity even though on many occasions the balancing discriminates against religious minorities within Islam. Thus, this policy has created a vicious cycle of conflicts and tensions with respect to the religious freedom of religious minorities within Islam in Indonesia. In this process, members of society usually put their religion into force as a legal mechanism to solve legal and human rights disputes. In this context, solidarity on the common ground of religion (Islam) is significant to create a web of common understanding among Muslims, who usually use Islam as the primary source for validating the rights of religious minorities within Islam. They consider a certain minority right, such as building a place of worship, should be eliminated to avoid tensions in society. Thus, after forming a violent mob, the majority generally targets a particular place of worship which belongs to a minority as a symbol of the minority's existence.[6]

6 Al Khanif, 'The Paradox of Religious (in)Tolerance in Indonesia' (*The Jakarta Post* 16 October 2015). Since the application of Islamic law in 2004, many cases of religious persecutions usually occurred between Muslims as the majority and Christians as religious minorities, rather than affecting the rights of religious minorities within Islam. *Qanun jinayat* or Islamic criminal

The findings of this book have highlighted that practising non-mainstream religions is considered to be criminal in social and legal terms. Thus, religious minorities within Islam who practise non-mainstream Islamic teachings are considered as rebelling against a well-established religious community, namely the Indonesian version of Islamic orthodoxy.[7] This shows that Islam, even though it is not formally declared as the main state religion, has become a part of the collective structure of Indonesian society, which results in a communal sense of religious rights for people. As a result, the religious domain for most members of Indonesian society represents a strong communal-religious character because the majority Muslims are bound by Islamic orthodoxy. Every individual in Indonesia not only belongs to the state but is also related to a traditional faith group and community. People's rights and responsibilities depend on their existence in a group. People are connected through a matrix of human relationships and are therefore integrally connected to their society.[8]

These realities indicate that protecting the rights of religious minorities within Islam in Indonesia, especially their religious rights, should take cognisance of both Islamic values and legal tradition within a particular society. Religious values and legal tradition are imposed by a politically organised society to determine a certain binding right and obligation for all community members. A breach of any such obligation would result in social repercussions such as moral condemnation, withdrawal of cooperation, exclusion from activities, demand for compensation or the infliction of punishment as well as expulsion.[9] For example, all persons accused of being criminal offenders, including those who practise non-mainstream religions, must show their willingness to restore social harmony in their community as a result of their actions, because most people believe that proper rights are rights which do not merely emphasise liberalism as asserted by international human rights law but are the rights that also consider an obligation towards values within society. Thus, relying only on formal state law and international human rights law may not lead to legal enforcement to protect the rights of religious minorities within Islam because Islamic orthodoxy and legal tradition are more feasible to most Muslims than human rights provisions are. This signifies the need to factor the Indonesian legal tradition, which primarily consists of the family spirit, deliberation and consensus for public good (*maslahah*), into the process.

In this context, justice and fairness in Indonesian legal terms does not solely mean punishment for criminal offences but should also consider the restoration

law was applied frequently in the case of gambling, adultery, drinking liquor and dating in public. See more detail in Arskal Salim, *Contemporary Islamic Law in Indonesia: Sharia and Legal Pluralism* (Edinburgh University Press 2015) 80–89.

7 Al Khanif, 'Tolikara: Majority-Minority Ties and Its Discontent' (*The Jakarta Post* 25 July 2015).

8 Padmo Wahyono, 2003. 'Indonesian Human Rights', in David Bourchier and Vedi Hadiz (eds), *Indonesian Politics and Society: A Reader* (Routledge 2014) 238.

9 Michael Barry Hooker, *Adat Law in Modern Indonesia* (Oxford University Press 1978) 146.

of harmony among people due to the recognition of the communitarian principle, which gives privilege to the community over individuals. Most Indonesian citizens believe that all persons are members of society and are bound by consensus prescription and cannot act differently from its precepts, hence non-compliance with unwritten rules would result in social and legal alienation.[10] The restriction of religious minorities within Islam indicates that constitutional and international human rights guarantees are generally not put into force because government officials essentially prefer to follow social order rather than deviate from the collective majority. This social order in fact protects the communitarian rights of all community members to alienate individuals who perform non-mainstream religious beliefs. Thus, this book suggests that the two instruments are more supplementary, because people do not seek human rights norms from the law made by the state but generally seek them from the living tradition within a particular society.

It can be asserted that the main character of Indonesian human rights law is that it generally perceives a combination of rights and obligations.[11] Most members of society believe that individuals may have freedom as long as they respect their obligation to their community. Thus, the concept of crime is not only limited to criminal matters but also to actions considered as transgressing established socio-religious values, such as the practice of theological difference and manifesting different interpretations of religious doctrines contrary to established orthodox understandings. Conflicts of opinion usually occur because the majorities prefer to use blasphemy law and stand by the orthodox interpretation of Islamic jurisprudence while the minorities stick to constitutional human rights provisions and international human rights instruments This legal fragmentation hence results in the rights of religious minorities within Islam being at stake, because the state generally favours and stands by the greater interest of the community rather than protecting minority rights in accordance with their expectations solely under international human rights provisions.

Bibliography

An-Na'im AA, 'Why Muslims Need the Secular State' (ABC Religion & Ethics 15 November 2011).

Benda-Beckmann F von, 'Scape-Goat and Magic Charm' (1989) 21 *The Journal of Legal Pluralism and Unofficial Law* 129.

Bourchier D and Hadiz V, *Indonesian Politics and Society: A Reader* (Routledge 2014).

Davidson J and Henley D, 'Introduction: Radical Conservatism – The Protean Politics of Adat', in Jamie S Davidson and David Henley (eds), *The Revival of Tradition in*

10 For further explanation of consensus prescription, see Franz von Benda-Beckmann, 'Scape-Goat and Magic Charm' (1989) 21 *The Journal of Legal Pluralism and Unofficial Law* 129, 138.

11 Jamie Davidson and David Henley, 'Introduction: Radical Conservatism – The Protean Politics of Adat', in Jamie Davidson and David Henley (eds), *The Revival of Tradition in Indonesian Politics: The Deployment of Adat from Colonialism to Indigenism* (Routledge 2007) 3.

Indonesian Politics: The Deployment of Adat from Colonialism to Indigenism (Routledge 2007) 3.

Hirschl R, 'Juristocracy vs. Theocracy: Constitutional Courts and the Containment of Sacred Law' (2009) 1 *Middle East Law and Governance* 129.

Hooker MB, *Adat Law in Modern Indonesia* (Oxford University Press 1978).

Khanif A, 'The Paradox of Religious (in)Tolerance in Indonesia' (*The Jakarta Post* 16 October 2015).

———, 'Tolikara: Majority-Minority Ties and Its Discontent' (*The Jakarta Post* 25 July 2015a).

Marshall J, 'Conditions for Freedom? European Human Rights Law and the Islamic Headscarf Debate' (2008) 30 *Human Rights Quarterly* 631.

Salim A, *Contemporary Islamic Law in Indonesia: Sharia and Legal Pluralism* (Edinburgh University Press 2015).

Taylor PM, *Freedom of Religion: UN and European Human Rights Law and Practice* (Cambridge University Press 2005).

Index

For Product Safety Concerns and Information please contact our EU representative GPSR@taylorandfrancis.com
Taylor & Francis Verlag GmbH, Kaufingerstraße 24, 80331 München, Germany

www.ingramcontent.com/pod-product-compliance
Ingram Content Group UK Ltd.
Pitfield, Milton Keynes, MK11 3LW, UK
UKHW022132190926
475702UK00013B/1770
9780367500764